UNDERSTANDING PUBLIC POLICY

second / UNDERSTANDING
edition / PUBLIC POLICY.

THOMAS R. DYE
Florida State University

Prentice-Hall, Inc., Englewood Cliffs, New Jersey

Library of Congress Cataloging in Publication Data

Dye, Thomas R
    Understanding public policy.

    Includes bibliographies.
    1. United States—Social policy.   2. United
States—Social conditions—1960-   I. Title.
HN65.D9 1975   320.4   74-17125
ISBN 0-13-936179-0

© 1975 by Prentice-Hall, Inc., Englewood Cliffs, New Jersey

PRINTED IN THE UNITED STATES OF AMERICA

10 9 8 7 6 5 4 3 2 1

Prentice-Hall International, Inc., London
Prentice-Hall of Australia, Pty. Ltd., Sydney
Prentice-Hall of Canada, Ltd., Toronto
Prentice-Hall of India Private Limited, New Delhi
Prentice-Hall of Japan, Inc., Tokyo

CONTENTS

v

14 POLICY IMPACT:
finding out what happens after a law is passed
327

PREFACE

If this book has a thesis, it is that political science can be "relevant" to public policy questions without abandoning its commitment to scientific inquiry; that social relevance does not require us to reject systematic analysis in favor of rhetoric, polemics, or activism; that knowledge about the forces shaping public policy and the consequences of policy decisions is socially relevant.

This volume is concerned with "who gets what" in American politics and, more important, "why" and "what difference it makes." We are concerned not only with *what* policies governments pursue but also *why* governments pursue the policies they do, and *what* the consequences of these policies are.

Political science, like other scientific disciplines, has developed a number of concepts and models to help describe and explain political life. These models are not really competitive in the sense that any one could be judged "best." Each focuses on separate elements of politics and each helps us to understand different things about political life.

We begin with a brief description of seven analytic models in political science and the potential contribution of each of them to the study of public policy. They are:

the institutional model
the group model
the elite model
the rational model

the incremental model
the game theory model
the systems model

We then attempt to describe and explain public policy by the use of these various analytic models. The reader is not only informed about public policy in a variety of key domestic policy areas but, more important, he is encouraged to utilize these conceptual models in political science to explain the causes and consequences of public policies in these areas. The policy areas studied are:

civil rights	urban affairs and housing
crime, violence, and repression	government spending
welfare and social security	budgeting and taxing
antipoverty and economic opportunity	national defense
education	state and local spending and services

Most public policies are a combination of rational planning, incrementalism, competition, group activity, elite preferences, systematic forces, and institutional influences. Throughout this volume we employ these models, both singly and in combination, to describe and explain public policy. However, certain chapters rely more on one model than another.

Any of these policy areas might be studied profitably by employing more than one model. Frequently our selection of a particular analytic model to study a specific policy area was based as much upon pedagogical considerations as anything else. We simply wanted to demonstrate how political scientists employ analytical models. Once the reader is familiarized with the nature and uses of analytic models in political science, he may find it interesting to explore the utility of models other than the ones selected by the author in the explanation of particular policy outcomes. For example, we use an elitist model to discuss civil rights policy, but the reader may wish to view civil rights policy from the perspective of group theory. We employ the language of game theory to discuss national defense policy, but the reader might enjoy reinterpreting defense policy in a systems model.

Each chapter concludes with a series of propositions, which are derived from one or more analytic models, and which attempt to summarize the policies discussed. The purposes of these summaries are to suggest the kinds of policy explanations that can be derived from analytic models and to tie the policy material back to one or another of our models.

In short, this volume is not only an introduction to the study of public policy, but also an introduction to the models political scientists use to describe and explain political life.

THOMAS R. DYE
Florida State University

UNDERSTANDING PUBLIC POLICY

Federally-ordered busing, Augusta, Georgia. UPI Photo

1 POLICY ANALYSIS:

the thinking man's response
to demands for relevance

POLICY ANALYSIS IN POLITICAL SCIENCE

This book is about public policy. It is concerned with what governments do, why they do it, and what difference it makes. It is also about political science and the ability of this academic discipline to describe, analyze, and explain public policy.

Public policy is whatever governments choose to do or not to do.[1]

[1] More elaborate definitions of public policy are found in the literature, of course, but on examination they seem to boil down to the same thing. David Easton defines public policy as "the authoritative allocation of values for the whole society"—but it turns out that only the government can "authoritatively" act on the "whole" society, and everything the government chooses to do or not to do results in the "allocation of values." Lasswell and Kaplan defines policy as "a projected program of goals, values, and practices," and Carl Friedrich says, "It is essential for the policy concept that there be a goal, objective, or purpose." These definitions imply a difference between specific government actions and an overall program of action toward a given goal. The problem, however, in insisting that government actions must have *goals* in order to be labeled "policy" is that we can never be sure whether or not a particular action has a goal. We generally assume that if a government chooses to do something there must be a goal, objective, or purpose, but all we can really observe is what governments choose to do or not to do. Realistically, our notion of public policy must include *all* actions of government—and not just stated intentions of governments or government officials. Finally, we must also consider government inaction—what a government chooses not to do—as public policy. Obviously government inaction can have as great an impact on society as government action. See: David Easton, *The*

1

Governments do many things: they regulate conflict within society; they organize society to carry on conflict with other societies; they distribute a great variety of symbolic rewards and material services to members of the society; and they extract money from society, most often in the form of taxes. Thus, public policies may be regulative, organizational, distributive, or extractive—or all these things at once.

Public policies may deal with a wide variety of substantive areas—defense, foreign affairs, education, welfare, police, highways, taxation, housing, social security, health, economic opportunity, urban development, inflation and recession, and so on. They may range from the vital to the trivial—from the allocation of tens of billions of dollars for an antiballistic missile system to the designation of an official national bird.

Public policy is not a new concern of political science: the earliest writings of political philosophers reveal an interest in the policies pursued by governments, the forces shaping these policies, and the impact of these policies on society. Yet the major focus of attention of political science has never really been on policies themselves, but rather on the institutions and structures of government and on the political behaviors and processes associated with policy making.

"*Traditional*" political science focused its attention primarily on the institutional structure and philosophical justification of government. This involved the study of constitutional arrangements, such as federalism, separation of power, and judicial review; powers and duties of official bodies, such as Congress, president, and courts; intergovernmental relations; and the organization and operation of legislative, executive, and judicial agencies. Traditional studies described the *institutions* in which public policy was formulated. But unfortunately the linkages between important institutional arrangements and the content of public policy were largely unexplored.

Modern "*behavioral*" political science focused its attention primarily on the processes and behaviors associated with government. This involved the study of the sociological and psychological bases of individual and group behavior; the determinants of voting and other political activities; the functioning of interest groups and political parties; and the description of various processes and behaviors in the legislative, executive and judicial arenas. Although this approach described the *processes* by which public policy was determined, it did not deal directly with the linkages between various processes and behaviors and the content of public policy.

Political System (New York: Knopf, 1953), p. 129; Harold D. Lasswell and Abraham Kaplan, *Power and Society* (New Haven: Yale University Press, 1970), p. 71; and Carl J. Friedrich, *Man and His Government* (New York: McGraw-Hill, 1963), p. 70.

Today the focus of political science is shifting to *public policy*—to the *description and explanation of the causes and consequences of government activity.* This involves a description of the content of public policy; an assessment of the impact of environmental forces on the content of public policy; an analysis of the effect of various institutional arrangements and political processes on public policy; an inquiry into the consequences of various public policies for the political system; and an evaluation of the impact of public policies on society, in terms of both expected and unexpected consequences. For example: What is the impact of war and depression on the growth of government activity? What are the real priorities among defense and domestic policy needs, and what forces affect the determination of priorities? Can aggression be deterred by threat of nuclear retaliation? Do arms limitations agreements make the world a safer or more dangerous place to live? What is the best mix of conventional and nuclear weapons in America's defense strategy? What forces operate to maintain the status quo in government's programs and policies, and what forces operate to induce change? What is the impact of racial and religious group activity on the allocation of public monies to schools and colleges? What are the consequences for ghetto blacks of laws prohibiting discrimination in the sale or rental of housing? Does greater party competition and increased voter participation bring about more liberal policies in welfare, health, or education? Will a guaranteed minimum income for all American families reduce or increase joblessness and social dependency? Can black students in ghetto schools receive a quality education through improvements in their neighborhood schools, or must they be bused out of the ghetto environment for an equal educational opportunity? Who gains and who loses from the present distribution of tax burdens and "tax loopholes"? Will reforms in governmental organizations result in any significant alleviation of urban problems—blight, pollution, congestion, crime, or fiscal crisis? What are the political consequences of establishing federally funded community action programs to fight poverty? Does it make any differences in the content of public policy whether Democrats or Republicans win control of government? Does violence bring about change in public policy, and if so, in what direction? These are the *kinds* of questions that can be dealt with in policy analysis.

WHY STUDY PUBLIC POLICY?

Traditionally, Americans have assumed that once they *passed a law* and *spent money,* the purposes of the law and the expenditure would be achieved. They assumed that when Congress adopted a policy and appropriated money for it, and when the Executive Branch organized a program, hired people, spent money, and carried out the activities designed to implement the policy, the effects of the policy would be felt by society and the effects would be those intended by the policy. Traditionally, Americans have been optimistic about what public policy can achieve: they believed that governments could eliminate poverty, end racism, insure peace, prevent crime, restore cities, clean the air and water, and so on, if only they would adopt the right policies. But now there is a growing uneasiness among policy-makers and scholars about the effectiveness of governments. The national experiences with the Vietnam War, the poverty programs, public housing, urban renewal, manpower training, public assistance, and many other public programs indicate the need for a careful appraisal of the real impact of public policy. We have learned from these experiences that America's problems cannot always be resolved by passing a law and throwing a few billion dollars in the general direction of the problem in the hope that it will go away. Social scientists themselves have been growing uneasy about the validity of many programs being developed under the umbrella of "applied social science." The result has been a sudden awakening of interest in policy studies.

Why should political science devote greater attention to the study of public policy? First of all, public policy can be studied for purely *scientific reasons:* to gain an understanding of the causes and consequences of policy decisions improves our knowledge about society. Public policy can be viewed as a *dependent variable,* and we can ask what environmental forces and political system characteristics operate to shape the content of policy. Or public policy can be viewed as an *independent variable,* and we can ask what impact public policy has on the environment and the political system. By asking such questions we can improve our understanding of the linkages between environmental forces, political processes, and public policy. An understanding of these linkages contributes to the breadth, significance, reliability, and theoretical development of social science generally.

Public policy can also be studied for *professional reasons:* an understanding of the causes and consequences of public policy permits us to apply social science knowledge to the solution of practical problems. Factual knowledge is a prerequisite to prescribing for the ills of society. If certain end values are desired, then the question of what policies would best implement these ends is a factual question requiring scientific study. In other words, policy studies can produce professional advice, in terms of "if . . . then . . ." statements, about how to achieve desired goals.

Finally, public policy can be studied for *political purposes:* to insure that the nation adopts the "right" policies to achieve the "right" goals. It is frequently argued that political science cannot be silent or impotent in the face of great social and political crises, and that political scientists have a moral obligation to advance specific public policies. An exclusive focus on institutions, processes, or behaviors is frequently looked upon as "dry," "irrelevant," and "amoral," because it does not direct attention to the really important policy questions facing American society. Policy studies can be undertaken not only for scientific and professional purposes but also to inform political discussion, advance the level of political awareness, and improve the quality of public policy. Of course, these are very subjective purposes—Americans do not always agree on what constitutes the "right" policies or the "right" goals—but we will assume that knowledge is preferable to ignorance, even in politics.

POLICY ANALYSIS AND POLICY ADVOCACY

Whether one chooses to study public policy for scientific, professional, or political reasons, it is important to distinguish *policy analysis* from *policy advocacy. Explaining* the causes and consequences of various policies is not equivalent to prescribing what policies governments ought to pursue. Learning *why* governments do what they do and what the consequences of their actions are is not the same as saying what governments *ought* to do, or bringing about changes in what they do. Policy advocacy requires the skills of rhetoric, persuasion, organization, and activitism. Policy analysis encourages scholars and students to attack critical policy issues with the tools of systematic inquiry. There is an implied assumption in policy analysis that developing scientific knowledge about the forces shaping public policy and the consequences of policy designs is itself a socially relevant activity, and that such analysis is a prerequisite to prescription, advocacy, and activism. In short, policy analysis might be labeled the "thinking man's response" to demands that social science become more "relevant" to the problems of our society.

Specifically, *public analysis* involves:

1. *A primary concern with explanation rather than prescription.* Policy recommendations—if they are made at all—are subordinate to description and explanation. There is an implicit judgment that understanding is a prerequisite to prescription, and that understanding is best achieved through careful analysis rather than rhetoric or polemics.
2. *A rigorous search for the causes and consequences of public policies.* This

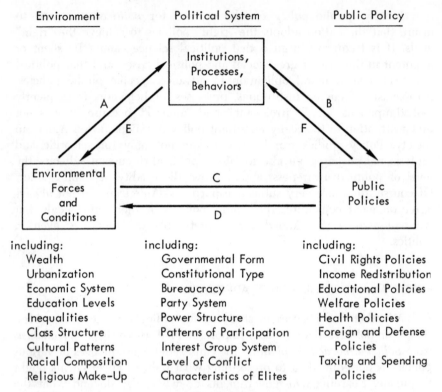

Fig. 1-1 *Linkages in Policy Analysis*

Linkage A: The effect of environmental forces and conditions on political and governmental institutions, processes, and behaviors.

Linkage B. The effect of political and governmental institutions, processes, and behaviors on public policies.

Linkage C: The effect of environmental forces and conditions on public policies.

Linkage D: The effect (feedback) of public policies on environmental forces and conditions.

Linkage E: The effect (feedback) of political and governmental institutions, processes, and behaviors on environmental forces and conditions.

Linkage F: The effect (feedback) of public policies on political and governmental institutions, processes, and behaviors.

search involves the use of scientific standards of inference. Sophisticated quantitative techniques may be helpful in establishing valid inferences about causes and consequences, but they are not really essential.

3. *An effort to develop and test general propositions about the causes and consequences of public policy and to accumulate reliable research findings of general relevance.* The object is to develop general theories about public policy that are reliable and that apply to different governmental agencies

and different policy areas. Policy analysts clearly prefer to develop explanations that fit more than one policy decision or case study—explanations that stand up over time in a variety of settings.

Policy analysis contrasts with many of the currently popular approaches to policy questions—rhetoric, rap sessions, dialogue, confrontation, or direct action. Policy analysis offers the serious student an approach to society's problems that is both scientific and relevant. The insistence on explanation as a prerequisite to prescription, the use of scientific standards of inference, and the search for reliability and generality of knowledge can hardly be judged "irrelevant" when these ideas are applied to important policy questions.

POLICY ANALYSIS IN ACTION—THE COLEMAN REPORT
AND AMERICAN EDUCATION

One of the more interesting examples of policy analysis in recent years is the influential report on American education by James S. Coleman, *Equality of Educational Opportunity,* frequently referred to as the "Coleman Report." [2] The Coleman Report dealt primarily with the linkage between educational policy and the aspiration and achievement levels of pupils (roughly speaking, Linkage D in Figure 1-1). Although Coleman's study is not without its critics, [3] it is nonetheless the most comprehensive analysis of the American public school system ever made. The Coleman Report was eighteen months in the making; it cost $2 million to produce; and it included data on 600,000 children, 60,000 teachers, and 4,000 schools. This report, and the reaction to it, can help us to understand both the problems and possibilities of systematic policy analysis.

The results of Coleman's study undermined much of the conventional wisdom about the impact of public educational policies on student learning and achievement. Prior to the study, legislators, teachers, school administrators, school board members, and the public generally, assumed that factors such as the number of pupils in the classroom, the amount

[2] James S. Coleman, *Equality of Educational Opportunity* (Washington, D.C.: Government Printing Office, 1966).

[3] For reviews of the Coleman Report, see Robert A. Dentler, "Equality of Educational Opportunity: A Special Review," *The Urban Review* (December 1966); Christopher Jenks, "Education: The Racial Gap," *The New Republic* (October 1, 1966); James K. Kent, "The Coleman Report: Opening Pandora's Box," *Phi Delta Kappan* (January 1968); James S. Coleman, "Educational Dilemmas: Equal Schools or Equal Students," *The Public Interest* (Summer 1966); James S. Coleman, "Toward Open Schools," *The Public Interest* (Fall 1967); and a special issue devoted to educational opportunity of *Harvard Educational Review,* Vol. 38 (Winter 1968).

of money spent on each pupil, library and laboratory facilities, teachers' salaries, the quality of the curriculum and other characteristics of the school affected the quality of education and educational opportunity. But systematic analysis revealed that these factors had *no* significant effect on student learning or achievement. "Differences in school facilities and curriculum . . . are so little related to differences in achievement levels of students that, with few exceptions, their effects fail to appear even in a survey of this magnitude." Moreover, learning was found to be unaffected by the presence or absence of a "track system," ability grouping, guidance counseling, or other standard educational programs. Even the size of the class was found to be unrelated to learning, although educators had asserted the importance of this factor for decades. Finally, the Coleman study reported that the quality of teaching was not a very significant factor in student achievement compared to family and peer-group influences. In short, the things that "everybody knew" about education turned out not to be so!

The only factors that were found to affect a student's learning to any significant degree were his family background and the family background of his fellow students. Family background affected the child's verbal abilities and attitudes toward education, and these factors correlated very closely with scholastic achievement. Of secondary but considerable significance were the verbal abilities and attitudes toward education of the child's classmates. Peer-group influence had its greatest impact on children from lower-class families. Teaching excellence mattered very little to children from upper- and middle-class backgrounds; they learned well despite mediocre or poor teaching. Children from lower-class families were slightly more affected by teacher quality.

Coleman also found that schools serving black pupils in this nation were not physically inferior to schools serving predominately white student bodies. In the South, in fact, black schools were somewhat newer than white schools. Black teachers have about the same education and teaching experiences as white teachers, and their pay is equal. Black teachers, however, score lower than white teachers on verbal tests, and their morale was reported to be lower than that of white teachers.

Reanalyzing Coleman's data for the U.S. Civil Rights Commission, Thomas F. Pettigrew and others found that black students attending predominantly black schools had lower achievement scores and lower levels of aspiration than black students *with comparable family backgrounds* who attended predominantly white schools.[4] When black students attending predominantly white schools were compared with black students attending predominantly black schools, the average difference in levels of

---

[4] U.S. Commission on Civil Rights, *Racial Isolation in the Public Schools*, 2 vols. (Washington, D.C.: Government Printing Office, 1967).

achievement amounted to more than *two grade levels*. On the other hand, achievement levels of white students in classes nearly half black in composition were *not* any lower than those of white students in all-white schools. Finally, special programs to raise achievement levels in predominantly black schools were found to have no lasting effect.

The Coleman Report made no policy recommendations. But, like a great deal of policy research, policy recommendations can easily be implied from its conclusions. First of all, if the Coleman Report is correct, it seems pointless to simply pour more money into the present system of public education—raising per-pupil expenditures, increasing teachers' salaries, lowering the number of pupils per classroom, providing better libraries and laboratories, adding educational frills, or adopting any specific curricula innovations. These policies were found to have no significant impact on learning.

The findings of the Coleman Report are particularly important for Title I of the Elementary and Secondary Education Act (see Chapter 9). This piece of Congressional legislation authorizes a billion-dollar-plus per year assistance for "poverty impact" schools. The purpose of this program is to remedy learning problems of disadvantaged children by increasing spending for special remedial programs. But the Coleman Report implies that compensatory programs have little educational value. They may have symbolic value for ghetto residents, or political value for officeholders who seek to establish an image of concern for the underprivileged, but they are of little educational value for children.[5]

The U.S. Commission on Civil Rights used the Coleman Report to buttress its policy proposals to end racial imbalance in public schools in both the North and the South. Inasmuch as money, facilities, and compensatory programs have little effect on student learning, and inasmuch as the socioeconomic background of the student's *classmates* does affect his learning, it seemed reasonable to argue that the assignment of lower-class black students to predominantly middle-class white schools would be the only way to improve educational opportunities for ghetto children. Moreover, because the findings indicated that the achievement levels of middle-class white students were unaffected by blacks in the classroom (as long as blacks were less than a majority), the Commission concluded that assigning ghetto blacks to predominantly white schools would not adversely affect the learning of white pupils. Hence, the Commission

---

[5] Professor Coleman himself did not believe that integration was the only answer, despite the data, and later urged that educators continue to search for other means to increase the achievement levels of disadvantaged black children. Other commentators noted that Coleman never tested for the effects of *drastically* reduced classroom size (6 to 8 pupils for example), nor was the impact of teaching quality fully explored (using measures other than experience, degrees, training, etc.). (See footnote 3.)

called for an end to neighborhood schools and the busing of black and white children to racially balanced schools.

The reaction of professional educators was largely one of silence. Perhaps they hoped the Coleman Report would disappear into history without significantly affecting the longstanding assumptions about the importance of money, facilities, classroom size, teacher training, and curricula. Perhaps they hoped that subsequent research would refute Coleman's findings. Daniel Moynihan writes:

> The whole rationale of American public education came very near to crashing down, and would have done so had there not been a seemingly general agreement to act as if the report had not occurred. But it had, and public education will not now be the same. The relations between resource input and educational output, which all school systems, all legislatures, all executives have accepted as given, appear not to be given at all. At very least what has heretofore been taken for granted must henceforth be proved. Without in any way purporting to tell mothers, school teachers, school board superintendents what *will* change educational outcomes, social science has raised profoundly important questions as to what does not.[6]

The reactions of black leaders were mixed.[7] Militant blacks were strongly offended by the Report and its implications for public policy. The findings regarding compensatory education efforts were said to deal a "death blow to all black children" in the ghetto. They reasoned that integrated education is a physical impossibility in many big-city school systems with few white pupils, and it is a political impossibility in many other cities. Hence, to discredit compensatory education is to threaten the only hope for improvement in ghetto education.

A more emotional reaction was the attack on the Report as "racist" because it implied that ghetto black children could only learn by contact with middle-class white children. One commentator exclaimed: "I don't subscribe to the view that a black kid must sit next to a white kid to learn. The report is based on the myth of white supremacy."

Since its publication, the Coleman Report has been frequently cited by proponents of "busing"—those urging deliberate government action to achieve racial balance in public schools. Courts and school officials in Northern and Southern cities have cited the Coleman Report as evidence that racial imbalance denies equality of educational opportunity to black children, and as evidence that deliberate racial balancing in the schools, or "busing," is required to achieve equal protection of laws.

[6] Daniel P. Moynihan, *Maximum Feasible Misunderstanding* (New York: Free Press, 1969), p. 195.

[7] See James K. Kent, "The Coleman Report: Opening Pandora's Box," pp. 244–45.

But in 1972, Harvard sociologist David Armor shocked the academic world with a careful review of the available evidence of the effect of busing on the achievement levels of black students.[8] His conclusions: black students bused out of their neighborhoods to predominantly white schools do not improve their performance relative to white students, even after three or four years of integrated education. His interpretation of the impact of busing on the achievement levels of black students indicated that black students were not being helped "in any significant way" by busing, and he urged consideration of the question of whether psychological harm was being done to black students by placing them in a situation where the achievement gap was so great.

Note that Armor was not contradicting the Coleman Report. Coleman was observing black children who were attending predominantly white schools not as a result of deliberate government action, but rather within the previously existing pattern of "neighborhood schools." In contrast, Armor was observing black children who had been deliberately reassigned to integrated schools by government action.

The policy implications of Armor's work appear to support opponents of government-mandated racial balancing. Other social scientists have disputed Armor's review of the relevant research findings, including Thomas F. Pettigrew who originally used the Coleman data in support of busing.[9] They contend that Armor's work undermines progress toward an integrated society and reinforces racism. But Armor replies that social science findings cannot be used only when they fit the political beliefs of social scientists, and ignored when their policy implications are painful.[10]

Still another reaction to the Coleman Report is found in the work of Harvard educator Christopher Jencks. Jencks reanalyzed Coleman's data and conducted additional research on the impact of schooling on economic success.[11] He found that school quality has little effect on an individual's subsequent success in earning income. He concluded, therefore, that no amount of educational reform would ever bring about economic equality. Jencks assumed that *absolute equality* of income is the goal of society, not merely *equality of opportunity* to achieve economic success. Because the schools cannot insure that everyone ends up with the same income, Jencks concludes that nothing short of a radical re-

[8] David J. Armor, "The Evidence on Bussing," *The Public Interest*, Number 28 (Summer, 1972), pp. 90–126.

[9] Thomas F. Pettigrew, et al., "Bussing: A Review of 'The Evidence,'" *The Public Interest*, Number 31 (Spring 1973), pp. 88–113.

[10] David J. Armor, "The Double Double Standard," *The Public Interest*, Number 31 (Spring 1973), pp. 119–31.

[11] Christopher Jencks, *Inequality: A Reassessment of the Effect of Family and Schooling in America* (New York: Basic Books, 1972).

distribution of income (steeply progressive taxes and laws preventing individuals from earning more than others) will bring about true equality in America. Attempts to improve the educational system, therefore, are a waste of time and effort. Thus, the Coleman findings have been used to buttress *radical* arguments about the ineffectiveness of *liberal* reforms.

The point of this brief discussion of the Coleman Report is that policy analysis sometimes produces unexpected and even embarrassing findings, that public policies do not always "work" as intended, and that different political interests will interpret the findings of policy research differently—accepting, rejecting, or using these findings as they fit their own purposes.

POLICY ANALYSIS AND THE QUEST FOR "SOLUTIONS"
TO AMERICA'S PROBLEMS

It is questionable that policy analysis can ever provide "solutions" to America's problems. War, ignorance, crime, poor health, poverty, racial cleavage, inequality, poor housing, pollution, congestion, and unhappy lives have afflicted men and societies for a long time. Of course, this is no excuse for failing to work toward a society free of these maladies. But our striving for a better society should be tempered with the realization that "solutions" to these problems may be very difficult to find. There are many reasons for tempering our enthusiasm for policy analysis, some of which are illustrated in the battle over the Coleman Report.

First of all, it is easy to exaggerate the importance, both for good and for ill, of the policies of governments. It is not clear that government policies, however ingenious, could cure all or even most of society's ills. Governments are constrained by many powerful environmental forces— wealth, technology, population growth, patterns of family life, class structure, child-rearing practices, religious beliefs and so on. These forces are not easily managed by governments, nor could they be controlled even if it seemed desirable to do so. In the final chapter of this volume we will examine policy impacts, but it is safe to say here that some of society's problems are very intractable. For example, it may be that the *only* way to insure equality of opportunity is to remove children from disadvantaged family backgrounds at a very early age, perhaps before they are six months old. The weight of social science evidence suggests that the potential for achievement may be determined at a very young age. However, a policy of removing children from their family environment at such an early age runs contrary to our deepest feelings about family attachments. The forcible removal of children from their mothers is "unthinkable" as a governmental policy. So it may turn out that we never really provide equality of opportunity because cultural forces prevent us from pursuing an effective policy.

Second, policy analysis cannot offer "solutions" to problems when there isn't general agreement on what the problems are. The Coleman Report assumed that raising achievement levels (measures of verbal and quantitative abilities) and raising aspiration levels (the desire to achieve by society's standards) were the "problems" to which our efforts should be directed. But others have contended that such achievement and aspiration levels are really middle- or upper-class white norms, and that the education of black ghetto children should be adapted toward totally different goals. Some have argued that the educational system should *not* be organized to facilitate the entry of children into middle-class society; instead they have urged that the policies of ghetto schools be to prepare children for life in the ghetto. In other words, there is no real agreement on what societal values should be implemented in educational policy. Policy analysis is not capable of resolving value conflicts. At best it can advise on how to achieve a certain set of end values; it cannot determine what those end values should be.

Third, policy analysis deals with very "subjective" topics and must rely upon "interpretation" of results. Professional researchers frequently interpret the results of their analyses differently. For example, some scholars may wish to focus on Coleman's findings that a child's attitudes toward education are the most important variable and that programs should be undertaken to improve the ghetto child's attitude toward his school. Or some may focus on the effect of placing disadvantaged black children in middle-class white schools. Obviously, quite different policy recommendations can emerge from alternative interpretations of the results of research.

There is also the problem of public attitudes toward research, particularly social science research. Social science research cannot be "value-free." Even the selection of the topic for research is affected by one's values about what is "important" in society and worthy of attention. As Louis Wirth explained,

> The distinctive character of social science discourse is to be sought in the fact that every assertion, no matter how objective it may be, has ramifications extending beyond the limits of science itself. Since every assertion of a "fact" about the social world touches the interests of some individual or group, one cannot even call attention to the existence of certain "facts" without courting the objections of those whose very raison d'être in society rests upon a divergent interpretation of the "factual" situation period.[12]

[12] Louis Wirth, Preface to Karl Mannheim, *Ideology and Utopia: An Introduction to the Sociology of Knowledge* (New York: Harcourt Brace Jovanovich, 1936).

For example, in recent years blacks have assumed that social science research findings would generally support their views of the problems confronting American society, and therefore by implication support their policy claims. But in the case of the Coleman Report the published findings tended to undermine the view that ghetto schools could be improved by channeling additional educational funds and services to them. Blacks supporting improvements of ghetto schools tended to reject as "false" the social science research suggesting that the removal of a child from the ghetto school environment would have greatest impact on his achievement.[13] In short, disadvantaged groups as well as established elites may not always agree with the findings of policy research.

Another set of problems in systematic policy analysis centers about inherent limitations in the design of social science research. It is not really possible to conduct some forms of controlled experiments on human beings. For example, the Coleman researchers could not order middle-class white children to go to ghetto schools for several years just to see if it had an adverse impact on their achievement levels. Instead, social researchers must find situations in which educational deprivation has been produced "naturally" in order to make the necessary observations about the causes of such deprivation. Because we cannot control all the factors that go into a real-world situation, it is difficult to pinpoint precisely what it is that causes educational achievement or nonachievement. Moreover, even where some experimentation is permitted, human beings frequently modify their behavior simply because they know they are being observed in an experimental situation. For example, in educational research it frequently turns out that children perform well under *any* new teaching method or curricula innovation. It is difficult to know whether the improvements observed are a product of the new teaching method or curricula improvement or merely a product of the experimental situation. Finally, it should be noted that the people doing policy research are frequently program administrators who are interested in proving the positive "results" of their programs. It is important to separate research from policy implementation, but this is a difficult thing to do.

Perhaps the most serious reservation about policy analysis is the fact that social problems are so complex that social scientists are unable to make accurate predictions about the impact of proposed policies.

---

[13] Many blacks also reacted negatively to the controversial Moynihan Report in 1965 which suggested that the historical experiences of blacks with slavery and segregation had weakened the structure of black families and this weakness in turn affected other conditions of life among blacks. Daniel P. Moynihan, *The Negro Family: The Case for National Action* (Washington, D.C.: Government Printing Office, 1965). See Rainwater and Yancy, eds., *The Moynihan Report and the Politics of Controversy* (Cambridge: M.I.T. Press, 1967).

Social scientists simply do not know enough about individual and group behavior to be able to give reliable advice to policy-makers. Occasionally policy-makers turn to social scientists for "solutions," but social scientists do not have any "solutions." Most of society's problems are shaped by so many variables that a simple explanation of them, or remedy for them, is rarely possible. A detailed understanding of such a complex system as human society is beyond our present capabilities. The fact that social scientists give so many contradictory recommendations is an indication of the absence of reliable scientific knowledge about social problems. Although some scholars argue that no advice is better than contradictory or inaccurate advice, policy-makers still must make decisions, and it is probably better that they act in the light of whatever little knowledge social science can provide than that they act in the absence of any knowledge at all. Even if social scientists cannot predict the impact of future policies, they can at least attempt to measure the impact of current and past public policies and make this knowledge available to decision-makers.

It is important to recognize these limitations on policy analysis. However, it seems safe to say that reason, knowledge, and analysis are still appropriate tools in the consideration of policy questions. Policy analysis is not likely to provide "solutions" to America's problems. But we do not need to rely exclusively on "rules of thumb" or "muddling through" or "rap sessions" or "sounding off" or emotional outpourings of one kind or another in approaching policy questions. We can try systematically to describe and explain the causes and consequences of public policy in order to advance scientific understanding, to better prescribe for the ills of society, and to improve the quality of public policy.

BIBLIOGRAPHY

Dror, Yehezkel, *Public Policy-Making Re-examined.* San Francisco: Chandler, 1968.

Jones, Charles O., *An Introduction to the Study of Public Policy.* Belmont, Calif.: Wadsworth, 1970.

Lerner, Daniel, and Harold D. Lasswell, eds., *The Policy Sciences.* Stanford: Stanford University Press, 1960.

Ranney, Austin, ed., *Political Science and Public Policy.* Chicago: Markham, 1968.

Sharkansky, Ira, ed., *Policy Analysis in Political Science.* Chicago: Markham, 1970.

Welfare activists occupy Democrats-for-Nixon headquarters. UPI Photo

2 MODELS OF POLITICS:

some help in thinking about public policy

MODELS FOR POLICY ANALYSIS

Over the years political science, like other scientific disciplines, has developed a number of concepts and models to help us understand political life. The purpose of these is (1) to simplify and clarify our thinking about government and politics, (2) to identify important political forces in society, (3) to communicate relevant knowledge about political life, (4) to direct inquiry into politics, and (5) to suggest explanations for political events and outcomes.

Throughout this volume we will try to see whether the concepts and models of political scientists have any utility in the study of public policy. Specifically we want to examine public policy from the perspectives of systems theory, elite theory, group theory, rational decision-making theory, incrementalism, game theory, and institutionalism. Each of these terms identifies a major conceptual approach to politics which can be found in the literature of politcial science. None of these models was derived especially to study *public policy*. Yet each offers a separate way of thinking about policy and even suggests some of the general causes and consequences of public policy.

These models are not competitive, in the sense that any one of them could be judged "best." Each one provides a *separate* focus on political life, and each can help us to understand *different* things about public policy. Although some policies appear at first glance to lend themselves to explanation by one particular model, most policies are a combination of rational planning, incrementalism, interest group activity, elite preferences, systemic forces, competition, and institutional influences. In later chapters these models will be employed, singularly and in combination, to describe and explain specific policies. Following is a brief description of each model, with particular attention to the separate ways in which public policy can be viewed.

INSTITUTIONALISM: POLICY AS INSTITUTIONAL ACTIVITY

Governmental structures and institutions have long been a central focus of political science. Traditionally, political science has been defined as the study of governmental institutions. Political activities generally center about particular governmental institutions—Congress, the presidency, courts, states, municipalities, political parties, etc. The activities of individuals and groups are generally directed toward governmental institutions. Public policy is authoritatively determined, implemented, and enforced by governmental institutions.

The relationship between public policy and governmental institutions is very close. Strictly speaking, a policy does not become a *public* policy until it is adopted, implemented, and enforced by some governmental institution. Governmental institutions give public policy three distinctive characteristics. First of all, government lends *legitimacy* to policies. Governmental policies are generally regarded as legal obligations which command the loyalty of citizens. Men may regard the policies of other groups and associations in society—corporations, churches, professional organizations, civic associations, etc.—as important and even binding. But only government policies involve legal obligations. Second, government policies involve *universality*. Only government policies extend to all people in a society; the policies of other groups or organizations only reach a part of the society. Finally, government monopolizes *coercion* in society—only government can legitimately imprison violators of its policies. The sanctions that can be imposed by other groups or organizations in society are more limited. It is precisely this ability of government to command the loyalty of all its citizens, to enact policies governing the whole society, and to monopolize the legitimate use of force that encourages individuals and groups to work for enactment of their preferences into policy.

Traditionally, the institutional approach in political science did *not* devote much attention to the linkages between the structure of governmental institutions and the content of public policy. Instead, institutional studies usually described specific governmental institutions—their structures, organization, duties, and functions—without systematically inquiring about the impact of institutional characteristics on policy outputs. Constitutional and legal arrangements were described in detail, as were the myriad government offices and agencies at the federal, state, and local level. Public policies were sometimes described, but seldom analyzed. The linkage between structure and policy remained largely unexamined.

Despite the narrow focus of early institutional studies in political science, the structural approach is not necessarily an unproductive one. Governmental institutions are really structured patterns of behavior of individuals and groups. By "structured" we mean that these patterns of behavior tend to persist over time. These stable patterns of individual and group behavior may affect the content of public policy. Institutions may be so structured as to facilitate certain policy outcomes and to obstruct other policy outcomes. They may give advantage to certain interests in society and withhold advantage from other interests. Certain individuals and groups may enjoy greater access to government power under one set of structural characteristics than under another set. In short, the structure of governmental institutions may have important policy consequences.

The institutional approach need not be narrow or descriptive. We can ask what relationships exist between institutional arrangements and the content of public policy, and we can investigate these relationships in a comparative, systematic fashion. For example, in the area of urban affairs we can ask: Are the policies of federal agencies (Congress, President, Department of Housing and Urban Development, etc.) more responsive to urban problems than are the policies of state or local governments? How does the division of responsibility for urban services among federal, state, and local governments affect the content of urban policy? What is the relationship between reformed structures of city government (city managers, nonpartisan elections, at-large constituencies) and taxing and spending policies of cities? Are unreformed city governments (mayor-councils, partisan elections, and constituencies) more responsive in policy decisions to minority group demands than reformed cities? These policy questions can be dealt with systematically and involve a focus on institutional arrangements. In Chapter 8 we shall direct ourselves to these questions about urban policy, and in Chapter 9 we will examine the overall growth of government activity in America and the distribution of functions between federal, state, and local governments.

It is important to remember that the impact of institutional arrangements on public policy is an empirical question that deserves investigation. Too frequently, enthusiastic reformers have asserted that a particular

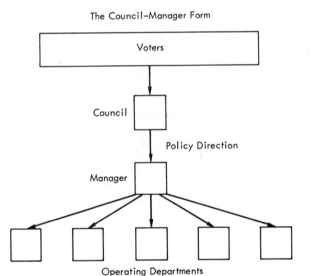

The Mayor–Council Form

Voters

Mayor

Council

Policy Direction

Operating Departments

The Council–Manager Form

Voters

Council

Policy Direction

Manager

Operating Departments

Fig. 2-1 *An Institutional Model: Forms of City Government*

change in institutional structure would bring about changes in public policy without investigating the true relationship between structure and policy; they have fallen into the trap of *assuming* on the basis of a priori logic that institutional changes will bring about policy changes. We must be cautious in our assessment of the impact of structure on policy. We may discover that both structure and policy are largely determined by environmental forces, and that tinkering with institutional arrangements will have little independent impact on public policy if underlying environmental forces—social, economic, and political—remain constant.

GROUP THEORY: POLICY AS GROUP EQUILIBRIUM

Group theory begins with the proposition that interaction among groups is the central fact of politics.[1] Individuals with common interests band together formally or informally to press their demands upon government. According to political scientist David Truman, an interest group is "a shared-attitude group that makes certain claims upon other groups in the society"; such a group becomes political "if and when it makes a claim through or upon any of the institutions of government."[2] Individuals are important in politics only when they act as part of, or on behalf of, group interests. The group becomes the essential bridge between the individual and his government. Politics is really the struggle among groups to influence public policy. The task of the political system is to *manage group conflict by* (1) establishing rules of the game in the group struggle, (2) arranging compromises and balancing interests, (3) enacting compromises in the form of public policy, and (4) enforcing these compromises.

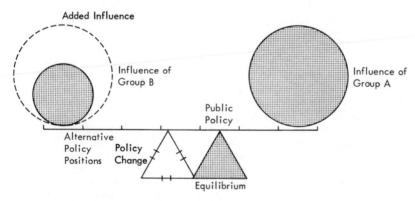

Fig. 2-2 *The Group Model*

According to group theorists, public policy at any given time is the equilibrium reached in the group struggle. This equilibrium is de-

---

[1] Group theory is explained at length in David B. Truman, *The Governmental Process* (New York: Knopf, 1951).

[2] *Ibid.*, p. 37.

termined by the relative influence of interest groups. Changes in the relative influence of any interest groups can be expected to result in changes in public policy; policy will move in the direction desired by the groups gaining in influence and away from the desires of groups losing influence. Political scientist Earl Latham describes public policy from the group theory viewpoint as follows:

> What may be called public policy is actually the equilibrium reached in the group struggle at any given moment, and it represents a balance which the contending factions or groups constantly strive to tip in their favor. . . . The legislature referees the group struggle, ratifies the victories of the successful coalition, and records the terms of the surrenders, compromises, and conquests in the form of statutes.[3]

The influence of groups is determined by their numbers, wealth, organizational strength, leadership, access to decision-makers, and internal cohesion.

Modern group theory is not very much different from the theory of "faction" described by James Madison two hundred years ago. Madison believed that differences among men generated "factions," which he defined as numbers of citizens united by a common interest that is adverse to the interests of other citizens. Controlling "faction" was "the principal task of modern legislation." Madison describes the causes of faction and the major factions encountered in society:

> The latent causes of faction are thus sown in the nature of man; and we see them everywhere brought into different degrees of activity, according to the different circumstances of civil society. A zeal for different opinions concerning religion, concerning government, and many other points, as well of speculation as of practice; an attachment to different leaders ambitiously contending for pre-eminence and power; or to persons of other descriptions whose fortunes have been interesting to human passions, have, in turn, divided mankind into parties, inflamed them to mutual animosity, and rendered them much more disposed to vex and oppress each other than to cooperate for their common good. So strong is this propensity of mankind to fall into mutual animosity, that where no substantial occasion presents itself, the most frivolous and fanciful distinctions have been sufficient to kindle their unfriendly passions and excite their most violent conflicts. But the most common and durable source of factions has been the various and unequal distribution of property. Those who hold and those who are without property have ever formed distinct interests in society. Those who are creditors and those who are debtors, fall under a like discrimination. A landed interest, a

---

[3] Earl Latham, "The Group Basis of Politics," in Heinz Eulau, Samuel J. Eldersveld, and Morris Janowitz, eds., *Political Behavior* (New York: Free Press, 1956), p. 239.

manufacturing interest, a mercantile interest, a moneyed interest, with many lesser interests, grow up of necessity in civilized nations, and divide them into different classes, actuated by different sentiments and views.[4]

Group theory purports to describe all meaningful political activity in terms of the group struggle. Policy-makers are viewed as constantly responding to group pressures—bargaining, negotiating, and compromising, among competing demands of influential groups. Politicians attempt to form a majority coalition of groups. In so doing, they have some latitude in determining what groups are to be included in the majority coalition. The larger the constituency of the politician, the greater the number of diverse interests, and the greater his latitude in selecting the groups to form a majority coalition. Thus, Congressmen have less flexibility than Senators who have larger and generally more diverse constituencies; and the president has more flexibility than Congressmen and Senators. Executive agencies are also understood in terms of the groups' constituencies.

Parties are viewed as coalitions of groups. The Democratic Party coalition from the Roosevelt era until recently was composed of labor, central-city dwellers, ethnic groups, Catholics, the poor, liberal intellectuals, blacks, and Southerners. The difficulties of the Democratic Party today can be traced largely to the weakening of this group coalition—the disaffection of the South and the group conflict between white labor and ethnic groups and blacks. The Republican coalition has consisted of rural and small-town residents, the middle class, whites, Protestants, white-collar workers, and suburbanites.

The whole interest group system—the political system itself—is held together in equilibrium by several forces. First of all, there is a large, nearly universal, *latent group* in American society which supports the constitutional system and prevailing "rules of the game." This group is not always visible but can be activated to administer overwhelming rebuke to any group that attacks the system and threatens to destroy the equilibrium.

Second, *overlapping group membership* helps to maintain the equilibrium by preventing any one group from moving too far from prevailing values. Individuals who belong to any one group also belong to other groups, and this fact moderates the demands of groups who must avoid offending their members who have other group affiliations.

Finally, the *checking and balancing resulting from group competition* also helps to maintain equilibrium in the system. No single group constitutes a majority in American society. The power of each

[4] *The Federalist*, No. 10, Modern Library Edition, pp. 55–56.

group is checked by the power of competing groups. "Countervailing" centers of power function to check the influence of any single group and protect the individual from exploitation.

Throughout this volume we will describe group struggles over public policy. A particularly interesting example of group conflict over policy is found in the discussion of federal aid to education in Chapter 7. We will examine the role of racial and religious group conflict over federal educational policy, educational interests at the community level, and the struggle over educational opportunity for children in the nation's black ghettos.

ELITE THEORY: POLICY AS ELITE PREFERENCE

Public policy may also be viewed as the preferences and values of a governing elite.[5] Although we often assert that public policy reflects the demands of "the people," this may express the myth rather than the reality of American democracy. Elite theory suggests that "the people" are apathetic and ill-informed about public policy, that elites actually shape mass opinion on policy questions more than masses shape elite opinion. Thus, public policy really turns out to be the preferences of elites. Public officials and administrators merely carry out the policies decided upon by the elite. Policies flow "downward" from elites to masses; they do not arise from mass demands.

Elite theory can be summarized briefly as follows:

1. Society is divided into the few who have power and the many who do not. Only a small number of persons allocate values for society; the masses do not decide public policy.
2. The few who govern are not typical of the masses who are governed. Elites are drawn disproportionately from the upper socioeconomic strata of society.
3. The movement of nonelites to elite positions must be slow and continuous to maintain stability and avoid revolution. Only nonelites who have accepted the basic elite consensus can be admitted to governing circles.
4. Elites share consensus in behalf of the basic values of the social system and the preservation of the system. In America, the bases of elite consensus are the sanctity of private property, limited government, and individual liberty.
5. Public policy does not reflect demands of masses but rather the prevailing

---

[5] Elite theory is explained at length in Thomas R. Dye and Harmon Zeigler, *The Irony of Democracy* (Belmont, Calif.: Wadsworth, 1970).

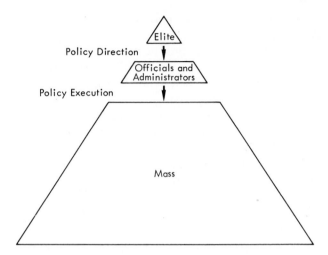

Fig. 2-3 *The Elite Model*

values of the elite. Changes in public policy will be incremental rather than revolutionary.

6. Active elites are subject to relatively little direct influence from apathetic masses. Elites influence masses more than masses influence elites.

What are the implications of elite theory for policy analysis? First of all, elitism implies that public policy does not reflect demands of "the people" so much as it does the interests and values of elites. Therefore, change and innovations in public policy come about as a result of redefinitions by elites of their own values. Because of the general conservatism of elites—that is, their interest in preserving the system—change in public policy will be incremental rather than revolutionary. Public policies are frequently modified but seldom replaced. Changes in the nature of the political system occur when events threaten the system, and elites, acting on the basis of enlightened self-interest, institute reforms to preserve the system and their place in it. The values of elites may be very "public-regarding." A sense of "noblesse oblige" may permeate elite values, and the welfare of the masses may be an important element in elite decision making. Elitism does not mean that public policy will be against mass welfare, but only that the responsibility for mass welfare rests upon the shoulders of elites, not masses.

Second, elitism views the masses as largely passive, apathetic and ill-informed; mass sentiments are more often manipulated by elites, rather than elite values being influenced by the sentiments of masses; and for the most part, communication between elites and masses flows downward.

Therefore, popular elections and party competition do not enable the masses to govern. Policy questions are seldom decided by the people through elections or through the presentation of policy alternatives by political parties. For the most part these "democratic" institutions—elections and parties—are important only for their symbolic value. They help tie the masses to the political system by giving them a role to play on election day and a political party with which they can identify. Elitism contends that the masses have at best only an indirect influence over the decision-making behavior of elites.

Elitism also asserts that elites share in a consensus about fundamental norms underlying the social system, that elites agree on the basic "rules of the game," as well as the continuation of the social system itself. The stability of the system, and even its survival, depends upon elite consensus in behalf of the fundamental values of the system, and only policy alternatives that fall within the shared consensus will be given serious consideration. Of course, elitism does not mean that elite members never disagree or never compete with each other for preeminence. It is unlikely that there ever was a society in which there was no competition among elites. But elitism implies that competition centers around a very narrow range of issues and that elites agree on more matters than they disagree.

In America elite consensus includes constitutional government, democratic procedures, majority rule, freedom of speech and press, freedom to form opposition parties and run for public office, equality of opportunity in all segments of life, the sanctity of private property, the importance of individual initiative and reward, and the legitimacy of the free enterprise, capitalist, economic system. Masses may give superficial support to democratic symbols, but they are not as consistent or reliable in their support for these values as elites.

In Chapter 3 we will examine civil rights policy largely from the perspective of elite theory. We will portray the civil rights movement as an effort of established liberal elites to insure that the benefits of the American system would be available to those blacks who accept the prevailing consensus and exhibit middle-class values. Opposition to civil rights is centered among white masses; virtually none of the progress in civil rights since World War II (Brown vs. Topeka, Civil Rights Act of 1964, Fair Housing, etc.) would have taken place if white masses rather than white elites determined public policy. Public-regarding elites were prepared to eliminate legal barriers to provide equality of opportunity under law for individual blacks. However, in Chapter 4 we will observe that established elites reacted negatively when black masses in ghettos violated the "rules of the game" in civil disorders, riots, and violence.

RATIONALISM: POLICY AS EFFICIENT GOAL ACHIEVEMENT

A rational policy is one that is correctly designed to maximize "net value achievement." [6] By "net value achievement" we mean that all relevant values of a society are known, and that any sacrifice in one or more values that is required by a policy is more than compensated for by the attainment of other values. This definition of rationality is interchangeable with the concept of efficiency—efficiency is the ratio between valued inputs and valued outputs. We can say that a policy is rational when it is most *efficient*—that is, if the ratio between the values it achieves and the values it sacrifices is positive and higher than any other policy alternative. One should *not* view efficiency in a narrow dollars-and-cents framework—in which basic social values are sacrificed for dollar savings. Our idea of efficiency involves the calculation of *all* social, political, and economic values sacrificed or achieved by a public policy, not just those that can be measured by quantitative symbols.

To select a rational policy, policy-makers must (1) know all the society's value preferences and their relative weights; (2) know all the policy alternatives available; (3) know all the consequences of each policy alternative; (4) calculate the ratio of achieved to sacrificed societal values for each policy alternative; (5) select the most efficient policy alternative.[7] This rationality assumes that the value preferences of *society as a whole* can be known and weighted. It is not enough to know and weigh the values of *some* groups and not others. There must be a complete understanding of *societal* values. Rational policy making also requires *information* about alternative policies, the *predictive capacity* to foresee accurately the consequences of alternate policies, and the *intelligence* to calculate correctly the ratio of costs to benefits. Finally, rational policy making requires a *decision-making system* that facilitates rationality in policy formation. A diagram of such a system is shown in Figure 2-4.

Many types of rational decision models are found in the literature of economics, political science, management, administrative science, and budgeting.[8] An example of a rational approach to resource allocation policy is portrayed in Figure 2-5. This model assumes that a society has an

---

[6] See Robert Henry Haveman, *The Economics of the Public Sector* (New York: John Wiley, 1970).

[7] See Yehezkel Dror, *Public Policy-Making Re-examined*, Part IV, "An Optional Model of Public Policy-Making" (San Francisco: Chandler, 1968).

[8] L. L. Wade and R. L. Curry, Jr., *A Logic of Public Policy: Aspects of Political Economy* (Belmont, Calif.: Wadsworth, 1970).

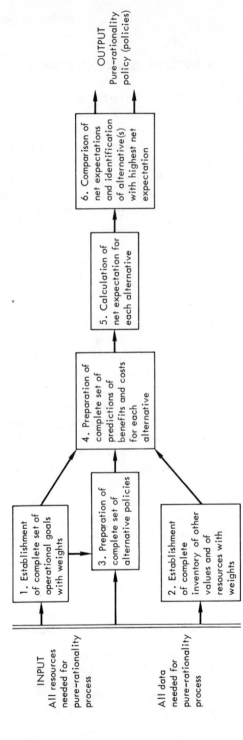

Fig. 2-4 *A Rational Model of a Decision System*

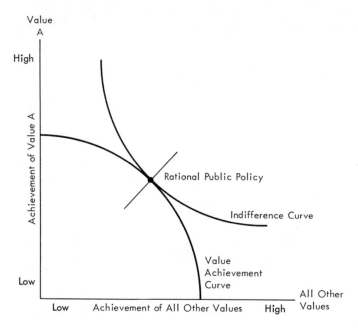

Fig. 2-5 *A Rational Resource-Allocation Model*

"indifference curve" which represents the combination of values to which society is indifferent. The indifference curve slopes in a convex fashion from the upper left (a high return of Value A at the expense of lower returns on other values) to the lower right (a lower return on Value A in exchange for higher returns of other values). Any point on the curve is assumed to be equally satisfactory to society. Of course, all combinations on a higher indifference curve are preferable to those on a lower indifference curve. But we can assume that society does not have sufficient resources to achieve high levels of Value A *and* high levels of all other values. We can plot this assumption with a "value achievement curve" which represents the combination of values which it is possible for government to produce given the limitations of resources. The value achievement curve always slopes in a concave fashion from upper left (a high achievement of Value A at the sacrifice of other values) to lower right (a lower achievement of Value A but a higher achievement of other values). Any point on the curve is possible for society to achieve. A rational public policy would be determined by the intersection of society's indifference curve and its value achievement curve. This point represents the highest level of indifference (satisfaction) allowable within society's resources.

There are many barriers to such rational decision making.[9] In fact, there are so many barriers to rational decision making that it rarely takes place at all in government. Yet the model remains important for analytic purposes because it helps to identify barriers to rationality. It assists in posing the question: Why is policy making not a more rational process? At the outset we can hypothesize several important obstacles to rational policy making:

1. There are no *societal* values that are usually agreed upon, but only the values of specific groups and individuals, many of which are conflicting..

2. The many conflicting values cannot be compared or weighted; for example, it is impossible to compare or weigh the value of individual dignity against a tax increase.

3. The environment of policy-makers, particularly the power and influence system, renders it impossible for them to see or accurately weigh many societal values, particularly those values which have no active or powerful proponents.

4. Policy-makers are not motivated to make decisions on the basis of societal goals, but instead try to maximize their own rewards—power, status, re-election, money, etc.

5. Policy-makers are not motivated to *maximize* net goal achievement, but merely to *satisfy* demands for progress; they do not search until they find "the one best way" but halt their search when they find an alternative that "will work."

6. Large investments in existing programs and policies ("sunk costs") prevent policy-makers from reconsidering alternatives foreclosed by previous decisions.

7. There are innumerable barriers to collecting all the information required to know all possible policy alternatives and the consequences of each alternative, including the cost of information gathering, the availability of the information, and the time involved in its collection.

8. Neither the predictive capacities of the social and behavioral sciences nor the predictive capacities of the physical and biological sciences are sufficiently advanced to enable policy-makers to understand the full range of consequences of each policy alternative.

9. Policy-makers, even with the most advanced computerized analytical techniques, do not have sufficient intelligence to calculate accurately cost-benefits ratios when a large number of diverse political, social, economic, and cultural values are at stake.

[9] See Charles E. Lindblom, "The Science of Muddling Through," *Public Administration Review*, 19 (Spring 1959), 79–88; David Braybrooke and Charles E. Lindblom, *A Strategy of Decision* (New York: Free Press, 1963); Aaron Wildavsky, *The Politics of the Budgetary Process* (Boston: Little, Brown, 1964).

10. Policy-makers have personal needs, inhibitions, and inadequacies which prevent them from performing in a highly rational manner.
11. Uncertainty about the consequences of various policy alternatives compels policy-makers to stick as closely as possible to previous policies to reduce the likelihood of disturbing, unanticipated consequences.
12. The segmentalized nature of policy making in large bureaucracies makes it difficult to coordinate decision making so that the input of all of the various specialists is brought to bear at the point of decision.

We cannot illustrate all the problems of achieving rationality in public policy. In Chapters 5 and 6 we will describe the general design of alternative strategies to deal with welfare and poverty in America. We will observe how these strategies were implemented in public policy, and analyze some of the obstacles to the achievement of the goal of eliminating poverty.

INCREMENTALISM: POLICY AS VARIATIONS
ON THE PAST

Incrementalism views public policy as a continuation of past government activities with only incremental modifications. Economist Charles E. Lindblom first presented the incremental model in the course of a critique of the traditional rational model of decision making.[10] According to Lindblom, decision-makers do *not* annually review the whole range of existing and proposed policies, identify societal goals, research the benefits and costs of alternative policies in achieving these goals, rank-order preferences for each policy alternative in terms of the ratio of benefits to costs, and then make a selection on the basis of all relevant information. On the contrary, constraints of time, intelligence, and cost prevent policy-makers from identifying the full range of policy alternatives and their consequences. Constraints of politics prevent the establishment of clear-cut societal goals and the accurate calculation of cost-benefit ratios. The incremental model recognizes the impractical nature of "rational-comprehensive" policy making, and describes a more conservative process of decision making.

Incrementalism is conservative in that existing programs, policies, and expenditures are considered as a base, and attention is concentrated on new programs and policies and on increases, decreases, or modifications of current programs. Policy-makers generally accept the legitimacy of established programs and tacitly agree to continue previous policies.

They do this, first of all, because they do not have the time, intelligence, or money to investigate all the alternatives to existing policy. The

[10] Charles E. Lindblom, "The Science of Muddling Through," pp. 79–88.

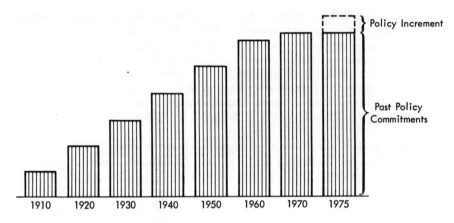

Policy Increment

Past Policy Commitments

Fig. 2-6 *The Incremental Model*

cost of collecting all this information is too great. Policy-makers do not have sufficient predictive capacities, even in the age of computers, to know what all the consequences of each alternative will be. Nor are they able to calculate cost-benefit ratios for alternative policies when many diverse political, social, economic, and cultural values are at stake. Thus completely "rational" policy may turn out to be "inefficient" (despite the contradiction in terms) if the time, intelligence, and cost of developing a rational policy are excessive.

Second, policy-makers accept the legitimacy of previous policies because of the uncertainty about the consequences of completely new or different policies. It is safer to stick with known programs when the consequences of new programs cannot be predicted. Under conditions of uncertainty, policy-makers continue past policies or programs whether or not they have proven effective.

Third, there may be heavy investments in existing programs ("sunk costs" again) which preclude any really radical change. These investments may be in money, buildings, or other hard items, or they may be in psychological dispositions, administrative practices, or organizational structure. It is accepted wisdom, for example, that organizations tend to persist over time regardless of their utility, that they develop routines that are difficult to alter, and that individuals develop a personal stake in the continuation of organizations and practices, which makes radical change very difficult. Hence, not all policy alternatives can be seriously considered, but only those which cause little physical, economic, organizational, and administrative dislocation.

Fourth, incrementalism is politically expedient. Agreement comes easier in policy making when the items in dispute are only increases or decreases in budgets, or modifications to existing programs. Conflict is heightened when decision making focuses on major policy shifts involving great gains or losses, or "all or nothing," "yes or no" policy decisions. Because the political tension involved in getting new programs or policies passed *every* year would be very great, past policy victories are continued into future years unless there is a substantial political realignment. Thus incrementalism is important in reducing conflict, maintaining stability, and preserving the political system itself.

The characteristics of policy-makers themselves also recommend the incremental model. Rarely do human beings act to maximize all their values; more often they act to satisfy particular demands. Men are pragmatic: they seldom search for the "one best way" but instead end their search when they find "a way that will work." This search usually begins with the familiar—that is, with policy alternatives close to current policies. Only if these alternatives appear to be unsatisfactory will the policy-maker venture out toward more radical policy innovation. In most cases modification of existing programs will satisfy particular demands, and the major policy shifts required to maximize values are overlooked.

Finally, in the absence of any agreed-upon societal goals or values, it is easier for the government of a pluralist society to continue existing programs rather than engage in overall policy planning toward specific societal goals.

We will give special attention to incrementalism in our discussion of taxing and spending policy in Chapter 10. Specifically, we will examine the federal government's budgeting and appropriations processes and federal tax policy, within the context of the incremental model.

GAME THEORY: POLICY AS RATIONAL CHOICE IN COMPETITIVE SITUATIONS

Game theory is the study of rational decisions in situations in which two or more participants have choices to make and the outcome depends on the choices made by each of them. It is applied to policy making where there is no *independently* "best" choice that one can make—where the "best" outcomes depend upon what others do.

The idea of a "game" is that decision-makers are involved in choices that are interdependent. Each "player" must adjust his conduct to reflect not only his own desires and abilities but also his expectations about what others will do. Perhaps the connotation of a "game" is unfortunate—suggesting that game theory is not really appropriate for *serious* conflict situations. But just the opposite is true: game theory can be applied to decisions about war and peace, the use of nuclear weapons, international diplomacy, bargaining and coalition building in Congress or the United Nations, and a variety of other important political situations. A "player" may be an individual, a group, or a national government—indeed, any body with well-defined goals that is capable of rational action.

Game theory is an abstract and deductive model of policy making. It does not describe how people actually make decisions, but rather how they would go about making decisions in competitive situations if they were completely rational. Thus, game theory is a form of rationalism, but it is applied in *competitive* situations where the outcome depends on what two or more participants do.

The *rules of the game* describe the choices that are available to all the players. The choices are frequently portrayed in a "matrix"—a diagram which presents the alternative choices of each player and all the possible outcomes of the game. A two-by-two matrix is the simplest of all: there are only two players and each player has only two alternatives to choose from:

PLAYER A

		Alternative A₁	Alternative A₂
	Alternative B₁	outcome	outcome
PLAYER B	Alternative B₂	outcome	outcome

There are four possible outcomes to this simple game, each represented by a cell in the matrix. The actual outcome depends upon the choices of both Player A and Player B.

In game theory, payoff refers to the values that each player receives as a result of his choices and those of his opponent. Payoffs are frequently represented by numerical values placed on each outcome; these numerical values are placed inside each cell of the matrix and presumably correspond to the values each player places on each outcome. Because players value different outcomes differently, there are two numerical values inside each cell—one for each player.

Consider the game of "chicken." Two adolescents drive their cars toward each other at high speed, each with one set of wheels on the center line of the highway. If neither veers off course they will crash. Whoever veers is "chicken." Both drivers prefer to avoid death but they also want to avoid the "dishonor" of being "chicken." The outcome depends on what both drivers do, and each driver must try to predict how the other will behave. This form of "brinkmanship" is common in international relations (see Figure 2-7).

Inspection of the payoff matrix suggests that it would be better for both drivers to veer in order to minimize the possibility of a great loss (−10). But the matrix is too simple. One or both players may place dif-

DRIVER A

		Stay on course	Veer
DRIVER B	**Stay on Course**	A: —10 B: —10	A: —5 B: +5
	Veer	A: +5 B: —5	A: —1 B: —1

Fig. 2-7 *A Game-Theoretic Matrix for the Game of "Chicken"*

The game theorist himself supplies the numerical values to the payoffs. If Driver A chooses to stay on course and Driver B chooses to stay on course also, the result might be scored as —10 for both players. But if Driver A chooses to stay on course and Driver B veers, then Driver A might get +5 ("Courage") and Driver B —5 ("Dishonor"). If Driver A veers but Driver B stays on course, the results would be reversed. If both veer, each is dishonored slightly (—1) but not as much as when one or the other stayed on course.

ferent values on the outcomes than is suggested by the numbers. For example, one player may prefer death to dishonor in the game. Each player must try to calculate the values of the other and neither has complete information about the values of his opponent. Moreover, bluffing or the deliberate misrepresentation of one's values or resources to an opponent is always a possibility. For example, a possible strategy in the game of chicken is to allow your opponent to see you drink heavily before the game, stumble drunkenly toward your car, and mumble something about having lived long enough in this rotten world. The effect of this communication on your opponent may increase his estimate of your likelihood of staying on course, and hence provide incentive for him to veer and allow you to win.

A key concept in game theory is that of *strategy*. Strategy refers to rational decision making in which a set of moves is designed to achieve optimum payoff even after consideration of all of the opponent's possible moves. Game theorists employ the term "minimax" to refer to the rational strategy that either *minimizes the maximum loss or maximizes the minimum gain* for a player, regardless of what his opponent does. The minimax strategy is designed to protect a player against his opponent's best play. It might be viewed as a conservative strategy in that it is designed to reduce losses and insure minimum gains rather than to seek maximum gains at the risk of great losses. But most game theorists view minimax as the best rational strategy. (The rational player in the game of chicken will veer, because this choice minimizes his maximum loss.)

It should be clear from this discussion that game theory embraces both very complex and very simple ideas. The crucial question is whether any of these game theory ideas is really useful in studying public policy.

Game theory is more frequently proposed as an *analytic* tool by social scientists than as a practical guide to policy making by government officials. The conditions of game theory are seldom approximated in real life. Seldom do policy alternatives present themselves neatly in a matrix. More importantly, seldom can policy-makers know the real payoff values for themselves or their opponents of various policy alternatives. Finally, as we have already indicated, there are many obstacles to rational policy making by governments.

Yet game theory provides an interesting way of thinking clearly about policy choices in conflict situations. Perhaps the real utility of game theory in policy analysis at the present time is in suggesting interesting questions and providing a vocabulary to deal with policy making in conflict situations. Our own use of game theory ideas in describing and explaining national defense policy in Chapter 11 will be limited to these purposes.

SYSTEMS THEORY: POLICY AS SYSTEM OUTPUT

Another way to conceive of public policy is to think of it as a response of a political system to forces brought to bear upon it from the environment.[11] Forces generated in the environment which affect the political system are viewed as *inputs*. The *environment* is any condition or circumstance defined as external to the boundaries of the political system. The political *system* is that group of interrelated structures and processes which functions authoritatively to allocate values for a society. *Outputs* of the political system are authoritative value allocations of the system, and these allocations constitute *public policy*.

This conceptualization of political activity and public policy can be diagramed as in Figure 2-8. This diagram is a simplified version of the idea of the political system described at great length by political scientist David Easton. The notion of a political system has been employed, either implicitly or explicitly, by many scholars who have sought to analyze the causes and consequences of public policy.

Systems theory portrays public policy as an output of the political *system*. The concept of "system" implies an identifiable set of institutions and activities in society that function to transform demands into authoritative decisions requiring the support of the whole society. The concept of "system" also implies that elements of the system are interrelated, that the system can respond to forces in its environment, and that it will do so in order to preserve itself. Inputs are received into the political system in the

---

[11] This conceptualization is based upon David Easton, "An Approach to the Analysis of Political Systems," *World Politics*, 9 (1957), 383–400; and Easton, *A Framework for Political Analysis* (Englewood Cliffs, N.J.: Prentice-Hall, 1965).

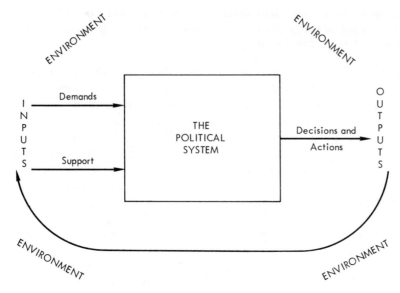

Fig. 2-8 *The Systems Model*

form of both demands and support. Demands occur when individuals or groups, in response to real or perceived environmental conditions, act to affect public policy. Support is rendered when individuals or groups accept the outcome of elections, obey the laws, pay their taxes, and generally conform to policy decisions. Any system absorbs a variety of demands, some of which conflict with each other. In order to transform these demands into outputs (public policies), it must arrange settlements and enforce these settlements upon the parties concerned. It is recognized that outputs (public policies) may have a modifying effect on the environment and the demands arising from it, and may also have an effect upon the character of the political system. The system preserves itself by (1) producing reasonably satisfying outputs, (2) relying upon deeply rooted attachments to the system itself, and (3) using, or threatening to use, force.

The value of the systems model to policy analysis lies in the questions that it poses:

1. What are the significant dimensions of the environment that generate demands upon the political system?
2. What are the significant characteristics of the political system that enable it to transform demands into public policy and to preserve itself over time?
3. How do environmental inputs affect the character of the political system?
4. How do characteristics of the political system affect the content of public policy?

5. How do environmental inputs affect the content of public policy?
6. How does public policy affect, through feedback, the environment and the character of the political system?

In Chapters 12 and 13 we will examine these questions with particular reference to public policies in the American states. We will assess the impact of various environmental conditions—particularly wealth, urbanization, and education—on levels of spending, benefits, and services in education, welfare, highways, police, corrections, and finance. We will see how federal policy sometimes tries to offset the impact of environmental variables on domestic policy in the states. We will examine the impact of political system characteristics—pluralism and reformism—on levels of taxing, spending, benefits, and service, and attempt to compare the impact of these system characteristics on public policy with the impact of environmental conditions. Finally, we will investigate what goes on in the "black box" labeled "political system" and the policy impact of various elements of the political system itself, including mass opinion, elite attitudes, parties, interest groups, and bureaucratic, executive, and legislative interaction.

MODELS: HOW TO TELL IF THEY ARE HELPING
OR NOT

A model is merely an abstraction or representation of political life. When we think of political "systems," or "elites," or "groups," or "rational decision making," or "incrementalism," or "games," we are abstracting from the real world in an attempt to simplify, clarify, and understand what is really important about politics. Before we begin in our study of public policy, let us set forth some general criteria for evaluating the usefulness of concepts and models.

1. Certainly the utility of a model lies in its ability to *order and simplify* political life so that we can think about it more clearly and understand the relationships we find in the real world. Yet too much simplification can lead to inaccuracies in our thinking about reality. If a concept is too narrow or identifies only superficial phenomena, we may not be able to use it to explain public policy. On the other hand, if a concept is too broad, and suggests overly complex relationships, it may become so complicated and unmanageable that it is not really an aid to understanding. In other words, some theories of politics may be too complex to be helpful, while others may be too simplistic.
2. A model should also *identify* the really significant aspects of public policy. It should direct attention away from irrelevant variables or circumstances, and focus upon the "real" causes and "significant" consequences of public

policy. Of course, what is "real," "relevant," "significant" is to some extent a function of an individual's personal values. But we can all agree that the utility of a concept is related to its ability to identify what it is that is really important about politics.

3. Generally, a model should be *congruent with reality*—that is to say, it ought to have real empirical referents. We would expect to have difficulty with a concept that identifies a process that does not really occur, or symbolizes phenomena that do not exist in the real world. On the other hand we must not be too quick to dismiss "unrealistic" concepts *if* they succeed in directing our attention to why they are unrealistic. For example, no one contends that government decision making is completely rational—public officials do not always act to maximize societal values and minimize societal costs. Yet the concept of "rational decision making" may be still useful, albeit "unrealistic," if it makes us realize how irrational government decision making really is and prompts us to inquire about why it is irrational.

4. A concept or model should also *communicate* something meaningful. If too many people disagree over the meaning of a concept, its utility in communication is diminished. For example, if no one really agrees on what constitutes an "elite," then the concept of an elite does not mean the same thing to everyone. If one defines an "elite" as democratically elected public officials who are representative of the general public, then he is communicating a different idea in using the term than one who defines an elite as an unrepresentative minority that makes decisions for society based on its own interests.

5. A model should help to *direct inquiry and research* into public policy. A concept should be operational—that is, it should refer directly to real-world phenomena that can be observed, measured, and verified. A concept, or a series of interrelated concepts (which we refer to as a "model") should suggest relationships in the real world that can be tested and verified. If there is no way to prove or disprove the ideas suggested by a concept, then the concept is not really useful in developing a science of politics.

6. Finally, a model approach should *suggest an explanation* of public policy. It should suggest hypotheses about the causes and consequences of public policy—hypotheses that can be tested against real-world data. A concept that merely *describes* public policy is not as useful as a concept that *explains* public policy, or at least suggests some possible explanations.

BIBLIOGRAPHY

DYE, THOMAS R., and HARMON ZEIGLER, *The Irony of Democracy*. Belmont, Calif.: Wadsworth, 1970.

EASTON, DAVID, *A Framework for Political Analysis*. Englewood Cliffs, N.J.: Prentice-Hall, 1965.

TRUMAN, DAVID B., *The Governmental Process*. New York: Knopf, 1971.

WADE, L. L., and R. L. CURRY, JR., *A Logic of Public Policy: Aspects of Political Economy*. Belmont, Calif.: Wadsworth, 1970.

WILDAVSKY, AARON, *The Politics of the Budgetary Process*. Boston: Little, Brown, 1964.

Marching to protest cutbacks of daycare funds. UPI Photo

3 CIVIL RIGHTS:

elite mass interaction

The central domestic issue of American politics over the long history of the nation has been the place of the black man in American society. In describing this issue we have relied heavily on the elite model—because elite and mass attitudes toward civil rights differ a great deal, and public policy appears to reflect the attitudes of *elites* rather than masses. Civil rights policy is a response of a national elite to conditions affecting a small minority of Americans, rather than a response of national leaders to majority sentiments. Policies of the national elite in civil rights have met with varying degrees of resistance from states and communities. We will contend that national policy has shaped mass opinion more than mass opinion has shaped national policy.

ELITE MASS ATTITUDES AND CIVIL RIGHTS

White America has long harbored an ambivalence toward black America—a recognition of the evils of inequality but a reluctance to take steps to eliminate it. Gunnar Myrdal, writing in 1944, captured the essence of the American racial dilemma:

> The "American dilemma" . . . is the ever-raging conflict between, on the one hand, the valuations preserved on the general plane which we shall call the "American creed," where the American thinks, talks, and acts under the influence of high national and Christian precepts, and, on

41

the other hand, the valuation on specific planes of individual and group living, where personal and local interests; economic, and social, and sexual jealousies; considerations of community prestige and conformity; group prejudices against particular persons or types of people; all sorts of miscellaneous wants, impulses, and habits dominate his outlook.[1]

The attitudes of white masses toward blacks in America are ambivalent. Most whites believe that blacks suffer injustices and that discrimination is wrong. Yet even though they admit the injustices of discrimination, an overwhelming majority of whites believe that blacks are moving "too fast." [2] In general, whites are willing to support laws eliminating discrimination and guaranteeing equality of opportunity. But what about compensatory efforts to overcome the effects of past discrimination and uplift the black community? Here the evidence is that most whites are not prepared to make any special effort to change the conditions of blacks. Louis Harris asked a national sample:

> Some Negroes have suggested that since Negroes have been discriminated against for one hundred years, they should be given special consideration in jobs, that they should actually be given a preference for a job opening, such as the veteran gets today in a government job. Do you agree or disagree with the idea of job preference for Negroes? [3]

Whites responded with a resounding "No!" Fully 90 percent of the national sample of whites opposed special consideration for blacks in jobs; only 4 percent favored it.

In general, white Americans are much more sympathetic to Negro rights today than they were a decade or two ago. A national sample of white Americans was asked the question, "Do you think white students and Negro students should go to the same schools or separate schools?" in 1942, 1956, 1963, and 1966 (see Table 3-1). In 1942, not one American white in three approved of integrated schools. Even in the North, a majority was opposed to school integration, while in the South only two whites in a hundred supported integration. In 1956, two years after the historic *Brown vs. Topeka*, white attitudes had shifted markedly. Nationwide support for integration characterized about half of the white population; in the North it was the majority view, and

---

[1] Gunnar Myrdal, *An American Dilemma: The Negro Problem and Modern Democracy* (New York: McGraw-Hill, 1944), vol. I, xxi.

[2] Survey results are derived from the text and Appendix of William Brink and Louis Harris, *Black and White: A Study of U.S. Racial Attitudes Today* (New York: Simon and Schuster, 1967); with updating from William Brink and Louis Harris, "Report from Black America," *Newsweek,* June 30, 1969. The data were collected in national surveys conducted in 1963, 1966, and 1969.

[3] Brink and Harris, *Black and White,* p. 126.

Table 3-1   *Attitude Change Among Whites: White and Negro Students Should Attend the Same Schools, 1942–66*

PERCENTAGE YES

	1942	1956	1963	1966	1973
Total whites	30	49	62	67	82
Northern whites	40	61	73	78	84
Southern whites	2	15	31	36	65

Source: Paul B. Sheatsley, "White Attitudes Toward the Negro," *Daedalus*, 95, No. 1 (Winter 1966). Updated from *Gallup Opinion Index*, No. 100, October 1973.

in the South the proportion supporting integration had risen to one in seven. By 1963, two out of every three whites believed in integrated schools, and, even more noteworthy, one out of three Southern whites believed in integration. Since 1963 there has been a continuation of the upward trend in the proportion of white Americans who favor school integration. Additional survey information suggests that whites are becoming increasingly accommodating toward equal rights for blacks over time in other areas as well. But it should be noted that white opinion generally follows public policy, rather than leading it.

There is a wide gap between the attitudes of masses and elites on the subject of the black revolution. The most hostile attitudes toward blacks are found among the less privileged, less educated whites. Low-income whites are much less willing to have contact with blacks than high-income whites, whether it is a matter of using the same public restrooms, or going to a movie or restaurant, or living next door. It is the affluent, well-educated American who is most concerned with discrimination against blacks and who is most willing to have contact with them.

The political implication of this finding is obvious: opposition to civil rights legislation and to black advancement in education, jobs, income, housing, and so on, is likely to be strongest among low-income whites. Within the white community, support for civil rights will continue to come from the educated, affluent American.

The black revolution has deeply divided white America. Although it is true that there is a wide gulf between blacks and whites in terms of the speed of progress, the tactics of the revolution, and perhaps even the ultimate objective of the revolution, there is also a wide gulf between poor and affluent whites in their response to the Negro struggle. The better educated, more privileged whites are much more sympathetic toward black aspirations than are poorly educated, low-income whites. Less privileged whites do not agree that the condition of the

Negro in America is worse than the condition of whites, or that Negroes are discriminated against.

	PERCENT AGREEING		
	All Whites	**Low Income**	**Affluents**
Negro housing worse than white	65	46	69
Negroes discriminated against	60	46	78
Negroes laugh a lot	56	66	49
Negroes smell different	52	61	45
Negroes have looser morals	50	56	46
Sympathize with Negro protests	46	24	57
Negroes want to live off handouts	43	53	33
Negro education worse than white	40	27	58

Less privileged whites hold stereotyped beliefs about Negroes—that they smell different, have looser morals, and are lazy. There is far less willingness to have contact with blacks among poor whites. As Louis Harris notes: "If there are two races in this country poles apart on the race issue, then it is equally true there are two white societies just as far apart." [4]

THE DEVELOPMENT OF CIVIL RIGHTS POLICY

The initial goal in the struggle for equality in America was the elimination of Jim Crow. This required the development of a national civil rights policy to eliminate direct discrimination and segregation in public and private life. First, discrimination and segregation practiced by governments had to be prohibited, particularly in voting and public education. Then direct discrimination in all segments of American life—in transportation, theaters, parks, stores, restaurants, businesses, employment, and housing—came under legal attack.

At the outset it is important to realize that the elimination of direct, lawful discrimination, does not in itself ensure equality. The civil rights policies of the national government do not affect the conditions of equality in America as directly as we might suppose. Civil rights laws have not dramatically affected the living conditions of the masses of blacks in either the North or the South. The problem of racial inequality—inequality between blacks and whites in income, health, housing, employment, education, and so on—is more than a problem of direct legal discrimination even though the first important step toward equality was

[4] *Ibid.*, p. 137.

the elimination of Jim Crow. The movement to end direct discrimination laid the foundation for the politics of equality in the future.

The Fourteenth Amendment declares:

> All persons born or naturalized in the United States, and subject to the Jurisdiction thereof, are citizens of the United States and of the State wherein they reside. No State shall make or enforce any law which shall abridge the privileges or immunities of citizens of the United States; nor shall any State deprive any person of life, liberty, or property, without due process of law; nor deny to any person within its jurisdiction the equal protection of the laws.

The language of the Fourteenth Amendment and its historical context leaves little doubt that its original purpose was to achieve the full measure of citizenship and equality for black Americans. Some radical Republicans were prepared in 1867 to carry out in Southern society the revolution this amendment implied. But by 1877, it was clear that Reconstruction had failed; the national government was not prepared to carry out the long, difficult, and disagreeable task of really reconstructing society in the eleven states of the former Confederacy. In what has been described as the Compromise of 1877, the national government agreed to end military occupation of the South, give up its efforts to rearrange Southern society, and lend tacit approval to white supremacy in that region. In return, the Southern states pledged their support of the Union, accepted national supremacy, and, of course, agreed to permit the Republican candidate to assume the presidency after the disputed election of 1876.

The Supreme Court adhered to the terms of the compromise. The result was a complete inversion of the meaning of the Fourteenth Amendment so that it became a bulwark of segregation. State laws segregating the races were upheld as long as persons in each of the separated races were protected equally. The constitutional argument in behalf of segregation under the Fourteenth Amendment was that the phrase "equal protection of the laws" did not prevent state-enforced separation of the races. Schools and other public facilities that were "separate but equal" won constitutional approval. This separate but equal doctrine became the Supreme Court's interpretation of the Equal Protection Clause of the Fourteenth Amendment in *Plessy* v. *Ferguson:*

> The object of the [14th] Amendment was undoubtedly to enforce the absolute equality of the two races before the law, but in the nature of things it could not have been intended to abolish distinctions based upon color, or to enforce social, as distinguished from political, equality, or a commingling of the two races upon terms unsatisfactory to either. Laws permitting, and even requiring, their separation in places where they are

liable to be brought into contact do not necessarily imply the inferiority of either race to the other, and have been generally, if not universally recognized as within the competency of the state legislatures in the exercise of their police power. The most common instance of this is connected with the establishment of separate schools for white and colored children, which has been held to be a valid exercise of the legislative power. . . .[5]

As a matter of fact, of course, segregated facilities, including public schools, were seldom if ever equal, even with respect to physical conditions. In practice, the doctrine of segregation was "separate and unequal." The Supreme Court began to take notice of this after World War II. Although it declined to overrule the segregationist interpretation of the Fourteenth Amendment, it began to order the admission of individual blacks to white public universities where evidence indicated that separate Negro institutions were inferior or nonexistent.[6]

Leaders of the newly emerging civil rights movement in the 1940s and 1950s were not satisfied with court decisions that examined the circumstances in each case to determine if separate school facilities were really equal. Led by Roy Wilkins, executive director of the National Association for the Advancement of Colored People, and Thurgood Marshall, chief counsel for the NAACP, the civil rights movement pressed for a court decision that segregation itself meant inequality within the meaning of the Fourteenth Amendment, whether or not facilities were equal in all tangible respects. In short, they wanted a complete reversal of the "separate but equal" interpretation of the Fourteenth Amendment, and a holding that laws *separating* the races were unconstitutional.

The civil rights groups chose to bring suit for desegregation in Topeka, Kansas, where segregated Negro and white schools were equal with respect to buildings, curricula, qualifications, and salaries of teachers, and other tangible factors. The object was to prevent the Court from ordering the admission of blacks because *tangible* facilities were not equal, and to force the Court to review the doctrine of segregation itself.

On May 17, 1954, the Court rendered its decision in *Brown* v. *Board of Education of Topeka, Kansas:*

Segregation of white and colored children in public schools has a detrimental effect upon the colored children. The impact is greater when it has the sanction of law, for the policy of separating the races is usually interpreted as denoting the inferiority of the Negro group. A form of

[5] *Plessy* v. *Ferguson,* 163 U.S. 537 (1896).
[6] *Sweatt* v. *Painter,* 339 U.S. 629 (1950).

inferiority affects the motivation of a child to learn. Segregation with the sanction of law, therefore, has a tendency to retard the educational and mental development of Negro children and to deprive them of some of the benefits they would receive in a racially integrated school system.

Whatever may have been the extent of psychological knowledge of the time of *Plessy* v. *Ferguson*, this finding is amply supported by modern authority. Any language in *Plessy* vs. *Ferguson* contrary to this source is rejected.[7]

The symbolic importance of the original *Brown* v. *Topeka* decision cannot be overestimated. Although it would be many years before any significant number of black children would attend formerly segregated white schools, the decision by the nation's highest court undoubtedly stimulated black hopes and expectations. Sociologist Kenneth Clark writes:

> This [civil rights] movement would probably not have existed at all were it not for the 1954 Supreme Court school desegregation decision which provided a tremendous boost to the morale of Negroes by its *clear* affirmation that color is irrelevant to the rights of American citizens. Until this time the Southern Negro generally had accommodated to the separatism of the black from the white society.[8]

MASS RESISTANCE TO CIVIL RIGHTS POLICY

The Supreme Court had spoken forcefully in the Brown case in 1954 in declaring segregation unconstitutional. From a constitutional viewpoint, any state-supported segregation of the races after 1954 was prohibited. Article VI of the Constitution declares that the words of that document are "the supreme law of the land . . . anything in the constitution or laws of any state to the contrary notwithstanding."

From a political viewpoint, however, the battle over segregation was just beginning. Segregation would remain a part of American life, regardless of its constitutionality, until effective elite power was brought to bear to end it. The Supreme Court, by virtue of the American system of federalism and separation of powers, has little formal power at its disposal. Congress, the president, state governors and legislatures, and the people have more power at their disposal than the federal judiciary. The Supreme Court must rely largely on the other branches of the federal government, on the states, and on private individuals and organizations to effectuate the law of the land.

Yet in 1954 the practice of segregation was widespread and deeply

[7] *Brown* v. *Board of Education of Topeka, Kansas,* 347 U.S. 483 (1954).
[8] Kenneth B. Clark, *Dark Ghetto* (New York, Harper & Row, 1965), pp. 77–78.

ingrained in American life. Seventeen states required the segregation of the races in public schools. These seventeen states were

Alabama	North Carolina	Kentucky
Arkansas	South Carolina	Maryland
Florida	Tennessee	Missouri
Georgia	Texas	Oklahoma
Louisiana	Virginia	West Virginia
Mississippi	Delaware	

The Congress of the United States required the segregation of the races in the public schools of the District of Columbia. Four additional states— Arizona, Kansas, New Mexico, and Wyoming—authorized segregation upon the option of local school boards.

Thus, in deciding *Brown* v. *Topeka*, the Supreme Court struck down the laws of twenty-one states and the District of Columbia in a single opinion. Such a far-reaching decision was bound to meet with difficulties in implementation. In an opinion delivered the following year regarding the question of relief for Brown and others similarly situated, the Supreme Court said:

> Full implementation of these constitutional principles may require solution of varied local school problems. School authorities have the primary responsibility for elucidating, assessing, and solving these problems; courts will have to consider whether the action of school authorities constitutes good faith implementation of the governing constitutional principles.

Thus, the Supreme Court did not order immediate nationwide desegregation, but instead turned over the responsibility for desegregation to state and local authorities under the supervision of federal district courts. The way was open for extensive litigation, obstruction, and delay by states that chose to resist desegregation.

The six border states with segregated school systems—Delaware, Kentucky, Maryland, Missouri, Oklahoma, West Virginia—together with the school districts in Kansas, Arizona, and New Mexico that had operated segregated schools, chose not to resist desegregation formally. The District of Columbia also desegregated its public schools the year following the Supreme Court's decision. Progress in desegregation in the border states proceeded fairly well; by 1964 over half of the black children in these states were attending integrated schools.

However, resistance to school integration was the policy choice of the eleven states of the Old Confederacy. Refusal of a school district to desegregate until it was faced with a federal court injunction was the most common form of delay. Segregationists also pressed for state

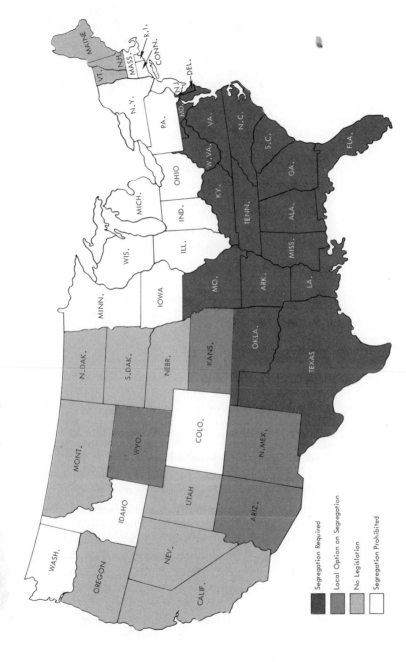

Fig. 3-1 Segregation Laws in the United States in 1954

Segregation Required

Local Option on Segregation

No Legislation

Segregation Prohibited

49

laws that would create an endless chain of litigation in each of the nearly 3,000 school districts in the South in the hope that these integration efforts would drown in a sea of protracted court controversy. Some other schemes included state payment of private school tuition in lieu of providing public schools, amending compulsory attendance laws to provide that no child shall be required to attend an integrated school, requiring schools faced with desegregation orders to cease operation, and the use of pupil placement laws to avoid or minimize the extent of integration. State officials attempted to prevent desegregation on the grounds that it would endanger public safety, and actually precipitated and encouraged violent resistance through attempts to "interpose" and "nullify" federal authority within their states. Of all delaying tactics, the most successful was the pupil placement law. Under this law each child was guaranteed "freedom of choice" in the selection of his school. School authorities relied on the fact that most blacks and most whites selected the schools they had previously attended—that is, segregated schools.

On the whole, those states that chose to resist desegregation were quite successful in doing so during the ten-year period from 1954 to 1964. In late 1964 only about 2 percent of the Negro school children in the eleven southern states were attending integrated schools! The effectiveness of state and local governments in resisting the policy of the Supreme Court for over a decade is an important commentary on the power of states and communities in our federal system.

In the Civil Rights Act of 1964, Congress finally entered the civil rights field in support of court efforts to achieve desegregation. Among other things, the Civil Rights Act of 1964 provided that every federal department and agency must take action to end segregation in all programs or activities receiving federal financial assistance. It was specified that this action was to include termination of financial assistance if states and communities receiving federal funds refused to comply with federal desegregation orders. Thus, in addition to court orders requiring desegregation, states and communities faced administrative orders or "guidelines" from federal executive agencies, particularly the U.S. Office of Education, threatening loss of federal funds for noncompliance. Acting under the authority of Title VI, the U.S. Office of Education required all school districts in the seventeen formerly segregated states to submit desegregation plans as a condition of federal assistance. "Guidelines" governing the acceptability of these plans were frequently unclear, often contradictory, and always changing, yet progress toward desegregation was speeded up.

In 1969 the last legal justication for delay in implementing school desegregation collapsed when the Supreme Court rejected a request by

Mississippi school officials for a delay in implementing school desegregation in that state. School officials, with the support of the Nixon Administration, contended that immediate desegregation in several southern Mississippi counties would encounter "administrative and legislative difficulties." The Supreme Court stated that no delay could be granted because "continued operation of segregated school under a standard of allowing 'all deliberate speed' for desegregation is no longer constitutionally permissible." [9] The Court declared that every school district was obligated to end dual school systems "at once" and "now and hereafter" to operate only unitary schools. The effect of the decision—fifteen years after the original Brown case—was to eliminate any further legal justification for the continuation of segregation in public schools.

By 1970 Southern school desegregation had proceeded to the point where more black pupils were attending integrated schools in the South than in the North. The Department of Health, Education and Welfare reported that 58.3 percent of black pupils in the *South* were attending school with whites (up from 15.9 percent in 1967), whereas only 42.6 percent of black pupils in the *North* were attending integrated schools. This is an important comparison between the diminishing impact of segregation by law in the South and the continuing impact of de facto segregation in the North. If the issue is posed as one of "racial isolation," then by 1970 the efforts of the federal courts and executive agencies toward eliminating the last vestiges of segregation by law had reduced racial isolation in the South to the point where it was less than racial isolation in the North.

"DE FACTO" SCHOOL SEGREGATION AND BUSING

In *Brown* v. *Board of Education of Topeka,* the Supreme Court quoted approvingly the view that segregation had "a tendency to retard the educational and mental development of Negro children and to deprive them of some of the benefits they would receive in a racially integrated school system." In 1967 the U.S. Commission on Civil Rights reported that even when the segregation was *de facto*—that is, the product of segregated housing patterns and neighborhood schools rather than direct discrimination—the adverse effects on black students were still significant.[10] Black students attending predominantly black schools had lower achievement scores and lower levels of aspiration than blacks with comparable socioeconomic backgrounds who attended predomi-

[9] *Alexander* v. *Holmes County Board of Education,* 396 U.S. 19 (1969).
[10] U.S. Commission on Civil Rights, *Racial Isolation in the Public Schools* (Washington, D.C.: Government Printing Office, 1966).

nantly white schools. When a group of black students attending school with a majority of advantaged whites was compared to a group of blacks attending school with a majority of disadvantaged blacks, the average difference in levels of achievement amounted to more than two grade levels. On the other hand, the Commission found that the achievement levels of white students in classes roughly half white in composition were not substantially different from those of white students in all-white schools. This finding comprises perhaps the best single argument for ending de facto segregation in Northern urban systems.

Racial isolation of public school pupils is widespread throughout the nation. The U.S. Commission on Civil Rights reported that 75 percent of the black elementary school pupils in seventy-five large cities attended predominantly black schools (those with 90 percent or more black enrollment). However, ending de facto segregation would require drastic changes in the prevailing concept of "neighborhood schools." Schools would no longer be a part of the neighborhood or the local community but rather part of a larger citywide or areawide school system. Students would have to be bused into and out of the ghettos on a massive scale. In several large cities where blacks comprise the overwhelming majority of public school students, desegregation would require city students to be bused to the suburbs and suburban students to be bused to the core city. Many suburbanites moved out of the central city in order to get their children out of city schools, and these persons are highly unlikely to favor any proposal to bus their children back into the ghettos. Finally, the ending of de facto segregation would require school districts to classify students on the basis of race and to use racial categories as a basis for school placement. Although this would supposedly be a benign form of racial classification, nevertheless it would represent a return to both government-sponsored racial classification and the differential application of laws to the separate races (in contrast to the notion that the law should be "color-blind").

The argument for busing is that it is the most effective and efficient method of providing minority groups with equal opportunities in education. Currently, black ghetto schools do not provide the same educational opportunities that are provided in predominantly white outer-city and suburban schools. As a black city councilman in Detroit put it:

> It's pragmatic. We don't have any desire to be close to white people just for the sake of being close to white people. We want the same thing everyone else wants so we can have the same opportunities for our kids to learn and grow.[11]

[11] *Time,* November 15, 1971, p. 64.

Blacks have a constitutional right to equal educational opportunities. Busing is an inconvenience, but it certainly is a minor inconvenience compared with the value of equal educational opportunity. Many proponents of busing argue that busing was frequently used in the South to maintain segregation and many black children were bused past white schools closer to their home in order to attend all-black segregated schools. Now it is argued that the same busing mechanisms should be used to achieve integration rather than segregation. Moreover, many supporters of busing argue that de facto segregation has indeed been abetted by government policies—for example, federal housing programs that build low-income public housing in central cities and promote middle-class home ownership in suburbs; transportation policies that make it easier for affluent white middle-class residents to leave the central city for homes in the suburbs while retaining their jobs in the cities, etc.—and therefore governments have a clear responsibility to take affirmative steps including busing to integrate public schools. Suburban residents contributed to de facto segregation in the central city when they moved to the suburbs, and now it is only fair that their children be bused back and forth between the suburbs and the ghettos in order to rectify the resulting racial imbalance.

Opposition to busing is widespread. Not all of this opposition is "racist." Middle-class parents feel that busing their children to ghetto schools will expose them to the social problems of ghettos—crimes, drugs, and violence. White parents fear that their children will be exposed to what blacks themselves are trying to escape—the rapes, rip-offs, robberies, and dope addiction that have turned many inner-city schools into blackboard jungles. Middle-class whites who have moved to a suburb for the sake of its school system resent the fact that courts will order their children to be bused back to the poorer-quality city schools. A Michigan mother argues, "I don't see any reason why they've got a right to come in here and tell me my kids can't use the school I bought and paid for." [12] The greatest opposition to busing comes when white middle-class children are ordered to attend ghetto schools; opposition is greatly reduced when ghetto children are ordered to attend predominantly white middle-class schools (see Table 3-2). Most whites do not believe in sending youngsters from a good school to a bad school in order to achieve racial integration. Busing also destroys the concept of a neighborhood school, where children are educated near their homes under the guidance of their parents. Neighborhood schools are said to stimulate community involvement in the educational process—bringing teachers and parents and students together

12 *Ibid.*, p. 57.

Table 3-2 *Mass Opinion on School Integration*

Question: Would you, yourself, have any objection to sending your children to a school where a few of the children are Negroes? Where half are Negroes? Where more than half are Negroes?

	Northern White Parents	Southern White Parents
Where a few are Negroes?		
1963	10%	61%
1970	6	16
1973	6	16
Where half are Negroes?		
1963	33%	78%
1970	24	43
1973	23	36
Where more than half are Negroes?		
1963	53%	86%
1970	51	69
1973	63	69

Source: Data derived from *Gallup Opinion Index* (October 1973), p. 14.

more frequently. In addition, busing involves educational time wasted in riding buses, educational funds spent on buses rather than learning materials, and an unnecessary increase in the risk of accidents to many children. Proponents of busing argue that it brings children of different cultures together and teaches them to live and work and play with others who are different from themselves. But opponents of busing cite the record of racial violence in mixed schools. It is difficult to justify placing the burden of racial integration of American society on school children; opponents of busing argue that the parents should first achieve an integrated community and then there would be no need for busing. Besides, racial balancing does not always result in genuine integration; as one Pennsylvania high school student remarked after a citywide busing program, "I thought the purpose of busing was to integrate the schools, but in the long run, the white kids sit in one part of the bus and the black kids in another part." [13]

The question of equality in public education, however, is a constitutional question that is likely to be resolved by federal courts rather than public opinion or presidential or Congressional action. The Fourteenth Amendment guarantees "equal protection of the laws." If the Supreme Court requires busing and racial balancing in all public schools in order to fulfill the constitutional mandate of the Fourteenth Amend-

[13] *Ibid.,* p. 63.

ment, then only another amendment to the Constitution specifically prohibiting busing and racial balancing could overturn that decision.

To date, however, the Supreme Court has not held that there is any affirmative duty of school officials to correct de facto racial imbalances in public schools as long as racial imbalances are not a product of present or past actions of state or local governments. However, where racial imbalance and de facto segregation may be in part a product of past discriminatory practices by states or school districts, school officials have a duty to eliminate all vestiges of segregation, and this responsibility may entail "busing" and deliberate racial balancing to achieve integration in education. Thus, in the important case of *Swann* v. *Charlotte-Mecklenburg Board of Education*,[14] the Supreme Court held that Southern school districts have a special affirmative duty under the Equal Protection Clause of the Fourteenth Amendment to eliminate all vestiges of dual school systems and to take whatever steps are necessary, including busing, to end all manifestations of segregation. Moreover, the Supreme Court held that the racial composition of the school in a Southern district that had previously segregated by law could be used as evidence of violation of constitutional rights, and busing to achieve racial balance could be imposed as a means of ending all traces of dualism in the schools. The Supreme Court was careful to say, however, that racial imbalance in a school is not itself grounds for ordering busing unless it is also shown that some present or past government action has contributed to that imbalance. Thus, the impact of the Swann decision falls largely on *Southern* schools.

The constitutional question in *Northern* cities is somewhat different from that in Southern cities; most Northern have no history of direct discrimination by law, and it is difficult to prove that de facto segregation in these cities is a product of any government actions. In 1974, the Supreme Court decided by a 5 to 4 vote that the Fourteenth Amendment does *not* require busing across city-suburban school district boundaries to achieve integration. Where central city schools are predominantly black, and suburban schools are predominantly white, cross-district busing is not required, unless it is shown that some official action brought about this segregation. The Supreme Court threw out a lower federal court order for massive busing of students between Detroit and 52 suburban school districts. Although Detroit city schools are 70 percent black, none of the Detroit area school districts segregated students *within* their own boundaries. This important decision means that largely black central cities, surrounded by largely white suburbs, will remain de facto segregated, because there are not enough white students living within the city to achieve integration.

[14] *Swann* v. *Charlotte–Mecklenburg Board of Education*, 39 L.W. 4437 (1971).

CONGRESS AND THE CIVIL RIGHTS ACT OF 1964

The initial objective of the civil rights movement in America was to prevent discrimination and segregation as practiced by or supported by *governments*, particularly states, municipalities, and school districts. But even while important victories for the civil rights movement were being recorded in the prevention of discrimination by governments, particularly in the Brown case, the movement began to broaden its objectives to include the elimination of discrimination in *all* segments of American life, private as well as public. Civil rights was redefined to mean not merely a legal but an actual possibility of developing human capacities and sharing in the goods a society has produced and the way of life it has built. This was a more positive concept of civil rights. It involved not merely restrictions on government, but a positive obligation of government to act forcefully to end discrimination in public accommodations, employment, housing, and all other sectors of private life. When the civil rights movement turned to combating private discrimination, it had to carry its fight into the legislative branch of government. The federal courts could help restrict discrimination by state and local governments and school authorities, but only Congress, state legislatures, and city councils could restrict discrimination practiced by private owners of restaurants, hotels and motels, private employers, and other individuals who were not government officials.

A new militancy, expressed in Martin Luther King's call for nonviolent direct action, appeared in the civil rights movement in the mid-1950s. Between 1941 and 1954, Negro protests were primarily in the form of legal cases brought by the NAACP to federal courts; negotiation and bargaining with white businessmen and government officials, often by the National Urban League; and local lobbying in behalf of Negro constituents by Negro political leaders in Northern communities. But in 1955 the Negro community of Montgomery, Alabama, began a year-long boycott with frequent demonstrations against the Montgomery city buses over segregated seating practices. The dramatic appeal and the eventual success of the boycott in Montgomery brought nationwide attention to a local Negro minister, Martin Luther King, and led to the creation in 1956 of the Southern Christian Leadership Conference. In 1960, Negro students from the North Carolina Agricultural and Technical College began a "sit in" demonstration at the segregated Woolworth lunch counter in Greensboro, North Carolina. Soon, "sit-ins" in restaurants, "read-ins" in libraries, "pray-ins" in white churches spread throughout the South, generally under the leadership of the Southern Christian Leadership Conference which followed nonviolent techniques.

Perhaps the most dramatic confrontation between the civil rights movement and Southern segregationists occurred in Birmingham, Alabama in the spring of 1963. In support of a request for desegregation of downtown eating places and the formation of a biracial committee to work out the integration of public schools, Martin Luther King led several thousand Birmingham Negroes in a series of orderly street marches. The demonstrators were met with strong police action, including fire hoses, police dogs, and electric cattle prods. Newspaper pictures of Negroes being attacked by police and bitten by dogs were flashed all over the world. More than 25,000 demonstrators, including Dr. King, were jailed.

The year 1963 was probably the most important for nonviolent direct action. The Birmingham action set off demonstrations in many parts of the country; the theme remained one of nonviolence, and it was usually whites rather than Negroes who resorted to violence in these demonstrations. Responsible black elites remained in control of the movement and won widespread support from the white liberal community. The culmination of the nonviolent philosophy was a giant, yet orderly march on Washington, held on August 28, 1963. More than 200,000 blacks and whites participated in the march, which was endorsed by many labor leaders, religious groups, and political figures. It was in response to this march that President Kennedy sent a strong civil rights bill to Congress, which was later passed, after his death—the famous Civil Rights Act of 1964.

The Civil Rights Act of 1964 passed both houses of Congress by better than a two-thirds favorable vote; it won the overwhelming support of both Republican and Democratic Congressmen. It was signed into law on July 4, 1964. It ranks with the Emancipation Proclamation, the Fourteenth Amendment, and *Brown* v. *Topeka* as one of the most important steps toward full equality for the Negro in America.

The Civil Rights Act of 1964 provides that:

1. It is unlawful to apply unequal standards in voter registration procedures, or to deny registration for irrelevant errors or omissions on records or applications.
2. It is unlawful to discriminate or segregate persons on the grounds of race, color, religion, or national origin in any public accommodation, including hotels, motels, restaurants, movies, theaters, sports areas, entertainment houses, and other places that offer to serve the public. This prohibition extends to all establishments whose operations affect interstate commerce or whose discriminatory practices are supported by state action.
3. The attorney general shall undertake civil action on behalf of any person denied equal access to a public accommodation to obtain a federal district court order to secure compliance with the act. If the owner or manager of a public accommodation should continue to discriminate, he would be in

contempt of court and subject to peremptory fines and imprisonment without trial by jury. (This mode of enforcement gave establishments a chance to mend their ways without punishment, and it also avoided the possibility that Southern juries would refuse to convict persons for violations of the act.)

4. The attorney general shall undertake civil actions on behalf of persons attempting orderly desegregation of public schools.
5. The Commission on Civil Rights, first established in the Civil Rights Act of 1957, shall be empowered to investigate deprivations of the right to vote, study, and collect information regarding the discrimination in America, and make reports to the president and Congress.
6. Each federal department and agency shall take action to end discrimination in all programs or activities receiving federal financial assistance in any form. This action shall include termination of financial assistance.
7. It shall be unlawful for any employer or labor union with 25 or more persons after 1965 to discriminate against any individual in any fashion in employment, because of his race, color, religion, sex, or national origin, and that an Equal Employment Opportunity Commission shall be established to enforce this provision by investigation, conference, conciliation, persuasion, and if need be, civil action in federal court.

The civil rights movement invented new political techniques for minorities in American politics. In 1963 a group of Alabama clergymen petitioned Martin Luther King, Jr., to call off mass demonstrations in Birmingham. King, who had been arrested in the demonstrations, replied in his famous "Letter from Birmingham Jail":

> In no sense do I advocate evading or defying the law as the rabid segregationist would do. This would lead to anarchy. One who breaks an unjust law must do it *openly, lovingly* (not hatefully as the white mothers did in New Orleans when they were seen on television screaming "nigger, nigger, nigger") and with a willingness to accept the penalty. I submit that an individual who breaks a law that conscience tells him is unjust, and willingly accepts the penalty by staying in jail to arouse the conscience of the community over its injustice, is in reality expressing the very highest respect for law.[15]

It is important to note that Martin Luther King's tactics relied primarily on an appeal to the conscience of white elites. The purpose of demonstrations was to call attention to injustice and stimulate established elites to remedy the injustice by lawful means. The purpose of civil disobedience was to dramatize injustice; only *unjust* laws were to be broken "openly and lovingly," and punishment was accepted to demonstrate sincerity. King did not urge black masses to remedy injustice themselves by

---

[15] A public letter by Martin Luther King, Jr., Birmingham, Alabama, April 16, 1963.

any means necessary; and he did not urge the overthrow of established elites.

NATIONAL "FAIR HOUSING" POLICY

For many years "fair housing" had been considered the most sensitive area of civil rights legislation. Discrimination in the sale and rental of housing was the last major civil rights problem on which Congress took action. Discrimination in housing had not been mentioned in any previous legislation—not even in the comprehensive Civil Rights Act of 1964. Prohibiting discrimination in the sale or rental of housing affected the constituencies of Northern members of Congress more than any of the earlier, Southern-oriented legislation.

Moreover, there was reason to believe that a majority of white Americans opposed laws prohibiting discrimination in sale or rental housing. When the California legislature passed a fair housing law, the state's voters replied by overwhelmingly supporting a state constitutional amendment, known as Proposition 14, which prohibited the legislature from abridging the rights of citizens to sell, lease, or rent to the person of their choice. The effect of this constitutional amendment was to nullify the state's fair housing law, and it won a statewide referendum in California by a two to one margin of voters! Later the California Supreme Court held Proposition 14 to be a violation of the Fourteenth Amendment of the United States Constitution and in effect threw out the results of the referendum; but nonetheless the vote itself was clear evidence of widespread popular opposition to fair housing.

Thus, the prospects for a fair housing law were not very good at the beginning of 1968. However, when Martin Luther King, Jr. was assassinated on April 4 the mood of Congress changed dramatically and many leaders felt that Congress should pass a fair housing law as a tribute to the slain civil rights leader. The final version of the Civil Rights Bill of 1968 included amendments that made it a crime for persons to travel in interstate commerce with intent to incite or take part in a riot or to manufacture or transport firearms and explosives for use in a civil disorder. These "antiriot" amendments won crucial support for the bill.

The Civil Rights Act of 1968 prohibited the following forms of discrimination:

Refusal to sell or rent a dwelling to any person because of his race, color, religion, or national origin.

Discrimination against a person in the terms, conditions, or privileges of the sale or rental of a dwelling.

Advertising the sale or rental of a dwelling indicating a preference or discrimination based on race, color, religion, or national origin.

Inducing persons to sell or rent a dwelling by referring to the entry into the neighborhood of persons of a particular race, religion, or national origin (the "blockbusting" technique of real estate selling).

EQUALITY AND BLACK-WHITE "LIFE CHANCES"

Although the great gains of the civil rights movement have been immensely important, it must be recognized that they are *symbolic* rather than *actual* changes in the conditions under which most blacks live in America. Racial politics today center about the actual inequalities between blacks and whites in incomes, jobs, housing, health, education, and other conditions of life.

The problem of inequality is usually posed as differences in the "life chances" of blacks and whites. Figures can reveal only the bare outline of the Negro's "life chances" in American society (see Table 3-3). The average income of a black family is only two-thirds of the average white family's income. One-third of all black families are below the recognized poverty line. Home ownership is greater among whites than blacks. The black unemployment rate is almost twice as high as the white unemployment rate. The average black does not acquire as much education as the average white. Blacks are far less likely to hold prestigious white-collar jobs in professional managerial, clerical, or sales work. They do not hold many skilled craft jobs in industry, but are concentrated in operative, service, and laboring positions. Black women not only have more children, but they have them earlier. And too many children too early make it difficult for parents to finish school. Thus a cycle is at work in the ghettos; low education levels produce low income levels, which prevent parents from moving out of the ghettos, which deprives children of educational opportunities, and then the cycle is repeated.

Daniel P. Moynihan has argued persuasively that one of the worst effects of slavery and segregation has been their impact on Negro family life.[16] The black male was most humiliated by segregationist practices. Segregation, with its implications of inferiority and submissiveness, damaged the male more than the female personality; the black female was a threat to no one. Not surprisingly, the female-headed black family emerges as one of the striking features of life in the ghetto. Over 25 percent of all black families are headed by women. For the young black male brought up in a matriarchal setting in the ghetto, the future is often

[16] Daniel P. Moynihan, *The Negro Family: The Case for National Action* (Washington, D.C.: Government Printing Office, 1965).

Table 3-3 *Black-White Life Chances*

	BLACK	WHITE
Median Family Income	$6,864	$11,549
Percent of Families with Incomes Under $3,000	19	7
Percent of Families with Incomes Over $10,000	30	54
Poverty percentage	32	9
Median Income—Men 25-54		
Less under 8 yrs.	$4,743	$ 6,618
High School 4 yrs.	6,789	8,613
College 4 yrs.	8,715	12,354
Unemployment Rate (%)		
1970	8.2	4.5
1972	10.0	5.0
Occupation (%)		
Professional	9.5	14.6
Managerial	3.7	10.6
Sales	2.2	7.1
Clerical	14.4	17.8
Craftsmen	8.7	13.8
Operatives	23.7	17.0
Laborer	9.9	4.6
Service	27.2	11.8
Farm	3.0	3.8
Education, Persons 25 to 34		
Males Completing High School (%)	59.0	71.0
Females Completing High School (%)	63.0	80.0
Males Completing College (%)	8.3	22.6
Females Completing College (%)	7.5	15.0
Home Ownership (%)	42	65
Infant Mortality Rate		
(per 1,000 live births)	34.6	19.2
Female-Headed Families (%)	26.8	9.1
Fertility Rate		
(births per 1,000 women 15 to 44)	115	82
Voter Participation		
(% reported they voted)	44	56

Source: Bureau of the Census, *The Social and Economic Status of Negroes in the United States,* Current Population Reports, Series P-23, No. 38 (1970) and No. 46 (1973).

depressing, with defeat and frustration repeating themselves throughout his life. He may drop out of school in the ninth grade to protest his lack of success. If he fails his armed forces qualification test (and a majority of young men from the ghetto do fail it), he may never again have an opportunity for further education or job training. Lacking parental supervision and with little to do, he may soon get into trouble with the police. A police record will further hurt his chances of getting a job. The ghetto male with limited job skills enters the job market seriously handicapped. His pay is usually not enough to support a family, and he has little hope of advancement. He may tie up much of his income in installment payments for a car, a television set, or the other conveniences that he sees in widespread use among middle-class Americans. Because of his low credit rating, he will be forced to pay excessive interest rates, and sooner or later his creditors will garnish his salary. If he marries, he is likely to have five or more children, and he and his family will live in overcrowded substandard housing. As pressures and frustrations mount, he may decide to leave his family, either because he has found his inability to support his wife and children humiliating or because only in this way will his wife and children be eligible for welfare payments. Welfare policy also strengthens the role of the female in the black family because she can get the family on welfare (particularly Aid to Families with Dependent Children) while the male cannot. In fact, his remaining with his family is often an obstacle to its receiving welfare payments.

PUBLIC POLICY AND BLACK-WHITE "LIFE CHANCES"

The civil rights movement opened up new opportunities for black Americans. But equality of *opportunity* is not the same as *absolute* equality. In a significant speech to the graduating class of Howard University in 1965, President Lyndon B. Johnson identified the fundamental problem of equality in America today:

> You do not take a person who for years has been hobbled by chains and liberate him, bring him up to the starting line of a race, and say, "You are free to compete with all the others," and still justly believe that you have been completely fair.
> Thus it is not enough to open the gates to opportunity. All our citizens must have the ability to walk through those gates.
> This is the next and most profound stage of the battle for civil rights . . . the task is to give twenty million Negroes the same choice as every other American to learn, to work, and share in society, to develop their abilities—physical, mental, and spiritual—and to pursue their individual happiness.[17]

But the complexity of this task is enormous. The problems are manifold—how to overcome the interlocking effects of deprivation in educa-

[17] President Lyndon B. Johnson, address to graduating class, Howard University, June 4, 1965.

tion, job training, health, housing, employment, crime and delinquency, and human motivation.

Can deprivation resulting from unequal treatment of Negroes in the past be eliminated without preferential treatment for present-day victims? And if preferential programs are begun, how will we know when blacks have been brought to the starting line? What about blacks who do succeed in joining the affluent American middle class—will they suffer from feelings of guilt in leaving most of their black brothers behind in the ghetto? Will integration of middle-class Negroes result in a "skimming off of the cream" of potential leadership of Negro masses?

The rapid equalization of life chances of blacks and whites in America would most certainly involve a massive public effort in redistributing income, education, jobs, and other resources. It is not our intention here to review all the proposed or existing public programs that may contribute to a reduction of inequality in American society. In Chapter 6 we will describe social insurance and welfare policies, and the difficulties involved in developing rational approaches to the care of the poor. In Chapter 5 we will examine the Economic Opportunity Act of 1964, the core of the widely heralded "war on poverty," which constituted the national government's most direct attempt to cope with the complex problems of poverty and inequality. The experience of the Economic Opportunity program is an instructive example of the complex political issues involved in public efforts aimed at equalizing "life chances." There is no guarantee that equality can be achieved *even if* the government embarks upon a multibillion dollar effort to do so.

Another problem: "Integration" assumes that individual blacks will acquire the skills, education, jobs, and income requisite for a secure position in affluent middle-class America, and it assumes that the values and institutions of this America are looked upon as legitimate and desirable by most blacks. Negros in the past have not had much of a share in shaping these institutions or determining these values; the most they can expect is a greater share in their joint determination in the future. Given these conditions, can we assume that blacks will voluntarily choose to join affluent white America? Once the right to choose has been established, will blacks choose to be "integrated" or will they choose separation?

Another problem: Does preferential treatment of blacks in university admissions and scholarships, job hiring and promotion, or other opportunities for advancement in life, result in discrimination against whites competing for the same opportunities? Does the Equal Protection Clause of the Fourteenth Amendment protect whites who have been bypassed in preference to blacks? Government agencies, private employers, and colleges and universities are under pressure from federal officials to take "affirmative action" to assure equal opportunity for blacks. Federal officials generally measure "progress" in "affirmative action" in terms of the numbers of blacks employed, admitted, aided, or promoted. Federal officials are usually very careful *not* to establish rigid "quotas"—to do so would imply that blacks were not competing on an equal basis with whites. But the pressure to show "progress" in "affirmative action" frequently does result in preferential treatment of blacks and discrimination against whites with equal or better qualifications. The Supreme Court has avoided deciding the tough question of whether "affirmative action," preferential treatment of black applicants violates the Fourteenth Amendment's Equal Protection guarantee of competing whites. (In a 5-4 decision the Court refused to hear the case of Marco DeFunis, Jr. whose application to the University of Washington Law School was rejected while blacks with lower grades and test scores were admitted; a lower federal court had ordered DeFunis admitted and since he was near graduation when the case finally reached the Supreme Court, it was declared moot.) But eventually the Supreme Court will have to rule in this difficult area.

Occasionally, the rhetoric of politics suggests that the conditions of blacks in America are worsening, that America is hopelessly "racist," and that there is no possibility of real progress. This is not true. Blacks have made great progress over the last decade in income, jobs, education, housing, and other conditions of life—not only in absolute terms but also in narrowing the gap between themselves and whites.

Median black family income was only slightly more than half the median white family income in the 1950s, but by 1970 black family income had increased to 64 percent of white family income (see Table 3-4).

Table 3-4 *Change in Black-White Life Chances*

| | Median Income of Families | | | | |
	1947	1960	1968	1970	1972
White	$4,916	$6,857	$8,937	$10,236	$11,549
Negro	$2,514	$3,794	$5,590	$6,516	$6,864

Median Income of Families of Negro and Other Races
as a Percent of White Family Income

1950	54	1966	60
1955	55	1968	63
1960	55	1970	64
1964	56	1972	62

Persons Below Poverty Level

| | MILLIONS | | PERCENT OF TOTAL | |
	Negro	White	Negro	White
1959	11.0	28.5	56	18
1965	10.7	22.5	47	13
1970	7.7	17.5	32	10
1972	8.3	16.2	32	9

Occupation: Negro and Other Races as a Percent
of All Workers in Selected Occupations
(*Note:* Negroes compose 10.6 percent of total employed)

	1960	1969	1972
Professional	4	6	6.6
Medical	4	8	8.0
Teachers	7	10	9.2
Managers	2	3	4.0
Clerical	5	8	8.7
Sales	3	4	3.6
Craftsmen	5	7	6.9
Operatives	12	14	13.2
Nonfarm laborers	27	24	20.2
Private household	46	44	40.7
Other service	20	19	18.5
Farm	16	11	8.6

Percent of Persons 25 to 29 Years Old
Who Completed 4 Years of High School or More

| | MALE | | FEMALE | |
	Negro	White	Negro	White
1960	37	64	42	66
1968	55	78	58	77
1971	59	81	63	80

Percent of Persons 25 to 34 Years Old
Who Completed 4 Years of College or More

| | MALE | | FEMALE | |
	Negro	White	Negro	White
1960	4.1	15.8	4.0	8.3
1967	4.5	20.9	6.4	12.3
1972	8.3	22.6	7.5	15.0

Source: Bureau of the Census, "The Social and Economic Status of Negroes in the United States," Current Population Reports. Series No. 38 (1970) and No. 46 (1973).

In a single decade the proportion of blacks living below the recognized poverty line had fallen from 56 percent of all blacks to 32 percent. Blacks increased their percentage of professional, managerial, sales, clerical, and other white-collar jobs and reduced their percentage of laborers, service workers, and farmers. The proportion of blacks living in substandard housing fell from nearly one-half to less than one-quarter. Blacks also narrowed the gap in education: the proportion of young black males who completed high school rose from 37 percent to over 59 percent in a single decade; the proportion of black college graduates has doubled. It is important that we do not mistake failure to progress fast enough with failure to progress at all. American society has moved toward equality very rapidly over the last decade. Of course whites have made progress too, and in every measure of "life chances" blacks remain below average white levels. Doubtlessly the progress made by blacks in recent years has been long overdue, and no rate of progress can be considered fast *enough*. But progress has been very impressive.

Will progress toward equality continue at the same pace of the 1960s? There is some disturbing evidence that suggests a recent slowdown in the march toward equality. Figures on income and poverty for the early 1970s suggest that black economic progress may be slowing down. For example, black family income slipped in relation to white family income from 64 to to 62 percent. Black poverty remained at 32 percent of the black population, while white poverty continued to decline. But black educational progress has continued, and so has black movement into professional and managerial positions.

Thus, despite long-term progress in narrowing black-white "life chances" in America, there is no justification for complacency. Continued progress will require a healthy economy and conscious efforts by blacks and whites to insure equality of opportunity.

SUMMARY

Let us try to set forth some propositions that are consistent with elite theory and assist in describing the development of civil rights policy:

1. Elites and masses in America differ in their attitudes towards blacks. Support for civil rights legislation has come from educated affluent whites in leadership positions. Working-class whites believe that blacks are moving "too fast."
2. Mass opinion toward civil rights has generally followed public policy, and not led it. Mass opinion did not oppose legally segregated schools until after elites had declared national policy in *Brown* v. *Topeka*.
3. The greatest impetus to the advancement of civil rights policy in this cen-

tury was the U.S. Supreme Court's decision in *Brown* v. *Topeka*. Thus, a white elite group, nonelected and enjoying life terms in office, assumed the initiative in civil rights policy. Congress did not take significant action until ten years later.

4. Resistance to the implementation of *Brown* v. *Topeka* was centered in states and communities that had the *largest* black population percentages. Resistance to national policy was remarkably effective for over a decade, and blacks were not admitted to white schools in the South in large numbers until all segments of the national elite—Congress and the executive branch, as well as the judicial branch—acted in support of desegregation.

5. The elimination of legal discrimination and the guarantee of equality of opportunity in the Civil Rights Act of 1964 was achieved largely through the dramatic appeals of middle-class black leaders to consciences of white elites. Black leaders did not attempt to overthrow the established order, but to open opportunities for blacks to achieve success within the American system.

6. National elites legally guaranteed nondiscrimination in the sale or rental of housing in 1968, an action that was clearly at variance with the preferences of white masses.

7. Elite support for *equality of opportunity* does not satisfy the demands of black masses for *absolute* equality. White elites are not yet prepared to undertake a massive public effort to redistribute income, education, jobs, housing, and other resources in order to achieve the equalization of "life chances" among blacks and whites. Nonetheless, individually blacks are making impressive gains within the existing economic system.

BIBLIOGRAPHY

BERMAN, DANIEL M., *It Is So Ordered*. New York: W. W. Norton, 1966.

CARMICHAEL, STOKELY, and CHARLES V. HAMILTON, *Black Power*. New York: Random House, 1968.

CLARK, KENNETH B., *Dark Ghetto*. New York: Harper & Row, 1965.

DYE, THOMAS R., *The Politics of Equality*. New York: Bobbs-Merrill, 1971.

PARSONS, TALCOTT, and KENNETH B. CLARK, eds., *The Negro American*. Boston: Beacon Press, 1965.

WALTON, HANES, JR., *Black Politics*. Philadelphia: Lippincott, 1972.

Philip and Daniel Berrigan watch baskets of draft board records burn. UPI Photo

4 CRIME, VIOLENCE, AND REPRESSION:

elite response to mass disorder

Crime, violence, and disorder are central problems confronting any society. So also is the problem of government repression. For thousands of years, men have wrestled with the question of balancing governmental power against individual freedom. How far can individual freedom be carried without undermining the stability of society, threatening the safety of others, and risking anarchy? The early English political philosopher, Thomas Hobbes (1588–1679), believed that society must establish a powerful "Leviathan"—the state—in order to curb the savage instincts in men.[1] He believed that a powerful authority in society was needed to prevent men from attacking each other for personal gain—"a war of every man against every man" where "notions of right and wrong, justice and injustice, have no place." According to Hobbes, without law and order there is no real freedom—the fear of death and destruction permeates every act of life: "every man is enemy to every man"; "force and fraud are the two cardinal virtues"; and "the life of man is solitary, poor, nasty, brutish, and short." It is clear, then, that freedom is *not* the absence of law and order. On the contrary, law and order are required if there is to be any freedom in society at all.

But what happens when a government becomes too strong for the liberties of its citizens? Men agree to abide by law and accept restrictions on their personal freedom in order to secure peace and self-preservation;

[1] Thomas Hobbes, *Leviathan*, Collier Classics Edition (New York: Macmillan, 1967).

69

but how much liberty must be surrendered in order to secure an orderly society? This is the classic dilemma of free government: men must create laws and governments to protect freedom; the laws and governments themselves restrict freedom.

VIOLENCE IN BLACK GHETTOS

Civil disorder and violence are not new on the American scene. The nation itself was founded in armed revolution. And violence as a form of political protest has continued intermittently in America to the present day. Yet even though domestic violence has played a prominent role in America's history, the ghetto riots of the 1960s shocked the nation with massive and widespread civil disorders. All these riots involved black attacks on established authority—policemen, firemen, National Guardsmen, whites in general, and property owned by whites. Three of these riots—Watts, California, in 1965 and Newark and Detroit, in 1967—amounted to major civil disorders.

The Watts riot in August 1965 was described in the McCone Commission's report:

> In the ugliest interval . . . perhaps as many as 10,000 Negroes took to the streets in neurotic bands. They looted stores, set fires, beat up white passers-by whom they had hauled from stopped cars, many of which were turned upside-down and burned, exchanged shots with law enforcement officers, and stoned and shot at firemen. The rioters seemed to have been caught up in an insensate rage of destruction. By Friday, disorder spread to adjoining areas, and ultimately, an area covering 46.5 square miles had to be controlled with the aid of military authority before public order was restored. . . . Of the 34 killed, one was a fireman, one was a deputy sheriff, and one a Long Beach policeman . . . [the remainder were Negroes].[2]

In the Newark riot in the summer of 1967 snipers fired at police and firemen, looters made off with the inventories of scores of stores, and arsonists set fire to large portions of commercial property in the black section of that city. New Jersey's governor proclaimed Newark "in open rebellion," declared a state of emergency, and called out the National Guard. More than 4,000 city policemen, state troopers, and National Guardsmen were required to restore order. Before the riot was over, 23 persons had been killed, and property damage was widespread. Of the

[2] Governor's Commission on the Los Angeles Riots, John A. McCone, Chairman, *Violence in the City—An End or a Beginning* (Sacramento, Calif.: Office of the Governor of California, 1965), pp. 3–5.

Michigan National Guardsmen in Detroit's Riot-Torn West Side, July 1967. UPI Photo

dead, only two were white—a policeman and a fireman. Of the Negro dead, two were children and six were women.

But it was Detroit that became the scene of the bloodiest racial violence of the twentieth century. A week of rioting in Detroit, July 23–28, 1967, left 43 dead and more than 1,000 injured. Whole sections of the city were reduced to charred, smoky ruins. Firemen who tried to fight fires were stoned and occasionally shot by ghetto residents. Over 1,300 buildings were totally demolished and 2,700 businesses sacked.

Detroit's upheaval began when police raided an after-hours club and arrested the bartender and several customers for selling and consuming alcoholic beverages after authorized closing hours. A force of 15,000 city and state police, National Guardsmen, and finally federal troops fought to quell the violence. Most of the looted retail businesses were liquor stores, groceries, and furniture stores. Many Negro merchants scrawled "Soul Brother" on their windows in an attempt to escape the wrath of the black mobs.

In the end, homes and shops covering a total area of fourteen square miles were gutted by fire. Of the 43 persons killed during the riot, 33 were Negro and 10 were white. Among the dead were one National Guardsman, one fireman, one policeman, and one Negro private guard. Both the violence and the pathos of the ghetto riots were reflected in the following report from Detroit:

A Negro plain clothes officer was standing in an intersection when a man threw a Molotov cocktail into a business establishment on the corner. In the heat of the afternoon, fanned by the 20–25 mile per hour winds of both Sunday and Monday, the fire reached the home next door within minutes. As its residents uselessly sprayed the flames with garden hoses, the fire jumped from roof to roof of adjacent two- and three-story buildings. Within the hour the entire block was in flames. The ninth house in the burning row belonged to the arsonist who had thrown the Molotov cocktail. . . .

Employed as a private guard, fifty-five year old Julius L. Dorsey, a Negro, was standing in front of a market, when accosted by two Negro men and a woman. They demanded he permit them to loot the market. He ignored their demands. They began to berate him. He asked a neighbor to call the police. As the argument grew more heated, Dorsey fired three shots from his pistol in the air.

The police radio reported: "Looters, they have rifles." A patrol car driven by a police officer and carrying three National Guardsmen arrived. As the looters fled, the law enforcement personnel opened fire. When the firing ceased, one person lay dead. He was Julius L. Dorsey. . . .[3]

The National Advisory Commission on Civil Disorders concluded:

1. No civil disorder was "typical" in all respects. . . .
2. While civil disorders of 1967 were racial in character, they were not *inter*-racial. The 1967 disorders, as well as earlier disorders of the recent period, involved action within Negro neighborhoods against symbols of white American society—authority and property—rather than against white persons.
3. Despite extremist rhetoric there was no attempt to subvert the social order of the United States. Instead, most of those who attacked white authority and property seemed to be demanding fuller participation in the social order and the material benefits enjoyed by the vast majority of American citizens.
4. Disorder did not typically erupt without pre-existing causes, as a result of a single "triggering" or "precipitating" incident. Instead, it developed out of an increasingly social atmosphere, in which typically a series of tension-heightening incidents over a period of weeks or months became linked in the minds of many in the Negro community with a shared network of underlying grievances.
5. There was, typically, a complex relationship between the series of incidents, and the underlying grievances. For example, grievances about allegedly abusive police practices . . . were often aggravated in the minds of many Negroes by incidents involving the police, or the inaction of municipal authorities on Negro complaints about police action.
6. Many grievances in the Negro community resulted from discrimination, prejudice, and powerlessness which Negroes often experience. . . .
7. Characteristically the typical rioter was not a hoodlum, habitual criminal, or riff-raff. . . . Instead, he was a teenager or young adult, a life-long resident of the city in which he rioted, high school drop-out—but somewhat better than his Negro neighbor—and almost invariably under-employed or employed in a menial job. He was proud of his race, extremely hostile to both whites and middle class negroes and, though

[3] National Advisory Commission on Civil Disorders, *Report* (Washington, D.C.: Government Printing Office, 1968), p. 4.

informed about politics, highly distrustful of the political system and of political leaders.

8. Numerous Negro counter-rioters walked the street, urging the rioters to "cool it." . . .

9. Negotiation between Negro and white officials occurred during virtually all of this disorder. . . .

10. . . . Some rioters may have shared neither the conditions nor the grievance of their Negro neighbors; some may have coolly and deliberately exploited the chaos created by others; some may have been drawn into the melee merely because they identified with, or wished to emulate, others.

11. The background of disorder in the riot cities was typically characterized by severely disadvantaged conditions for Negroes, especially as compared with those of whites. . . .

12. In the immediate aftermath of disorder, the status quo of daily life before the disorder generally was quickly restored. Yet despite some notable public and private efforts, little basic change took place in the conditions underlying the disorder. In some cases, the result was increased dislike between blacks and whites, diminished inter-racial communication, and the growth of Negro and white extremist groups.[4]

ASSESSING THE CAUSES OF RIOTS

One explanation of urban violence is that it is a product of the "relative deprivation" of ghetto residents.[5] "Relative deprivation" is the discrepancy between people's expectations about the goods and conditions of life to which they are justifiably entitled and what they perceive to be their *chances* for getting and keeping what they feel they deserve. Relative deprivation is not just a complicated way of saying that people are deprived and therefore angry because they have less than what they want; it is more complex than that. Relative deprivation focuses on (1) what people think they *deserve*, not just what they want in an ideal sense, and (2) what they think they have a *chance of getting*, not just what they have.

Relative deprivation differs considerably from the "absolute deprivation" hypothesis. The absolute deprivation idea suggests that the individuals who are most deprived are most likely to rise up. Of course, it is

---

[4] *Ibid.*, pp. 110–12.

[5] For a full discussion of the "relative deprivation" explanation as well as alternative explanations, see Dan R. Bowen and Louis H. Masotti, "Civil Violence: A Theoretical Overview," in *Riots and Rebellion*, Masotti and Bowen, eds. (Beverly Hills, Calif.: Sage Publications, 1968); see also James C. Davies, "Toward a Theory of Revolution," *American Sociological Review*, 27 (February 1962), 6; and Ted Gurr, *Why Men Rebel* (Princeton: Princeton University Press, 1970).

true that conditions in America's ghettos provide the necessary environment for violence. Racial imbalance, de facto segregation, slum housing, discrimination, unemployment, poor schools and poverty all provide excellent kindling for the flames of violence. But these underlying conditions for violence existed for decades in America, and the nation never experienced simultaneous violent uprisings in nearly all its major cities before the 1960s. This suggests the deprivation itself is not a sufficient condition for violence. Some new ingredients were added to the incendiary conditions in American cities that touched off the violence of the 1960s.

Relative deprivation focuses on the distance between one's current status and his expectation level. According to this hypothesis, it is neither the wholly downtrodden—who have no aspirations—nor the very well off—who can satisfy theirs—who represent a threat to civil order. The threat is posed by those whose expectations about what they deserve outdistance the capacity of the political system to satisfy them. Often rapid increases in expectations are a product of minor or symbolic improvements in conditions. This leads to the apparent paradox of violence and disorder occurring at the very time that improvements in the conditions of blacks are being made. It is hope, not despair, that generates civil violence and disorder. Masotti and Bowen remark: "The reason why black Americans riot is because there has been just enough improvement in their condition to generate hopes, expectations, or aspirations beyond the capacities of the system to meet them." [6]

The civil rights movement made many blacks acutely aware of discrimination in American society and reduced their tolerance for injustice. The civil rights movement increased the aspiration level of Negro masses and inspired impatience and hostility toward the "white establishment." The civil rights movement had to awaken blacks to their plight in American society before progress could be made in eliminating discrimination; but the price of this awakening was a major increase in aspiration levels and the risk of frustration and bitterness when aspirations were unfulfilled. The breakthroughs made by the established civil rights movement in public accommodations, employment, voting, and office holding in the 1960s may have opened new opportunities for the educated middle class. But the undereducated Negro poor, living in the ghetto environment, could not really take advantage of many of these opportunities. The movement increased their expectation level, but it failed to alter significantly their condition in life. Thus, it is no coincidence that the urban disorders followed on the heels of some of the most significant legislative gains in the civil rights struggle.

Once racial violence has broken out anywhere in the nation, the

[6] Masotti and Bowen, *Riots and Rebellion*, pp. 24–25.

mass media play an important role in disseminating images of violence as well as the symbols and rationalizations of the rioters. Television offers the rioter a mass audience. It was not unknown for rioters to leave the scene temporarily to hurry to their TV sets to see themselves. Moreover, television images may reinforce predispositions to participate and even to legitimate participation. Television enables blacks in one ghetto to see what blacks in another ghetto are doing, and explains simultaneous rioting in ghettos across the nation.

ELITE AND MASS REACTION TO RACIAL VIOLENCE

Blacks and whites disagree over the causes and cures of urban violence. Whites are far more likely to believe that the main cause of civil disorder has been "radicals," looters and other undesirables, and "Communists." Very few blacks take this view. Blacks tended to cite discrimination and unfair treatment, unemployment, inferior jobs, and housing. Only about half as many whites cited these underlying socioeconomic conditions as "the main cause" of riots. A clear majority of blacks believed that the civil disturbances were "mainly a protest against unfair conditions" and very few blacks believed that the riots were "mainly a way of looting and things like that." Although many whites recognized the protest nature of the riots, whites were far more likely to believe that disturbances were mainly a way of looting.

Blacks and whites differed even more sharply on how to prevent riots. Whites tended to call for more repressive measures, "more police control," while blacks called for improvements in socioeconomic conditions, "better employment," and "discrimination." Whites and blacks also differed substantially in their assessment of the impact of the riots. More blacks believed the disturbances helped rather than hurt the cause of Negro rights. In contrast, the overwhelming majority of whites believed the riots hurt the Negro cause (see Table 4-1).

Although more blacks believed the riots helped rather than hurt their cause, it important to point out that the great majority of blacks in cities do not believe that violence is "the best way for Negroes to gain their rights." On the contrary, most blacks are prepared to put their faith in "laws and persuasion" and "nonviolent protest." When asked "if a disturbance like the one in Detroit or Newark last summer broke out here, do you think you would join, or would try to stop it, or would you stay away from it," three out of every four urban blacks said they would "stay away." Only a tiny fraction said they would join in, and a nearly equal fraction said they would try to stop it. Yet even though the overwhelming majority of Negroes renounced violence, they expressed sym-

Table 4-1 *Black and White Perceptions of Civil Disorder in Large Cities*

	NEGRO		WHITE	
	Men	Women	Men	Women

Some people say these disturbances are mainly a protest by Negroes against unfair conditons. Others say they are mainly a way of looting and things like that. Which seems more correct to you?

	NEGRO Men	NEGRO Women	WHITE Men	WHITE Women
Mainly protest	56	59	38	48
Mainly looting	9	10	33	24
50/50 mixture	30	25	25	24
Don't know	5	6	4	4

On the whole, do you thing the disturbances have helped or hurt the cause of Negro rights, or would you say they haven't made much difference?

	NEGRO Men	NEGRO Women	WHITE Men	WHITE Women
Helped	37	30	13	14
Hurt	22	24	69	59
Helped and hurt equally	12	11	7	7
Made no difference	21	28	9	17
Don't know	8	7	2	3

What do you think was the main cause of these disturbances?

	NEGRO Men	NEGRO Women	WHITE Men	WHITE Women
Discrimination, unfair treatment	49	48	22	27
Unemployment	23	22	13	13
Inferior jobs	13	10	5	5
Bad housing	23	20	15	15
Poor education	10	9	7	7
Poverty	10	8	11	9
Police brutality	10	4	2	1
Black power, "radicals," Communists	4	5	33	26
Looters and other undesirables	11	11	34	34

What do you think is the most important thing the city government could do to keep a disturbance like the one in Detroit from breaking out here?

	NEGRO Men	NEGRO Women	WHITE Men	WHITE Women
Better employment	26	24	11	9
End discrimination	14	15	2	3
Better housing	8	8	4	4
Other social and economic improvements	7	5	4	3
Better police treatment	6	1	0	1
Improve communications between Negroes and whites	12	13	10	13
More police control	9	8	51	42
Can't do anything	3	5	8	8
Don't know	15	21	10	17

Source: Supplemental Studies for the National Commission on Civil Disorders (Washington, D.C.: Government Printing Office, 1968).

pathy for those who do join in riots. In summary, most urban blacks look upon the riots as protest activity. A majority feels sympathetic toward the rioters, but only a small minority is willing to join the riots themselves. Most blacks reject violence as a means of securing their rights, but more believe that the riots helped rather than hurt their cause.

The reaction of elites to rioting was mixed. It was not until July 1967 that President Johnson publicly acknowledged the extent of civil disorder and condemned rioting. His statement was typical of those of many public officials who were actively engaged in the suppression of a riot:

> Let there be no mistake about it—the looting, arson, plunder, and pillage which have occurred are not part of the civil rights protest. There is no American right to loot stores, burn buildings, to fire rifles from rooftops. This is a crime. . . .
>
> Criminals who have committed these acts of violence against the people deserve to be punished—they must be punished.[7]

Later the president cited the riots as an additional reason for Congress to pass administration-backed urban programs to alleviate the ills of cities. But many Congressmen were concerned that large-scale increases in federal expenditures in the ghettos might appear to reward rioting. Congress reacted by passing overwhelmingly a bipartisan antiriot bill, making it a federal crime to cross state lines to incite a riot.

There is little likelihood that violence will produce the attitude change among white elites necessary for progress in the struggle for equality. On the contrary, violence has resulted in a negative reaction among whites. It has served to reinforce prejudice and to justify antagonisms against blacks rather than to affect any attitude changes. Violence in the urban ghettos in the 1960s failed to shock white Americans into action in behalf of equality or even to scare them into such action. Instead, the urban violence led to a strong "law and order" movement which was reflected in local, state, and national politics. The violence provided white masses with an opportunity to express hostile stereotypes about Negroes; e.g., that the riots were "mainly a way of looting and things like that." The riots also gave white elites a new political theme— "law and order."

The reaction of most government officials was negative also. Both the president and Congress pointedly ignored the recommendations of the Advisory Commission on Civil Disorders for more jobs, housing, and educational programs in the ghettos. There was substantial fear that new

[7] President Lyndon B. Johnson in a speech broadcast over national television networks, July 27, 1967.

public programs might appear to "reward violence." No more money was poured into the ghettos. Both Congress and the president became disenchanted with the Poverty Program. The rhetoric of government officials emphasized "law and order" rather than massive programs aimed at equalizing black and white living standards.

THE PROBLEM OF CRIME

Crime rates are the subject of a great deal of popular discussion. Very often they are employed to express the degree of social disorganization or even the effectiveness of law enforcement agencies. Crime rates are based upon the Federal Bureau of Investigation's *Uniform Crime Reports*, but the FBI reports are based on figures supplied by state and local police agencies (see Table 4-2). The FBI has succeeded in establish-

Table 4-2 *Crime Rates in the United States; Offenses Known to the Police (Rates per 100,000 Population)*

	1960	1965	1970	1972	PERCENT INCREASE 1960–1972
Murder and non-negligent manslaughter	5	5	8	9	80
Forcible rape	9	12	18	22	144
Robbery	52	61	172	180	246
Aggravated assault	82	107	162	187	128
Burglary	465	605	1,068	1,126	142
Larceny	271	393	859	883	226
Auto theft	179	251	454	423	136
Total crimes against person	148	185	360	398	169
Total crimes against property	916	1,250	2,381	2,432	166

Source: FBI, *Uniform Crime Reports*, 1966–1971.

ing a uniform classification of the number of serious crimes per 100,000 people that are known to the police—murder and nonnegligent manslaughter, forcible rape, robbery, aggravated assault, burglary, larceny, and theft, including auto theft. But record keeping is still a problem, and one should be cautious in interpreting official crime rates. They are really a function of several factors: the diligence of police in detecting crime, the adequacy of the reporting system tabulating crime, and the amount of crime itself. Yet the evidence seems inescapable that crime in the

United States is increasing at a rapid pace. The greatest increase in crime rates occurs in nonviolent crimes—burglary, larceny, theft—and lesser increases are found in crimes involving violence against the person—murder and nonnegligent manslaughter and robbery.

Police statistics vastly understate the real amount of crime. Citizens do not report many crimes to police. The National Opinion Research Center of the University of Chicago asked a national sample of individuals whether they or any member of their household had been a victim of crime during the past year. This survey revealed that the actual amount of crime is several times greater than that reported by the FBI. There are more than twice as many crimes committed as reported to the police. The number of forcible rapes was more than three and one-half times the number reported, burglaries three times, aggravated assaults and larcenies more than double, and robbery 50 percent greater than the reported rate. Only auto theft statistics were reasonably accurate, indicating that most people call the police when their cars are stolen.

Interviewees gave a variety of reasons for their failure to report crime to the police. The most common reason was the feeling that police could not be effective in dealing with the crime. This is a serious comment about police protection in America today. Other reasons included the feeling that the crime was "a private matter" or that the victim did not want to harm the offender. Fear of reprisal was mentioned much less frequently, usually in cases of assaults and family crimes.

The current system of criminal justice is certainly no serious deterrent to crime. Most behavioral research suggests that it is not the severity of punishment that affects behavior but the establishment of a sure linkage between the errant behavior and punishment. In other words, crime is more likely to be deterred by making punishment sure rather than severe. However, the best available estimates of the ratio between crime and punishment suggest that the likelihood of an individual being jailed for a serious crime is less than one in a hundred (see Figure 4-1). Most crimes are not even reported by the victim. Police are successful in clearing only about one in five reported crimes by arresting the offender. The judicial system only convicts about one in four of the persons arrested and charged; others are not prosecuted, are handled as juveniles, are found not guilty, or are permitted to plead guilty to a lesser charge and released. Only about half of convicted felons are given prison sentences.

CRIME AND THE COURTS

Chief Justice Warren E. Burger has argued persuasively that rising crime in America is partly due to inadequacies in our system of criminal

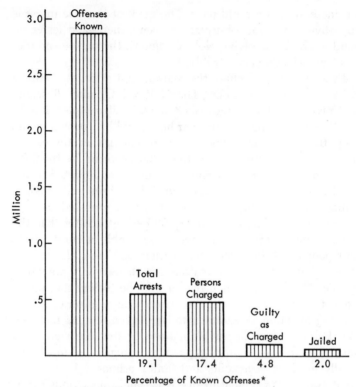

Fig. 4-1 *Law Enforcement in Relation to Crime*

Source: Statistical Abstract of the United States, 1973 (Washington, D.C.: U.S. Government Printing Office), p. 152.

justice. "The present system of criminal justice does not deter criminal conduct," he said in a special State of the Federal Judiciary Message. "Whatever deterrent effect may have existed in the past has now virtually vanished." [8] He urged major reform in law enforcement, courts, prisons, probation, and parole.

A major stumbling block to effective law enforcement is the current plight of America's judicial machinery.

[8] Chief Justice Warren Burger, Address on the State of the Federal Judiciary to the American Bar Association, August 10, 1970.

Major congestion on court dockets that delays the hearing of cases months or even years. Moreover, actual trials now average twice as long as ten years ago.

Failure of courts to adopt modern management and administrative practice to speed and improve justice.

Increased litigation in the courts. Not only are more Americans aware of their rights, but more are using every avenue of appeal. Seldom do appeals concern the guilt or innocence of the defendant; they usually focus on procedural matters.

Excessive delays in trials. According to Burger, "Defendants, whether guilty or innocent, are human; they love freedom and hate punishment. With a lawyer provided to secure release without the need for a conventional bail bond, most defendants, except in capital cases, are released pending trial. We should not be surprised that a defendant on bail exerts a heavy pressure on his court-appointed lawyer to postpone the trial as long as possible so as to remain free. These postponements—and sometimes there are a dozen or more—consume the time of judges and court staffs as well as of lawyers. Cases are calendared and reset time after time while witnesses and jurors spend hours just waiting."

Excessive delays in appeals. "We should not be surprised at delay when more and more defendants demand their undoubtedly constitutional right to trial by jury because we have provided them with lawyers and other needs at public expense; nor should we be surprised that most convicted persons seek a new trial when the appeal costs them nothing and when failure to take the appeal will cost them freedom. Being human, a defendant plays out the line which society has cast him. Lawyers are competitive creatures and the adversary system encourages contention and often rewards delay; no lawyer wants to be called upon to defend the client's charge of incompetence for having failed to exploit all the procedural techniques which we have deliberately made available."

Excessive variation in sentencing. Some judges let defendants off on probation for crimes that would draw five- or ten-year sentences by other judges. Although flexibility in sentencing is essential in dealing justly with individuals, perceived inconsistencies damage the image of the courts in the public mind.

Excessive "plea bargaining" between the prosecution and the defendant's attorney in which the defendant agrees to plead guilty to a lesser offense if the prosecutor will drop more serious charges.

The Warren Court—the Supreme Court of the 1950s and 1960s, under the guidance of Chief Justice Earl Warren—greatly strengthened the rights of accused persons in criminal cases. Several key decisions were made by a split vote on the Court, and drew heavy criticism from law enforcement officers and others as hamstringing police in their struggle with lawlessness. These decisions included the following:

Mapp v. *Ohio* (1961)—Barring the use of illegally seized evidence in criminal cases by applying the Fourth Amendment guarantee against unreasonable searches and seizures. Even if the evidence seized proves the guilt of the accused, the accused goes free because the police committed a procedural error.

Gideon v. *Wainwright* (1963)—Ruling that equal protection under the Fourteenth Amendment requires that free legal counsel be appointed for all indigent defendants in all criminal cases.

Escobedo v. *Illinois* (1964)—Ruling that a suspect is entitled to confer with counsel as soon as police investigation focuses on him, or once "the process shifts from investigatory to accusatory."

Miranda v. *Arizona* (1966)—Requiring that police—before questioning a suspect—must inform him of all his constitutional rights including the right to counsel, appointed free, if necessary, and the right to remain silent. Although the suspect may knowingly waive these rights, the police cannot question anyone who at any point asks for a lawyer or indicates "in any manner" that he does not wish to be questioned. If the police commit an error in these procedures, the accused goes free, regardless of the evidence of guilt.

It is very difficult to ascertain to what extent these decisions have really hampered efforts to halt the rise in crime in America. The Supreme Court under Chief Justice Burger has not reversed any of these important decisions. So whatever progress is made in law enforcement will have to be made within the current definition of the rights of defendants. It is important to note that Chief Justice Burger's recommendations for judicial reform center on the speedy administration of justice and not on changes in the rights of defendants.

One of the more heated debates in correctional policy today concerns capital punishment. Opponents of the death penalty argue that it is "cruel and unusual punishment" in violation of the Eighth Amendment of the U.S. Constitution. They also contend that nations and states that have abolished the death penalty have not experienced higher homicide rates, and hence there is no concrete evidence that the death penalty discourages crime. They argue as well that the death penalty is applied unequally. A large proportion of those executed have been poor, uneducated, and nonwhite. In contrast, there is a strong sense of justice among many Americans that demands retribution for heinous crimes—a life for a life. A mere jail sentence for a multiple murderer or a rapist-murderer seems unjust compared to the damage inflicted upon society and the victims. In most cases, a life sentence means less than ten years in prison under the current parole and probation policies of many states. Convicted murderers have been set free, and some have killed again. Moreover, prison guards and other inmates are exposed to convicted murderers who have "a license to kill" because they are already serving life sentences and have nothing to lose by killing again. Public opinion polls continue to support the death penalty, although opponents have been gaining supporters over time.

In 1972, the Supreme Court ruled that capital punishment *as currently imposed* violates the Eighth and Fourteenth Amendment prohibitions against cruel and unusual punishment and due process of law. The decision was made by a narrow 5 to 4 of the justices, and the reasoning in the case is very complex. Only two justices—Brennan and Marshall—declared that capital punishment itself is cruel and unusual. The other three justices in the majority—Douglas, White, and Stewart—felt that death sentences had been applied unfairly: a few individuals were receiving the death penalty for crimes for which many others were receiving lighter sentences. These justices left open the possibility that capital punishment would be constitutional if it were specified for certain kinds of crime and applied uniformly. All four Nixon appointees on the Court—Burger, Blackman, Powell, and Renquist—dissented, mainly on the ground that the abolition of the death penalty is a decision that should be left to the people and their elected representatives, and not a decision for the Supreme Court to impose upon the nation. Some states can be expected to rewrite their laws on capital punishment to try to insure fairness and uniformity in the application of this penalty; so even though the death penalty is currently in abeyance, the issue will continue to be debated in state capitals and federal courts.

FEDERAL LAW ENFORCEMENT POLICY

Historically, state and local governments have exercised principal responsibility for law enforcement in America. The Federal Bureau of Investigation and the Justice Department were charged with the responsibility of enforcing only federal law. The federal government employs less than 50,000 persons in all law enforcement activities, compared with over 500,000 state and local law enforcement personnel. Federal prisons contain 25,000 inmates, compared with 200,000 in state prisons. Federal involvement in state and local law enforcement, however, is growing.

In the Crime Control and Safe Street Act of 1968, Congress created the Law Enforcement Assistance Administration within the Department of Justice to channel federal grants-in-aid to the states for use in upgrading state and local law enforcement programs. Most of these funds come to the states as "bloc grants" to be employed by the states as they see fit in improving state or local law enforcement. The money may be spent on court reform and correctional programs as well as on police protection. Although it is too early to evaluate the effectiveness of this grant program, critics have charged that the states do not always channel this money into the cities where crime rates are highest.

Congress has the opportunity to lead the nation in fighting urban crime in the District of Columbia. Responsibility for the governance of the District of Columbia rests with Congress itself, and this area has one of the highest crime rates in the nation. In 1970 Congress enacted a series of proposals by the Nixon administration to reduce crime in the area and provide a model for urban law enforcement throughout the nation. Among other things, the District of Columbia Court Reorganization and Criminal Procedure Act of 1970

1. Established a modern independent court system for the District of Columbia with an executive officer to manage court operations;
2. Lowered to fifteen the age at which a juvenile charged with a felony could be tried as an adult;
3. Authorized a life sentence for a third felony conviction and set a minimum five-year sentence for a second armed crime of violence;
4. Authorized "no-knock" search-and-arrest warrants if police have "probable cause to believe" that notice was likely to result in the destruction of evidence, danger to police, or escape;
5. Authorized pretrial detention of up to sixty days of a defendant so dangerous that no conditions of release (bail) would assure the community's safety.

It is still too early to judge the effectiveness of these provisions, but critics have challenged both their constitutionality and their effectiveness. Although many crimes are committed by persons out on bail, pretrial detention of "dangerous" suspects might be questioned as a violation of the Eighth Amendment guarantee against excessive bail; the no-knock" provisions might violate the Fourth Amendment prohibition on "unreasonable" searches and seizures. Yet it is clear that states and communities are increasingly turning to Washington for guidance and assistance in the fight against crime.

MASS UNREST AND ELITE REPRESSION:
THE WHITE HOUSE "HORRORS"

Elites as well as masses can infringe upon democratic values. When governing elites feel threatened by external forces ("national security threats") or internal movements ("subversion" or "revolutionary violence and disruption"), they may respond in an antidemocratic fashion themselves. Indeed, mass activism and elite repression frequently interact to create multiple threats to democracy. Mass activism—riots, demonstrations, extremism, violence—generate fear and insecurity among governing elites, who respond by curtailing freedom and strengthening police and security forces, generally in the name of "national security" or "law and order."

The Watergate hearings—the hearings before the Senate Select Committee on Campaign Practices chaired by Senator Samuel J. Ervin, Jr.—provide a revealing insight into the origins of repressive acts by governments. We do not intend to describe the full history of the Watergate affair, or try to establish the guilt or innocence of the president or anyone else. Our interest is the process by which governing elites determine that repressive tactics are necessary and proper to preserve the political system. We are concerned with the origin of the *policy* of repression. Thus, we are more concerned with the whole series of repressive tactics—the White House "horrors"—which preceded the bugging and burglary of the Democratic National Headquarters in June 1972, than we are with determining guilt or innocence.

To understand Watergate, one must first understand the climate of mass unrest in the 1960s which threatened the security of governing elites. A decade of disorder began with the assassination of President John F. Kennedy in 1963; to be followed by the assassinations of Martin Luther King and Robert F. Kennedy in 1968, and the attempted assassination of George C. Wallace in 1972. Mass demonstrations and civil disobedience were developed and refined as political tactics in the civil rights movement. The ghetto riots which began in Watts in 1965, climaxed in the summer of 1967 in Newark and Detroit, and flowered anew in many cities after the death of Martin Luther King in 1968, invited a repressive "law and order" movement. The concern of elites over the increasing legitimation of violence among the masses was reflected in the establishment of two separate presidential commissions—the National Advisory Commission on Civil Disorders and the National Commission on the Causes and Prevention of Violence.

But racial unrest and social change were not the only forces contributing to mass unrest. Humiliation and defeat in a prolonged and fruitless military effort in Vietnam was also undermining the legitimacy of the government. The Democratic National Convention in Chicago in 1968 featured violent antiwar protest outside the convention hall; the police responded with counterviolence of their own. Fears of violence were heightened in 1969 when "Weathermen" sponsored their "days of rage" in Chicago, during which time they destroyed property and fought with police. Soon bomb scares became commonplace and bombings increasingly frequent. College protest activity, which had remained nonviolent for most of the decade, became increasingly violent in 1970. Radical elements argued that the use of violence was justified.

The masses, confused and indignant over student unrest, concluded that only harsh and punitive measures could control students. Many Americans openly applauded police violence against students, arguing that students had only themselves to blame if they were killed by police during disruptive or violent protests. In May 1970, national guardsmen were sent to Kent State University after the ROTC building had been set afire. When students defied an order to disperse, some guardsmen fired their weapons; four students were killed and nine were wounded. On May 9, 1970 more than 60,000 people, most of them students, assembled in Washington for an antiwar demonstration. Although most demonstrators were nonviolent, a radical minority pledged to "close down the government" and atempted to incite violence. In the inevitable reaction, Washington authorities conducted mass arrests in violation of established procedures.

At the same time, there was a serious split among elites about the handling of the war. Though everyone agreed that the war should be terminated, the president's critics did not believe that he was moving fast enough toward that goal. In 1971, the *New York Times* and the *Washington Post* published the so-called "Pentagon Papers," which had been stolen from the files of the Department of Defense by a former Defense Department Advisor, Daniel Ellsberg. The president and his senior advisors were convinced that this important segment of the nation's elite—the influential newsmakers—had acted outside the established "rules of the game" in their effort to end the war quickly.

Thus, by the early 1970s, all the conditions for elite repression existed: (1) racial unrest and violence, (2) mass protests and demonstrations, (3) the approval and encouragement of violence by vocal counterelites, (4) defeat and humiliation in war, (5) sporadic counterelite violence, including bombings and arson, and (6) attacks from segments of the elite that went beyond the established "rules of the game."

The testimony of H. R. Haldeman, former White House Chief of Staff, John D. Ehrlichman, former Presidential Domestic Affairs Advisor, and reports by the president himself, all make it clear that the White House "horrors" revealed in the Watergate investigation were reactions of a governing elite to perceived threats to the political system.

Let us turn first to the testimony of H. R. "Bob" Haldeman to understand the origins of Watergate in elite fears about mass disruption:

> It has been alleged that there was an atmosphere of fear at the White House regarding security matters. I can state categorically that there was no climate of fear at all. There was, however, a healthy and valid concern for a number of matters in the general area of national security and for a number of other matters in the general area of domestic security. . . .
>
> With regard to leaks of information, especially in the area of national

security, it became evident in 1969 that leaks of secret information were taking place that seriously jeopardized a number of highly sensitive foreign policy initiatives. . . . In order to deal with these leaks, a program of wiretaps was instituted in 1969 and continued into early 1971.

In 1970, the domestic security problem reached critical proportions as a wave of bombings and explosions, rioting and violence, demonstrations, arson, gun battles, and other disruptive activities took place across the country—on college campuses primarily, but also in other areas.

In order to deal with this problem, the president set up an interagency committee consisting of the directors of the FBI, the CIA, the Defense Intelligence Agency, and the National Security Agency. This committee was instructed to prepare recommendations for the President . . . for expanded intelligence operations.[9]

This group submitted a forty-three-page report calling for (1) intensified electronic surveillance of both domestic security threats and foreign diplomats, (2) monitoring of American citizens using international communications facilities, (3) increased legal and illegal opening and reading of mail, (4) more informants on college campuses, (5) the lifting of restrictions on "surreptitious entry" (burglary), and (6) the establishment of an interagency group on domestic intelligence. The president approved the report but later FBI Director J. Edgar Hoover objected to it—not because he opposed such measures, but because the FBI was not given exclusive control of the program. Hoover's opposition resulted in the formal withdrawal of the plan, but the plan itself clearly reflected elite thinking about the appropriate means of dealing with threats to the political system.

Despite withdrawal of the plan, the White House still believed that the political system was endangered by disruptive and subversive elements, and that "extraordinary" measures were required to protect it. As Mr. Haldeman explains:

> In mid-1971, *The New York Times* started publication of the so-called Pentagon Papers, which had been stolen from the sensitive files of the Department of State and Defense and the CIA and which covered military and diplomatic moves in a war that was still going on. The implications of this security leak were enormous and it posed a threat so grave as to require, in the judgment of the president and his senior advisors, extraordinary action. As a result, the president approved creation of the Special Investigation Unit within the White House which later became known as "the plumbers." [10]

The Special Investigation Unit within the White House was placed under the supervision of John Ehrlichman and his assistant, Egil Krough.

[9] Testimony of H. R. Haldeman, former White House Chief of Staff, before the U.S. Senate Select Committee on Campaign Practices, July 30, 1973, reprinted in *Congressional Quarterly Weekly Report*, August 4, 1973, pp. 2125–34.

[10] *Ibid.*

The Plumber's Unit soon included ex-CIA agent and author of spy novels, E. Howard Hunt, Jr. and former FBI agent G. Gordon Liddy. The Plumber's Unit worked independently of the FBI and the CIA (although it received occasional assistance from the CIA) and reported directly to Ehrlichman. It undertook a variety of repressive activities—later referred to as White House "horrors"—including the investigation of Daniel Ellsberg and the burglary of his psychiatrist's office to learn more about his motives in the theft of the Pentagon Papers; investigation (and later forgery) of the record of the events surrounding the assassination of South Vietnam's President Diem during the administration of John F. Kennedy; investigation of national security leaks that affected the U.S. negotiating position in the SALT talks; and other undisclosed domestic and foreign intelligence activities. There is additional evidence that the Plumber's Unit also undertook investigations of other White House domestic "enemies," which included antiwar protesters, critical reporters and television commentators, assorted liberals and radicals, and even an investigation of the Chappaquiddick scandal and Edward M. Kennedy.

The Watergate break-in itself—the burglarizing and wiretapping of the Democratic National Headquarters in the Watergate apartment building in Washington, D.C.—was an outgrowth of earlier elite fears and repressive measures. The work of the Plumber's Unit tapered off at the end of 1971, and Hunt and Liddy found new jobs with the president's reelection campaign organization, the Committee to Reelect the President, headed by former Attorney General John M. Mitchell. The "security coordinator" for this committee (CREEP) was James W. McCord, Jr., who had served seven years as an FBI agent and nineteen years as a CIA agent. It was easy for Hunt, Liddy, and McCord to confuse threats to national security with threats to the reelection of the incumbent president, and to employ well-known "national security" tactics, including bugging and burglary, against the president's opponents.

The White House cover-up of the Watergate affair stemmed in part from the same motives that led to the original repressive measures—elite concerns with mass disorders and threats to national security. It was probably not so much political embarrassment or fear of prosecution that led the White House to attempt a cover-up so much as concern over exposure of the whole series of repressive acts undertaken earlier. The great blunder of the Watergate operation was that certain individuals who were caught in the petty political burglary of the Democratic National Committee—Liddy, Hunt, and McCord—had previously served with the Special Investigation Unit of the White House and with the CIA. The Watergate burglary mixed partisan politics with national security affairs. The president and his top White House aids were prepared to defend repressive tactics employed in defense of "national security"—that is to say, repressive tactics used against radicals, subversives, and antiwar zealots who were leaking national defense secrets to the press. Indeed, it is likely that the president would have found widespread support among both the elites and the masses for the use of repressive tactics against such opponents. But the use of these same tactics against the Democratic Party clearly violated the established "rules of the game" in American politics.

The president's major concern was to separate the partisan political act of the break-in of the Democratic National Committee from the more important "national security" activities. Not only was the Watergate affair a political embarrassment, but it also threatened to expose the whole series of repressive measures undertaken by the White House over several years.

The president's official statements on the Watergate affair clearly indicate his desire to *deplore* the partisan political act while at the same time to *defend* the earlier "national security" measures. In the words of the president:

> The purpose of this statement is . . . to draw the distinction between national security operations and the Watergate case. . . .
>
> In citing these national security matters, it is not my intention to place a national security "cover" on Watergate, but rather to separate them out from Watergate—and at the same time to explain the context in which certain actions took place that were later misconstrued or misused.
>
> Long before the Watergate break-in, three important national security operations took place which have subsequently become entangled in the Watergate case.
>
> The first operation begun in 1969 was a program of wire-taps. All were legal, under the authorities then existing. They were undertaken to find and stop serious national security leaks.
>
> The second operation was a reassessment, which I ordered in 1970, of the adequacy of internal security measures. This resulted in the plan in a directive to strengthen our intelligence operations. They were protested by Mr. Hoover, and as a result of his protest, they were not put into effect.
>
> The third operation was the establishment, in 1971, of a special investigation unit in the White House. Its primary mission was to plug leaks of vital security information. . . .[11]

In explaining the cover-up, then, the president contended:

> The burglary and bugging of the Democratic National Committee Headquarters came as a complete surprise to me. . . . I wanted justice done

---

[11] Statement of President Richard M. Nixon, May 22, 1973, reprinted in *Congressional Quarterly Weekly Report*, May 26, 1973, pp. 1265–69.

with regard to Watergate; but in the scale of national priorities with which I had to deal . . . I also had to be deeply concerned with insuring that neither the covert operations of the CIA nor the operations of the special investigation unit should be compromised.[12]

In summary, the Watergate affair is important because it illustrates elite behavior in the face of perceived threats to the political system. Repressive behavior is typical of elites in crisis situations. There are many other historical examples of such repression—the Alien and Sedition Acts in the administration of John Adams, the suspension of due process rights by Abraham Lincoln during the Civil War, the "red scare" roundup of suspected "Bolsheviks" in the administration of Woodrow Wilson, the mass incarceration of thousands of Japanese-American families by the Roosevelt Administration, the persecution of suspected Communists and "fellow travelers" during the Truman and Eisenhower Administrations. Most of the practices revealed in the Watergate hearings—extensive wiretapping, monitoring of mail, paid informants, surveillance of suspected subversives, infiltration of radical organizations, "surreptitious entry," and so forth—have been longstanding practices of federal security agencies. The mass media, the Democratic opposition, and the academic community may contend that the Nixon Administration was especially blameworthy; and there is no need to dispute this contention. But government repression is a continuing threat to democratic values. And this threat will always be greater in periods of mass unrest, when elites convince themselves that their repressive acts are necessary to preserve the political system.

SUMMARY

In this chapter we have examined crime, violence, and disorder, and government policies designed to cope with these social ills. We have also examined government repression—government activities that infringe on traditional democratic values in the interests of "national security" or "law and order."

1. The civil rights movement, although well within the established elite consensus in goals and tactics, awakened the black masses to their condition in American society. The result was a major increase in their aspiration levels and subsequent frustration and bitterness because these new aspirations were unfulfilled. The traditional apathy of the black masses was replaced with an activism that was unstable and violence-prone.

2. The change from apathy to activism occurred as a result of rising expectations of the black masses. The civil rights movement had to awaken blacks

12 *Ibid.*

to their plight in American society to begin to make progress in the elimination of discrimination. But the price of this awakening was a major increase in the aspiration levels of the masses and a subsequent frustration and bitterness when these aspirations were not fulfilled.

3. Police in the ghetto are recruited from white masses rather than white elites, and thus reflect white mass attitudes toward blacks. Police are frequently unsympathetic toward black aspirations, and their experiences in the ghetto reinforce unsympathetic attitudes.

4. Elite reaction to rioting was mixed. Some white elites cited rioting and violence as evidence of the social maladies of cities and called for massive public programs to improve housing, health, education, employment, and so on. But no new massive public programs were undertaken. Generally established elites, who had supported the elimination of legal discrimination and efforts to achieve equality of opportunity, reacted negatively when black masses violated the accepted consensus about "rules of the game." They condemned rioters as "criminals," passed a law making it a federal crime to cross a state line to incite the masses to riot, and called for improved police tactics and training in quelling mass disturbances. A strong "law and order" movement developed in local, state, and national politics.

5. Crime is a serious social problem in America, particularly when we consider that most crimes are not even reported to the police. But courts must weigh the values of individual liberty and due process of law against demands for increased public safety. Generally, the Supreme Court has insisted on protection of the rights of defendants regardless of evidence of guilt. Chief Justice Burger has emphasized better administration of the courts as a means of speedy justice.

6. Congress and the president, reacting to demands that something be done to protect "law and order," have supported stronger anticrime measures, including pretrial detention, "no-knock" raids, and stiffer penalties.

7. Governing elites themselves can pose a threat to due process of law when they resort to repressive tactics in the face of mass unrest and disorder. The Watergate hearings suggest that the conditions for repressive acts include racial unrest and violence, mass protests and demonstrations, the approval and encouragement of violence by vocal counterelites, defeat and humiliation in war, sporadic violence, and perceived threats to national security.

BIBLIOGRAPHY

Congressional Quarterly, *Watergate: Chronology of a Crisis.* Washington, D.C.: Congressional Quarterly Reporting Service, 1973.

GURR, TED, *Why Men Rebel.* Princeton: Princeton University Press, 1970.

MASOTTI, LOUIS H., and DON R. BOWEN, eds., *Riots and Rebellion.* Beverly Hills, Calif.: Sage Publications, 1970.

National Advisory Commission on Civil Disorders, *Report.* Washington, D.C.: Government Printing Office, 1968.

WILSON, JAMES Q., *Varieties of Police Behavior.* Cambridge: Harvard University Press, 1968.

Poverty. UPI Photo

5 POVERTY:

the search for a rational strategy

The first obstacle to a rational approach to poverty lies in the conflict over the definition of the problem. Measuring the extent of poverty in America is itself a political activity. Proponents of programs for the poor frequently make high estimates of the number of poor. They view the problem of poverty as a persistent one, even in an affluent society; they contend that many millions of poor people suffer from hunger, exposure, and remedial illness, and that some of them even starve to death. Their definition of the problem practically mandates immediate and massive public programs.

On the other hand, others minimize the number of poor in America. They see poverty diminishing over time without major public programs; they view the poor in America as considerably better off than the middle class of fifty years ago and even wealthy by the standards of most other societies in the world; and they deny that anyone needs to suffer from hunger, exposure, remedial illness, or starvation if they make use of the services and facilities available to them. This definition of the problem minimizes demands for public programs to fight poverty.

According to the U.S. Social Security Administration there are about 25 million poor people in the United States. This is approximately 12 percent of the population. This is the number of Americans falling *below* the poverty line which is set at: [1]

[1] U.S. Bureau of the Census, *Current Population Reports,* Series P-60 "Poverty in the United States: 1959–1968" (1969), p. 11.

93

| | ANNUAL CASH INCOME |
Year	Nonfarm Family of Four
1975 est.	$4,750
1972	4,275
1970	3,968
1968	3,553
1965	3,223
1960	3,022

This definition of the poverty line by the Social Security Administration was derived by careful calculation of costs of food, housing, clothing, and other items for rural and urban families of different sizes. The dollar amounts on these lines are flexible to take into account the effect of inflation; these amounts can be expected to rise each year with the rate of inflation.

There are several problems in this definition of poverty. First of all, it does not take account of regional differences in the costs of living, or climate, or accepted style of living. Second, it does not account for family assets—for example, a family that owns its own home does not usually devote as much income to housing as a family that rents. Third, there are many families and individuals whose particular circumstances may place them officially among the poor but who do not think of themselves as "poor people"—students, for example. Doubtless there are others whose income is above the poverty line but who have special problems—such as serious or chronic sickness—which leave them impoverished. Finally, the official definition of poverty does not recognize the problems of those who spend their incomes unwisely. If money goes for liquor, or dope, or expensive used cars, or if money is siphoned off by loan sharks, impoverished relatives and friends, or high prices charged by ghetto storeowners, then even a reasonably high income family can live in poverty. Yet despite these problems, the Social Security Administration definition has provided the best available estimate of poverty in America.

How poor is "poor"? There is reason to believe that the 25 million Americans living in official poverty do not all suffer hardship and privation.[2] About 45 percent own cars, 42 percent own their own homes, and more than half have some savings. Nearly 80 percent of the poor have television sets and 75 percent have refrigerators or freezers. Over three-quarters have hot water, access to a telephone for receiving calls, kitchen with cooking equipment, a flush toilet, and a bath. Yet the diets of the poor are nutritionally bad, whether from ignorance or poverty. The poor

[2] Herman P. Miller, "The Dimensions of Poverty," in Ben B. Seligman, ed., *Poverty as a Public Issue* (New York: Free Press, 1965).

do not seek medical attention except in emergencies. The result is a great deal of preventable illness and malnutrition.

Table 5-1 *Population, by Categories, with Income Below Poverty Level (Based on Total Population)*

	NUMBER (IN MILLIONS)	PERCENT OF TOTAL IN CATEGORY
Total	24.5	11.9
White population	16.2	9.0
Black population	7.7	33.3
Those living in central cities	7.8	11.3
Those living in suburbs	5.1	5.3
Those living in rural areas	11.5	12.3
Under age 25	13.1	14.3
Ages 25–65	7.6	8.7
Over age 65	3.7	18.6
Families with male head	12.9	7.4
Families with female head	11.6	36.9

Source: U.S. Bureau of the Census, *Characteristics of the Low-Income Population* Series P-60, No. 88 (Washington, D.C.: Government Printing Office, 1973).

Who are the poor? Poverty occurs in many different kinds of families and in all environmental settings. However, the incidence of poverty varies sharply among groups living under different circumstances, and several groups experience poverty in greater proportions than the national average. First of all, the likelihood of *blacks* experiencing poverty is three times greater than whites; the percentage of the black population of the United States falling under the poverty line is 33.3 compared to 9.0 percent for the white population. Second, *female-headed families* experience poverty far more frequently than do male-headed families; 36.9 percent of all female-headed families live below the poverty line. Third, the *aged* experience more poverty than persons of working age; 25.0 percent of the population over 65 lives below the poverty line. Although we think of poverty as a characteristic of persons living in large, central-city ghettos, actually *rural* families experience more poverty more frequently than central-city families. On the other hand, central cities have more poverty than their surrounding suburbs.

Are the poor disappearing? In Franklin D. Roosevelt's second inaugural address in 1937 he said, "I see one-third of a nation ill-housed, ill-clad, ill-nourished." Since that time the American political and economic system has succeeded in reducing the proportion of poor to about 12 percent. If current rates in the reduction of poverty in America con-

POVERTY IN THE UNITED STATES

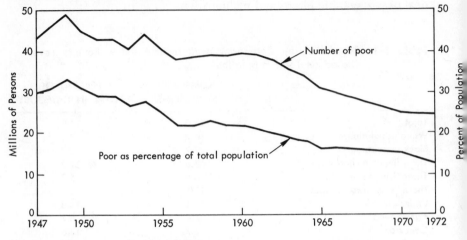

Fig. 5-1 *Poverty in the United States*

Source: Redrawn after G. Bach, *Economics,* 7th Ed. (Englewood Cliffs, N.J.: Prentice-Hall, Inc., © 1971), Fig. 37-1, p. 535. Data from Council of Economic Advisers and Social Security Administration.

tinue in the future, there will be virtually no poverty remaining in 25 to 50 years.

Table 5-2 provides a closer look at the change in the number and

Table 5-2 *Changes in the Number of Poor Over Time*

| | POPULATION (IN MILLIONS) LIVING BELOW POVERTY LEVEL | | | |
	1959	1963	1967	1972
Total	39.5	36.4	27.8	24.5
White	28.5	25.2	19.0	16.2
Nonwhite	11.0	11.2	8.8	8.2

Source: U.S. Bureau of the Census, *Current Population Reports,* Series P-60, No. 88 (Washington, D.C.: Government Printing Office, 1973).

percentage of poor over the last decade.[3] All these figures account for the effect of inflation, so there is no question that the number and percentage of the population living in poverty is declining, despite increases in the population. Both white and black poverty is declining, although the rate

[3] U.S. Bureau of the Census, *Current Population Reports.*

of decline among blacks has not been as great as the rate of decline among whites.

POVERTY AS INEQUALITY

It is possible to define poverty as "a state of mind"—some people think they have less income or material possessions than most Americans, and they believe they are entitled to more. Their sense of deprivation is not tied to any *absolute* level of income. Instead, their sense of deprivation is *relative* to what most Americans have, and what they, therefore, feel they are entitled to. Even fairly substantial incomes may result in a sense of relative deprivation in a very affluent society when commercial advertising and the mass media portray the "average American" as having a high level of consumption and material well-being.

Today the poor are not any more deprived, relative to the nonpoor, than in the past. However, they *feel* more deprived—they perceive the gap to be wider, and they no longer accept the gap as legitimate. Blacks are overrepresented among the poor; the civil rights movement made blacks acutely aware of their position in American society relative to whites. Thus, the black revolution contributed to a new awareness of the problem of poverty in terms of relative differences in income and conditions of life.

Defining poverty as relative deprivation really defines it as *inequality* in society. As Victor Fuchs explains:

> By the standards that have prevailed over most of history, and still prevail over large areas of the world, there are very few poor in the United States today. Nevertheless, there are millions of American families who, both in their own eyes and in those of others, are poor. As our nation prospers, our judgment as to what constitutes poverty will inevitably change. When we talk about poverty in America, we are talking about families and individuals who have much less income than most of us. When we talk about reducing or eliminating poverty, we are really talking about changing the distribution of income.[4]

Thus, eliminating poverty if it is defined as relative deprivation would mean achieving absolute equality of incomes and material possessions in America.

Let us try systematically to examine poverty as relative deprivation. Economists have already provided us with a way of measuring income

[4] Victor R. Fuchs, "Redefining Poverty and Redistributing Income," *The Public Interest* (Summer 1967), p. 91.

distributions within political systems.[5] Income distributions may be observed by means of a Lorenz curve, which shows the cumulative proportions of aggregate income (on the vertical or y axis) accruing to cumulative proportions of the population ranging in order from the lowest to highest income earners (on the horizontal or x axis). The total area on a diagram that falls between the Lorenz curve, representing the actual income distribution, and the straight diagonal line, representing perfect income equality, expresses the extent of income inequality within a political system. This area is measured by Gini coefficient or a Gini index, which ranges from a plus 1.00 (theoretically perfect inequality) to 0.00 (theoretically perfect equality) as illustrated in Figure 5-2. Inequality in

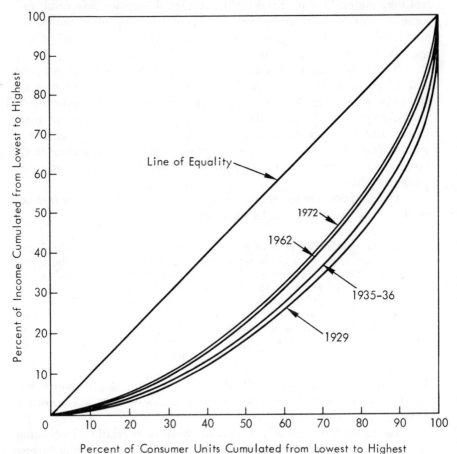

Fig. 5-2 *Lorenz Curves for the Distribution of Family Personal Income*

America is decreasing over time. However, the rate of decrease is not very rapid. Certainly poverty as relative deprivation is not disappearing at the same rate as absolute poverty. Figure 5-2 shows that the Lorenz curve is moving closer to the line of perfect equality over time, but that changes in the curve are not very great.

A closer view of changes in income inequality over time is presented in Table 5-3. This table divides all American families into five groups—

Table 5-3 *Percent Distribution of Family Personal Income [1] by Quintiles and Top 5 Percent of Consumer Units,[2] Selected Years, 1947–1972*

QUINTILES	1947	1950	1951	1954	1956	1959	1962	1968	1972
Lowest	5.0	4.8	5.0	4.8	4.8	4.6	4.6	5.7	5.5
Second	11.0	10.9	11.3	11.1	11.3	10.9	10.9	12.4	12.0
Third	16.0	16.1	16.5	16.4	16.3	16.3	16.3	17.7	17.4
Fourth	22.0	22.1	22.3	22.5	22.3	22.6	22.7	23.7	23.5
Highest	46.0	46.1	44.9	45.2	45.3	45.6	45.5	40.6	41.6
Total	100.0	100.0	100.0	100.0	100.0	100.0	100.0	100.0	100.0
Top 5 percent ratio	20.9	21.4	20.7	20.3	20.2	20.2	19.6	14.0	14.4
Gini concentration	.40	.40		.39	.39		.40	.37	.36

[1] Family personal income includes wage and salary receipts (net of social insurance contributions), other labor income, proprietors' and rental income, dividends, personal interest income, and transfer payments. In addition to monetary income flows, it includes certain nonmonetary or imputed income such as wages in kind, the value of food and fuel produced and consumed on farms, net imputed value of owner-occupied homes, and imputed interest. Personal income differs from national income in that it excludes corporate profits taxes, corporate saving (inclusive of inventory valuation adjustment), and social security contributions of employers and employees, and includes transfer payments (mostly governmental) and interest on consumer and government debt.

[2] Consumer units include farm operator and nonfarm families and unattached individuals. A family is defined as a group of two or more persons related by blood, marriage, or adoption, and residing together.

Source: U.S. Bureau of the Census, *Current Population Reports,* Series P-60, No. 80.

from the lowest one-fifth, in personal income, to the highest one-fifth —and shows the percentage of total family personal income received by each of these groups over the years. (If perfect income equality existed, each fifth of American families would receive 20 percent of all family personal income, and it would not even be possible to rank fifths from highest to lowest.) The poorest one-fifth received 5 percent of all family personal income in 1947; in 1972, this group had increased its percentage of all family personal income to 5.5. The highest one-fifth of American families in personal income received 46 percent of all family personal income in 1947; in 1972, this percentage had declined to 41.6. This was the only income group to lose in relation to other income groups. The middle classes improved their relative income position even more than the poor. Another measure of income equalization over time is the decline in the percentage of income received by the top 5 percent in America. The top 5 percent received 21 percent of all family personal incomes in 1947, but only 14.4 percent in 1972. The Gini coefficient of income inequality declined from .40 to .36 in that same time period. Income differences in America are decreasing over time, but only very slowly.

It is unlikely that income differences will ever disappear completely —at least not in a society that rewards skill, talent, risk taking, and ingenuity. If the problem of poverty is defined as relative deprivation—that is, *inequality*—then the problem is not really capable of solution. Regardless of how well-off the poor may be in absolute terms, there will always be a lowest one-fifth of the population receiving something less than 20 percent of all income. Income differences may decline over time, but *some* differences will remain, and even minor differences can acquire great importance and hence pose a "problem."

In describing federal antipoverty programs, we will be dealing with policies that were designed primarily to raise the poor above the poverty line. Policies dealing with income redistribution are discussed in Chapter 10.

THE CURATIVE STRATEGY—THE WAR ON POVERTY

The war on poverty was an attempt to apply a "curative strategy" to the problems of the poor. In contrast to the alleviative strategy of public assistance, or the preventative strategy of social security, the curative strategy stresses efforts to help the poor and unemployed become self-supporting and capable of earning adequate incomes by bringing about changes in the individuals themselves or in their environment. The curative strategy was the prevailing approach to poverty in the administrations of Presidents John F. Kennedy and Lyndon B. Johnson. It is represented in the Economic Development Act of 1965, Appalachian Regional Development Act of 1965, the Manpower Training and Development Act of 1962, and the Economic Opportunity Act of 1964, all of which are discussed below.

The rationale of the curative strategy was described in a very influential book, *The Affluent Society*, by economist and Presidential Advisor John Kenneth Galbraith.[6] Writing in 1957, Galbraith first called the attention of the intellectual community to the existence of widespread poverty in the midst of an affluent society. Although only a small minority of

[6] John K. Galbraith, *The Affluent Society* (Boston: Houghton Mifflin, 1958).

Americans are poor, the poverty they experience is a very bitter kind of poverty because the majority of Americans are so rich.

In attempting to identify the causes of poverty in America, Galbraith distinguishes between "case poverty" and "area poverty." Case poverty is largely a product of the personal characteristics of affected persons. Some persons have been unable to participate in the nation's prosperity because of old age, illiteracy, inadequate education, lack of job skills, poor health, inadequate motivation, or racial discrimination. Area poverty is a product of economic deficiency relating to a particular sector of the nation, such as West Virginia or much of the rest of Appalachia, and large parts of rural America. Urbanization, industrialization, and technological development appear to have passed up many of these areas, creating high rates of unemployment and large numbers of low-income families. The decline in employment in the coal industry, the exhaustion of iron-ore mines, the squeezing out of the small farmer from the agricultural market, and other such economic factors create "pockets of poverty" or "depressed areas" throughout the nation. People in these areas suffer many of the problems of case poverty because the two types of poverty are not mutually exclusive. But both case poverty and area poverty differ from the "mass poverty" of the 1930s or the mass poverty predicted for capitalist societies by Marxian doctrine. Today's poverty afflicts only a minority of Americans, and it does not disappear even when the economy expands and the nation is prosperous.

The Economic Development Act is an attempt to cope with area poverty.[7] In 1961, President John F. Kennedy launched a four-year program of assistance for "depressed areas," in which the Department of Commerce provided long-term loans at low interest to attract businesses to these areas, as well as loans and grants to local governments for public facilities needed to attract businesses. This Area Redevelopment Act was essentially a "trickle-down" approach to poverty, with most of the direct benefits going to businesses rather than to the poor. Republicans charged that the program was a pork barrel to help elect Democrats, and many specific ARA projects were criticized for failing to alleviate poverty. In 1965, President Johnson requested Congress to replace ARA with an expanded and broadened program for depressed areas under the Economic Development Act of 1965. It authorized grants and loans for public works, development facilities, technical assistance, and other activities to help economically depressed areas and to stimulate planning for economic development. In this Act, the responsibility is placed upon local and state governments to apply for economic development assistance from the

[7] For an excellent summary of public policies in the war on poverty, see James E. Anderson, "Poverty, Unemployment, and Economic Development: The Search for a National Anti-Poverty Policy," *Journal of Politics*, 29 (February 1967), 70–93.

Economic Development Administration and to create multicounty and multistate development areas and districts for the purposes of planning economic development. The Economic Development Administration can make direct grants to communities for such projects as water systems, waste disposal plants, industrial development parks, airports, or other facilities that will improve employment opportunities in a depressed area; but it insists on regional planning and requires any community proposal to "substantially further the objectives of the war on poverty."

The Appalachian Regional Redevelopment Act in 1965 was another federal approach to the problem of area poverty. The name "Appalachia" denoted an eleven-state region centering around the Appalachian mountains from southern New York to mid-Alabama. It was generally conceded to be the largest economically depressed area in the nation, although it did contain "pockets of prosperity." The focus of the Appalachia Act is on highway construction, which was believed necessary to open up the region to economic development although it may make it even easier for the residents to leave. Programs under the Appalachia Act will be carried out by

Shacks, Appalachia. Photo by Michael Mauney

existing national and state agencies, such as the U.S. Bureau of Public Roads and state highway departments. However, the entire program is coordinated by the Appalachian Regional Commission, comprised of the governor of each state in the region or his representative, and a federal representative chosen by the president. This arrangement was designed to secure state participation and better adaptation of programs to local conditions. Needless to say, the Appalachian program stirred the interest of Congressmen from *other* regional areas.

FEDERAL MANPOWER PROGRAMS

In an approach to case poverty, the federal government has undertaken a variety of manpower training programs. These programs are designed to increase the skills and employment opportunities of the poor to enable them to become productive members of the nation's work force. The programs provide skill training, transitional employment experience, job placement assistance, and even related child-care, social, and health services.

This approach to poverty began with the Manpower Training and Development Act of 1962, which authorized federal grants to state employment agencies and private enterprise for on-the-job training programs to help workers acquire new job skills. Additional manpower training programs were authorized under the Economic Opportunity Act of 1964 and directed at persons living below the poverty line. In 1973 all manpower programs were brought together under the Comprehensive Employment and Training Act (CETA).

Federal manpower programs under CETA provide for both institutional (classroom) and on-the-job type training. On-the-job training is provided by private and governmental employers who recruit and train low-skilled persons to fill regular job vacancies. The employers are reimbursed for the costs of training, remedial education, counseling, and supportive services. More than half the costs of the program have been for enrollee allowances—payments to participants during their training period. In the past the CETA program concentrated on retraining technologically displaced workers, but in recent years it has also attempted to teach skills to unemployed persons with little or no work experience.

The Job Corps is a specialized program for disadvantaged youth. It provides education, vocational training, and work experience in rural conservation camps for unemployable youth between the ages of sixteen and twenty-one. It is not a simple manpower training effort; Job Corps enrollees are considered to lack the attitudes and basic education required to gain and hold a job. Reading and basic arithmetic are taught, as well as auto mechanics, clerical work, and the use of tools. Health care and personal guidance and counseling are also provided. Removing the enrollees from their home environment is considered helpful in breaking habits and associations that are obstacles to useful employment. It is very difficult to measure the effectiveness of the program; its dropout rate is very high; the cost of the program per enrollee is very high; and there is no solid evidence that Job Corps alumni do better in the labor market than they would have done without Job Corps experience. The Job Corps was begun as part of the 1964 Economic Opportunity Act "war on poverty," but it is now operated by the Department of Labor under CETA.

Federal Work-Study programs help students from low-income families remain in school by giving them federally paid part-time employment with cooperating public or private agencies. Many universities and colleges are participants in this program; they benefit from the federally paid labor and students benefit from the part-time jobs created.

Two manpower programs designed specifically to deal with disadvantaged adults are the Work Incentive Program (WIN) and the Concentrated Employment Program (CEP). Participants in these programs are poor; they generally have few skills and little or no work experience. CEP was established to deal with hard-core unemployed; the WIN program was mandated for all employable welfare recipients in 1972. It is very difficult to evaluate the success of these programs. Numerically, very few individuals have escaped poverty and found rewarding jobs as a direct result of them. However, programs like these have tried to assist long-term public assistance recipients, unusual offenders, narcotic addicts, and alcoholics, and the very difficulty of the task precludes high success rates.

In addition to the programs mentioned above, the Department of Health, Education and Welfare provides federal grants to states to undertake vocational rehabilitation programs for physically or mentally handicapped persons, and the Veterans Administration operates a vocational rehabilitation program for disabled veterans.

Finally, the federal government funds the Federal-State Employment Service with its network of 2,300 local offices providing job-placement services for nearly 10 million persons per year. Although these placement services are available to everyone, not just the poor, special efforts are given to placing disadvantaged persons.

THE ECONOMIC OPPORTUNITY ACT

The most important legislation in the "war on poverty" was the Economic Opportunity Act of 1964. The Office of Economic Opportunity

(OEO) was established directly under the president with authority to support varied and highly experimental techniques for combating poverty at the community level. The focus was upon case poverty and the objective was to help the poor and unemployed become self-supporting and capable of earning adequate incomes by bringing about changes in the individuals themselves or in their environment. The strategy was one of "rehabilitation, not relief." OEO was given no authority to make direct grants to the poor as relief or public assistance. All of its programs were aimed, whether accurately or inaccurately, at curing the causes of poverty rather than alleviating its symptoms.

The core of the Economic Opportunity Act was a grassroots "Community Action Program" to be carried on at the local level with federal financial assistance, by public or private nonprofit agencies. Communities were urged to form community action agencies composed of representatives of government, private organizations, and most importantly, the poor themselves. It was originally intended that OEO would *support antipoverty programs* devised by the local community action agencies. Projects might include (but were not limited to) literacy training, health services, homemaker services, legal aid for the poor, neighborhood service centers, manpower vocational training, and childhood development activities. The Act also envisioned that a community action agency would help *organize the poor* so that they could avail themselves of the many public programs designed to serve the poor. Finally, the Act attempted to *coordinate federal and state programs for the poor* in each community.

Community action was to be "developed, conducted, and administered with the maximum feasible participation of the residents of the areas and members of the groups served." This was one of the more controversial phases in the Act itself. Militants within the OEO administration frequently cited this phase as authority to "mobilize" the poor "to have immediate and irreversible impact on the communities." This language implied that the poor were to be organized as a political force by federal antipoverty warriors using federal funds. Needless to say neither Congress nor the Democratic Administration of President Lyndon Johnson intended to create in these communities rival political organizations that would compete for power with local governments. But some OEO administrators thought that the language of the Act gave them this authority.

The typical Community Action Agency was governed by a board consisting of public officials (perhaps the mayor, a county commissioner, a school board member, public health officer, etc.), prominent public citizens (from business, labor, civil rights, religious, and civil affairs organizations), and representatives of the poor (in some cases elected in agency-sponsored elections but more often hand-picked by ministers, social workers, civil rights leaders, etc.). A staff was to be hired, including a full-time director, and paid from an OEO grant for administrative expenses. A target area would be defined—generally it was the low-income area of the county or the ghetto of a city. Neighborhood centers were established in the target area, perhaps with general counselors, employment assistance, a recreation hall, a child-care center, and some sort of health clinic. These centers assisted the poor in contacting the school system, the welfare department, employment agencies, the public housing authority, and so on. Frequently, the centers and the antipoverty workers who manned them acted as intermediaries between the poor and public agencies. The jargon describing this activity was "outreach."

Community action agencies also devised specific antipoverty projects for submission to Washington offices of OEO for funding. The most popular of these projects was "Operation Head Start"—usually a cooperative program between the community action agency and the local school district. Preschool children from poor families were given six to eight weeks of special summer preparation before entering kindergarten or first grade. The idea was to give these disadvantaged children a "head start" on formal schooling. Congress (as well as the general public) was favorably disposed toward this program and emphasized it in later budget appropriations to OEO. However, studies of the academic progress of disadvantaged children who participated in Head Start revealed that these children did no better in the long run than disadvantaged children who had not participated in the program.

Another popular antipoverty project was the "legal services program." Many community action agencies established free legal services to the poor to assist them in rent disputes, contracts, welfare rules, minor police actions, housing regulations, and so on. The idea was that the poor seldom have access to legal counsel and they are frequently taken advantage of because they do not understand their rights. Congress amended the Act in 1967 to insure that no OEO funds would be used to defend any person in a criminal case. But antipoverty lawyers using federal funds have been active in bringing suit against city welfare departments, housing authorities, public health agencies, and other government bodies.

Other kinds of antipoverty projects funded by OEO include family planning programs—the provision of advice and devices to facilitate family planning by the poor; homemaker services—advice to poor families on how to stretch low family budgets; manpower training—special outreach efforts to bring hard-core unemployed into more established manpower programs; "Follow Through"—to remedy the recognized failures of Head Start and continue special educational experiences for poor children after they enter school; "Upward Bound"—educational counseling for poor children; etc.

WHY WE LOST THE WAR ON POVERTY

The war on poverty failed to produce any notable victories. In 1969 the Office of Economic Opportunity was "reorganized" by the Nixon Administration, transferring its educational and manpower training programs—the Head Start program, the Job Corps, and Manpower Training—to other federal agencies and relegating OEO to the status of a "laboratory agency." In 1973, President Nixon recommended that OEO be abolished, that federal support for local community action agencies be discontinued, and that remaining programs, including legal services, be transferred to other agencies. Congress has not yet acted decisively on the future of OEO, and the courts have prevented the president from discontinuing OEO on his own initiative. Nonetheless, the future of Economic Opportunity programs looks very bleak.

The demise of the economic opportunity programs cannot be attributed to political partisanship. The war on poverty had become the unpopular stepchild of the Johnson Administration long before LBJ left office. The reasons for the failure of this effort to implement a curative strategy are complex.[8] President Nixon has declared:

> In the past, OEO suffered from a confusion of roles and from a massive attempt to do everything at once, with the same people performing many conflicting functions: coordinating old programs, doing new research, setting up demonstration projects, evaluating results and serving as advocates for the poor. As a result, inefficiency, waste and resentment too often clouded the record of even its best accomplishments.[9]

The Office of Economic Opportunity was always the scene of great confusion. New and untried programs were organized at breakneck speed. There was a high turnover in personnel. There was delay and confusion in releasing funds to local community action agencies. There was an excess of scandal and corruption, particularly at the local level. Community action agencies with young and inexperienced personnel frequently offended experienced governmental administrators as well as local political figures. Congressional action was uncertain, the Community Action Program's life was extended for a year at a time, and appropriations were often delayed. But most damaging of all, even though programs were put in operation, there was little concrete evi-

[8] The most important and controversial analysis of the difficulties in the war on poverty is Daniel P. Moynihan's *Maximum Feasible Misunderstanding: Community Action in the War on Poverty* (New York: Free Press, 1969), on which the following analysis relies.

[9] President Richard M. Nixon, Message to Congress, October 2, 1969.

dence that these programs were successful in their objectives—that is, in eliminating the causes of poverty.

The community action effort in Syracuse, New York, was illustrative of the difficulties which all too frequently plagued the war on poverty. In a city of 222,000, with only 16,000 Negroes, the Syracuse Crusade for Opportunity, the local community action agency, was established with a white majority on its governing board. Simultaneously, however, the OEO gave Syracuse University a grant to establish a Community Action Training Center to experiment with new approaches for enabling the poor to participate in the management of antipoverty programs such as the Crusade for Opportunity. The Training Center worked primarily with blacks, and soon agitation was begun among the Negro poor that Negroes "take over" Crusade for Opportunity. Early in 1966 the white Jewish executive director resigned the $19,000 job (a very substantial salary from the perspective of the poor clientele) and was replaced by a militant black. Soon blacks acquired a majority on the board. In the eyes of the public the war on poverty was now a "black program." At this point the public demands and the rhetoric emanating from Crusade for Opportunity became more and more abrasive to the white community. For example, remedial reading manuals in literacy classes informed readers: "no ends are accomplished without the use of force. . . . Squeamishness about force is the mark not of idealistic but moonstruck morals." The local NAACP charged that such materials were "geared to rioting," but militant poverty workers responded that the NAACP head was a "house nigger."

While the struggle for power went on over Crusade for Opportunity, the actual antipoverty projects floundered. A job-training program was rated "a dismal failure" by its head. Politically the organization failed to assist the poor in bringing about a more responsive government. A Republican mayor was reelected, not only in spite of but probably because of the intense opposition, even harassment, by antipoverty workers. The finances of the organization soon became a scandal; substantial sums went unaccounted for. Then it was revealed that $7 million of the $8 million expended by Crusade for Opportunity up to mid-1967 went for salaries of antipoverty workers. It was difficult to see what the organization had done for the poor of Syracuse.

Daniel P. Moynihan summarized the community action experiences as follows:

> Over and again the attempts by official and quasi-official agencies (such as the Ford Foundation) to organize poor communities led first to the radicalization of the middle-class persons who began the effort; next to a certain amount of stirring among the poor, but accompanied by

heightened radical antagonism *on the part of the poor* if they happened to be black; next to retaliation from the larger white community; where-upon it would emerge that the community action agency, which had talked so much, been so much in the headlines, promised so much in the way of change in the fundamentals of things, was powerless. A creature of a Washington bureaucracy, subject to discontinuation without notice. Finally, much bitterness all around.[10]

Community experiences such as that in Syracuse were bound to reverberate in Washington. The Democratic administration under President Johnson had never intended to finance a conflict between poor blacks and Democratic big-city mayors and party organization. The Democratic administration did not wish to stir up antagonism in cities between blacks and low-income white labor and ethnic groups, which had made up the winning Democratic party coalition since the days of FDR. Local power structures are not without influence in Washington; they could strike at the financial roots of the program in Washington without risking direct confrontations at the local level. Even before Johnson left office, the war on poverty had been substantially down-graded in policy priorities. The Nixon administration began a gradual dismantling of OEO. The final verdict on the war on poverty is not yet in. But the interim report is very negative.

In an obvious reference to public policies affecting the poor and the black in America, Aaron Wildavsky wrote:

A recipe for violence: Promise a lot; deliver a little. Lead people to believe they will be much better off, but let there be no dramatic improvement. Try a variety of small programs, each interesting but marginal in impact and severely underfinanced. Avoid any attempted solution remotely comparable in size to the dimensions of the problem you are trying to solve. Have middle-class civil servants hire upper-class student radicals to use lower-class Negroes as a battering ram against the existing local political systems; then complain that people are going around disrupting things and chastise local politicians for not cooperating with those out to do them in. Get some poor people involved in local decision-making, only to discover that there is not enough at stake to be worth bothering about. Feel guilty about what has happened to black people; tell them you are surprised they have not revolted before; express shock and dismay when they follow your advice. Go in for a little force, just enough to anger, not enough to discourage. Feel guilty again; say you are surprised that worse has not happened. Alternate with a little suppression. Mix well, apply a match, and run. . . .[11]

[10] *Maximum Feasible Misunderstanding*, pp. 134–35.

[11] Aaron Wildavsky, "The Empty-Headed Blues: Black Rebellion and White Reaction," *The Public Interest* (Spring 1968), p. 3.

It would be difficult to find a better summary of the unintended consequences of public programs for the poor and the black.

SUMMARY

The difficulties of rational policy making are evidenced in policies and programs dealing with the poor.

1. Contrasting definitions of the problem of poverty constitute an obstacle to national policy making. Official government sources define poverty in terms of minimum dollar amounts required for food, housing, clothing, and other necessary items. Poverty, by this definition, is declining over time.

2. If poverty is defined in relative terms, then the problem of poverty is nearly insoluble. Income inequality is slowly decreasing over time. However, unless all incomes in America are equalized among all persons, there will aways be some individuals who fall below average income levels. Even if the differences in incomes are substantially narrowed, small differences may come to have great symbolic value and the problem of "poverty" will remain.

3. The "war on poverty" was designed as a curative strategy to help poverty-stricken individuals and areas become self-supporting. The Economic Development Act and the Appalachian Regional Development Act were designed to cure area poverty, while the Manpower Training and Development Act and the Economic Opportunity Act were designed to assist individuals in fighting poverty.

4. Several antipoverty programs dealt with young people—Job Corps, Work Study, Head Start, etc. The strategy appeared to be aimed at breaking the cycle of poverty at an early age. However, the impact of these programs is difficult to discern.

5. Community action programs had multiple objectives—mobilize the poor to become participating members of the community and to pressure community agencies to better serve their needs; coordinate federal and state programs for the poor in each community; and support a variety of local antipoverty projects. Frequently these objectives conflicted, particularly when community action agencies threatened to mobilize the poor as a political force in competition with existing community political structures.

6. The war on poverty promised the poor, especially the poor blacks, a great deal—but it failed to bring about any significant change in their condition. Frustration and bitterness was a frequent product of antipoverty efforts. Community action programs were characterized by confusion, turnover, inexperience, scandal, and racial and political controversy.

BIBLIOGRAPHY

Budd, Edward C., *Inequality and Poverty*. New York: W. W. Norton, 1967.
Galbraith, John K., *The Affluent Society*. Boston: Houghton Mifflin, 1958.
Kershaw, Joseph A., *Government Against Poverty*. Chicago: Markham, 1970.

LEVINE, ROBERT A., *The Poor Ye Need Not Have With You*. Cambridge: M.I.T. Press, 1970.

MOYNIHAN, DANIEL P., *Maximum Feasible Misunderstanding: Community Action and the War on Poverty*. New York: Free Press, 1969.

WILCOX, CLAIR, *Toward Social Welfare*. Homewood, Ill.: Richard D. Irwin, 1969.

Welfare lines, New York City. UPI Photo

6 WELFARE AND HEALTH:

the limits of rationalism

RATIONALITY AND IRRATIONALITY IN WELFARE POLICY

Approximately 7 percent of the nation's population—15 million people—receive welfare payments. This is nearly twice the number of people on welfare rolls a few years ago. The welfare population of New York City exceeds the total population of a city the size of Baltimore. In Boston, one person out of every five receives some form of public assistance; in Newark the figure is one person out of every four. In New York and San Francisco, one out of every seven persons receives welfare. And these figures may represent only *half* of the persons eligible for welfare assistance in this nation!

The costs of welfare and the growth of social dependency outrage many working, tax-paying Americans, but their outrage is matched by that of the recipients themselves, who claim that the payments are inadequate to maintain a decent standard of living. Nationwide, welfare payments are well below poverty levels established by the Social Security Administration. The welfare bureaucracy is a nightmare—long lines, endless forms, insensitive officials, and pointless regulations. No one is more bitter about the welfare system in America than the recipients themselves. Even the welfare officials who operate the system are offended by it. Turnover among caseworkers is high. Caseworkers are assigned so many cases that they can rarely be of direct assistance to families. All they can do is process forms and send checks. Finally, the

113

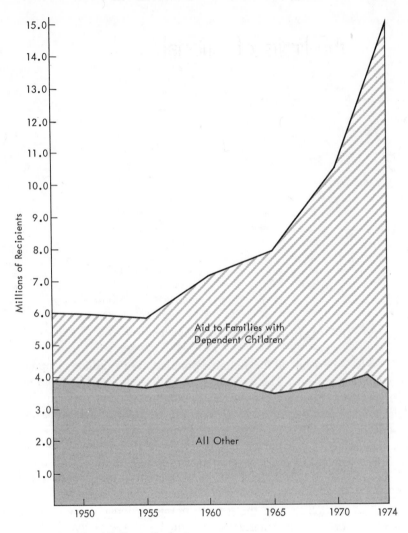

Fig. 6-1 *The Welfare Explosion*

greatest inequity in the welfare system is its total exclusion of the *work-ing* poor—those millions of American families who live in poverty but cannot receive government assistance because one member of the family is working.

Racial antagonisms are another part of the welfare dilemma. About 25 percent of the nation's black population receives public assistance of one kind or another; only about 4 percent of the white population is on welfare. In the nation's large cities the welfare rolls are overwhelmingly black. Hence, conflict over welfare is closely related to racial problems.

Incredibly enough, today's welfare dilemma is the product of more than thirty years of rational planning. Social security, public assistance, Medicaid and Medicare, manpower training, the "war on poverty," and a variety of other programs and policies were initially presented to the nation as rational approaches to the problems of the poor. Yet none of these programs has succeeded in eliminating poverty or even reducing public demands that "something be done" about "the welfare mess." All these programs have produced serious, unanticipated consequences. Welfare rolls continue to rise, both in absolute numbers and in percentage of the population. This is true despite an expanding economy and the absence of any national economic depression. The rapidly rising costs of many current welfare programs are resented by working taxpayers. Many current welfare policies are denounced by the officials and caseworkers who must administer them. Welfare assistance does not get to many Americans who deserve it. It is frequently accepted with bitterness by those who were intended to benefit from it.

It is not really possible in this chapter to describe all the problems of the poor in America or to describe all the difficulties in developing rational health and welfare policies. But it is possible to describe the general design of alternative strategies to deal with poverty in America, to observe how these strategies have been implemented in public policy, and to outline some of the obstacles to a rational approach to the problems of the poor.

THE PUNITIVE STRATEGY—EARLY WELFARE POLICY

Public welfare has been a recognized responsibility of governments in English-speaking nations for almost four hundred years. Prior to the 1930s, care of the poor in the United States resembled the early patterns of poor relief established as far back as the Poor Relief Act of 1601 by the English Parliament. Early "Elizabethan" welfare policy was a combination of punitive as well as alleviative strategies that discouraged all but the most desperately poor from seeking aid, and provided only minimal assistance to those persons clearly unable to care for themselves. Primary reliance was placed upon institutional care—county workhouses, poorhouses, or almshouses. The "able-bodied poor," those we call the unemployed, were sent to county workhouses; while the "worthy poor"—widows, aged, orphans, and handicapped—were sent to poorhouses. Indigent persons who were mentally or physically ill were often kept in the same institutions. Destitute children were kept in county orphanages or sent to foster homes. Thus, public welfare was limited almost exclusively to institutional care; the distribution of food or clothing or other aid to homes of the poor was left to private charities. Whatever relief was provided by the public could never exceed the value of the income of the lowest-paid person in the community who was not on relief. Poor rolls were made public, and relief was forthcoming only if there were no living relatives who could be legally required to support a destitute member of their family.

Under Elizabethan law, the care of the poor was the responsibility of the local governments rather than the state and local governments. The parish in England, and the township and county in the United States, had to care for their poor out of their general tax funds. Because local governments wished to make certain that they were not caring for the poor of other communities, residence requirements were established for welfare care, and communities generally limited their support to those who had been born in the area or who had lived there for some time.

The rationale behind Elizabethan policy—a rationale that has not altogether disappeared from the welfare scene today—was that poverty was a product of moral or character deficiencies in the individual. Only a punitive strategy would dissuade people from indolence and keep poverty to a minimum. The great English economist of the nineteenth century, T. R. Malthus, wrote that the poor

> are themselves the causes of their own poverty; that the means of redress are in their own hands, and in the hands of no other person whatever; that the society in which they live and the government which presides over it, are without any direct power in this respect.[1]

In America, the popular sociologist Herbert Spencer opposed any public assistance because it interfered with the natural laws of selection. Natural evolution would wipe out poverty over time, he believed, by simply wiping out the poor, who were "good-for-nothings, who . . . live on the good-for-somethings—vagrants and sots, criminals and those who are on their way to crime. . . ."[2] However, Spencer's simple solution never really prevailed in public policy. Soft-hearted public officials and charitable organizations contrived to keep the poor alive with a trickle of public and private aid.

During the period of rapid industrialization and heavy immigration,

---

[1] T. R. Malthus, *An Essay on the Principle of Population* (London, 1826); quoted in Sidney Fine, *Laissez Faire and the General Welfare State* (Ann Arbor: University of Michigan Press, 1956), p. 7.

[2] Herbert Spencer, *The Man Versus the State* (London, 1892); quoted in Fine, *Laissez Faire*, p. 38.

roughly 1870 to 1920, the big city political "machines" and "bosses" also interfered with natural selection by assisting the impoverished (according to the bosses' own sense of political rationality). The political machine operated as a large, although inefficient, brokerage organization. It traded off baskets of food, bushels of coal, minor patronage, and petty favors in exchange for the votes of the poor. To get funds to pay for this primitive welfare assistance, it traded off city contracts, protection, and privileges to business interests, who paid off in cash. The machine was not very efficient as a welfare organization, because a great many middlemen came between the cash paid for a business franchise and the Christmas turkey sent to Widow O'Leary. But it worked. Recipients of such assistance were spared much of the red tape and delays experienced by recipients of public assistance today. More importantly, the aid was provided in a very personal fashion without making the recipient feel inferior or dependent. They were trading something valuable—their votes—for the assistance they received.

Prior to the 1930s most people believed the federal government had no legitimate role to play in the welfare field. The federal government provided only for needy veterans, Indians, and merchant seamen.

The Depression brought about significant changes in attitudes toward public welfare and in the policies and administration of welfare programs. Millions who had previously considered welfare recipients to be unworthy of public concern now joined in the breadlines themselves. One out of four Americans was unemployed and one out of six was receiving some sort of welfare care. No longer were many people willing to believe that poverty was a product of the individual's moral or character faults. This widespread experience with poverty changed public attitudes toward welfare and led to a change away from Elizabethan policy.

THE PREVENTATIVE STRATEGY—SOCIAL SECURITY

The administration of President Franklin D. Roosevelt lent legitimacy to the concept of national planning. In the broadest sense national planning meant attempts by the federal government to develop rational programs to achieve societal goals. Roosevelt himself was a master at articulating broad national purposes that could enlist the support of a large cross-section of the national public. However, Roosevelt was something less than a master in devising specific rational policy alternatives to achieve these purposes. Despite a great deal of New Deal rhetoric implying rationality and consistency in solving national problems, the actual record of the Roosevelt administration indicated pragmatism, experimentalism, and improvisation. According to Roosevelt, the times required full, persistent experimentation. If it fails, admit it frankly and try something else. But above all, try something. The millions who are in want will not stand by silently forever until the things to satisfy their needs are within easy reach.[3]

Yet there was an underlying logic to the most important piece of legislation of the New Deal—the Social Security Act of 1935. In this Act, the federal government undertook to establish the basic framework for welfare policies at the federal, state, and local level and, more importantly, to set forth a new approach to the problem of poverty. The Depression convinced the national leadership, and a great many citizens, that indigency could result from forces over which the individual had no control— loss of his job, old age, death of the family breadwinner, or physical disability. The solution was to require individuals to purchase insurance against their own indigency resulting from any of these misfortunes.

The *social insurance* concept, devised by the New Deal planners, was designed to prevent poverty resulting from unemployment, old age, death of a family breadwinner, or physical disability. Social insurance was based on the same notion as private insurance—the sharing of risks and the setting aside of money for a rainy day. Social insurance was not to be charity or public assistance; it was to be preventative. It relied upon the individual's (compulsory) contribution to his own protection. In contrast, public assistance is only alleviative, and relies upon general tax revenues from all taxpayers. Indeed, when the Roosevelt Administration presented the social insurance plan to Congress in the Social Security Act of 1935, it was contended that it would eventually abolish the need for any public assistance program, because individuals would be compelled to protect themselves against poverty!

The distinction between a *social insurance* program and a *public assistance* program is an important one, and has on occasion been a major political issue. If the beneficiaries of a government program are required to have made contributions to it before claiming any of its benefits, and if they are entitled to the benefits regardless of their personal wealth, then the program is said to be financed on the *social insurance* principle. On the other hand, if a program is financed out of general tax revenues, and if the recipients are required to show they are poor before claiming its benefits, then the program is said to be financed on the *public assistance* principle.

One of the key features of the Social Security Act is the Old Age Survivors' Disability Insurance (OASDI) program; this is a compulsory social insurance program financed by regular deductions from earnings, which gives individuals a legal right to benefits in the event of certain

[3] Richard Hofstadter, *American Political Tradition* (New York: Knopf, 1948), p. 316.

occurrences that cause a reduction of their income: old age, death of the head of household, or permanent disability. OASDI is based on the same principle as private insurance—sharing the risk of the loss of income—except that it is a government program that is compulsory for all workers. OASDI is not public *charity*, but a way of compelling people to provide *insurance* against a loss of income. OASDI now covers about nine out of every ten workers in the United States. Both employees and employers must pay equal amounts toward the employees' OASDI insurance. Upon retirement, an insured worker is entitled to monthly benefit payments based upon his age at retirement and the amount he has earned during his working years. However, average monthy payments are really quite modest: the average monthly amount for a retired worker, aged 65, with a wife, is less than $300. So OASDI has not eliminated poverty from the ranks of the retired in America.

OASDI also insures benefit payments to survivors of an insured worker, including his widow if she has dependent children. But if she has no dependent children, her benefits will not begin until she herself reaches retirement age. Finally, OASDI insures benefit payments to persons who suffer permanent and total disabilities that prevent them from working for more than one year. However, on the whole, payments to survivors and disabled workers are just as modest as those provided retired workers.

OASDI is a completely federal program, administered by the Social Security Administration in the Department of Health, Education and Welfare. But OASDI has an important indirect effect on state and local welfare programs: by compelling people to insure themselves against the possibility of their own poverty, social security has doubtlessly reduced the welfare problems that state and local governments would otherwise face.

Social Security benefits are specifically exempted from federal income tax liability. This tax-free provision is of some benefit to the aged. Persons over 65 also receive a double personal exemption on the federal income tax.

The second feature of the Social Security Act of 1935 was that it induced states to enact unemployment compensation programs through the imposition of the payroll tax on all employers. A federal unemployment tax is levied on the payroll of employers of four or more workers, but employers paying into state insurance programs that meet federal standards may use these state payments to offset most of their federal unemployment tax. In other words, the federal government threatens to undertake an unemployment compensation program and tax, if the states do not do so themselves. This federal program succeeded in inducing all fifty states to establish unemployment compensation programs. However, the federal standards are flexible and the states have considerable freedom in shaping their own unemployment programs. In all cases, unemployed workers must report in person and show that they are willing and able to

Table 6-1 *Social Security, 1940–1975*

	1940	1950	1960	1965	1970	1972	1975
Numbers of bene-ficiaries (in thousands)	222	3,477	14,845	20,867	25,312	30,556	31,598
Average monthly benefit, retired worker	$23	$44	$74	$84	$100	$117	$183
Social insurance receipts of federal government (in millions)	n.a.	$5,500	$11,248	$17,359	$38,914	$53,914	$85,600
Social insurance receipts as percent of all federal receipts			15.9	19.1	22.5	24.0	29.0
Medicare expenditures (in millions)	0	0	0	0	$6,800	$8,819	$14,191

Source: *The Budget of the United States Government, 1975* (Washington, D.C.: Government Printing Office, 1974), and past issues of U.S. Bureau of the Census, *Statistical Abstract of the United States.*

work in order to receive unemployment compensation benefits, and states cannot deny workers benefits for refusing to work as strike-breakers or refusing to work for rates lower than prevailing rates. But basic decisions concerning the amount of benefits, eligibility, and the length of time that benefits can be drawn are largely left to the states.

INTENDED AND UNINTENDED CONSEQUENCES
OF SOCIAL SECURITY

The framers of the Social Security Act of 1935 created an OASDI trust fund with the expectation that a reserve would be built up from social insurance premiums from working persons. The reserve would earn interest, and the interest and principal would be used in later years to pay benefits. Benefits for an individual would be in proportion to his contributions. General tax revenues would not be used at all. It was intended that the system would resemble the financing of private insurance. But it turned out not to work that way at all.

The social insurance system is now financed on a pay-as-you-go, rather than a reserve, system. Political pressure to raise benefit levels while keeping payments low reduced the reserve to a very minor role in social security finance. Today the income from all social insurance programs—over $75 billion—matches the outgo in social security benefits. Today, this generation of workingmen is paying for the benefits of the last generation, and it is expected that this generation's benefits will be financed by the next generation of workers. Social security trust fund revenues are now lumped together with general tax revenues in the federal budget.

Congress has gradually increased the social security payroll tax from 3 percent combined employee and employer contributions on the first $3,000 of wages, to an expected 12 percent combined contribution on the first $14,000. To keep up with the generous benefits which Congress finds politically expedient to vote year after year, the social security tax is now the *third largest source of federal revenue.* More important, it is also *the fastest-growing source of federal revenue.* Social insurance and welfare payments are now *the largest expenditure of the federal government,* surpassing expenditures for national defense.

The decline of the insurance concept began in the very first years of the program when FDR's planners quickly realized that building a reserve was taking money from the economy and adding to the Depression. The plan to build a large self-financing reserve fund was abandoned in 1939. The generosity of Congress has raised benefit levels an average of 400 percent since 1940. Now Congress regularly alters the levels of benefits and the formula for their computation, a practice very much at variance with sound insurance practices. More and more groups of workers have been given coverage under social security. Benefits are no longer really proportionate to contributions; they are figured more generously for those whose wages were low than for those whose wages were high. The proportion of benefits actually purchased by the contributions of those retiring in the system to date have averaged less than 10 percent! The only remaining aspect of an insurance program is that individuals must have paid into the system to receive its benefits, and beneficiaries are not required to prove they are needy. Most Americans view their benefits as a right.

The social security tax is highly regressive. It takes a much larger share of the income of the poor than the rich. This was not a serious factor when the payments amounted to very little, but today the size of social security revenues—fully one-quarter of the federal government's income —have an important impact on the total revenue structure. The tax is only on wages, not total *income.* And wages *above* certain levels ($14,000 in 1975) are completely untaxed.

Despite rises in benefit levels, the average monthly payment for a retired couple remains below $300. This is below the recognized poverty level of the 1970s of $4,000 per year. Without additional retirement or investment income, all social security recipients would live in poverty, and a significant proportion of them have no such additional income. Although there is no question that social security has reduced the amount of poverty that would exist in the absence of the program, it has failed to eliminate poverty.

MEDICAL CARE FOR THE AGED AND POOR

American's problems in health and medicine are severe. Although the United States is the richest nation in the world, it ranks well down on the list of nations in medical care provided the average citizen, number of physicians available, infant death rates, average life span, and other indicators of national health and medical care. One particularly difficult problem is the small number of physicians graduated by the nation's medical schools. Moreover, as professional specialization becomes of more interest to doctors, the result is shortages in the ranks of general practitioners. It is ironic that the United States, the richest nation in the world, must turn to graduates of foreign medical schools for more than one-fourth of its hospital residents and interns.

Public health and sanitation are among the oldest functions of government. Local public health departments are directly concerned with the *prevention* of disease. They engage in a compulsory vaccination, immunization, and quarantine, as well as regulatory activity in the processing of milk and the safeguarding of water supplies. In addition to the preventive activities of the public health departments, state and local governments also provide extensive, tax-supported hospital care. State and local governments provide both general and specialized hospitals, health centers, and nursing homes, and very often subsidize private hospitals and medical facilities as well.

The federal government is also deeply involved in public health. The U.S. Public Health Service, now part of the Department of Health, Education and Welfare, is one of the oldest agencies of the federal government, having been created in 1798 to provide medical and hospital care for merchant seamen. Today, the Service provides medical care and hospital facilities to many categories of federally aided patients, enforces quarantine regulations, licenses biological products for manufacture and sale, engages in and sponsors medical research, and, most important of all, administers federal grant-in-aid programs to states and communities for the improvement of health and hospital services. Federal grants-in-aid are available to promote the construction of hospitals, nursing homes, diagnostic centers, rehabilitation centers, medical schools, and other medical centers. Federal grants for hospital construction began in earnest with the passage of the Hill-Burton Act in 1946; these funds are usually made available on a matching basis of approximately two-to-one, with local communities carrying the heavier burden. The federal government's Veterans Administration also provides extensive medical and hospital care.

Direct federal involvement in hospital and medical care did not come until the passage of Medicare and Medicaid in 1965. Persons concerned with the state of the nation's health, and particularly the medical care problems of the poor and the aged, had urged the federal government for many years to undertake a broad national health-care program. Proponents of the national health program generally shunned the English system of government-owned and government-operated hospitals and government-employed doctors in favor of a compulsory medical *insurance* program closely linked to the Social Security Act. They envisioned a program in which all Americans would be required to insure themselves against the possibility of their medical indigency; the program would resemble private medical and hospital insurance, except that it would be compulsory. Individuals would continue to choose their own doctors, but their bills would be paid in whole or in part through their government medical insurance policy. Opponents of a national health program, led by the prestigious American Medical Association representing the nation's physicians, strongly opposed a national health program linked to social security. They deemed it "socialized medicine" and argued that it would interfere with the "sacred doctor-patient relationship." They argued that a large proportion of the population was already covered by voluntary private medical insurance plans and that charity hospitals and charitable services of doctors were readily available to the poor. Many physicians worried that if the Social Security Administration paid insured persons' doctors' bills, it would begin to set maximum prices for physicians' services; the AMA feared that this would lead to the subservience of physicians to a government agency. Proponents of national health care waged a war of statistics, arguing that the poor and the aged were not receiving adequate medical care and that private insurance companies did not enroll these segments of the population.

Congress enacted a historic comprehensive medical care act in 1965 for persons over 65, which became known as "Medicare." Passed over the opposition of the American Medical Association, Medicare provides for prepaid hospital insurance for the aged under Social Security, and low-cost voluntary medical insurance for the aged under federal administration. Medicare includes (1) a compulsory basic health insurance plan covering hospital costs for the aged, which is financed through payroll taxes collected under the social security system; and (2) a voluntary but supplemental medical program that will pay doctors' bills and additional medical expenses, financed in part by contributions from the aged and in part by the general tax revenues. So far only aged persons are covered by Medicare provisions.

Congress also passed a Medical Assistance Program in 1965, known as "Medicaid," which provides federal funds to enable states to guarantee medical services to all public assistance recipients. Each state operates its own Medicaid program. Unlike Medicare, Medicaid is a welfare program designed for needy persons; no prior contributions are required, and recipients of Medicaid services are generally welfare recipients. States can extend coverage to other medically needy persons if they choose to do so. The cost of this program has far exceeded all original estimates, which suggests that the poor in America require much more medical attention than they have received in the past.

One consequence of Medicare and Medicaid has been to place increased medical purchasing power into the hands of the aged and the poor. The result has been to greatly increase the demand for the nation's fairly stable supply of medical resources. The supply of medical services increases relatively slowly because it takes a long time to train a doctor or build a hospital, in part because the medical profession has strict rules about who can do what, and in part because medical technology is becoming ever more complex and expensive. Moreover, the availability of both government and private medical insurance has relieved both hospitals and patients of the need to keep costs down. As any student of basic economics might have predicted (but as government policy failed to anticipate), the result of Medicare and Medicaid has been an extraordinary rapid price increase in medical care and heavy pressure on available resources. Proposed reforms have concentrated on the delivery of health care: perhaps medical paraprofessionals (equivalent to military "medics") could do some of the things currently reserved for doctors; perhaps greater use should be made of out-patient clinics to relieve hospitals of some of the burden; perhaps greater emphasis should be placed on preventive medicine; perhaps medical service centers could treat patients at any time of the day or night without burdening doctors or hospitals; perhaps payment mechanisms could be improved to provide incentives for cost control.

Today debate continues over the issue of compulsory national health insurance. Medicare and Medicaid apply only to the aged and the poor; the question confronting decision-makers is whether a national health insurance program should be devised for the entire population, and if so, how the program should be designed and financed.

THE ALLEVIATIVE STRATEGY—PUBLIC ASSISTANCE

The Social Security, Unemployment Compensation, and Medicare programs were based upon the insurance strategy for preventing indigency, but the federal government also undertook in the Social Security Act of 1935 to help the states in providing public assistance payments to certain needy persons to alleviate the conditions of poverty. This strategy was clearly alleviative; there was no effort to attack the causes of poverty. The notion was to provide a minimum level of subsistence to certain categories of needy adults—the aged, blind, and disabled—and to provide for the care of dependent children. This was to be done by providing small amounts of cash in monthly payments through state-administered welfare programs. The grant-in-aid device was employed because welfare functions traditionally had been the responsibility of state and local governments, and the constitutional arrangements under American federalism made direct federal administration improbable. The entire federal effort in public assistance was supposed to be temporary in duration, declining in importance as social insurance took over the burden of assuring security.

Today the federal government directly aids three categories of welfare recipients—the aged, the blind, and the disabled. The federal government also provides grants to the states to assist the fourth and largest category—families with dependent children. Within broad outlines of the federal policy, states retain considerable discretion in the Aid to Families with Dependent Children (AFDC) program in terms of the amounts of money appropriated, benefits to be paid to recipients, rules of eligibility, and rules of the programs. Each state may choose to grant assistance beyond the amounts supported by the national government. Each state establishes its own standards to determine "need." As a result, there is a great deal of variation among the states in ease of access to welfare rolls and in the size of welfare benefits.

It is important to note that the federal government aids only four categories of welfare recipients. Only dependent children or persons who are aged, blind, or disabled fall within the categories of recipients eligible for federal support. Aid to persons who do not fall into any of these categories but who, for one reason or another, are "needy," is referred to as "general assistance." General assistance programs are entirely state-financed and state-administered. Without federal participation, these programs differ radically from state to state in terms of the persons aided, the criteria for eligibility, the amount and nature of benefits, and administration of financing. Many of these programs continue to resemble Elizabethan welfare policy. The average general assistance payment is lower than comparable payments in federally supported programs.

States also continue to maintain institutions to care for those individuals who are so destitute, alone, or ill that money payments cannot meet their needs. These institutions include state orphanages, homes for the aged, and homes for the ill. They are, for the most part, state-financed as well as state-administered. Persons living in these tax-supported institutions normally are not eligible for federal assistance, although they may receive old age payments for medical care received in a nursing home. This feature of federal welfare policy has provided incentive for the states to turn their indigent institutions into nursing homes. The quality of these homes and of the people employed to care for their residents varies enormously from state to state.

Federal standards for state AFDC programs, which are established as a prerequisite to receiving federal aid, allow considerable flexibility in state programs. Federal law requires the states to make financial contributions to their public assistance programs and to supervise these programs either directly or through local agencies. Whatever standards a state adopts must be applicable throughout the state, and there must be no discrimination in these welfare programs. The Social Security Administration demands periodic reporting from the states, insists that states administer federally supported programs under a merit personnel system, and prevents the states from imposing unreasonable residence requirements on recipients. But in important questions of administration, standards of eligibility, residence, types of assistance, and amounts of payments, the states are free to determine their own welfare programs. Beginning in 1972, the federal government required "employable" welfare recipients to register for the Work Incentive (WIN) Program; individuals prepared for work are referred to jobs while others are enrolled in training or job experience programs. But the definition of "employable" generally excludes the aged, the ill, and mothers of preschool children; indeed, only a tiny fraction of all welfare recipients have participated in the WIN program.

Public assistance recipients are generally eligible for participation in a variety of social service programs. These include Medicaid, public housing, school lunch and milk, manpower training, Office of Economic Opportunity antipoverty programs, various educational and child-care programs and services, and the food stamp program. Many of the programs are described elsewhere in this volume (public housing, Chapter 8; manpower and antipoverty programs, Chapter 5; educational programs, Chapter 7).

The *food stamp program* now distributes nearly $4 billion in federal monies to improve food and nutrition among the poor. Eligible persons may purchase food stamps, generally from county welfare departments, at a small fraction of their value in foodstuffs. The stamps may then be used to purchase food at supermarkets. This program has mushroomed very rapidly since 1972, with expansions in eligible population and increases in the costs of food. Eligibility for food stamps now extends to many low-income persons who are not poor enough to qualify for cash public assistance payments. Of course, food stamps are also made available to public assistance recipients. Federal expenditures for food stamps are rapidly approaching federal expenditures for the AFDC program, making food stamps a major subsidy for low-income families.

The effect of these multiple social service programs on the alleviation of poverty is considerable. Indeed, it is difficult to determine just how "poor" the poor really are, because it is difficult to add up the dollar value of the many separate programs serving the poor.

THE WELFARE MESS: CONSEQUENCES UNINTENDED

Public assistance turned out to be politically one of the most unpopular programs ever adopted by Congress. It is disliked by national, state, and local legislators who must vote the skyrocketing appropriations for it; it is resented by the taxpayers who must bear the ever-increasing burdens of it; it is denounced by the officials and caseworkers who must administer it; and it is accepted with bitterness by those who were intended to benefit from it.

Certainly our public assistance programs have not succeeded in reducing dependency. In the last decade the number of welfare recipients has more than doubled, and public assistance costs have quadrupled. Interestingly, it has not been programs for the aged, blind, or disabled, or even the general assistance programs that have incurred the greatest burdens. It is the Aid to Families with Dependent Children (AFDC) program that is the largest, most expensive, and most rapidly growing of all welfare programs, and the most controversial.

This growth in welfare rolls has occurred during a period of high employment; it cannot be attributed to economic depression. The acceleration has occurred because more people are applying for public assistance. They have been aided by the activities of civil rights and welfare rights organizations, Office of Economic Opportunity-supported community action agencies, and comparable groups, which have informed eligible persons of the law and encouraged them to apply for assistance. Increases in assistance levels, relaxation of eligibility requirements, and a more sympathetic attitude on the part of welfare administrators have also contributed to the increase in welfare rolls. So also has the movement of

Photo by Fred W. McDarrah

Table 6-2 *Growth of Public Assistance Programs*

	TOTAL	AFDC	AGED	DISABLED	BLIND	GENERAL ASSISTANCE
			(Millions of Recipients)			
1950	6.0	2.2	2.8	.1	.1	.9
1955	5.8	2.2	2.5	.2	.1	.7
1960	7.0	3.1	2.3	.4	.1	1.2
1965	7.8	4.4	2.1	.6	.1	.7
1970	10.4	6.7	2.0	.87	.1	.8
1971	13.5	9.5	2.0	1.0	.1	.9
1972	15.0	10.8	2.1	1.0	.1	1.0
1973	15.3	11.1	1.9	1.2	.1	1.0
1975	16.6	11.5	2.4	1.6	.1	1.0

Source: Special Analysis of the Budget of the United States, 1975 (Washington, D.C.: Government Printing Office, 1974), and past issues of U.S. Bureau of the Census, Statistical Abstract of the United States.

persons from Southern and rural areas, where welfare administration is tighter, to Northern urban areas, where access to welfare rolls is less restricted.

Despite increased dependency upon welfare and the growing burden of welfare costs, a majority of the nation's poor do *not* receive public assistance. Depending on one's definition of poverty, there were between 25 and 40 million poor people in America in 1970, yet only 14 million persons on welfare rolls. Most of the nation's poor are *working poor,* who are ineligible for welfare assistance because they hold jobs, even though these jobs pay very little. A low-income family, headed by the father, is not eligible to receive AFDC payments if the father is working, regardless of how poor the family may be.

State administration of welfare has resulted in wide disparities among the states in eligibility requirements and benefits levels. For example, in 1972 average AFDC monthly payments ranged from a high of $335 per family in New Jersey to a low of $53 per family in Mississippi. Monthly old age assistance payments ranged from a high of $143 in Wisconsin to a low of $52 in South Carolina. A state's income is the single most important variable determining the level of welfare benefits. In terms of welfare payments, it is far better to be poor in a wealthy state than in a poor one.

Operating policies and administration of welfare have produced a whole series of problems, including disincentives to family life and work. Until recently, most states denied AFDC benefits if a man was living with his family, even though he had no work. This denial was based on the assumption that an employable man in the household meant that children were no longer "dependent" upon the state. Thus, if a man lived with his family, he could watch them go hungry; if he abandoned them, public assistance would enable them to eat. Moreover, an unmarried mother could get on welfare rolls easier than a married mother (who had to prove she was not receiving support from her husband). Occasionally enforcement of the "man in the house" rule led to sensational reports of welfare caseworkers making surprise nighttime calls to discover whether a woman had a partner in her bed. These rules have been relaxed in recent years, but it is still more difficult for whole families to get on public assistance than for fatherless families.

In most states, if a recipient of assistance takes a full-time job, assistance checks are reduced or stopped. If the recipient is then laid off, it may take some time to get back on the welfare roll. In other words, employment is uncertain, while assistance is not. More importantly, the jobs available to most recipients are very low-paying jobs which do not produce much more income than does assistance, particularly when transportation, child care, and other costs of working are considered. All these facts discourage people from looking for work.

The merits of cash versus goods and services as a form of public assistance have long been debated. It is frequently argued that cash payments are ineffective in alleviating poverty because recipients are often unable to manage household money. They fall prey to advertising which encourages them to spend money for non-essential items and to overlook the food and clothing needs of themselves and their children. Assistance in the form of goods (for example, food stamps which could only be used to purchase basic food items) and services (for example, health care, day care for children, home management counseling) might represent a more effective approach. However, recipients themselves resent the goods and services approach, charging that it is paternalistic, that it curtails flexibility in family spending, and that it implies irresponsibility on the part of the recipient. Today most caseworkers argue for joint provision of cash and goods and services; they contend that cash is more effective when accompanied by services, and services are more effective when accompanied by cash.

Welfare administration is made difficult by the heavy load assigned to caseworkers, many of whom are recent college graduates. They spend much of their time determining eligibility, computing payments, and filling out an avalanche of proper forms. With caseloads averaging up to 100 or 200 families, their contacts with recipients must be hurried, infrequent, and impersonal. Caseworkers are unable to develop any close bonds of friendship or rapport with persons in need of help. Recipients often come to view caseworkers with distrust or worse. The strain on caseworkers is very great; big city welfare departments report high turn-over among caseworkers.

Fraudulent welfare claims are a source of concern for federal and state administrators. The U.S. Office and Management and Budget cites survey studies which indicate that 40 percent of all welfare claims under the AFDC program are inaccurate.[4] About 10 percent of AFDC recipients are not eligible for any payment, 23 percent are receiving greater payments than they should, and another 8 percent are underpaid. The food stamp program experiences about the same proportion of ineligibles and overpayments as the AFDC program. Most of these inaccuracies are technical errors rather than outright fraud. Recent tightening of management procedures has noticeably slowed the growth rate of AFDC spending.

Social dependency and disincentives to work are magnified by the pyramiding effect of separate public assistance and social service programs. A family on the welfare rolls is generally entitled to participate in the food stamp program, to receive health care through Medicaid, to gain access to free or low-rent public housing, to receive free lunches in public schools, and to receive a variety of other social and educational benefits at little or no cost to themselves. These benefits and services available to the poor are not counted as income, yet the non-poor must pay for similar services out of their own earnings. If a family head on welfare takes a job, he not only loses welfare assistance, but, more importantly perhaps, becomes ineligible for food stamps, Medicaid, public housing, and many other social services.

One study reported that a family of four in New York City would have to earn more than $7,000 per year to live as well as a family receiving just four basic social benefits—public assistance, food stamps, school lunches, and Medicaid.[5] The report argues that the level of benefits from multiple social programs discourages work unless the anticipated earnings are $8,000 or more. The study also reported that female-headed families were far better off than male-headed (or "intact") families because of eligibility rules for various social programs. Another estimate by the U.S. General Accounting Office places the total value of all social services available to an urban family of four on welfare at over $11,000 per year. Thus, only a fairly well-paying job would justify going off the welfare rolls.

Do current welfare programs destroy the work ethic and increase

[4] *The Budget of the United States Government, 1975* (Washington, D.C.: Government Printing Office, 1974), pp. 128–29.

[5] Report prepared for the Joint Economic Subcommittee on Fiscal Policy released July 8, 1973, reported in Congressional Quarterly, *The Future of Social Programs* (Washington, D.C., Congressional Quarterly, 1973), p. 87.

social dependency? What *are* the effects of alternative welfare strategies on the behavior of the poor? At first glance it would appear that social science could help to answer such questions and thereby contribute to the development of rational public policy. Indeed, the Office of Economic Opportunity employed social scientists to conduct large-scale experiments of the effect of a guaranteed annual income on the work incentives of the poor (see Chapter 14, "Experimental Policy Research: The Guaranteed Income Experiment"). But as we shall observe later, attempts to systematically assess the impact of welfare policies on the poor have proven very difficult. Policy research has not yet made any significant contribution to rationalizing welfare policy.

NEW STRATEGIES FOR INCOME MAINTENANCE

There is fairly wide agreement about what is wrong with the existing welfare system. President Richard M. Nixon summarized the nation's welfare policies as "a colossal failure":

> Whether measured by the anguish of the poor themselves or by the drastically mounting burden on the taxpayer, the present welfare system has to be judged a colossal failure.
> Our states and cities find themselves sinking in a welfare quagmire as caseloads increase, as costs escalate and as the welfare system stagnates enterprise and perpetuates dependency. What began on a small scale in the depression '30's has become a monster in the prosperous '60's. The tragedy is not only that it is bringing states and cities to the brink of financial disaster, but also that it is failing to meet the elementary human, social and financial needs of the poor.
> It breaks up homes. It often penalizes work. It robs recipients of dignity. And it grows.
> Benefit levels are grossly unequal. . . .
> The present system creates an incentive for desertion. . . .
> The present system often makes it possible to receive more money on welfare than on a low-paying job. This creates an incentive not to work; it also is unfair to the working poor. . . .[6]

There is fairly wide agreement on the goals for income maintenance: to raise the income of the poor, to narrow disparities among states in benefit levels, to assist the working as well as the nonworking poor, to increase incentives to work, to keep families together, and to reduce bureaucratization and impersonality in welfare administration. We might expect this general agreement on goals to facilitate a rational

[6] President Richard M. Nixon, Address on national television networks, August 12, 1969.

approach to devising a new income maintenance program. However, reform has proven a very difficult task.

At least three major strategies have been proposed for revamping America's welfare system. The first might be described as "welfare reform" because it envisions making the existing welfare system more uniform and more nearly adequate. The agenda for reform typically includes federal action to put a floor under benefit levels paid by the states. Frequently reformers call for total federal financing of welfare costs, relieving states and cities from the burden of cost sharing. Federal intervention is also advocated to raise benefit levels and expedite welfare payments: elimination of "man in the house" rules, substituting simplified affidavits for complex and demeaning investigations to establish eligibility, and elimination of residence requirements.

A different basic approach is set forth by advocates of a "negative income tax." This group argues that reforming welfare is hopeless, and that welfare payments will always mean punitive rules, meddling social workers, and humiliation of the poor. They favor scrapping the welfare system altogether in favor of a general system of income payments entirely separate from any other kind of social service. The negative income tax would guarantee everyone a minimum income, and it would encourage recipients to work by allowing them to keep a proportion of their earnings without deducting them from the minimum guarantee. For example, a guarantee might be set at $3,000 for a family of four with an earnings deduction of 50 percent. Under such a system a family with no earnings would receive a payment of $3,000; a family with $2,000 in earnings would receive a payment of $2,000 for a total income of $4,000; and a family earning $6,000, the break-even point, would receive no government benefit. The proposal seems like a logical extension of the progressive income tax. Everyone would file a declaration of income as they do now; most would pay taxes as they do now, but those at the low end of the income scale would receive payments (negative taxes) just as those who overpay their tax do now (except that negative taxes would be paid monthly rather than at the end of the tax year).

A third approach under active discussion is the "children's allowance." Advocates of this strategy reject both welfare payments and a negative income tax because both involve an income test. They argue that the simplest and most dignified way to insure a minimum income for needy children is to give an allowance to all children regardless of need. Such an allowance would go to all families with children but it would contribute a great deal to raising the income of the poor. However, because it would go to all families regardless of need, it would appear to be an extremely inefficient way of getting money to the poor.

Moreover, it might be viewed as an inducement to the poor to have more children.

In 1970, President Nixon proposed a "Family Assistance Plan" which paralleled the negative income tax proposals that had been discussed for years in liberal circles:

> I propose that we abolish the present welfare system and adopt in its place a new family assistance system. Initially, this new system would cost more than welfare. But unlike welfare, it is designed to correct the condition it deals with and thus to lessen the long-range burden. . . .
>
> Its benefits would go to the working poor as well as the nonworking; to families with dependent children headed by a father as well as to those headed by a mother, had a basic federal minimum would be provided, the same in every state.
>
> I propose that the Federal Government build a foundation under the income of every American family with dependent children that cannot care for itself—wherever in America that family may live. . . .
>
> . . . Outside earnings would be encouraged, not discouraged. The new worker could keep the first $60 a month of outside earnings with no reduction in his benefits, and beyond that his benefits would be reduced by only 50 cents for each dollar earned.
>
> By the same token, a family head already employed at low wages could get a family assistance supplement, those who work would no longer be discriminated against. . . .
>
> Thus, for the first time, the government would recognize that it has no less of an obligation to the working poor than to the nonworking poor, and for the first time, benefits would be scaled in such a way that it would always pay to work.
>
> With such incentive, most recipients who can work will want to work. This is part of the American character.
>
> But what of the others—those who can work but choose not to?
>
> The answer is very simple.
>
> Under this proposal, everyone who accepts benefits must also accept work or training provided suitable jobs are available, either locally or at some distance if transportation is provided. The only exceptions would be those unable to work and mothers of preschool children. Even mothers of preschool children, however, would have the opportunity to work—because I am also proposing along with this a major expansion of day-care centers to make it possible for mothers to take jobs by which they can support themselves and their children.[7]

The proposed Family Assistance Program is clearly designed to remedy many of the dysfunctional consequences of previous welfare policy—disincentives to work, discouragement of family life, inequalities among the states, and discrimination against the working poor. But the long-run impact of such a policy reform is difficult to predict.

The first problem is cost: a negative income tax or a family assis-

[7] *Ibid.*

tance plan would double the cost of welfare over the current system and might run three to four times greater. There is no reliable information on the number of working poor who would apply for assistance. Moreover, Congress would be under constant pressure to raise the minimum income each year; already the National Welfare Rights Organization has called for a minimum of $6500.

Moreover, it is not certain whether this expansion of welfare assistance to many working families would increase or reduce economic dependency in America. It is conceivable that such an expansion in welfare assistance would destroy the "work ethic" and encourage dependency by making the acceptance of such assistance a common family practice, extending well up into the middle class. Certainly the percentage of the population receiving some form of public assistance would be greatly increased; it is conceivable that 20 percent of the population would eventually gain access to welfare rolls under a family assistance program. (Social science research on the effect of guaranteed income on the working behavior of the poor is discussed in Chapter 14.)

The work incentives of the family assistance proposal have been attacked as useless, and perhaps demeaning. Previous work incentive amendments to public assistance programs have not succeeded in reducing dependency. If welfare recipients could find good jobs, they would have done so long ago; the real problem is that they are unskilled, uneducated, and unprepared to function effectively in the work force. Perhaps the work incentives would encourage some recipients to accept more poorly paid, economically marginal jobs—maid service, gardening, window washing, etc. But the social value of these jobs is limited, and this aspect of the reform proposal has been attacked as demeaning to the poor.

The family assistance plan does not tackle the problem of pyramiding welfare programs. Even if the prospect of keeping 50 cents on each dollar earned proved to be an incentive to work, nonetheless, the loss of benefits under other welfare programs would remain a powerful disincentive. Benefits under multiple income-test programs would be eliminated—notably, food stamps, child care, Medicaid, and public housing—again leaving the working poor worse off than the nonworking poor. Moreover, earnings would also be reduced by the costs of working—transportation, clothing, etc.—and social security contributions. If working provides little improvement in the lives of the poor over the nonworking, we can hardly expect them to join the labor force.

There is widespread agreement that the nation's welfare system is in urgent need of reform. But there is little agreement on the direction of reform. The proposed Family Assistance Program failed in Congress because of the combined opposition of those who felt it was too much welfare and those who felt it was not enough. Former Presidential Advisor, Harvard Professor Daniel P. Moynihan, an author of the Family Assistance Program, attributed its failure to Senate liberals and welfare organizations who hurt the plan by criticizing it as too little aid and backing instead unrealistically expensive alternatives. But President Nixon also lost interest in F.A.P. when Congressional amendments began to push up its anticipated cost. The failure of welfare reform illustrates again the political obstacles to rational policy making.

SUMMARY

A variety of seemingly "rational" strategies for dealing with the poor have been attempted over the years. Yet each strategy produced many unintended consequences, and none succeeded in eliminating poverty or even reducing the political controversy surrounding welfare efforts. Let us summarize the major directions of welfare policy in America and some of the difficulties encountered in coping effectively with the problems of the poor:

1. The strategy of early welfare policy was to discourage poverty by providing only minimal assistance, generally in institutions, to the most destitute in society. Heavy reliance was placed on local governments and upon private charity. Poverty was viewed as a product of moral deficiency in the individual, and it was reasoned that only a punitive strategy would dissuade people from indolence.
2. The widespread experience with poverty in the Depression led many people to reason that poverty was a product of personal misfortunes or economic conditions over which the individual had little control. Thus, the Depression discredited the punitive strategy.
3. The social insurance concept was designed as a preventive strategy to insure persons against indigency arising from old age, death of a family breadwinner, or physical disability. It was hoped that social security would eventually abolish the need for public welfare, because individuals would be insured against poverty.
4. Despite the fact that social insurance is now the second largest expenditure item of the federal government, welfare rolls are rising rather than declining. Average monthly payments under social security fall below recognized poverty levels. The trust fund concept has been abandoned. And the tax itself is highly regressive.
5. The federal government also undertook an alleviative strategy in helping the states provide public assistance payments to certain categories of needy persons—aged, blind, disabled, and dependent children. Federal grants-in-aid to the states assisted them in providing monthly cash payments to the needy.
6. Dependence upon public assistance in America is growing at a very rapid rate, despite a reasonably healthy economy. Aid to families with dependent

children is the largest, most expensive, and most rapidly growing of all welfare programs. Yet a majority of the nation's poor does not receive welfare payments, notably the working poor. Welfare benefits are uneven among the states. Program policies include disincentives to both family life and work. Cash payments are frequently misspent. Caseworkers are too overloaded for effective counseling, and administration is heavy with red tape. Multiplication of programs serving the poor mask the real income of the poor, and there is a pyramiding of disincentives to work.

7. A national strategy for health care was adopted in 1965. It included "Medicare" for the aged under the social security program, and "Medicaid" for welfare recipients under federal-state public assistance programs. The costs of both programs greatly exceed expectations. Moreover, the increased pressure on medical facilities and physicians services has caused skyrocketing prices and forced reconsideration of the entire system of health-care delivery in America.

8. Welfare reform—in terms of a family assistance plan or negative income tax—is another attempt at rationalizing welfare policy. It is designed to assist the working as well as the nonworking poor, to provide a federally guaranteed floor on minimum incomes, and to reduce dependency by work incentives. However, the outcomes are difficult to predict; the number of participants and future costs are difficult to estimate; the impact on social dependency is difficult to foresee; and the work incentives may turn out to be inappropriate or ineffective.

BIBLIOGRAPHY

Congressional Quarterly, *Future of Social Programs*. Washington, D.C.: Congressional Quarterly, 1973.

FISHMAN, LEO, ed., *Poverty Amid Affluence*. New Haven: Yale University Press, 1966.

HARRINGTON, MICHAEL, *The Other America: Poverty in the United States*. New York: Macmillan, 1962.

MARMOR, THEODORE R., ed., *Poverty Policy*. Chicago: Aldine-Atherton, 1971.

President's Commission on Income Maintenance Programs, *Poverty Amid Plenty*. Washington, D.C.: Government Printing Office, 1969.

Library-on-wheels for pre-schoolers. UPI Photo

7 EDUCATION:

the group struggle

Perhaps the most widely recommended "solution" to the problems that confront American society is more and better schooling. If there ever was a time when schools were only expected to combat ignorance and illiteracy, that time is far behind us. Today schools are expected to do many things: resolve racial conflict and build an integrated society; inspire patriotism and good citizenship; provide values, aspirations, and a sense of identity to disadvantaged children; offer various forms of recreation and mass entertainment (football games, bands, choruses, majorettes, and the like); reduce conflict in society by teaching children to get along well with others and to adjust to group living; reduce the highway accident toll by teaching students to be good drivers; fight disease and poor health through physical education, health training, and even medical treatment; eliminate unemployment and poverty by teaching job skills; end malnutrition and hunger through school lunch and milk programs; produce scientists and other technicians to continue America's progress in science and technology; fight drug abuse and educate children about sex; and act as custodians for teenagers who have no interest in education but whom we do not permit either to work or to roam the streets unsupervised. In other words, nearly all the nation's problems are reflected in demands placed on the nation's schools. And, of course, these demands are frequently conflicting.

Thus, educational policy affects a wide variety of interests, and stimulates a great deal of interest-group activity. We will describe the major interests involved in federal educational policy and examine the group struggle over federal aid to education. We will examine the constitutional provisions and court policies dealing with religion in the public schools. We will observe how both racial and religious group interests are mobilized in educational policy making, and we will see the importance of resolving group conflict in the development of educational policy. We shall also describe the structure of educational decision making and the resulting multiple points of group access in a fragmented federal-state-local educational system. We shall attempt to describe the broad categories of group interests—teachers, taxpayers, school board members, school administrators—involved in educational policy at the local level. We will also examine the governing and financing of public higher education—the nation's increasingly costly investment in state colleges and universities. Finally, we will attempt to unravel the complex issues and interests involved in providing equality of educational opportunity for children in the nation's black ghettos.

THE FEDERAL ROLE IN EDUCATION

The federal government's role in education is a longstanding one. In the famous Northwest Ordinance of 1787, Congress offered land grants for public schools in the new territories and gave succeeding generations words to be forever etched on grammar school cornerstones: "Religion, morality, and knowledge, being necessary to good government and the happiness of mankind, schools and the means for education should ever be encouraged." The earliest democrats believed that the safest repository of the ultimate powers of society was the people themselves. If the people made mistakes, the remedy was not to remove power from their hands but to help them in forming their judgment through education. If the common man was to be granted the right to vote, he must be educated to his task. This meant that public education had to be universal, free, and compulsory. Compulsory education began in Massachusetts in 1852 and was eventually adopted by Mississippi in 1918.

In 1862 the Morrill Land Grant Act provided grants of federal land to each state for the establishment of colleges specializing in agricultural and mechanical arts. These became known as "land grant colleges." In 1867 Congress established a U.S. Office of Education, which is now a part of the Department of Health, Education and Welfare. The Smith-Hughes Act of 1917 set up the first program of federal grants-in-aid to promote vocational education, enabling schools to provide training in agriculture, home economics, trades, and industries. In the National School Lunch and Milk Programs, begun in 1946, federal grants and commodity donations are made for nonprofit lunches and milk served in public and private schools. In the Federal Impacted Areas Aid Program begun in 1950, federal aid is authorized for "federally impacted" areas of the nation. These are areas in which federal activities create a substantial increase in school enrollments or a reduction in taxable resources because of a federally owned property. Federal funds can be used for construction, operation, and maintenance of schools in these public school districts. This program is an outgrowth of the defense-impacted area aid legislation in World War II.

In response to the Soviet Union's success in launching the first satellite into space, Congress became concerned that the American educational system might not be keeping abreast of advances being made in other nations, particularly in science and technology. The Russian space shot created an intensive debate over education in America, and prompted Congress to reexamine the responsibilities of the national government in public education. "Sputnik" made everyone realize that education was closely related to national defense. In the National Defense Education Act of 1958, Congress provided financial aid to states and public school districts to improve instruction in science, mathematics, and foreign languages; to strengthen guidance counseling and testing; and to improve statistical services. And also to establish a system of loans to undergraduates, fellowships to graduate students, and funds to colleges—all in an effort to improve the training of teachers in America.

Despite these many individual federal programs in education, prior to 1965 the overall contribution of the federal government to education was very small. No general federal aid to education bill was able to win Congressional approval, for reasons we will explore later. Federal programs were only peripheral in character and limited in impact—some aid to federally impacted areas; assistance in school lunch and milk programs; some support for vocational-technical education; some grants for science, mathematics, and foreign language projects; etc.—but no real general assistance to public and private schools in building classrooms or paying teacher salaries.

The Elementary and Secondary Education Act of 1965 marked the first real breakthrough in large-scale federal aid to education. ESEA is now the largest federal aid-to-education program. Yet even ESEA cannot be termed a *general* aid-to-education program—one that would assist all public and private schools with costs of school construction and teachers' salaries. The main thrust of ESEA is in "poverty-impacted" schools, instructional materials, and educational research and training.

The Elementary and Secondary Education Act provided for the following:

Title   I: Financial assistance to "local educational agencies serving areas with concentrations of children from low-income families" for programs "which contribute particularly to meeting the special needs of educationally deprived children." Grants would be made on application to the Office of Education on the basis of the number of children from poverty-stricken families.

Title II: Grants to "public and private elementary and secondary schools" for the acquisition of school library resources, textbooks, and other instructional materials.

Title III: Grants for public and private schools for "supplementary educational centers and services" including remedial programs, counseling, adult education, specialized instruction and equipment, etc.

Title IV: Grants to universities, colleges, or other nonprofit organizations for research or demonstration projects in education.

Title V: Grants to stimulate and strengthen state educational agencies.

Note that the Act does include private, church-related schools in some of its benefits, as long as the federal aid money is used for nonreligious purposes within such schools. However, the greatest amounts of money distributed under ESEA have been to public schools in poverty-impacted areas.

FEDERAL AID TO EDUCATION AND
THE GROUP STRUGGLE

The long struggle for federal aid to education is an excellent example of the power of interest groups in blocking legislation that has widespread public support, and the necessity of accommodating specific interest groups and finding workable compromises before a bill can be passed. Every year from 1945 to 1965—a period spanning two decades and the administrations of both Democratic and Republican presidents and both Democratic and Republican Congressional majorities—federal aid-to-education bills were introduced and debated at great length. Yet no general aid-to-education bill passed the Congress in this period. These bills were lost *despite* overwhelming public support for federal aid to education revealed in all national opinion polls during this period, and *despite* announced presidential support for such aid. The failure of federal aid to education under these conditions can be attributed to the conflict between major *racial* and *religious* group interests in America over the character of such aid. Federal aid to education became lost in the major racial and religious controversies in the nation. Not until these issues were resolved, and bargains struck with the influential interest groups involved, was it possible to secure the passage of the Elementary and Secondary Education Act of 1965.[1]

Leading the fight for federal aid to education was the National Education Association. The NEA represents school administrators, state departments of education, university schools of education, and often the interests of the dues-paying teachers as well. Whatever differences existed within these various categories of members, the NEA was united in its support of federal aid to education. The national office of NEA, located in a modern well-equipped office building in Washington, works closely with the Office of Education, located only a few blocks away. The NEA also has affiliates in every one of the fifty states and most local school districts in the nation. Although NEA was a strong advocate of federal aid, it actively opposed public funds for private church-related schools. Other groups supporting federal aid were the AFL-CIO (particularly its constituent union, the American Federation of Teachers, which frequently competes with NEA for the loyalties of classroom teachers), Americans for Democratic Action, National Congress of Parents and Teachers, and other library and professional groups.

The arguments by NEA and others in support of federal aid were:

1. Education is a national responsibility rather than a matter of mere local concern:

> Nations with the highest general level of education are those with the highest economic development. Schools more than natural resources are the basis of prosperity. . . .
>
> Where ignorance generates poverty, poverty perpetuates ignorance, and the whole nation is weaker. . . .
>
> A similar relationship appears in draft rejections. . . . The ability of American society to conduct its essential affairs—political, economic, and military—depends directly upon education.[2]

2. States and local school districts are already strained to the limits of their financial capacities. Only the national government has the tax resources—individual and corporate income taxes—to raise funds for education.

3. Only the national government can equalize educational opportunities throughout the country:

> The operation of the national industrial economy appears to insure that average per capita income will be unequal among the states. The poorest states, if left to their own resources, have no reasonable pros-

---

[1] A detailed account of the long struggle leading to the passage of the Elementary and Secondary Education Act of 1965 is found in Eugene Eidenberg and Roy D. Morey, *An Act of Congress* (New York: W. W. Norton, 1969).

[2] Educational Policies Commission, National Education Association, *National Policy and the Financing of Public Schools* (Washington, D.C.: National Education Association, 1962); p. 7.

pect of raising the funds to provide adequate education. Some form of equalization is needed, because it is vital to the nation that the children in the poorest states also be well-educated. Therefore, federal participation in the financing of their schools is essential.[3]

Opposition to the general idea of federal aid to education was limited to conservative groups, including the U.S. Chamber of Commerce, National Association of Manufacturers, American Farm Bureau Federation, American Legion, and the Daughters of the American Revolution. Generally this opposition argued:

1. The progress of states and school districts in meeting educational needs is impressive. The "educational crisis" is overrated.
2. Federal aid would inevitably lead to federal control, the creation of a powerful national education bureaucracy, and the dangerous erosion of state and local powers and responsibilities.

But this opposition was never really very strong in itself. The only hope for the opposition was to divide the proponents of federal aid.

The first divisive issue was that of *race*. The question of whether or not the federal government would assist racially segregated Southern schools was raised very early in the debates on federal aid. Southern Congressmen stood to gain from any federal aid program designed to equalize educational expenditures among the states, because Southern states are among the poorest in the nation. But the prospect of federal aid money being used as leverage to achieve integration was an anathema to this group. On the other hand, the NAACP and many liberal groups and Congressmen opposed any federal aid to schools operated on a racially segregated basis. The 1954 decision, in *Brown v. Board of Education of Topeka, Kansas,* that racial segregation in public schools was unconstitutional strengthened the resolve of the liberals to deny federal aid to segregated schools. In 1956 Representative Adam Clayton Powell of Harlem introduced an amendment to the federal aid-to-education bill barring such aid for segregated schools. The NEA, the AFL-CIO, and other education groups opposed the Powell Amendment, believing correctly that such an amendment would involve federal school aid in the sensitive segregation issue and thereby lead to its defeat. Once the Powell Amendment was part of the bill, the coalition of conservative Republicans and Southern Democrats defeated it. Similar cross-pressures affected federal aid bills in other years.

The Civil Rights Act of 1964 greatly assisted the movement for federal aid to education, even though it made no direct mention of such aid. Title VI of that Act specified that

[3] *Ibid.,* p. 11.

No person in the United States shall, on the grounds of race, color, or national origin, be excluded from participation in, be·denied the benefits of, or be subjected to discrimination under any program or activity receiving federal financial assistance.

In effect, this was a "Powell Amendment" covering *every* federal aid program. The Act also specified that every federal department and agency must take action to end segregation by issuing rules, regulations, and orders (later known as "guidelines"), and withholding federal aid from any programs that have failed to comply with terms. The Act was supported by large majorities of both Democrats and Republicans in the House and the Senate. The effect of the Act was to resolve the issue raised by Representative Powell and others, and clear the track of at least one obstacle to federal aid to education.

The second divisive issue in federal aid to education was *religion,* i.e., whether or not federal aid should go to private, church-related schools. The Catholic Church operates a very large elementary and secondary school system in the United States. Catholic groups, particularly the National Catholic Welfare Conference, generally refused to support any federal aid bill that did not include aid to parochial schools. The leading Catholic spokesman in two decades of struggle over federal aid to education was Francis Cardinal Spellman of New York. When President John F. Kennedy excluded church schools from his 1961 aid-to-education bill, Spellman responded:

I believe that I state that these recommendations are unfair to most parents of the nation's 6,800,000 parochial and private school children. Such legislation would discriminate against a multitude of America's children because their parents choose to exercise their constitutional right to educate them in accordance with their religious beliefs.

The requirements of the national defense as well as the general welfare of our country demand that, in educational opportunities, no child be treated as a second-class citizen. Hence, it is unthinkable that any American child be denied the Federal funds allotted to other children which are necessary for his mental development because his parents choose for him a God-centered education. . . .

I cannot believe that Congress would enact a program of financial assistance and secondary education unless all children were granted equal educational privileges, regardless of the school they attend.

By denying this measure of equality to church-related school children and their parents, the task force proposals are blatantly discriminating against them, depriving them of freedom of mind and freedom of religion.[4]

---

[4] Quoted in Hugh D. Price, "Race, Religion and the Rules Committee," in Alan F. Westin, ed., *The Uses of Power* (New York: Harcourt Brace Jovanovich, 1962), p. 23.

Yet many Protestant groups were equally convinced that federal aid to church-related schools would destroy the historic concept of separation of church and state. Many Protestant denominations, as well as the National Council of Churches, went on record against federal aid for parochial schools. A spokesman for the influential group of Protestants and Other Americans United for Separation of Church and State, stated:

> Cardinal Spellman has not changed his mind. His aim is still to compel Protestants, Jews, and others to suport a wholly controlled function of the Roman Catholic Church. The compulsion lies in the use of the taxing powers of the Federal Government to raise funds for Catholic schools. He has given us fair warning, so he should have our answer. American Protestants will never pay taxes to support Catholic schools. We will oppose enactment of laws which require such payments. If Congress is pressured into enacting such laws, we will contest them in the courts. If the courts reverse themselves and declare such laws constitutional, we will still refuse to pay these taxes, paying whatever price is necessary to preserve religious liberty in a pluralistic society.[5]

The failure of President Kennedy's aid-to-education bill is generally attributed to the religious conflict it engendered. In honoring a 1960 campaign pledge to Protestants, the nation's first Catholic president introduced a federal aid-to-education bill which *excluded* parochial schools.[6] To the school aid bill's usual enemies—conservative Republicans wary of federal bureaucracy and Southern Democrats wary of integration efforts—President Kennedy added a substantial bloc of Catholic Congressmen, many of whom had supported aid to education in the past. To reduce Southern fears, the Administration pledged *not* to withhold funds from segregated schools, and Representative Powell obliged a presidential request not to introduce the desegregation issue in the interest of passing a bill. But on crucial votes in the all-important Rules Committee of the House, Catholic Democratic committee members, who previously supported the Administration, joined the Republicans and some still-skeptical Southern Democrats to defeat the bill.

By 1965, twenty years of group struggle over federal aid to education convinced proponents of the policy that *compromise between major interest groups* was essential to its adoption.

---

[5] *Ibid.*, pp. 36–37.

[6] In a speech before the Greater Houston Ministerial Association in 1960 Kennedy stated: "I believe in an America where separation of Church and State is absolute . . . where no church or church school is granted any public funds or political preference."

ESEA: A CASE STUDY IN GROUP COMPROMISE

It is unlikely that the Elementary and Secondary Education Act (ESEA) would have become law had not President Lyndon B. Johnson taken great pains to arrange a compromise among the major interest groups involved. Because the Civil Rights Act of 1964 was the law of the land, it was unnecessary for the president to fight the civil rights issue directly. Though Southern Democrats would remain cool to voting for federal money that they knew would be used later as desegregation leverage, they were not placed in a position of voting directly on a bill to advance desegregation. Over 40 percent of Southern Democrats in the Congress would end up supporting the president's bill. In 1965 it was the *religious* issue that required the greatest skill in group negotiation and compromise.

Congress, particularly members of the House and Senate committees most directly concerned with education legislation, expected the Administration to work out the appropriate group compromise before Congress would consider a federal aid bill. In effect, Congress stood ready to legitimatize whatever compromise could be arranged among the major interests. Political scientists Eidenberg and Morey explained it as follows:

> The Congress and particularly the members of the committee who had experienced education fights before, feared they would have to resolve the church-state issue on Capitol Hill. The political consequences of taking sides on the "religious issue" was the greatest concern of most members. One Democratic member of the committee put it this way: "We were all sensitive to the start of another holy war. Politically, not many of us can afford a religious war—at least those of us from two-religion districts."
>
> In effect, the Democrats on the committee wanted and expected the Administration to work out the necessary agreements (whatever they might be) so that the principal factions were satisfied. Their failure on so many prior occasions to find agreement predisposed the leading congressional figures to leave these delicate negotiations in the hands of the Administration. Then the committee and the House would act to ratify those agreements.[7]

The key to success, then, was working out a compromise acceptable to the NEA and other educational groups, the National Catholic Welfare Conference and other representatives of the Catholic Church, and the National Council of Churches and other Protestant groups.

[7] Eidenberg and Morey, *An Act of Congress*, p. 77.

The Johnson Administration plan was to emphasize "aid to children" rather than aid to schools, and particularly aid to children from low-income families. It was hoped that by placing the emphasis on the child, the church-state issue could be submerged. The president identified the program with his "war on poverty" rather than with earlier aid-to-education efforts. The greatest proportion of ESEA funds would be given under Title I to *public* school districts with children from low-income families. But as a concession to Catholic interests, the president's bill allowed parochial schools to receive funds along with public schools under Title II and Title III for libraries, textbooks, and instructional materials, and for supplementary educational centers and services. This money was only for peripheral items—not classroom construction or teachers' salaries—and specifically prohibited the use of federal funds for sectarian instruction or worship.

The NEA accepted the compromise despite its longstanding opposition to giving any public funds to church schools. Eidenberg and Morey explain the NEA decision as follows:

> Fear over possible exclusion from the policy making process helped persuade the NEA to go along in 1965 with an aid formula that would see some funds channeled into the hands of private and parochial schools. In 1965, to be on the side of a minority when education legislation got passed would have left the NEA without influence during the critical period after passage when the administrative regulations were being drawn up. . . . If for no other reason, the NEA could not afford to be with the losers the year federal aid finally got enacted. Since the NEA's principal reason for being was the passage of federal aid to education legislation, the rival teacher organization's (the AFL-CIO-affiliated American Federation of Teachers) charges that the NEA had not been successful up to 1965 touched a sensitive chord.[8]

The National Council of Churches was not really enthusiastic about the Johnson bill; they very much preferred President Kennedy's 1961 bill which would have completely excluded Catholic schools from federal aid programs. Yet responsible spokesmen for Protestant churches in America did not want to be charged with having hurt public education in America or blocked assistance for impoverished school children. Arthur Flemming, former Secretary of HEW during the Eisenhower Administration and later president of the University of Oregon, testified before the House Education Committee as vice-president of the National Council of Churches:

> The church and state issue . . . has been one of the principal roadblocks standing in the way of constructive federal legislation in the areas

[8] *Ibid.,* p. 63.

of elementary and secondary education. It has likewise been a divisive factor in the life of our nation.

I hope that all concerned, both inside and outside of Congress, will analyze HR 2362 with the end in view of doing everything possible to make it an instrument of reconciliation. I believe that it can be. I believe that President Johnson and his associates should be commended for providing us with this opportunity of approaching an old unsolved problem with a new spirit.[9]

If this posture was not one of enthusiasm for the bill, at least it was not opposition.

Catholic education interests were defended on Capitol Hill by Speaker of the House John McCormack of Boston. Strong Catholic opposition to the bill might have meant failure. Catholic groups were also unenthusiastic about the bill. There was no guarantee that Catholic education would receive proportionately equal funding with public education under the legislation. Public school interests would be administering the grant money. It was not clear whether the bill was a victory for Catholics or whether it merely held out token support to Catholic education. But in the end the Catholic interests withheld their objections. In response to a direct question by a House Committee member as to whether or not the United States Catholic Conference (successor to the National Catholic Welfare Conference) endorsed the bill, director Monsignor Frederick G. Hochwalt said:

> It is a strong word (endorse), but it comes close to it. We look with favor upon those kinds of provisions and hope they can be worked out successfully. To say we endorse the whole thing line by line is a little too broad for us.[10]

Liberal groups were aware of the fact that ESEA was *not* a general aid-to-education bill. But they too were willing to accept the bill as a compromise. Andrew Biemiller, chief lobbyist for the AFL-CIO testified:

> I repeat . . . let's get started . . . and get a bill through here, and begin to get some money into our school systems where we now know it is badly needed, and then we can take another good look and get closer to the goal that both you and I want; and we make no bones about it; that we want a general education bill.[11]

Once support of the major interests was obtained, Congressional approval of ESEA was practically assured. Congressmen deliberately

[9] *Ibid.*, pp. 65–66.
[10] *Ibid.*, p. 68.
[11] *Ibid.*, pp. 105–106.

avoided any amendments that would upset the church-state compromise. The bill was introduced on January 12, 1965, and signed into law by the president on April 11, with very little change in the original wording. Most of the floor debate in the House and the Senate centered about minor variations in the aid formula. The ease and rapidity with which the bill passed Congress was a striking contrast to the bloody battles of earlier years. This turnabout in Congressional behavior would have mystified anyone who was not aware of the interest-group compromise.

READING, WRITING, AND RELIGION IN THE COURTS

The First Amendment to the Constitution of the United States contains two important guarantees of religious freedom: (1) "Congress shall make no law respecting an establishment of religion . . ." and (2) "or prohibiting the free exercise thereof." The Due Process Clause of the Fourteenth Amendment made these guarantees of religious liberty applicable to the states and their subdivisions as well as to Congress. Most of the debate over religion in the public schools centers around the "no establishment" clause of the First Amendment rather than the "free exercise" clause. However, it was respect for the "free exercise" clause that caused the Supreme Court in 1925 to declare unconstitutional an attempt on the part of a state to prohibit private and parochial schools and to force all children to attend public schools. In the words of the Supreme Court: "The fundamental theory of liberty upon which all governments in this Union repose excludes any general power of the state to standardize its children by forcing them to accept instruction from public teachers only. The child is not the mere creature of the state." [12] It is this decision that protects the entire structure of parochial schools in this nation.

A great deal of religious conflict in America has centered around the meaning of the "no establishment" clause, and the public schools have been the principal scene of this conflict. One interpretation of the clause holds that it does not prevent government from aiding religious schools or encouraging religious beliefs in the public schools, as long as it does not discriminate against any particular religion. Another interpretation of the "no establishment" clause is that it creates a "wall of separation" between church and state in America to prevent government from directly aiding religious schools or encouraging religious beliefs in any way.

---

[12] *Pierce* v. *The Society of Sisters*, 268 U.S. 510 (1925).

Those favoring government aid to parochial schools frequently refer to the language found in several cases decided by the Supreme Court, which appears to support the idea that government can *in a limited fashion* support the activities of church-related schools. In the case of *Pierce* v. *The Society of Sisters* (1925), the Court stated that the right to send one's children to parochial schools was a fundamental liberty guaranteed to all. In *Cochran v. the Board of Education* (1930), the Court upheld a state law providing free textbooks for children attending both public and parochial schools on the grounds that this aid benefited the *children* rather than the Catholic Church and hence did not constitute an "establishment" of religion within the meaning of the First Amendment.[13]

In *Everson* v. *Board of Education* (1947), the Supreme Court upheld bus transportation for parochial school children at public expense on the grounds that the "wall of separation between church and state" does not prohibit the state from adopting a general program which helps *all* children.[14] Interestingly, in this case even though the Supreme Court permitted the expenditure of public funds to assist children going to and from parochial schools, the Supreme Court voiced the opinion that the no establishment clause of the First Amendment should constitute a wall of separation between church and state. In the words of the Court:

> Neither a state nor the federal government can set up a church. Neither can pass laws which aid one religion, aid all religions, or prefer one religion over another. Neither can force nor influence a person to go to or to remain away from church against his will, or force him to profess a belief or disbelief in any religion. No person can be punished for entertaining or professing religious beliefs or disbeliefs, for church attendance or nonattendance. No tax in any amount, large or small, can be levied to support any religious activities or institutions, whatever they may be called, or whatever form they may adopt to teach or practice religion. Neither a state nor the federal government can, openly or secretly, participate in the affairs of any religious organizations or groups, and vice versa.[15]

So the Everson Case can be cited by those interests which support the allocation of public funds for assistance to children in parochial schools, as well as those interests which oppose any public support, direct or indirect, of religion.

The question of how much government aid can go to church schools and for what purposes is still unresolved. Recently, in response

---

[13] *Cochran* v. *Board of Education,* 281 U.S. 370 (1930).
[14] *Everson* v. *Board of Education,* 330 U.S. 1 (1947).
[15] *Ibid.*

to fiscal crises, Catholic church leaders have pressed hard for more aid from the federal government and the states. Many of these states have passed bills giving financial support to nonpublic schools for such purposes as textbooks, bus transportation, and remedial courses. Proponents of public aid for parochial schools argue that these schools render a valuable public service by instructing millions of children who would have to be instructed by the state, at great expense, if the parochial schools closed. There seemed to be many precedents for public support of religious institutions: church property has always been exempt from taxation; church contributions are deductible from federal income taxes; federal funds have been appropriated for the construction of religiously operated hospitals; chaplains are provided in the armed forces as well as in the Congress of the United States; veterans' programs permit veterans to use their educational subsidies to finance college educations in Catholic universities; federal grants and loans for college construction are available to Catholic as well as to public colleges, and so on.

Opponents of state aid to parochial schools challenge the idea that Catholic parents are being discriminated against when parochial schools are denied tax funds. They argue that free public schools are available to the parents of all children regardless of religious denomination. If Catholic parents are not content with the type of school that the state provides, they should expect to pay for the establishment and operation of special schools. The state is under no obligation to finance the religious preferences in education of Catholics or other religious groups. In fact, they contend that it is unfair to compel taxpayers to support religion directly or indirectly, and furthermore, the diversion of any substantial amount of public education funds to parochial schools would weaken the public school system. The public schools bring together children of different religious backgrounds and by so doing supposedly encourage tolerance and understanding. ·In contrast, church-related schools segregate children of different backgrounds, and it is not in the public interest to encourage such segregation. And so the dispute continues.

One of the most important Supreme Court decisions in the history of church-state relations in America came in 1971 in the case of *Lemon v. Kurtzman*.[16] The Supreme Court held that it was unconstitutional for a state (Pennsylvania) to pay the costs of teachers' salaries or instructional materials in parochial schools. The Court acknowledged that it had previously approved the provision of state textbooks and bus transportation directly to parochial school children. But the Court held that state payments to parochial schools involved "excessive entanglement between

[16] *Lemon* v. *Kurtzman*, 403 U.S. 602 (1971).

government and religion" and violate both the Establishment and Free Exercise clauses of the First Amendment. State payments to religious schools, the Court said, would require excessive government controls and surveillance to insure that funds were used only for secular instruction. Moreover, the Court expressed the fear that state aid to parochial schools would create "political divisions along religious lines . . . one of the principal evils against which the First Amendment was intended to protect."

Religious conflict in public schools also centers around the question of prayer and Bible-reading ceremonies conducted by public schools. A few years ago the practice of opening the school day with prayer and Bible-reading ceremonies was widespread in American public schools. Usually the prayer was a Protestant rendition of the Lord's Prayer and Bible reading was from the King James version. In order to avoid the denominational aspects of these ceremonies, the New York State Board of Regents substituted a nondenominational prayer, which it required to be said aloud in each class in the presence of a teacher at the beginning of each school day.

> Almighty God, we acknowledge our dependence upon Thee, and we beg Thy blessings upon us, our parents, our teachers, and our country.

New York argued that this prayer ceremony did not violate the "no establishment" clause, because the prayer was denominationally neutral and because student participation in the prayer was voluntary. However, in *Engle* v. *Vitale* (1962), the Supreme Court stated that "the constitutional prohibition against laws respecting an establishment of a religion must at least mean in this country it is no part of the business of government to compose official prayers for any group of the American people to recite as part of a religious program carried on by government." [17] The Court pointed out that making prayer voluntary did not free it from the prohibitions of the no establishment clause; that clause prevented the establishment of a religious ceremony by a government agency, regardless of whether the ceremony was voluntary or not:

> Neither the fact that the prayer may be denominationally neutral, nor the fact that its observance on the part of the students is voluntary can serve to free it from the limitations of the establishment clause, as it might from the free exercise clause, of the First Amendment, both of which are operative against the states by virtue of the Fourteenth Amendment. . . . The establishment clause, unlike the free exercise clause, does not depend on any showing of direct governmental compulsion and is violated by the enactment of laws which establish an official religion

[17] *Engle* v. *Vitale*, 370 U.S. 421 (1962).

whether those laws operate directly to coerce nonobserving individuals or not.

One year later in the case of *Abbington Township* v. *Schempp*, the Court considered the constitutionality of Bible-reading ceremonies in the public schools.[18] Here again, even though the children were not required to participate, the Court found that Bible reading as an opening exercise in the schools was a religious ceremony. The Court went to some trouble in its opinion to point out that it was not "throwing the Bible out of the schools," for it specifically stated that the study of the Bible or of religion, when presented objectively as part of a secular program of education, did not violate the First Amendment, but religious *ceremonies* involving Bible reading or prayer, established by a state or school district, did so.

THE FORMAL STRUCTURE OF EDUCATIONAL DECISION MAKING

The formal responsibility for public education in America rests with the fifty state governments. State laws create local school boards and provide a means for choosing their members, usually, but not always, by popular election. State laws authorize boards to lay and collect taxes, to borrow money, to engage in school construction, to hire instructional personnel, and to make certain determinations about local school policy. Yet in every state, the authority of local school districts is severely circumscribed by state legislation. State law determines the types and rates of taxes to be levied, the maximum debt that can be incurred, the number of years of compulsory school attendance, the minimum salaries to be paid to teachers, the types of schools to be operated by the local boards, the number of grades to be taught, the qualifications of teachers, and the general content of curricula. In addition, many states choose the textbooks, establish course outlines, fix styles of penmanship, recommend teaching methods, establish statewide examinations, fix minimum teacher-pupil ratios, and stipulate course content in great detail. Some states outlaw the mention of communism or the teaching of evolution in the classroom. In short, the responsibility for public education is firmly in the hands of our state governments.

State responsibility for public education is no mere paper arrangement. At one time there was no effective way state governments could insure that local school districts conformed to state policies; there were

18 *Abbington Township* v. *Schempp*, 374 U.S. 203 (1963).

no enforcement agencies or devices to guarantee enforcement of state regulations. But in recent years two devices have been utilized effectively by the states to help ensure that local districts do not deviate from state standards. The first device is the statewide administrative agency, sometimes called the state board of education, state department of education, or the superintendent of public instruction. The central task of these state administrative agencies is to oversee local school districts and ensure implementation of state policies. Although there are some variations among the states in the power vested in these agencies, one trend is common to all the states: state educational agencies are centralizing state control over education.

A second device for ensuring the implementation of state educational policies is state grants of money to local school districts. Every state provides grants in one form or another to local school districts to supplement locally derived school revenue. This places the superior taxing powers of the state in the service of public schools operated at the local level. In every state, an equalization formula in the distribution of state grants to local districts operates to help equalize educational opportunities in all parts of the state. Equalization formulas differ from state to state as do the amounts of state grants involved, but in every state, poorer school districts receive larger shares of state funds than wealthier districts. This enables the state to guarantee a minimum "foundation" program in education throughout the state. In addition, because state grants to local school districts are administered through state departments of education, state school officials are given an effective tool for implementing state policies—namely, withholding or threatening to withhold state funds from school districts that do not conform to state standards. The growth of state responsibility for school policy was accomplished largely by the use of state grants of money to local schools.

One of the most dramatic reorganization and centralization movements in American government in this century has been the successful drive to reduce, through consolidation, the number of local school districts in the United States. Over the last thirty-year period, three out of every four school districts have been eliminated through consolidation. Support for school district consolidation has come from state school officials in every state.

There is a slight tendency toward increased centralization in the poorer states and the states with lower adult education levels. It is in these states that the state governments have played a greater role in the financing of public schools and the school consolidation movement has made the greatest progress. State participation in school finance decreases among the more wealthy states and the states with educated

156 / understanding public policy

Table 7-1 *Federal, State, and Local Contributions to Public Elementary and Secondary Education*

PERCENT OF SCHOOL REVENUE RECEIVED FROM:

	Federal Sources	State Sources	Local Sources
1972	9.0	37.0	54.0
1970	7.3	40.7	52.0
1967	7.9	39.1	53.0
1963	4.4	39.3	56.4
1960	4.4	39.1	56.5
1957	4.0	39.4	56.6

Source: U.S. Bureau of the Census, Statistical Abstract of the United States, 1973 (Washington, D.C.: Government Printing Office, 1973), p. 127.

adult populations. Apparently the lack of economic resources is a stimulus toward state participation in school finance and school district consolidation. Affluence, on the other hand, enables smaller local school districts to function more effectively, reduces the need for state aid, and delays the movement toward school consolidation.

There are marked disparities between state educational programs. The decentralization of educational policy making in fifty separate state systems has meant a great deal of variation in the character of public education from state to state. States differ in educational expenditures per pupil, average teacher salaries, teacher-pupil ratios, dropout rates, and many other educational measures. For example, New York spends two and one-half times more than Mississippi on the education of an average pupil. California teachers receive twice the salary of teachers in South Dakota. Teacher-pupil ratios in the states range from fifteen to near thirty. Most of the differences in state educational systems are related to economic resources in the states (see Chapter 12).

THE INFORMAL STRUCTURE
OF EDUCATIONAL GROUPS

The formal structure of local school districts often obscures the realities of educational politics in communities. School politics will differ from one community to another, but it is possible to identify a number of political groups that appear on the scene in school politics in almost every community. There is, first of all, that small band of *voters* who turn out for school elections. It is estimated that, on the average, only about one-third of the eligible voters bother to cast ballots in school elections. Voter turnout at school bond and tax elections shows no groundswell of public interest in school affairs. Perhaps even more interesting is the finding that the larger the voter turnout in a school bond referendum, the more likely the defeat of proeducational proposals. In general, the best way to defeat a school bond referendum is to have a large turnout. Public support for education appears to have declined over the last decade. The proportion of bond referendums for financing schools that have won voter approval has declined from 89 percent in the early 1960s to 48 percent in the early 1970s.[19] Proponents of educational expenditures are better advised not to work for a large turnout, but for a better-informed and more educationally oriented electorate.

School board members constitute another important group of actors in school politics. School board members are generally better educated than their constituents. They are selected largely from among business owners, proprietors, and managers. There is some evidence that people who are interested in education and have some knowledge of what the schools are doing tend to support education more than do the less-informed citizens. However, the occupational background of school board members suggests that they are sensitive to tax burdens placed upon businessmen and property owners.

Many *professional educators* are distrustful of the laymen who compose the school boards; they often feel that educational policy should be in the hands of professional educators. They may feel that important decisions about curriculum, facilities, personnel, and finances should be the special province of persons trained in education. They view the school board's role as one of defending the schools against public criticism and persuading the community to open its pocketbook. Professional educators often support the idea that "politics" should be kept out of education; to them, this means that laymen should not interfere with decisions that professional educators wish to make for themselves. School boards and voters (those who supply the money for public schools and therefore feel that it is their legitimate right to control them) believe that citizen control of education is a vital safeguard of democracy. But professional educators sometimes feel that school board members are uninformed about school problems and unwilling or unable to support the needs of education. As a case in point, school board members throughout the nation were much less likely to support federal aid to education than were professional educators. Many school board members felt that the federal government would strip them of their local power over the schools, while professional educators were less fearful of dictation from Washington.

The professional educators can be divided into at least three distinct groups. Numerically the largest group (two and one-half million), yet

[19] Congressional Quarterly, *Education for a Nation* (Washington, D.C.: Congressional Quarterly Inc., 1972), p. 6.

politically the least significant, is the *school teachers*. The most powerful group is the professional *school administrators*, particularly the superintendents of schools. A third group consists of the *faculties of teachers colleges* and departments of education at universities. This latter group often has contacts with state departments of education, diffuses educational innovations and ideologies to generations of teachers, and influences requirements for teacher certification within the states.

State and local chapters of the National Education Association (NEA) represent both teachers and administrators. The participation of administrators in the National Education Association is one of the major criticisms of that organization made by the American Federation of Teachers (AFT).

The AFT has emerged as an important voice of teachers in the nation's largest cities. This labor union, representing classroom teachers, employs all the recognized techniques of labor organizations to achieve its goals. The AFT advocates collective bargaining for teachers and, whenever necessary, the strike. In the past, the much larger NEA viewed these techniques as unprofessional, and it criticized the AFT for its connection with other unions through the AFL-CIO. However, the growing membership of the AFT in large cities has brought about a greater degree of militancy by the NEA and its local and state chapters.

THE CHALLENGE OF SCHOOL FINANCE:
HAVES AND HAVE-NOTS

A central issue in the group struggle over public education is that of distributing the benefits and costs of education in an equitable fashion. Most school revenues are derived from *local* property taxes. In every state except Hawaii, local school boards must raise money from property taxes to finance their schools. This means that communities that do *not* have much taxable property cannot finance their schools as well as communities that are blessed with great wealth. Frequently, wealthy communities can provide better educations for their children at *lower* tax rates than poor communities can provide at *higher* tax rates, simply because of disparities in the value of taxable property from one community to the next.

Representatives of poor, black, and Spanish-speaking groups have charged that reliance on local property taxation for school finance discriminates against poor communities. In an important state decision—*Serrano* v. *Priest*—the California Supreme Court held that the California system of public school finance "with its substantial dependence on local property taxes and resultant wide disparities in school revenue, violates the equal protection clause of the Fourteenth Amendment (of the U.S. Constitution)." The California court cited, for example, disparities of tax rates and tax yields between Beverly Hills and Baldwin Park, two nearby communities in Los Angeles County. Property owners in wealthy Beverly Hills paid only $2.38 per $100 of assessed property value, while in poorer Baldwin Park residents paid $5.48 per $100. Yet Beverly Hills, because of its better tax base, was able to spend $1,232 on each pupil in its schools, compared to only $577 in Baldwin Park. "We have determined," the California court said, "that this funding arrangement discriminates against the poor because it makes the quality of a child's education a function of the wealth of his parents and neighbors." Decisions similar to this California case have been rendered recently in other states. Their effect should be to speed the movement toward *state* funding of the costs of public education. Note that the argument does not attack the use of property taxes, but rather the inequable distribution of property tax revenues from one jurisdiction to another. Presumably, if a *state* would collect all property taxes statewide and then distribute the revenues equally among all communities, there would be little objection from have-not groups.

The Supreme Court of the United States has declined to intervene in this struggle over educational finance. By a 5–4 vote in *Rodriguez* v. *San Antonio Independent School Board* (1973), the Supreme Court ruled that disparities in property values between jurisdictions relying on property taxes to finance education did *not* violate the equal protection clause of the Fourteenth Amendment. The Supreme Court declined to substitute its own judgment about how schools should be financed for the judgments of forty-nine states. Writing for the majority, Justice Lewis F. Powell said:

> We are urged to abrogate systems of financing public education presently in existence in virtually every state . . . [to declare unconstitutional] what many educators for half a century have thought was an enlightened approach to a problem for which there is no perfect solution. We are unwilling to assume for ourselves a level of wisdom superior to that of legislators, scholars, and educational authorities in 49 states, especially when the alternatives proposed are only recently conceived and nowhere yet tested.

It is likely that the struggle over educational finance will continue.

PUBLIC HIGHER EDUCATION

State governments have been involved in public higher education since the colonial era. State governments in the Northeast frequently made contributions to support private colleges in their states, a practice that continues today. The first state university to be chartered by a state legislature was the University of Georgia in 1794. Before the Civil War, Northeastern states relied exclusively on private colleges, and the Southern states assumed the leadership in public higher education. The antebellum curricula at Southern state universities, however, resembled the rigid classical studies of the early private colleges—Greek and Latin, history, philosophy, and literature.

It was not until the Morrill Land Grant Act of 1862 that public higher education began to make major strides in the American states. Interestingly, the Eastern states were slow to respond to the opportunity afforded by the Morrill Act to develop public universities; Eastern states continued to rely primarily on their private colleges and universities. The Southern states were economically depressed in the post–Civil War period, and leadership in public higher education passed to the Midwestern states. The philosophy of the Morrill Act emphasized agricultural and mechanical studies rather than the classical curricula of Eastern colleges, and the movement for "A and M" education spread rapidly in the agricultural states. The early groups of Midwestern state universities were closely tied to agricultural education, including agricultural extension services. State universities also took over the responsibility for the training of public school teachers in colleges of education. The state universities introduced a broad range of modern subjects in the university curricula—business administration, agriculture, home economics, education, engineering. It was not until the 1960s that the Eastern states began to develop public higher education.

Today public higher education enrolls three-quarters of the nation's college and university students. Perhaps more importantly, the nation's leading state universities can challenge the best private institutions in academic excellence. The University of California at Berkeley, the University of Michigan, and the University of Wisconsin are deservedly ranked with Harvard, Yale, Princeton, and Columbia.

Federal aid to colleges and universities comes in a variety of forms. Historically, the Morrill Act of 1862 provided the groundwork for federal assistance in higher education. In 1890 Congress activated several federal grants to support the operations of the land-grant colleges, and this aid, although very modest, continues to the present. The GI Bills following World War II and the Korean War (enacted in 1944 and 1952 respectively) were not, strictly speaking, aid-to-education bills, but rather a form of assistance to veterans to help them adjust to civilian life. Nevertheless, these bills had a great impact on higher education in terms of the millions of veterans who were able to enroll in college. In 1966 Congress finally acted to make veterans' education benefits a permanent program for "all those who risk their lives in our armed forces." The National Defense Education Act of 1958 also affected higher education by assisting superior students through loans and grants to continue undergraduate and graduate education, and by directly assisting institutions in which they enroll. Preference was given to undergraduate students intending to teach in elementary or secondary schools, particularly in science, mathematics, and modern foreign languages, and graduate students preparing to teach in college.

Federal support for scientific research has also had an important impact on higher education. In 1950 Congress established the National Science Foundation to promote scientific research and education. NSF has provided fellowships for graduate education in the sciences, supported the development of science institutes and centers at universities, funded training institutes for science teachers at all levels, supported many specific scientific research projects, and supported other miscellaneous scientific enterprises. In 1965, Congress established a National Endowment for the Arts and Humanities, but funded these fields at only a tiny fraction of the amount given to NSF. In addition to NSF, many other federal agencies—the Department of Defense, Atomic Energy Commission, Office of Education, Public Health Service, and so forth—have granted research contracts to universities for specific projects. Thus, research has become a very big item in university life.

The federal government directly assists institutions of higher education through the Higher Education Facilities Act of 1963 and the Higher Education Act of 1965. The first of these general support measures authorizes federal grants and loans for construction and improvement of both public and private higher education facilities; generally, matching grants are required from the institution. The 1965 act was much broader in scope, providing for federally insured student loans and scholarships, a National Teacher Corps, funds for library materials and specialized equipment, grants to expand university extension programs, and grants to strengthen colleges that "are struggling for survival and are isolated from the main currents of academic life."

In 1972, Congress amended the Higher Education Act to establish a new "basic educational opportunity grant" program. The program was intended to offer any college student in good standing a grant of $1,400 per year minus the amount his family would reasonably be expected to contribute to his educational expenses. To date however, the administration of the program has been clumsy: applications are difficult; the

Table 7-2 *Higher Education Finance*

SOURCES OF OPERATING FUNDS IN PERCENT

	Public Institutions %	Private Institutions %
Tuition and Student Fees	11.8	34.1
Federal Government	13.3	13.4
State Governments	40.3	1.1
Local Governments	4.9	0.5
Endowment Earnings	0.4	5.1
Private Gifts	0.4	7.8
Other General Revenue	7.5	9.6
Auxiliary Revenue	13.2	15.9
Student Aid Grants	2.5	3.9
Public Service Programs	5.7	8.6

Source: Statistical Abstract of the United States, 1973, p. 135.

family contribution schedule is complex; and accurately determining family assets is probably impossible. The program is potentially very costly, but each year Congress and the president have severely limited the funds available. As a result, the number of students aided has been small, and the maximum grant itself has been cut to less than $500. Congress also authorized a government-guaranteed loan program that sought to encourage private banks to make low-interest loans to students. The federal government would pay the interest changes while the student was in school and guaranteed repayment in the event the student defaulted on the payment after graduation. But again, results of the program were disappointing: banks found the interest rates too low and administrative details too cumbersome; student defaults ran higher than expected; and as a result, the number of student loans has fallen far below expectations.

Among the influential groups in public higher education—aside from the governors and legislators who must vote the funds each year—are the boards of trustees (or "regents") that govern public colleges and universities. Their authority varies from state to state. But in nearly every state, they are expected not only to set broad policy directions in higher education but also to insulate higher education from direct political involvement of governors and legislators.

Prominent citizens who are appointed to these boards are expected to champion higher education with the public and the legislature. In the past, there were separate boards for each institution and separate consideration by the governor's office and the legislature of each institution's budgetary request. But the resulting competition has caused state after state to create unified "university system" boards to coordinate higher education. These university system boards consolidate the budget requests of each institution, determine systemwide priorities, and present a single budget for higher education to the governor and the legislature. The stronger and more independent the university system board, the less likely that universities and colleges throughout the state will be distributed to cities and regions in a pork barrel fashion by legislators seeking to enhance their local constituencies.

Another key group in higher education is composed of university and college presidents and their top administrative assistants. Generally, university presidents are the chief spokesmen for higher education, and they must convince the public, the regents, the governor, and the legislature of the value of state colleges and universities. The president's crucial role is one of maintaining support for higher education in the state; he frequently delegates administrative responsibilities for the internal operation of the university to the vice-presidents and deans. Support for higher education among the public and its representatives can be affected by a broad spectrum of university activities, some of which are not directly related to the pursuit of knowledge. A winning football team can stimulate legislative enthusiasm and win appropriations for a new classroom building. University service-oriented research—developing new crops or feeds, assessing the state's mineral resources, advising state and local government agencies on administrative problems, analyzing the state economy, advising local school authorities, and so forth—may help to convince the public of the practical benefits of knowledge. University faculty may be interested in advanced research and the education of future Ph.D.s, but legislators and their constituents are more interested in the quality and effectiveness of undergraduate teaching.

The faculty of the nation's 2,500 colleges and universities—over two and one-half million strong—traditionally identified themselves as professionals with strong attachments to their institutions. The historic pattern of college and university governance included faculty participation in policy making—not only academic requirements but also budgeting, personnel, building programs, etc. But governance by faculty committee has proven cumbersome, unwieldy, and time-consuming in an era of large-scale enrollments, multi-million dollar budgets, and increases in the size and complexity of academic administration. Increasingly, concepts of public "accountability," academic "management," cost control, and centralized budgeting and purchasing have transferred power in colleges and universities from faculty to professional academic administrators.

The traditional organization of faculty has been the American Association of University Professors (AAUP); historically this group has confined itself to publishing data on faculty salaries and officially "censoring" colleges or universities that violated longstanding notions of academic freedom or tenure. (Tenure is the notion that a faculty member who has demonstrated his competence by service in a college or university position for three to seven years cannot thereafter be dismissed except for "cause"—a serious infraction of established rules or dereliction of duty, provable in an open hearing.) In recent years, the AFT has succeeded in convincing some faculty that traditional patterns of *individual* bargaining over salaries, teaching load, and working conditions in colleges and universities should be replaced by *collective* bargaining in the style of unionized labor. The AFT has only a few thousand college or university members, but its existence has spurred the AAUP on many campuses to assume a more militant attitude on behalf of faculty interests. Nonetheless, the AAUP itself has only about 100,000 members out of 2.5 million faculty. Faculty collective bargaining is complicated by the fact that faculty continue to play some role in academic governance—choosing deans and department heads, sitting on salary committees, etc.

EDUCATION IN THE GHETTO

Schools in the nation's urban ghettos present a special challenge to American education. Disadvantaged black pupils are behind whites in standard achievement tests in the primary grades, and they fall further behind as they move through school. By the twelfth grade, the average black pupil is more than two years behind the average white on standardized tests of achievement, the black dropout rate is more than double the white rate, and black pupil self-esteem is lower. The validity of achievement and intelligence tests can be disputed, but there is little doubt that many ghetto blacks are educationally ill-prepared for college, post–high school training, or the job market. The question of "equality of educational opportunity" is a serious one for urban schools and indeed for the entire nation (see Figure 7-1).

Government efforts at coping with ghetto educational deficiencies can be classified into three broad policy directions: (1) Ending de facto school segregation by racial balancing in the assignment of pupils to public schools and busing pupils wherever necessary to achieve racial balance

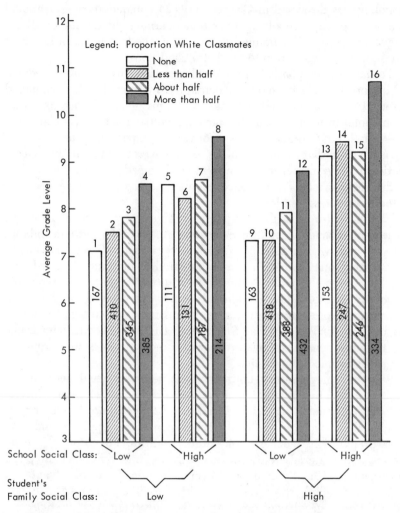

Fig. 7-1 *Average Grade Level Performance of Twelfth Grade Negro Students by Individual Social Class Origin, Social Class Level of School and Proportion White Classmates, Metropolitan Northeast*

Notes: The numbers used in the bars represent the number of cases. Data from the Coleman report is used by the U.S. Commission on Civil Rights to support the view that black pupils perform better academically in integrated schools. Note that performance of black children improves with the proportion of white classmates regardless of whether the black child's family social class is low or high, or whether the social class composition of the school is low or high. Note also that black children from higher family social class perform better academically than black children from lower family social class. Note also that black children from lower family social class perform better in *schools* with classmates of higher social class.

Source: U.S. Commission on Civil Rights, *Racial Isolation in the Public Schools*, Vol. 1 (Washington, D.C.: Government Printing Office, 1967), p. 90.

(this policy was discussed in Chapter 3); (2) compensatory educational programs in ghetto schools to overcome learning difficulties of disadvantaged children; (3) community control of ghetto schools in an effort to redesign public education to fit ghetto conditions.

To date, the emphasis in public policy relative to equality of educational opportunity has been on compensatory programs for disadvantaged children. Compensatory educational programs generally assume that environmental problems create learning difficulties for the disadvantaged pupil—verbal retardation, lack of motivation, experiential and sensory deprivation—and that these difficulties can be overcome in part by special educational programs. In addition to special remedial programs grafted onto the regular school experience, compensatory efforts have been attempted at the preschool level.

The major thrust of the compensatory movement came in Title I of the Elementary and Secondary Education Act of 1965 with its billion-dollar-plus per year assistance for "poverty impacted" schools. Public schools throughout the nation were stimulated to upgrade remedial programs for the poor under Title I. In addition, under the Economic Opportunity Act of 1964, community action agencies throughout the nation initiated preschool remedial programs for disadvantaged children under the popular Project Head Start. Project Head Start was later transferred to public school administration with funds and assistance from the Office of Economic Opportunity.

But the compensatory approach was seriously challenged in an influential report by Professor James Coleman of Johns Hopkins University in 1967 entitled *Equality of Educational Opportunity*.[20] This report concluded that formal educational inputs, such as per pupil expenditure, teacher preparation, teacher-pupil ratios, libraries, laboratories, special programs and materials, etc., make relatively *little* difference in pupil achievement and motivation. However, children from disadvantaged backgrounds (regardless of race) benefit from integration with advantaged children (regardless of race). Moreover, advantaged children are not harmed by such integration, particularly if the disadvantaged are not a majority in the classroom. The startling implication of the Coleman Report was that schools make relatively little difference except as a place where kids learn from each other, and money spent improving ghetto schools is unlikely to produce any meaningful results. Later the U.S. Civil Rights Commission in its report *Racial Isolation in the Public Schools* used the Coleman data as ammunition to support its conception that integration,

[20] James S. Coleman, *Equality of Educational Opportunity* (Washington, D.C.: Government Printing Office, 1966).

and not compensatory education, was the key to the problem of equal educational opportunities.[21]

Earlier we discussed the feasibility—politically and otherwise—of ending de facto segregation. Congress, the federal courts, and urban school districts are not enthusiastic about racial balancing or busing to overcome de facto segregation. The prospects for widespread urban school integration are very dim. This situation, together with the findings of the Coleman Report that compensatory education has little value,[22] has stimulated the search for some other approach to equality of educational opportunity.

Decentralization of big-city school systems and "community control" of local schools as an approach to equality in urban education has produced a great deal of controversy recently.[23] Proponents of "community control" have suggested that ghetto residents should be given control over ghetto schools in order to (1) shift from professional and administrative "dominance" of the schools to "a meaningful parental and community role in the education process," (2) deemphasize the acquisition of achievement skills (reading, writing, and arithmetic) in favor of "a humanistically oriented curriculum modifying the skill-performance standard by which educational quality is primarily measured," and (3) bring personnel into the schools who have "broader talents than the conventionally prepared career educator."

Support for the community control concept is found among black power advocates and black racial separatists, as well as educational reformers. Black militants have attacked desegregation because it implies that Negro pupils can learn well only by sitting next to white pupils. They want educational programs that emphasize black identity and self-awareness, and they reject programs designed to make black pupils "like" white pupils. More importantly, they want black political control of educational resources in the ghetto. Professor Marilyn Gittell explains:

> Community control implies a redistribution of power within the educational subsystem. It is directed toward achieving a modern mechanism

[21] U.S. Commission on Civil Rights, *Racial Isolation in the Public Schools* (Washington, D.C.: Government Printing Office, 1967).

[22] As one might expect, Coleman's explosive findings have been challenged. See Samuel Bowles and Henry M. Levin, "The Determinants of Scholastic Achievement—An Appraisal of Some Recent Evidence," *Journal of Human Resources*, 3 (Winter 1968), 3–24; Peter Schrag, "Why Our Schools Have Failed," *Commentary*, 45 (March 1968), 31–38.

[23] See Marilyn Gittell and Alan G. Hevesi, eds., *The Politics of Urban Education* (New York: Praeger, 1969).

for participatory democracy. It attempts to answer the political failure in education systems, and, as regards the educational failure, community control is intended to create an environment in which more meaningful educational policies can be developed and a wide variety of alternative solutions and techniques can be tested. It seems plausible to assume that a school system devoted to community needs and serving as an agent of community interests will provide an environment more conducive to learning.[24]

New York's unhappy experience with "community control" illustrates some of the problems involved in this concept.[25] In 1967 the Ford Foundation sponsored demonstration projects in community control in New York City, including a project in a ghetto area known as Ocean Hill–Brownsville. At the same time Mayor John Lindsay created an Advisory Panel on Decentralization of New York City Schools, headed by Ford Foundation President McGeorge Bundy. This advisory panel recommended a citywide program of school decentralization (the Bundy Plan).[26] An Ocean Hill–Brownsville Local Governing Board was established and proceeded to act with considerable autonomy from the New York City Board of Education. When school opened in September 1967, the Board appointed five principals who were not on the Civil Service list and thereby incurred the opposition of the Council of Supervisory Associations representing school administrators. During a citywide school strike over pay increases and smaller classes, Ocean Hill–Brownsville schools stayed open, thereby incurring the opposition of the United Federation of Teachers representing the city's teachers. Throughout the 1967–68 school year there was a growing hostility and an escalation of rhetoric between white teachers and administrators on the one hand and the Ocean Hill–Brownsville Governing Board on the other. The Board charged that certain white teachers were uncooperative and failed to understand ghetto problems. The teachers charged the Board with black racism and even anti-Semitism (many New York teachers and administrators are Jewish). In May 1968 the Board dismissed nineteen white teachers without notice or hearing, seven weeks before the end of the term, apparently because they were "out of tune with the political atmosphere in the community." The United

---

24 *Ibid.*, pp. 365–66.
25 *Ibid.*, pp. 305–77.
26 Mayor's Advisory Panel on Decentralization of the New York City Schools, *Reconnection for Learning: A Community Control System for New York City* (New York: Office of the Mayor, 1967); reprinted in Gittell and Hevesi, *Politics of Urban Education.*

Federation of Teachers called a citywide strike protesting the dismissals as violations of civil service regulations and due process of law. The strike seriously curtailed education in New York City during the 1968–69 school year. The issues of the strike were eventually mediated, but not without a tragic increase in distrust and suspicion between the races in the school system and the city at large.

Opponents of "community control"—particularly white teachers, teacher unions, and administrators—argue that decentralization creates administrative duplication, inefficiencies, and increased overhead costs. They contend that it results in wasted educational dollars, the destruction of the merit system, and the introduction of political and racial considerations in educational policies. Finally they contend that it promotes racial separatism and black militancy.

SUMMARY

Let us summarize educational policy with particular reference to the group interests involved:

1. Historically, educational policy has been decentralized in America, with states and communities carrying the major responsibility for public elementary and secondary and higher education. However, federal aid to education is nearly as old as the nation itself. Prior to 1865, federal aid was distributed for specific programs and services—vocational education; school lunch and milk; federally impacted schools; science, mathematics, and foreign language; higher-education facilities—rather than general support of education.

2. The Elementary and Secondary Education Act of 1965 was the first large-scale federal aid-to-education program. The long struggle over federal aid to education indicates the power of interest groups in blocking legislation that has widespread public support, and the necessity of accommodating specific interest groups in policy formation.

3. The difficulty in securing passage of a significant federal aid-to-education bill can be attributed to conflict between major racial and religious group interests over the character of such aid rather than to opposition to the idea of federal aid.

4. For many years the question of whether federal aid should be withheld from racially segregated schools divided proponents of federal aid to education. Only after the passage of the Civil Rights Act of 1965, barring the use of federal funds in *any* segregated program or activity, was this divisive issue removed as a direct obstacle to federal aid to education.

5. Another divisive issue over federal aid to education was that of whether or not such aid should be withheld from private, church-related schools. Catholic interests would not support a bill that excluded such schools from assistance, and Protestant interests, as well as the National Education Association, opposed the idea of federal aid to church schools.

6. Congress stood ready to enact whatever compromise the various religious and educational groups could agree upon. Experience clearly indicated that no policy of federal aid to education was possible without prior group compromise. The final compromise—enacted as the Elementary and Secondary Education Act of 1965—focused on "aid to children" in poverty-impacted areas, and allowed church-related schools to receive federal funds for specific nonreligious educational services and facilities.

7. Although educational decision making is still largely decentralized in America, state education departments are gradually centralizing policy making by means of state grants to local school boards, and gradually reducing by means of consolidation the number of local school boards.

8. Important groups in local school politics include taxpayers who vote in school board elections; school board members who are frequently owners of small businesses in the community; professional school administrators at the local level and from the state departments of education and faculties of teacher colleges; and school teachers. The American Federation of Teachers is a labor union representing many classroom teachers in large cities. The National Education Association, an older and larger "professional group," represents school administrators and teachers; it has become more militant in recent years in protecting teacher interests.

9. Educational and community groups are divided over how to improve education in the nation's black ghettos. Integrationists advise against exclusive reliance on compensatory education programs in the ghettos, because these programs do not attack the problem of de facto segregation. However, busing black students out of the ghetto to achieve racial balance in urban schools involves many problems—political, legal, administrative, and physical.

10. Decentralization of urban education and "community control" of ghetto schools has been supported by some reform groups as well as black militants. New York's experiment in community control has floundered in group conflict between white teachers and their union, black community activists, and educational administrators.

BIBLIOGRAPHY

COLEMAN, JAMES S., *Equality of Educational Opportunity.* Washington, D.C.: Government Printing Office, 1966.
EIDENBERG, EUGENE, and ROY D. MOREY, *An Act of Congress.* New York: W. W. Norton, 1969.

GITTELL, MARILYN, and ALAN G. HEVESI, eds., *The Politics of Urban Education.* New York: Praeger, 1969.

KIMBROUGH, RALPH B., *Political Power and Educational Decision-Making.* Chicago: Rand McNally, 1964.

ZEIGLER, HARMON, *The Political Life of American Teachers.* Englewood Cliffs, N.J.: Prentice-Hall, 1967.

Urban renewal project, Denver, Colorado. UPI Photo

8 URBAN AFFAIRS:

institutional arrangements and public policy

DILEMMAS OF URBAN POLICY

Urban life has come under severe criticism in recent years. A newspaperman describes the dangers of modern urban living:

> An observer of the sprawling urban scene today might be compelled to concede that the superficial monotony of physical similarity must be the least important of all the ailments of the squatting modern metropolitan region, whose air grows fouler and more dangerous by the day, whose water is threatened increasingly by pollution, whose mobility is undermined by accumulations of vehicles and withering transit, whose educational systems reel under a growing variety of economic, social, and national emergencies, and whose entire pattern is assuming an ominous shape and sociological form, with well-to-do whites in their suburban cities ringing poverty-ridden minority groups widening at the core.[1]

The urban "crisis" is really a series of interrelated problems which affect the nation as a whole. Poverty, poor housing, racial conflict, crime and delinquency, social dependency, poor health, overcrowding, joblessness, ignorance, white flight to the suburbs, and fiscal imbalance are national problems. Yet their impact is increasingly concentrated in the nation's large cities.

These problems are not a product of government organization or

[1] Mitchell Gordon, *Sick Cities: The Psychology and Pathology of American Urban Life* (Baltimore: Penguin, 1963), p. 3.

administration. However, we will observe in this chapter how institutional arrangements affect the ability of governments to deal effectively with urban problems. First, we will examine federal urban policy, with particular reference to the institutional arrangements that have affected federal programs in the nation's cities. Then we will examine the characteristics of city governments and the forces shaping the policies of cities.

The critical deficiency in federal urban policy is that there are no concrete goals or clear priorities in the hundreds of separate programs affecting cities. James Q. Wilson writes about urban policy: *"We do not know what we are trying to accomplish.* . . . Do we seek to raise standards of living, maximize housing choices, revitalize the commercial centers of our cities, and suburban sprawl, eliminate discrimination, reduce traffic congestion, improve the quality of urban design, check crime and delinquency, strengthen the effectiveness of local planning, increase citizen participation in local government? All these objectives sound attractive—in part, because they are rather vague—but unfortunately they are in many cases incompatible." [2]

The institutional arrangements of American government have proven remarkably well-suited for pursuing different policies toward contradictory goals simultaneously. Government can maintain the support of competing groups in society by allowing different federal agencies to pursue incompatible goals and by permitting local communities to follow competing policies with federal money.

For example, the two federal program areas that account for the greatest expenditure of dollars for the physical improvement of cities are (1) the federal highway and transportation programs, (2) the federal housing and urban renewal programs. The first is operated by the Department of Transportation (DOT) and the second by the Department of Housing and Urban Development (HUD). The urban portion of the interstate highway system is costing billions of federal dollars; the effect of these dollars is to enable people to drive in and out of the central city speedily, safely, and conveniently, and to open up suburban areas to business and residential expansion. Of course, these expressways also encourage middle-class (mostly white) families to move out of the central city and to enable commercial establishment to follow them. This leads to further racial segregation within the metropolitan region in housing and schools, and reduces the number of service jobs available to the poor living in the city. The encouragement of longer automobile trips from suburban residencies to downtown offices adds to pollution and congestion. Although federal investment in mass-transit facilities (subways, railways, buses) might reduce pollution and congestion, such investment

[2] James Q. Wilson, "The War on Cities," *The Public Interest* (Summer 1966), p. 10.

would still encourage suburbanization, "white flight," and de facto segregation.

At the same time, the Federal Housing Administration (in HUD) and the Veterans Administration are encouraging home ownership by insuring mortgages that are written on easy terms for millions of middle-class (mostly white) Americans. Most of these mortgages are for new homes because it is cheaper to build on vacant land and because so many prospective homeowners want to move to the suburbs. So it turns out that these programs actually facilitate the movement of middle-class people out of the central city.

And meantime, the Urban Renewal Administration (in HUD) is helping cities tear down slum dwellings, often displacing the poor who live there at considerable hardship, in order to make way for office buildings, hotels, civic centers, industrial parks, and middle-class luxury apartments. In part, this effort is intended to lure suburbanites back to the central city. Although urban renewal reduces the overall supply of housing to the poor in cities, the Housing Assistance Administration (in HUD) is assisting cities in building low-rent public housing units to add to the supply of housing for the poor.

Not only do different federal programs operate at cross-purposes, but the American system of federalism and the concern for local autonomy insure that different cities will use these programs in different ways. Wilson observes:

> Furthermore, the goals for most programs—especially urban renewal—were determined at the local level. This meant that urban renewal, in itself simply a tool, was used for very different purposes in different cities—in some places to get Negroes out of white neighborhoods, in others to bring middle-class people closer to downtown stores, in still other places to build dramatic civic monuments, and in a few places to rehabilitate declining neighborhoods and to add to the supply of moderately priced housing.[3]

Despite the emphasis in federal urban programs on the *physical* characteristics of cities, most observers now acknowledge that "the urban crisis" is not primarily, nor even significantly, a physical problem. It is not really housing, or highways, or urban rebuilding that lie at the heart of urban discontent. Instead when we think of the challenges confronting cities, we think of racial tension, crime, poverty, poor schools, residential segregation, rising welfare rolls, fiscal crisis—in short, all the major domestic problems facing the nation. In an urban society, *all* domestic problems become urban problems.

[3] *Ibid.*, p. 12.

HUD—MORTGAGE INSURANCE

The Department of Housing and Urban Development (HUD) is the federal agency concerned primarily with public housing, mortgage insurance, urban renewal, community facilities, mass transit, and related programs whose objectives are better houses and improved communities. HUD administers federal housing and urban affairs programs that were begun in the 1930s. The organization of HUD reflects the structure of these major federal programs:

Federal Housing Administration
FHA programs of mortgage insurance
Federal National Mortgage Association
FNMA ("Fanny Mae") secondary mortgage market operations for federally insured mortgages
Housing Assistance Administration
Low-rent public housing programs for low-income families
Urban Renewal Administration
Federal programs for slum clearance, urban renewal, and planning assistance
Community Facilities Administration
Federal grants and loans to municipalities for sewer, water, mass transit, and other public works

The Federal Housing Administration was created in 1934 to guarantee private mortagages against default by the individual homebuyer, thereby enabling banks, savings and loan associations, and other lending agencies to provide long-term, low-interest, low down-payment mortgages for Americans wishing to buy their own homes. After checking the credit rating of the prospective homebuyer, the FHA insures the private mortgage lender—bank, savings and loan company, insurance company, etc.—of repayment of the loan in case the homebuyer defaults. This reduces the risk and encourages mortgage lenders to make more loans at lower interest rates, lower down payments, and longer repayment periods. Although these advantages in borrowing assist middle-class homebuyers, note that the *direct* beneficiaries of the FHA program are the banks and mortgage lending companies that are insured against losses. The FHA also establishes minimum building standards for homes it insures and thus has raised the general quality of middle-class housing. The FHA adds a small charge to each mortgage to finance a revolving fund to repay defaulted mortgages. However, the record of Americans in mortgage repayment is so good that FHA has consistently returned premium payments to the U.S. Treasury.

FHA has been extremely successful in promoting home ownership among millions of middle-class Americans. Millions of families have financed their homes through FHA-insured mortgages, and millions more have financed their houses through mortgages insured by the Veterans Administration. A great many of these mortgages financed *suburban* homes. In fact the success of FHA and VA programs may have contributed to the deterioration of the nation's central cities by enabling so many middle-class white families to acquire homes in the suburbs and leave the city behind.

In recent years Congress has attempted to extend the benefits of FHA to moderate- and low-income families through several special programs. An FHA mortgage subsidy program, "Section 235," provides reduced interest rates for moderate- or low-income families. A related program, "Section 236," provides a mortgage subsidy to developers to cut their costs and thus lower rents for tenants. A below-market interest-rate program on rental housing, "Section 221(d) (3)," and a below-market home ownership program, "Section 221(h)," waive some traditional "economic soundness" requirements to finance the building or purchase of single- and multiple-family units for low-income families. Unfortunately, the result has been a startling increase in the rate of defaults and a resulting increase in the costs of the FHA program.

The Federal National Mortgage Association, FNMA or "Fanny Mae," was created in the 1930s to further assist the mortgage market. FNMA can buy mortgages on the open market, particularly FHA- and VA-insured mortgages, when private mortgage money dries up. When mortgage money becomes more plentiful, it sells its mortgages. These market operations help to stabilize the mortgage market and insure a steady flow of money for home buying.

HUD—PUBLIC HOUSING

The Housing Act of 1937 established a federal public housing agency, later named the Housing Assistance Administration, to provide low-rent public housing for the poor. The public housing program was designed for persons without jobs or incomes sufficient to enable them to afford home ownership even with the help of FHA. The Housing Assistance Administration does not build, own, or operate its own housing projects; rather it provides the necessary financial support to enable local communities to provide public housing for their poor if they choose to do so. The Housing Assistance Administration makes loans and grants to *local* housing authorities established by local governments to build, own, and operate low-cost public housing. Local housing authorities must keep rents low in relation to their tenants' ability to pay. No community is required to have a Public Housing Authority; it must apply to the Public

Housing Administration and meet federal standards in order to receive federal financial support.

Public housing has always been involved in more political controversy than FHA. Real estate and building interests, which support FHA because it expands their number of customers, have opposed public housing on the grounds that it is socialistic and wasteful. Although, in theory, public housing serves individuals who cannot afford private housing, private real estate interests contend that public housing hurts the market for older homes and apartments. In addition, owners of dwellings seldom welcome competition from federally supported housing authorities. Also, political difficulties have been encountered in the location of public housing units. Many Americans will support public housing for low-income persons as long as it is not located in their neighborhood. A large proportion of public housing occupants are blacks, and thus public housing is automatically involved in the politics of race.

In recent years, many of the earlier supporters of public housing, including minority groups, labor, social workers, charitable organizations, and big-city political organizations, have expressed doubts about its effect. Although it has provided improved living conditions, public housing has failed to eliminate poverty, ignorance, family disruption, juvenile delinquency, crime, and other characteristic troubles of slums. Very often, the concentration of large numbers of poor persons with a great variety of social problems in a single, mass housing project compounds their problems. Huge housing projects are impersonal and bureaucratic, and often fail to provide many of the stabilizing neighborhood influences of the old slums. Removing thousands of people from neighborhood environments and placing them in the institution-like setting of large public housing developments very often increases their alienation or separation from society and removes what few social controls exist in the slum neighborhood. Furthermore, black groups often complain that public housing is a new form of racial segregation, and indeed, the concentration of blacks among public housing dwellers does lead to a great deal of de facto segregation in housing projects. Finally, it should be noted that rural areas contain more substandard housing than city areas, but the dispersal of rural dwellers over large land areas makes the public housing approach difficult.

Requests by communities for federal aid for public housing have far exceeded the amount of money appropriated by Congress. The result in most communities is a long waiting list of persons eligible for public housing for whom no space is available. To alleviate this shortage and to correct some of the problems involved in large-site housing projects, Congress authorized three programs to supplement public housing—a rent subsidy program, a dispersed public housing site program, and a new "turnkey" approach to the acquisition of public housing units. The rent subsidy program authorizes federal grants to local housing authorities to provide cash grants to assist families to meet rents in "moderate-income" housing projects receiving FHA approval. The grants are paid to the housing owners; tenants are obliged to contribute only 25 percent of their annual income to rents. The dispersed public housing site program provides federal grants to local housing authorities to enable them to purchase or lease existing single homes or apartment buildings throughout the community for operation as public housing units. The "turnkey" approach to the acquisition of public housing units encourages private builders to build public housing on their own sites and then sell it to local housing authorities. The purpose of all these policies is to speed up the availability of public housing units and, perhaps more importantly, to eliminate dependence upon large, institutionlike public housing facilities and achieve more dispersal of public housing residents throughout the community. Opponents of these programs argue that the federal government is subsidizing "blockbusting" tactics in its attempt to disperse public housing dwellers, mostly Negros, throughout the community. It is, they argue, a subtle form of open-housing legislation aimed at de facto housing segregation.

In summary the record of federal housing policy is uneven. FHA mortgage insurance was successful when it served only middle-class house buyers; but when it began insuring low-income housing, the rate of default increased drastically and so did the costs of the program. Public housing in the form of large institution-like developments produce many undesirable social consequences; but dispersed public housing is more difficult and costly to administer. More importantly, public housing has never provided enough units to satisfy the need for low income housing.

The private homebuilding industry and mortgage market continues to play the dominant role in filling the nation's housing needs. Over two million new housing units are built each year in the United States. Only about 600,000 of these are financed through FHA or VA guaranteed mortgages. Only about 30,000 new public housing units are produced each year. Thus, the private sector continues to provide the bulk of housing and housing finance in America. The median sales price of a new single family home in the private market is now over $30,000; this price excludes almost half of the nation's families from the purchase of a *new* single family home. But private apartments play a major role in housing— slightly less than half of all new housing units are apartments.

The private sector also plays the major role in providing *low-cost* housing. The mobile home industry is generally ignored by public housing advocates, but in fact this industry has provided the great bulk of low-cost housing for America. Approximately 500,000 mobile home units are produced each year, compared to only 30,000 public housing units. If low-income Americans depended exclusively on public housing, most would be camping out in the cold. Fortunately the mobile home industry has filled the gap in low-income housing without government assistance.

HUD—URBAN RENEWAL

After World War II, the suburban exodus had progressed to the point where central cities faced gradual decay if large public efforts were not undertaken to rebuild obsolescent and deteriorating core areas. Urban renewal could not be undertaken by private enterprise because it was not profitable; suburban property was usually cheaper than downtown property and it did not require large-scale clearance of obsolete buildings. Moreover, private enterprise did not possess the power of eminent domain that enabled the city to purchase many separately owned tracts of land and insure an economically feasible new investment.

To save the nation's central cities, the Urban Renewal Administration was authorized to match local monies to acquire blighted land, demolish or modernize obsolete or dilapidated structures, and make downtown sites available for new uses. The federal government does not engage in these activities directly, but makes available financial assistance to local urban renewal authorities for renewal projects. When the sites are physically cleared of the old structures by the local urban renewal authority, they can be resold to private developers for residential, commercial, or industrial use. Two-thirds of the difference between the costs of acquisition and clearance and the income from the private sale to the developers is paid for by the federal government. In other words, local urban renewal authorities sustain a loss in their renewal activities and two-thirds of this loss is made up by federal grants; the rest must come from local sources. However, the local share may include noncash contributions in the form of land donations, schools, streets, or parks.

No city is required to engage in urban renewal, but if it wishes federal financial backing, it must show in its application a "workable program" for redevelopment and the prevention of future blight. It must demonstrate that it has adequate building and health codes, good zoning and subdivision control regulations, proper administrative structures for renewal and other government services, sufficient local financing and public support, and a comprehensive plan of development with provision for relocating displaced persons. Failure to meet federal standards can halt federal urban assistance; for example, Houston, the largest city without any zoning, cannot get urban renewal funds.

The key to success in urban renewal is to encourage private developers to purchase the land and make a heavy investment—in middle- or high-income housing or in commercial or industrial use. In fact, before undertaking a project, urban renewal authorities frequently "find a developer first, and then see what interests him." The city cannot afford to purchase land, thereby taking it off the tax rolls, invest in its clearance, and then be stuck without a buyer. Moreover, the private developer must be encouraged to invest in the property and thus enhance the value of the central city. So over time a city can more than pay off its own investment in urban renewal by increased tax returns from renewed property and hence make a "profit." Thus, many people can come out of a project feeling successful—the city increases its tax base and annual revenues, the private developer makes a profit, and mayors can point to the physical improvements in the city that occurred during their administration.

Moreover, there are many favorable "spillover effects" of a successful urban renewal project:

1. Each project stimulates jobs, not only during demolition and construction but also later in servicing the new housing, business, or industry.
2. The city increases its ability to attract and maintain middle-class residents as well as business and industry.
3. Universities, hospitals, cultural centers, etc., can be built or expanded when all or part of an urban renewal project is turned over to public purposes.
4. Downtown areas can be revitalized and attract private development in areas adjacent to urban renewal projects.

However, there are also drawbacks to urban renewal. The concern for "profit" frequently leads to fiscal conservatism on the part of urban renewal authorities. They do not undertake to renew the very worst slum areas because of the excessive costs involved and because private developers may not wish to go into these areas even after renewal. More importantly, the financial considerations often dictate the choice of profitable middle- or upper-income housing or commercial or industrial use of renewed land rather than low-cost private or public housing development. Developers make more profit on the former types of investments, and the city gets better tax returns. The effect of urban renewal is frequently to redistribute land from lower-income to higher-income purposes.

Relocation is the most sensitive problem in urban renewal. The vast majority of people relocated by urban renewal are poor and black. They have no interest in moving simply to make room for middle- or higher-income housing, or business or industry, or universities, hospitals, and other public facilities. Even though relocated families are frequently given priority for public housing, there is not nearly enough space in public housing to contain them all. They are simply moved from one slum to another. The slum landowner is paid a just price for his land, but the renter receives only a small moving allowance, averaging about one hundred dollars. Urban renewal officials assist relocated families in finding new housing and generally claim success in moving families to better housing. But frequently the result is higher rents, and urban renewal may actually help to create new slums in other sections of the city.[4] Small businessmen are especially vulnerable to relocation. They often depend on a small, well-known neighborhood clientele, and they cannot compete successfully when forced to move to other sections of the city.

Political support for urban renewal has come from mayors who wish to make their reputation as rigorous proponents by engaging in large-scale renewal activities that produce impressive "before" and "after" pictures of the city. Businessmen wishing to preserve downtown investments and developers wishing to acquire land in urban centers have provided a solid base of support for downtown renewal. Mayors, planners, the press, and the good-government forces have made urban renewal politically much more popular than public housing.

Originally, liberal reform groups and representatives of urban minorities supported urban renewal as an attack on the slum problem. Recently, however, they have become disenchanted with urban renewal, complaining that it has not considered the plight of the slum dweller. Too often, slum areas have been cleared and replaced with high-income residential developments or commercial or industrial developments that do not directly help the plight of the slum dwellers. Urban renewal authorities are required to pay landowners a just price for their land, but slum dwellers who rent their apartments are shoved about the city with only a minimal amount of support from the "relocation" division of urban renewal authority. Downtown areas have been improved in appearance, but usually at the price of considerable human dislocation. Thus, the slum dwellers and the landlords who exploit them often join forces to oppose urban renewal. When dislocated persons are poor and black, and the completed project is used for middle- or high-income white residences, the charge is leveled that urban renewal is simply "Negro removal."[5]

STRUCTURAL PROBLEMS IN FEDERAL URBAN POLICY

For over thirty years the federal government has been directly involved in housing and urban development programs. Yet today we con-

---

[4] See Chester Hartman, "The Housing of Relocated Families,' *Journal of the American Institute of Planners*, 30 (November 1964), 266–86.

[5] For a scathing attack on urban renewal, see Jane Jacobs, *The Death and Life of Great American Cities* (New York: Random House, 1961).

tinue to speak of the "urban crisis"—racial conflict, inadequate housing, air and water pollution, poor schools, crime and delinquency, crowded hospitals, traffic congestion, crippling city tax burdens, poorly paid policemen and other municipal workers, and so on.

The failure of federal urban policy to resolve these problems is *not* merely a product of structural or organizational defects in federal programs. Indeed, it is a serious difficulty of the institutional approach that it focuses on structural or organization problems when in fact the real issues are much more deeply rooted in social or economic dimensions of urban life. Poverty, racism, crime, pollution, overcrowding, and other serious maladies afflicting mankind are not likely to be cured by tinkering with the organizational structure of government.

Yet it is possible to identify briefly a number of organizational and administrative problems that are serious obstacles to the development of an effective federal policy in housing and urban affairs: [6]

1. First of all, the major thrust of federal policy is now and always has been a commitment to the physical aspects of urban life—the provision of housing and transportation, the rebuilding of central cities, and development of community facilities, etc. It may be that the "urban crisis" is not primarily or even significantly a problem of housing or transit or facilities. It may be a problem of human conflict in crowded, high-density, socially heterogenous areas.
2. Federal policy has frequently worked at cross-purposes, reflecting organizational fragmentation of programs. For example, urban renewal tries to save central cities, while federal highway policy builds expressways making possible the suburban exodus and FHA has helped suburbanites to buy their own homes.
3. The Public Housing Program has tried to increase the supply of low-rent housing for the poor, while the urban renewal program, together with highway building, has torn down low-rent housing.
4. Federal civil rights policy is committed to desegregation but many large public housing projects concentrate blacks in de facto segregated neighborhoods and schools.
5. Federal policy has stressed *local* administration with local autonomy, flexibility, and participation in decision making. Yet this has meant that housing and urban renewal have been employed in different places for different purposes—in some places to help get blacks out of white neighborhoods, in others to subsidize white middle-class residents to come back to the central city, in others to restore business to downtown department stores, in others to build dramatic civic monuments or assist university expansion, in others to build sports palaces, museums, or other middle-class centers, and in still others to improve the quality of life for urban blacks.

[6] For a more detailed critique of federal urban policy, see James Q. Wilson, "The War on Cities"; and Edward C. Banfield, *The Unheavenly City* (Boston: Little, Brown, 1970).

6. Direct federal-to-city grants for housing and urban renewal assist hard-pressed central cities, but generally overlook the possibilities for regional or metropolitan-wide housing and urban renewal programs. If it is true that segregation, slum housing, poverty, crime, and so on, are responsibilities of the entire metropolitan population, then grants to regional organizations for the implementation of housing and urban development policy would appear more appropriate than grants to cities.

7. Federal grant-in-aid programs provide money for specific purposes—frequently "new" or "innovative" or "demonstration" programs. Yet the real urban crisis may be occurring in the provision of traditional municipal services—policy protection, sewage disposal, sanitation—and what is required is the upgrading of existing services, not necessarily the initiation of "new" or "innovative" or "demonstration" programs.

8. The maze of federal grant-in-aid programs for cities (nearly 500 separate programs with separate purposes and guidelines) is uncoordinated and bureaucratic in character. Mayors and other municipal officials spend a great deal of time in "grantmanship"—learning where to find federal funds, how to apply, and how to write applications in such a way as to appear to meet the purposes and guidelines of the program.

9. The federal government has never set any meaningful priority among its hundreds of grant programs. The result is that too few dollars chase too many goals. Cities are sometimes pressured to apply for funds for projects they do not really need, simply because federal funds are available—while they may receive little or no federal assistance for more vital programs.

The reason for many of these administrative and organization problems is not merely incompetency on the part of government planners. Institutional analysis is misleading when it implies that these problems are strictly institutional. Frequently conflicting policies, incompatible goals, and competing government programs reflect underlying conflicts over public policy. Government institutions often accommodate conflict over public policy by enacting conflicting policies and establishing separate agencies to implement these policies. We can only admire a political system that so neatly accommodates conflicting demands!

The Model Cities Program, enacted in 1966, was an attempt to cope with some of the organizational and administrative problems in federal urban programs. Model Cities is not a new program or new approach to urban problems but rather an effort to reorganize old programs and approaches. The emphasis in Model Cities is upon "coordination" and "integrated planning" of federal programs in each participating city. The idea is to coordinate programs and grants in housing, urban renewal, and community facilities, with programs and grants in transportation, job training, education, economic opportunity, and related programs. A federal coordinator would be appointed for each participating city. Supplemental federal funds, in addition to existing federal grant programs, would be made available to participating cities as incentives for participation. However, it is doubtful that this reorganization and imposition of another layer of federal bureaucracy between urban needs and federal monetary resources will succeed in reducing existing organizational chaos, let alone solve any significant urban problems.

An alternative approach to the organizational and administrative problems in federal grant-in-aid programs is that of providing unrestricted *federal bloc grants* to states or cities with few or no strings attached. A related approach is that of *federal revenue sharing* where a certain percentage of federal tax collections would be turned back to states or cities for their own use. Bloc grants would be given by the federal government for stated purposes, such as education, health, welfare, transportation, or housing and urban development, and states or cities would spend the money for these purposes as they saw fit. Revenue sharing would give states and cities access to the fiscal resources of the federal government and ensure state and local control over the use of these funds.

The issue of bloc grants and revenue sharing extends well beyond the area of housing and urban development. Indeed, the structure of American federalism is vitally affected by the direction of federal grant-in-aid policy. Bloc grants and revenue-sharing proposals are generally supported by those groups that fear centralization of power in federal bureaucracies. In addition, state and local officials welcome the notion of assigning the federal government the unhappy task of collecting money, while retaining for themselves the more agreeable task of deciding how the money should be spent. Many mayors support bloc grants and revenue sharing only on the guarantee that federal money will be given directly to cities and not allocated to state governments. Some urban groups—notably, blacks and poor people—are distrustful of state and local decision making, and would probably prefer the present arrangements, however chaotic, to any organizational shifts that would threaten their interests. The federal bureaucracies themselves are less than enthusiastic about relinquishing too much control over policy making to state and local authorities.

URBAN ENVIRONMENT AND THE STRUCTURE
OF CITY POLITICS

City politics come in a variety of structural packages. Cities vary in the form of government—*mayor-council, commission,* or *council-manager.* Municipal election systems vary as to whether they are *partisan* or *nonpartisan,* and whether or not council constituencies are *at-large* or *by ward.* Finally, urban governmental structures differ in the extent of *consolidation* or *fragmentation* in metropolitan regions.

These structural differences in city politics are frequently associated with the political success or failure of the municipal reform movement.[7] The municipal reform movement developed over the last century to fight "city machines" and "bosses." The reformers wanted to eliminate "politics" from local government, and they supported a variety of structural changes to do so. The reform movement put forward a program that included city-manager government, nonpartisan elections, at-large constituencies, the elimination of many separately elected offices (the "short ballot"), the merit system of civil service, modern budget and planning practices, and the separation of the municipal government from state and national politics.

The *council-manager* form of government was put forward as a means of separating "politics" from "administration" in city government. Policy making would be vested in an elected council, but administration would be assigned to an appointed administrator known as a manager. The reform ethos included a belief that there is a "right" answer to public questions and that "politics" ought to be divorced from city government. City government should be placed in the hands of those who are best qualified, by training, ability, and devotion to public service, to manage public businesses. Popular control of government was to be guaranteed by making the managers' tenure completely dependent upon the will of the elected council. In contrast to the council-manager form of government, the mayor-council form is the more traditional and "political" structure.

The *nonpartisan ballot* was the most widely adopted reform ever put forward to curb the "machines" and ensure a "no party" style of politics. Nearly two-thirds of America's cities use a nonpartisan ballot to elect local officials. Reformers felt that nonpartisanship would take the "politics" out of local government and raise the caliber of candidates for elected offices. They believed that nonpartisanship would restrict local campaigning to local issues, and thereby remove extraneous state-national issues from local elections. They also believed that, by omitting party labels, local campaigns would emphasize the qualifications of the individual candidates rather than their party affiliations. Moreover, to eliminate traditional "ward politics" with its emphasis on neighborhood affiliations, the reform movement proposed that candidates for local office run in *at-large* rather than *ward* constituencies. This meant that all city councilmen would be elected by a citywide constituency, rather than each councilman being elected by a separate ward constituency.

What characteristics of the urban environment are associated with

---

[7] See Edward C. Banfield and James Q. Wilson, *City Politics* (Cambridge: Harvard University Press, 1963).

reformed or unreformed structures of city government? First of all, city-manager government is closely associated with the size of cities. Large cities show a distinct preference for the more "political" form of mayor-council government in contrast to the more "efficient" form of council-manager government. Most of the nation's large cities have mayor-council governments; the council-manager and commission forms of government are most popular in the middle-sized cities. The political environment of large cities is so complex that these cities require strong political leadership, which can arbitrate struggles for power, arrange compromises, and be directly responsible to the people for policy decisions. A large city requires a "political" form of government that can arbitrate the conflicting claims of diverse interests. On the other hand, smaller cities have fewer competing interests, more acceptance of a common public interest, and less division over community policy. A professional city manager would have less difficulty in recognizing cues about direct behavior in a small city than in a large city with a complex social and political structure. A single interest is more likely to dominate politics in a small city; therefore, such a city can use a professional administrator rather than a political negotiator. There is reason to believe that larger cities require political skills more than professional administration.

The mayor-council form of government is also associated with ethnicity in the population. When cities are compared, increases in the proportion of foreign-born persons coincide with increases in the incidence of unreformed political institutions. A study by sociologist Daniel N. Gordon shows that foreign-born population was a correlate of that form in 1960.[8] Moreover, this relationship persists under controls for region, economic base, population, size, and population change. It is interesting to note that unreformed political structures are associated with foreign-born populations but not necessarily with black populations. Apparently blacks have not allied themselves with machines and bosses to the extent that earlier Irish, Italian, and Slavic immigrants did. Yet the most obvious explanation for the relationship between ethnicity and "politicized" institutions is the fact that ethnic groups were especially dependent upon political activities for their advancement in society. Because the early immigrants to the city lacked wealth and social standing they came to value access to government, public office holding, and patronage. They supported the "political" governmental forms in preference to forms that were intended to reduce the value of one of their few resources—their votes.

Reformed governmental structures are more common in middle-class cities with large proportions of well-educated, white-collar work-

---

[8] Daniel N. Gordon, "Immigrants and Urban Governmental Form in American Cities, 1933–1960," *American Journal of Sociology*, 74 (September 1968), 158–71.

ers. Middle-class citizens are more likely to want government conducted in a businesslike fashion, with a council serving as a board of directors and a city manager as the president of a "municipal corporation." They are primarily concerned with efficiency, honesty, and saving their tax dollars. These values are not necessarily shared by labor and ethnic groups, which may prefer a government that grants them small favors, dispenses patronage jobs, awards representation and "recognition" to groups, and can be held directly responsible by the voters at election time.

There is also a relationship between reformed institutions in city politics and the rate of population growth and mobility.[9] Growing cities face more administrative and technical problems than cities whose population is stable. There is a strong relationship between population growth and council-manager government. A rapidly growing city faces many administrative problems in providing streets, sewers, and other services required by an expanding population. This creates a demand for a professional administrator. In contrast, the mayor-council form of government is associated with cities having relatively stable populations, in which the problems of growth are not quite so pressing but the problems of political conflict are well-defined and persistent. Cities with highly mobile populations are also much more likely to have the manager form of government. Mobile middle-class populations are less likely to settle into stable political factions that compete with each other and require "political" institutions. Instead, more mobile populations seem to demand efficient, businesslike, service-producing governments—and a structure more convenient to these goals.

URBAN GOVERNMENTAL STRUCTURES
AND PUBLIC POLICY

Does it make any difference in the policies adopted by cities whether a city's governmental structure is "reformed" or "unreformed"? Do council-manager cities pursue notably different policies than mayor-council cities? Are there any consistent policy differences between cities with nonpartisan, at-large electoral systems and cities with partisan ward type electoral systems? Are metropolitan policies in areas of fragmented local government any different from metropolitan policies in areas with consolidated governmental structures? It is difficult to come to grips with these questions because, as we have seen, there are significant environmental differences between cities with different governmental struc-

---

[9] See also Robert R. Alford and Harry M. Scoble, "Political and Socioeconomic Characteristics of American Cities," *Municipal Year Book* (Chicago: International City Manager's Association, 1965), pp. 82–97.

tures. This makes it difficult to sort out the effect of governmental structure from the effect of urban environment. For example, if reformed cities pursue noticeably different policies than unreformed cities, we must be careful in attributing these policy differences to reformism, because we already know that reformed and unreformed cities differ in their size and socioeconomic composition. It may be that the environmental variables really account for the differences in policy in reformed and unreformed cities, just as they account for differences in structure.

In general, the research described here suggests that *structural* characteristics of cities do have *some* independent effect on urban policy. It is also true that urban *environmental* variables have a *very important effect* on urban policies—an effect that is generally greater than structural characteristics. Nonetheless, there is evidence that the structure of government does affect the outcome of public policy, and this evidence lends validity to the structural approach.

In general, policies of reformed, manager governments are likely to be directed toward (1) promoting economic growth, and/or (2) providing life's amenities.[10] (Merely mantaining traditional services—caretaker government—is inconsistent with reformed, manager government.) Manager governments may be concerned with promoting economic growth through population expansion, industrial development, commercial activities, total wealth, and the like. This type of government is prepared to enact zoning regulations, reduce tax assessments, develop industrial parks, install utilities, and do whatever else may be required to attract business and industry and promote production. Another policy orientation of reformed manager governments is that of providing and securing life's amenities. The policies of these governments accent the home environment rather than the working environment; laws stress safety, slowness, quiet, beauty, convenience, and restfulness. Neighborhoods are defended by rigid zoning laws and building codes, open spaces are guarded, traffic is routed around the city, and noise and smoke are curtailed. Reformed manager governments may assume either of these two policy orientations: promoting economic growth or providing and securing life's amenities. The caretaker policy orientation is inconsistent with the reformed structure. A caretaker government is expected to provide minimum public services in the community and nothing more. Nothing new is ever tried and tax increases are steadfastly avoided. Pressing public problems are passed on to higher levels of government, given to private groups or charities, or ignored.

According to political scientists Oliver P. Williams and Charles R. Adrian, it is contrary to the professional orientation of manager governments to be content with cartetaker policies:

[10] Oliver P. Williams, "A Typology for Comparative Local Government," *Midwest Review of Political Science*, 5 (May 1961), 150–64.

It is against his [the manager's] professional code of ethics to let the city's physical plant deteriorate for the sake of low taxes. The clash between the manager plan and care-taker government does not stop with professional values however. Career advancements for managers are based upon concrete achievements, not simply satisfied councilmen.[11]

There is some evidence that urban renewal policies may be effected by manager versus mayor government. Political scientist George S. Duggar reports that mayor cities were quicker to respond to the lure of federal money than manager cities and got a faster start on their urban renewal programs.[12] This finding would testify to the political awareness of mayors. On the other hand, Duggar reports that once urban renewal programs were begun, manager cities experienced slightly greater program achievement than mayor cities. Duggar admits that population size is a more influential variable in urban renewal achievement than governmental structure: greater achievement is associated with greater size. However, the author concludes that governmental structure does have some independent effect on urban renewal policies.

The structure of city governments has been found to be related to outcomes in water fluoridation battles. In a comparative study of several hundred cities, sociologists Robert L. Crain and Donald B. Rosenthal found that fluoridation has a better chance of consideration and adoption in cities having a strong executive (a manager or a strong partisan mayor) and a relatively low level of direct citizen participation.[13] Broad population participation, particularly in the absence of strong executive leadership, frequently spelled defeat for fluoridation. Moreover, a mayor's public endorsement is closely correlated with fluoridation adoption, even when a referendum is held. Another structural variable—partisanship— is also related to fluoridation outcomes. In both mayor and manager cities, partisan electoral systems are marked by the largest proportion of adoptions of fluoridation laws by city councils.

REFORM AND PUBLIC POLICY

What are the policy consequences of reform government? In a very important study of taxing and spending in 200 American cities with populations of 50,000 or more, political scientists Robert L. Lineberry

---

[11] Oliver P. Williams and Charles R. Adrian, *Four Cities* (Philadelphia: University of Pennsylvania Press, 1963), p. 280.

[12] George S. Duggar, "The Relation of Local Government Structure to Urban Renewal," *Law and Contemporary Problem* (Winter 1961), pp. 55–65.

[13] Robert L. Crain and Donald B. Rosenthal, "Structure and Values in Local Political Systems: The Case of Fluoridation Decisions," *Journal of Politics,* 28 (February 1966), 169–95.

and Edmund P. Fowler found that reformed cities tended to tax and spend *less* than unreformed cities.[14] Cities with manager governments and at-large council constituencies were *less* willing to spend money for public purposes than cities with mayor-council governments and ward constituencies. (However, cities with partisan elections did not actually spend any more than cities with nonpartisan elections.) In short, reformism *does* save tax money.

Lineberry and Fowler also found that environmental variables had an important impact on tax and spending policies. For example they concluded that:

1. The more middle class the city, measured by income, education, and occupation, the lower the general tax and spending levels.
2. The greater the home ownership in a city, the lower the tax and spending levels.
3. The larger the percentage of religious and ethnic minorities in the population, the higher the city's taxes and expenditures.

What turned out to be an even more important finding in the Lineberry and Fowler study was the difference in *responsiveness* of the two kinds of city governments—reformed and unreformed—to the socioeconomic composition of their populations. Reformed cities (cities with manager governments, at-large constituencies, and nonpartisan elections) appeared to be unresponsive in their tax and spending policies to differences in income, educational, occupational, religious, and ethnic characteristics of their populations. In contrast, unreformed cities (cities with mayor-council governments, ward constituencies, and partisan elections) reflected class, racial, and religious composition in their taxing and spending decisions.

Reformism tends to reduce the importance of class, home ownership, ethnicity, and religion in city politics. It tends to minimize the role that social conflicts play in public decision making. In contrast, mayor-council governments, ward constituencies, and partisan elections permit social cleavages to be reflected in city politics and public policy to be responsive to socioeconomic factors. These findings suggest that reformed cities have gone a long way toward accomplishing the reformist goal—that is, "to immunize city governments from 'artificial' social cleavages—race, religion, ethnicity, and so on." Thus, political institutions seem to play an important role in policy formation

. . . a role substantially independent of a city's demography. . . . Nonpartisan elections, at-large constituencies, and manager governments are

[14] Robert L. Lineberry and Edmund P. Fowler, "Reformism and Public Policy in Cities," *American Political Science Review*, 61 (September 1967), 701–16.

associated with a lessened responsiveness of cities to the enduring conflicts of political life.[15]

As Table 8-1 shows, the strength of the correlation between environment and taxing and spending, by categories of reform, decreases regularly with an increase in reform government.

Table 8-1 *Environmental Characteristics and Tax and Spending Policy in Reformed and Unreformed Cities*

RELATIONSHIPS BETWEEN	CORRELATIONS BETWEEN ENVIRONMENTAL CHARACTERISTICS AND TAXING AND SPENDING IN:	
	Reformed Cities	**Unreformed Cities**
Taxes and		
Ethnicity	.62	.34
Private school attendance	.40	.25
Home ownership	−.70	−.44
Education	−.55	−.13
Expenditures and		
Ethnicity	.51	.05
Private school attendance	.46	.08
Home ownership	−.67	−.38
Education	−.49	−.37

Source: Adapted from figures in Robert L. Lineberry and Edmund P. Fowler, "Reformism and Public Policy in American Cities," *American Political Science Review,* 61 (September 1967), 701–16.

SUMMARY

The urban crisis is not only, or even primarily, a problem of governmental organization or administration. The institutional approach is misleading to the extent that it implies that reforming governmental institutions in the metropolis can solve problems of urban blight, inadequate housing, crime and delinquency, poverty and poor health, pollution, racial tension, and other urban ills. Yet institutional arrangements are linked to the nature of the urban environment and even to the content of urban policy. Let us summarize our ideas about these linkages:

1. Federal housing and urban development policy centers about direct federal-to-city grants-in-aid for public housing, urban renewal, community facilities and related programs, together with mortgage insurance programs admin-

[15] *Ibid.,* p. 715.

istered by the federal government itself. These programs are organized and administered separately from federal grants programs in education, welfare, economic opportunity, and transportation. These programs have emphasized the physical aspects of urban life.

2. Frequently federal programs in urban areas have worked at cross-purposes, reflecting organizational fragmentation. However, competing goals and conflicting policies reflect underlying conflicts over urban affairs rather than merely organizational problems.

3. The question of federal control versus state or local autonomy in urban policy raises broad questions of centralization and decentralization in the American federal system.

4. The municipal reform movement assumed that structural changes in city government would lead to a progressive middle-class policy orientation. The movement supported the city-manager form of government, nonpartisan elections, and at-large constituencies, in addition to other structural reforms.

5. The success of the reform movement in achieving these structural reforms is associated with characteristics of the urban environment: reformed cities are more likely to be middle-sized cities, with native-born white populations and rapid population growth.

6. Reformed structural characteristics of government do have some independent effect on urban policy, although the effect of environmental variables is generally greater. The policies of reformed, manager governments are likely to be directed toward promoting economic growth and providing life's amenities rather than resolving community conflict. Reformed city governments tax and spend less than unreformed governments.

7. There is some evidence that reformed governments are less responsive in policy matters to the characteristics of their populations. In contrast, the policies of unreformed cities (cities with mayor-council governments, ward constituencies, and partisan elections) tended to reflect the class, racial, and ethnic composition of their populations.

8. The extent of metropolitan fragmentation was not related to any observable policy dimensions; fragmentation does not increase or decrease per capita government spending for education, highways, welfare, health, police, fire, sanitation, housing, or other urban services.

BIBLIOGRAPHY

BANFIELD, EDWARD C., *The Unheavenly City*. Boston: Little, Brown, 1970.

BANFIELD, EDWARD C., and JAMES Q. WILSON, *City Politics*. Cambridge: Harvard University Press, 1963.

BOLLENS, JOHN C., and HENRY J. SCHMANDT, *The Metropolis*, 2nd ed. New York: Harper & Row, 1970.

HAWKINS, BRETT W., *Politics and Urban Policies*. New York: Bobbs-Merrill, 1971.

WOLMAN, HAROLD, *Politics of Federal Housing*. New York: Dodd, Mead, 1971.

Marching for surplus food and job action. UPI Photo

9 PRIORITIES AND PRICE TAGS:

dimensions
of institutional activity

DIMENSIONS OF GOVERNMENT SPENDING

Governments do many things that cannot be measured in dollars. Nevertheless, government expenditures are the best available measure of the overall dimensions of government activity. There are few public policies that do not require an expenditure of funds. Budgets represent government policies with price tags attached.

The expenditures of all governments in the United States—federal, state, and local—grew from 1.7 billion in 1902 to over 370 billion in 1972 (see Table 9-1). A great deal of the increase in government activity can be attributed to growth in the nation's population. And a great deal of the increase in dollar amounts spent by government is exaggerated by the diminishing value of the dollar—that is, by inflation. If we are to measure the growth of government activity accurately, we must examine government expenditures *per person*, and do so in *constant dollars*. This enables us to view past and present government activity in relation to the size of the population and the value of the dollar. It turns out that *per capita* expenditures of all governments *in constant dollars* increased from $84 to over $1,200 from 1902 to 1972. Thus, we note that the increase in government spending cannot be attributed merely to increases in population or the devaluation of the dollar; government activity has grown much faster than both the population and inflation.

An even more important yardstick of the growth of government

195

Table 9-1 *Growth in Population, Wealth, and Government Activities Over Seven Decades*

	Population Millions	GNP Billions	GNP Per Capita Constant Dollars	ALL GOVERNMENT SPENDING Billions	ALL GOVERNMENT SPENDING Per Capita Constant Dollars	ALL GOVERNMENT SPENDING Percent of GNP
1902	79.2	21.6	1,089	1.7	84	7.7
1913	97.2	39.1	1,308	3.2	107	8.2
1922	110.1	74.0	1,380	9.3	174	12.5
1927	119.0	96.0	1,637	11.2	190	11.6
1932	124.9	58.5	1,196	12.4	254	21.3
1936	128.2	82.7	1,561	16.8	316	20.8
1940	132.6	100.6	1,782	20.4	353	20.3
1944	138.9	211.4	2,747	109.9	1,429	52.0
1946	141.9	210.7	2,288	79.7	866	37.8
1950	152.3	284.6	2,401	70.3	593	24.7
1952	157.6	347.0	2,609	99.8	751	28.8
1955	165.9	397.5	2,737	110.7	762	27.9
1960	180.7	502.6	2,815	151.3	848	30.1
1962	186.6	554.9	2,943	175.8	933	31.7
1967	199.1	789.7	3,380	257.8	1,102	32.6
1970	203.2	959.6	3,557	312.1	1,156	32.5
1972	208.2	1,155.0	3,795	371.6	1,222	32.2

Source: U.S. Bureau of the Census, *Historical Statistics on Governmental Finances and Employment* (Washington, D.C.: Government Printing Office, 1967); updating from U.S. Bureau of the Census, *Statistical Abstract of the United States.*

activity is found in the relationship of government expenditures to the Gross National Product (GNP). The GNP is the dollar sum of all goods and services produced in the nation's economy. The growth of the GNP in the twentieth century reflects the expansion of the nation's economy: the GNP in dollar amounts grew from 21.6 billion dollars to over a trillion dollars in the early 1970s. Part of this growth, of course, was attributed to inflation and a growing population. But the GNP also increased in *per capital constant dollars* by more than 300 percent. Thus, the GNP has also grown much faster than the population, and much faster than inflation.

Government expenditures in relation to the Gross National Product have risen, somewhat bumpily, from 7.7 percent in 1902 to over 30 percent in the 1970s. If public programs financed by the government had grown at the same rate as private economic activities, this percentage figure would have remained at the same level over the years. But government activity over the long run has grown even *faster* than private enterprise. By any yardstick whatsoever, then, we find the growth of government activity in America has been substantial. Government activity now accounts for about one-third of all economic activity in the nation.

WARS, DEPRESSIONS, AND GOVERNMENT ACTIVITY

What accounts for the growth of government activity? Years ago, a European economist, Adolph Wagner, set forth a "law of increasing state activity" roughly to the effect that government activity increased faster than economic output in all developing societies.[1] He attributed his law to a variety of factors: increasing regulatory services required to control a more specialized, complex economy; increasing involvement of government in economic enterprise; increasing demands in a developed society for social services such as education, welfare, public health, etc. Thus the "law of increasing state activity" portrayed growth in government activity as an inevitable accompaniment of a developing society.

But the American experience raises serious doubts about the "law of increasing state activity." Although it is true that governmental activity has grown in relation to the economy over the last seven decades, this growth has occurred in spurts during crisis periods rather than as a steady acceleration. Government expenditures in relation to the GNP have *not* increased predictably as if governed by a "law"; instead they have remained stable over periods of time and then spurted upward in response to wars and depressions.

Wars and severe depressions bring about significant increases in government activity. National emergencies provide the opportunity for governments to increase the scope and magnitude of their activities, both in national defense and domestic service. When an emergency ends, government activities do not decline to their old levels. Post-crisis expenditures level out on a higher plateau than precrisis expenditures. Thus, national emergencies provide the occasion for government activities to rise to successively higher plateaus (see Figure 9-1). Government expenditures have grown through a series of leaps associated with international crises, principally wars, and, to a lesser extent, in the Depression.

Scholars have summarized the American experience as follows:

> Whether the rule of "normal peacetime" stability would continue over large periods without crisis is unknown; unfortunately, such periods have

---

[1] Adolph Wagner's major work is *Grundlegung der politischen oekonomie* (Leipzig, 1893). This work is discussed at length in Alan T. Peacock and Jack Wiseman, *The Growth of Public Expenditures in the United Kingdom* (Princeton: Princeton University Press, 1961).

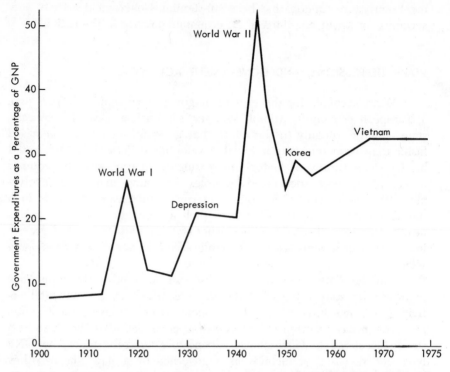

Fig. 9-1 *Government Expenditures as a Percentage of the Gross National Product*

in the past been of relatively short duration. The experience does, however, suggest a hypothesis that, over the short run at least, the political pressures in this democratic society are such as to prevent any substantial change in the total levels of expenditures upward or downward in relation to the economy as a whole. And it appears probable that the fixing of expenditure levels is a consequence of the stickiness of revenues, principally taxes, rather than of the shifting of expenditure needs. Crises, on the other hand, "unfreeze" revenue levels, permit them to rise and then, once the crises are past, they again congeal.

In sum, it is clear that expenditures of American governments have increased substantially by every measure, but that these increases have occurred spasmodically with the occurrences of international and domestic crises.[2]

Defense spending rises sharply during war, then declines after hostilities. During periods of peace, defense spending gradually declines

[2] Frederick C. Mosher and Orville F. Poland, *The Costs of American Governments* (New York: Dodd, Mead, 1964), pp. 28–29.

as a proportion of the GNP. In contrast, *domestic* spending declines during wartime. During peacetime periods it tends to rise.

Table 9-2 *Defense and Domestic Spending of Federal, State, and Local Governments as a Percentage of GNP*

	ALL GOVERNMENT SPENDING	DEFENSE [1]	DOMESTIC [2]	FEDERAL [3]	STATE-LOCAL
1902	7.7	1.6	6.1	2.6	5.1
1913	8.2	1.2	7.0	2.5	5.7
1922	12.5	3.2	9.3	5.0	7.5
1927	11.6	2.1	9.5	3.6	8.0
1932	21.3	3.8	17.4	7.1	14.2
1936	20.8	2.4	17.4	10.2	10,6
1940	20.3	2.5	17.8	9.8	10.5
1944	52.0	41.6	10.4	47.2	4.8
1946	37.8	27.0	10.8	31.7	6.1
1950	24.7	6.8	17.9	16.4	8.3
1955	27.9	11.2	16.7	18.1	9.8
1960	30.1	9.9	20.2	18.6	11.5
1965	31.7	8.2	23.5	18.1	13.6
1970	32.5	8.8	23.7	20.6	11.9
1975	32.9	6.3	26.6	20.9	12.0 (est.)

[1] Defense and international relations.
[2] All other, including social insurance.
[3] Including social insurance.
Source: *The Budget of the United States Government 1975* and past volumes of the *Statistical Abstract of the United States.*

These trends indicate that defense and domestic spending move in different patterns, and sometimes compensate for each other. During World War II *defense* spending grew to over 40 percent of the entire economic product of the nation. In contrast, during World War II *domestic* spending dropped to 10 percent of the GNP, from highs of nearly 18 percent during the Depression. After World War II, domestic spending gradually regained momentum, with a brief drop-off during the Korean War. War tends to displace domestic spending with defense spending during the period of hostilities. But war also conditions citizens to tolerate major increases in government activity, and thus, after the war, government activity remains on a higher plateau than before the war. Domestic spending gradually displaces defense spending during peacetime periods.

During the Vietnam War, a deliberate effort was made by the Johnson and Nixon administrations to prevent the war from becoming a

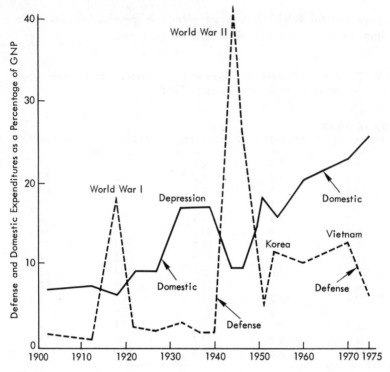

Fig. 9-2 *Defense and Domestic Expenditures as a Percentage of the Gross National Product*

drain on domestic programs. National policy stressed "guns *and* butter." The effort was successful. Domestic expenditures did *not* decline as percentage of the GNP, as had been the case in previous wars. Domestic expenditures continued to rise even in relation to the economy.

IDENTIFYING NATIONAL PRIORITIES

A great deal of political rhetoric centers about national "priorities." The problem is to separate rhetoric from reality. We must distinguish between what is *said* to be a national priority, from what is actually given priority in the allocation of national resources. To identify actual priorities, we have determined the percentage of national income devoted to various government activities. The results are summarized in Table 9-3. Obviously all private needs are given priority over all public needs, because total public expenditures of federal, state, and national governments are only about one-third of the Gross National Product. This is

Table 9-3 *Government Expenditures by Function in Relation to Gross National Product*

FEDERAL, STATE, & LOCAL GOVERNMENT EXPENDITURES	PERCENTS OF GROSS NATIONAL PRODUCT DEVOTED TO GOVERNMENT ACTIVITY BY FUNCTION					
	1950	**1955**	**1960**	**1968**	**1970**	**1975 est.**
Total	24.7	27.8	30.0	32.7	32.5	32.9
National Defense and International Relations	6.5	10.9	9.4	9.6	8.8	6.3
Space Research	0.0	0.0	0.1	0.5	0.3	.2
Postal Service	0.8	0.7	0.7	0.8	0.8	.7
Education	3.4	3.2	3.9	5.0	5.5	5.3
Higher Education	0.4	0.4	0.6	1.2	1.3	1.3
Elementary and Secondary	2.1	2.5	3.0	3.4	3.8	3.6
Other	0.9	0.3	0.2	0.5	0.4	0.4
Highways	1.4	1.6	1.9	1.7	1.7	1.5
Public Welfare	1.1	0.8	0.9	1.3	1.8	2.0
Hospitals	0.7	0.7	0.8	0.9	1.0	1.0
Health	0.2	0.2	0.2	0.3	0.4	0.5
Police	0.3	0.4	0.4	0.4	0.5	0.5
Fire	0.2	0.2	0.2	0.2	0.2	0.2
Sanitation	0.3	0.3	0.3	0.3	0.3	0.3
Natural Resources	1.8	1.6	1.7	1.1	1.1	1.1
Parks and Recreation	0.1	0.1	0.1	0.2	0.2	0.2
Housing and Urban Renewal	0.2	0.2	0.2	0.3	0.3	0.3
Veterans Services	1.2	0.8	0.8	0.5	0.5	0.5
Financial Administration				0.3	0.3	0.3
General Control	0.6	0.5	0.6	0.3	0.3	0.3
Interest	1.7	1.4	1.8	1.7	1.8	1.8
Other	1.1	1.1	1.4	1.7	1.7	1.6
Social Security	2.4	2.3	2.3	4.4	4.8	5.3

what one might reasonably expect in a private-enterprise, capitalist society.

The preference for private over public enterprise is not merely a myth. Over two-thirds of the GNP originates in the private sector. Traditionally expenditures in the *private* sector—whether for tobacco, alcohol, soda pop, automobiles, or housing—have been looked upon favorably in terms of economic growth. But expenditures in the *public* sector are generally supposed to be as low as possible. Most Americans approve of frugality in government spending, budgetary "austerity," and the elimination of "frills"; they prefer a government as small and as close to the people as possible.

Until recently, national defense was the nation's highest priority in public spending. But today "income security"—the combination of social security, welfare, and related social services—is the nation's largest public undertaking. It was during the Nixon Administration that income security overtook defense as the nation's top priority budget item. Defense spending has gradually declined as a proportion of the GNP and as a proportion of total government spending. The expansion of social security coverage and benefits is largely responsible for the growth of "income security" spending. Social security, including Medicare, is the fastest-growing large item of public spending. Welfare costs are also rising, not only in absolute dollars but also as a percentage of the GNP. Today welfare costs are nearly 2 percent of the GNP.

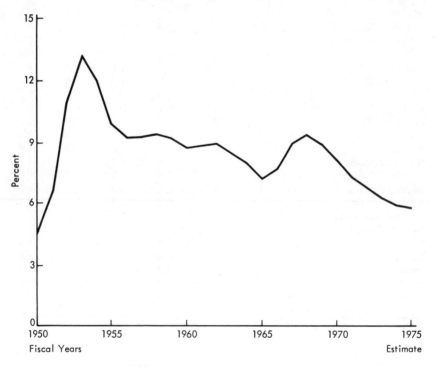

Fig. 9-3 *Defense Outlays as a Percent of GNP*

Source: The Budget of the United States Government, 1975

Education is the nation's third largest public undertaking. Although education is a very small proportion of the federal government's budget, it is the largest spending item of state and local governments. Over 5 percent of the GNP is devoted to education.

Note that some items that are the object of a great deal of political rhetoric actually receive little priority in the allocation of national re-

Jeeps stand in field in Philadelphia awaiting shipment overseas. Wide World Photos

sources. Despite concerns over the quality of urban life, less than three-tenths of 1 percent of the GNP is devoted to government housing and urban renewal efforts. Regarding the popular issue of environmental control, it is interesting to note that only two-tenths of 1 percent of GNP is devoted to parks and recreation and 1.3 percent to natural resources (and this latter category is a very broad one including many expenditures that do not contribute to the quality of the environment).

If we merge broad categories of government spending and again combine the spending of federal, state, and local government, we observe that the major objects of government spending are social security, health, and welfare; defense, veterans, and space; education; interest; general government; and highways and transportation (see Figure 9-4).

PUBLIC POLICY AND THE FEDERAL SYSTEM

At the beginning of the twentieth century, most government activity was carried on at the *local* level. Table 9-4 reveals that local governments once made about 59 percent of all government expenditures, compared to 35 percent for the federal government and 6 percent for state governments. Yet by the 1970s centralization in the American federal system had proceeded to the point where local governments were spending only 22 percent of all government expenditures, compared to 65 percent for the federal government and 13 percent for state governments.

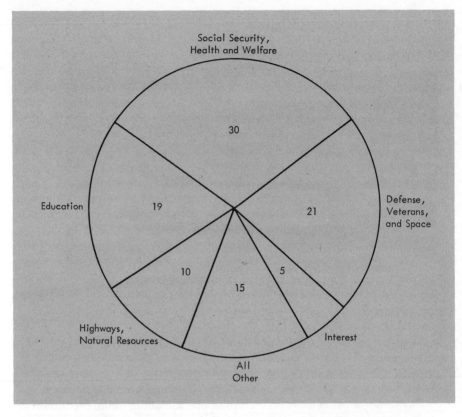

Fig. 9-4 *Total Government Spending by Major Category (Figures Show Percentage of Total)*

Wars and the Depression had a great deal to do with the shift away from local reliance on American government. During national emergencies, both foreign and domestic, Americans have turned to the federal government for help. After the emergency, federal activity decreases somewhat in relation to state and local activity, but federal activity never returns to the precrisis level. Thus, during World War I and World War II, and the Korean and Vietnamese Wars, the federal government increased its percentage of total government activity, while local and state government percentages declined. Because the federal government has the primary responsibility for national defense, we would expect this to occur during wartime. But the federal government also expands its activities in response to domestic crisis—it was during the 1930s that federal expenditures first surpassed those of all local governments.

Although foreign and domestic crises have brought about increasing centralization in American government, we noted that expanded federal

Table 9-4 *A Comparison of the Expenditures of Federal, State, and Local Governments Over Seven Decades*

PERCENTAGES OF TOTAL GENERAL EXPENDITURES [3]

	Federal [1]	State [2]	Local [2]
1902	35%	6%	59%
1913	31	9	60
1922	40	11	49
1927	31	13	56
1932	34	16	50
1936	50	14	36
1940	48	15	37
1944	91	3	7
1946	82	6	12
1948	64	13	23
1950	64	12	24
1952	71	9	20
1955	66	11	23
1960	62	**13**	25
1962	63	12	25
1967	65	12	23
1970	66	12	22
1972	65	13	22

[1] Figures include social security and trust fund expenditures.
[2] State payments to local governments are shown as local government expenditures; federal grants-in-aid are shown as federal expenditures.
[3] Figures may not total correctly because of rounding.

activity has not come at the expense of state and local activity. Federal power and state-local power are not at the opposite ends of a seesaw; the growth of federal power has not necessarily curtailed the power of states and localities. National activity has expanded in the twentieth century but so has the activity of state and local governments.

The extent of centralization of government activity in the American federal system varies widely according to policy area (see Table 9-5). In the fields of national defense, space research, and postal service, the federal government assumes almost exclusive responsibility. In all other fields state and local governments share responsibility and costs with the federal government. State and local governments assume the major share of the costs of education, highways, health and hospitals, sanitation, and fire and police protection. Welfare costs are being shifted to the federal government. The federal government assumes the major share of the costs of natural resource development and social security.

Over the years, the federal government has steadily increased its share of responsibility in every important policy area of American

Table 9-5 *Federal and State-Local Shares of Expenditures by Policy Areas, 1927–1967*

	1927		1938		1967		1972	
	Fed-eral [1]	State and Local	Fed-eral [1]	State and Local	Fed-eral [1]	State and Local	Fed-eral [1]	State and Local
National Defense	100	0	100	0	100	0	100	0
Space Research	100	0	100	0	100	0	100	0
Postal Service	100	0	100	0	100	0	100	0
Education	1	99	6	94	10	90	12	88
Highways	1	99	23	77	29	71	29	71
Welfare	6	94	13	87	58	42	59	41
Health and Hospitals	18	82	19	81	33	67	30	70
Natural Resources	31	69	81	19	80	20	82	18

[1] Federal grants-in-aid are shown as federal expenditures.

government (see Figure 9-5). Many feel that the date 1913, when the Sixteenth Amendment gave the federal government the power to tax-incomes directly, was the beginning of a new era in American federalism. Congress had been given the power to tax and spend for the general welfare in Article I of the Constitution. But the Sixteenth Amendment helped to shift the balance of financial power from the states to Washington when it gave Congress the power to tax the incomes of corporations and individuals on a progressive basis. The income tax gave the federal government the power to raise large sums of money, which it proceeded to spend for the general welfare as well as for defense. It is not coincidence that the first major grant-in-aid programs (agricultural extension in 1914, highways in 1916, vocational education in 1917, and public health in 1918) all came shortly after the inauguration of the federal income tax.

The federal "grant-in-aid" has become the principle instrument for the increased involvement of the federal government in domestic policy areas. The great depression of the 1930s put pressure on the national government to use its tax and spending powers in a wide variety of areas formerly reserved to states and communities. The federal government initiated grant-in-aid programs to states and communities for public assistance, unemployment compensation, employment services, public housing, urban renewal, and so on; it also expanded federal grants-in-aid programs in highways, vocational education, and rehabilitation. The inadequacy of state and local revenue systems to meet the financial crises

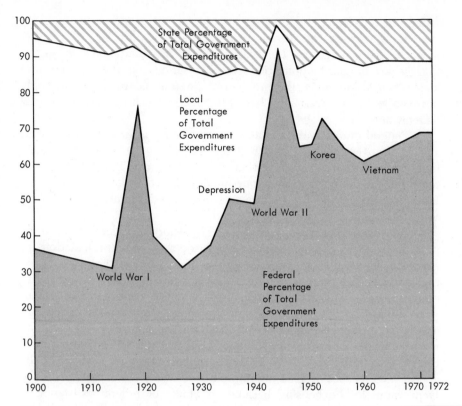

Fig. 9-5 *Federal, State, and Local Proportions of Total Governmental Expenditures*

created by the Depression contributed significantly to the development of cooperative federalism. States and communities called upon the superior taxing powers of the national government to assist them in many fields in which the federal government had not previously involved itself.

FEDERAL GRANTS-IN-AID

Today grant-in-aid programs are the single most important source of federal influence over state and local affairs. Approximately one-sixth of all state and local government revenues are from federal grants. This money is paid out through a staggering number and variety of programs. There are probably 500 different federal grant programs in existence today. So numerous and diverse are federal aid programs that a substantial information gap surrounds the availability, purpose, and requirements of these programs. Learning about their availability and mastering the art of grant application places a serious burden on state and local officials. Moreover, the problem of program coordination, not only between levels of government but also among federal agencies, is a truly difficult one.

Federal grants are available in nearly every major category of state and local government activity. Federal grants may be obtained to assist in everything from the celebration of the American Revolution Bicentennial to the drainage of abandoned mines, riot control, and school milk. However, federal aid for welfare and highways accounts for over two-thirds of total federal aid money.

Ira Sharkansky has observed that the history of federal grant-in-aid programs reflects in microcosm the contemporary policy orientations of American governments.[3] Prior to World War I, federal grants reflected the concerns of a rural, agricultural society—the Smith-Level Act of 1914 establishing agricultural extension programs; the Smith-Hughes Act of 1917 supporting vocational education with an emphasis on agriculture and home economics; and the early Federal Aid Highway Act designed to assist in the construction of farm-to-market, rural roads. In the 1930s federal grant programs, particularly the public assistance sections of the Social Security Act of 1935, attempted to alleviate the hardships of the Depression. Public housing became an object of federal assistance in the Housing Act of 1937. In the 1940s and 1950s, federal aid programs assumed labels that made them appear to be part of the nation's defense effort, e.g., the National Defense Highway Act of 1956; the National Defense Education Act of 1957. In the 1960s the emphasis of grant-in-aid legislation was on poverty, education, and urban affairs: the Elementary and Secondary Education Act of 1965 with aid for "poverty impacted" schools; the Economic Opportunity Act of 1964 with federal money to assist communities in fighting poverty; and the Model Cities Program in 1966. The Nixon Administration developed the notion of general revenue sharing—federal financial contributions to state and local governments with no strings attached—as a means of revitalizing state and local government and reducing bureaucratic control over grant programs.

Not only have federal grants-in-aid to the states expanded rapidly in terms of the numbers of programs and the dollar amounts involved,

---

[3] Ira Sharkansky, *The Politics of Taxing and Spending* (New York: Bobbs-Merrill, 1969), pp. 155–56.

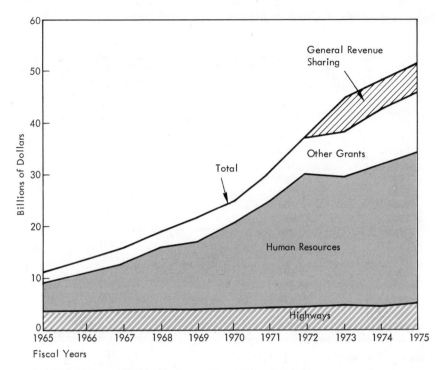

Fig. 9-6 *Federal Aid to State and Local Governments*

but states and communities have also come to *rely* on the national government for an ever-increasing share of their total revenues (see Table 9-6). Prior to the New Deal, federal grants amounted to only 2 or 3 percent of total state-local revenue. The New Deal itself, in spite of all of its innovations in federal aid programs, raised this proportion only to 7 or 8 percent. State-local reliance on federal aid has continued to increase over the last two decades, from 8 percent over total state-local revenues in 1946 to over 22 percent today. More than one-third of *state* revenues are derived from federal sources. Thus, no matter how it is measured—increased numbers of programs, increased dollar amounts, increased reliance by states and communities—federal aid has grown into a major influence over state and local governmental activity.

There are several reasons for this growth of federal aid.[4] First of

[4] See George F. Break, *Intergovernmental Fiscal Relations in the United States* (Washington, D.C.: Brookings Institution, 1967); Deil S. Wright, *Federal Grants-in-Aid: Perspectives and Alternatives* (Washington, D.C.: American Enterprise Institute, 1968).

Table 9-6 *Federal Grants-in-Aid and State-Local Finances*

	TOTAL FEDERAL GRANTS-IN-AID IN MILLIONS OF DOLLARS	FEDERAL GRANTS AS A PERCENTAGE OF STATE-LOCAL REVENUE
1902	7	*
1913	12	*
1922	118	2.1%
1927	123	1.6
1932	232	2.9
1938	800	7.2
1940	945	8.1
1944	954	6.8
1948	1,861	8.6
1950	2,486	9.7
1955	3,131	8.3
1960	6,974	11.6
1962	7,871	11.3
1967	15,366	14.0
1970	25,029	18.0
1972	35,940	21.3
1975	51,732	22.4

* Less than 1 percent.

all, these grants permit the federal government to single out and support those state and local government services in which it has a particular interest. Grants permit the national government to set national goals and priorities in all levels of government without formally altering the federal structure. Thus, as problems of public assistance, urban renewal, highway construction, education, poverty, and so on acquire national significance, they can be dealt with by the application of national resources.

Second, the grant-in-aid system helps to overcome the inadequacies of state-local revenue resources. Contrary to the political rhetoric charging the states with fiscal conservatism, the states have actually demonstrated a great deal of fiscal courage, effort, and ingenuity in trying to cope with money problems. In the last two decades state-local expenditures have risen at a faster *rate* than have federal expenditures. These fiscal efforts have meant increased income or sales tax rates in nearly every state in the past ten years as well as increased liquor and gasoline tax rates. Yet in spite of these near Herculean efforts by states, their fiscal problems continue to multiply.

States and communities must raise revenues and at the same time carry on interstate and interlocal competition for industry and wealth. Although the influence of tax considerations on industrial locations decisions may be overstated by most lawmakers, this overstatement itself is part of the political lore at statehouses and courthouses that operates to impede revenue raising. Not only do competitive considerations inhibit state-local taxing efforts but they also tend to push them in regressive directions.

Debates over finances in state capitals invariably include references to the "preemption" of income taxes by the national government. There are no compelling economic reasons for the argument that the federal income tax preempts this source of revenue for the states (particularly because the federal government permits the deduction of state income taxes from total taxable income). Nonetheless, in the minds of most state lawmakers and probably in the minds of their constituents as well, there is the belief that the federal government already takes all the income taxes they wish to pay. This means states are stuck with sales taxes and localities with property taxes, and, in contrast to income taxes, these taxes respond sluggishly to rises in the GNP.

Another argument in behalf of federal grants-in-aid centers about the greater progressivity of the federal tax structure. If a particular government program is funded through state and local taxes, it is funded on a tax structure that is regressive or only mildly progressive; but if it is funded out of federal taxes, it is funded on a more progressive basis. This may help to explain the "liberal" predisposition for federal financial involvement.

Finally, grants-in-aid provide an opportunity for the national government to insure a uniform level of public service throughout the nation as a minimum or foundation program. For example, federal grants-in-aid to help achieve equality in educational opportunity in all parts of the nation, or help to insure a minimum level of existence for the poverty-stricken regardless of where they live.[5] This aspect of federal policy as-

---

[5] The meaning of "equalization" in federal policy is more complex than it appears at first glance. Basically, equalization means some policy recognition of differences in the states' relative capacities to raise funds from their own resources, in order to achieve more uniform program standards throughout the nation. This means, first of all, equal federal grants per unit of need, whether the unit of need is defined as pupils, poverty-stricken families, ill-housed families, medically indigent, aged, etc. But exclusive reliance upon equal allocations per unit of need is likely to mean unequal program expenditures when state-local matching funds are required. This is because a grant offering Mis-

sumes that in some parts of the nation, state and local governments are unable, or perhaps unwilling to devote their resources to raising public service levels to minimum national standards.

Whenever the national government contributes financially to state or local programs, state and local officials have less freedom of choice than they would have without federal aid. They must adhere to federal standards or "guidelines," which invariably accompany federal grants-in-aid, if they are to receive their federal money. The national government gives money to states and communities only if they are willing to meet conditions specified by Congress. Often Congress delegates to federal agencies the power to establish the "conditions" that are attached to grants.

No state is required to accept a federal grant-in-aid. In other words, states are not required to meet federal standards or guidelines that are set forth as conditions for federal aid because they have the alternative of rejecting the federal money—and they have sometimes done so. But it is very difficult for states and communities to resist the pressure to accept federal money.

In short, through the power to tax and spend for the general welfare, and through "conditions" attached to federal grants-in-aid, the national government has come to exercise great powers in many areas originally "reserved" to the states—highways, welfare, education, housing, natural resources, employment, health and so on. Of course federal grants-in-aid have enabled many states and communities to provide necessary and desirable services that they could not have afforded otherwise. Federal guidelines have often improved the standard of administration, personnel policies, and fiscal practices in states and communities. More importantly, federal guidelines have helped to insure that states and communities will not engage in racial discrimination in federally aided programs.

---

sissippi $2 per person that has to be matched on a 50-50 basis requires a larger state tax effort relative to personal income from Mississippi citizens than a similar $2 per person grant offered to New York's wealthier citizens. In view of unequal tax resources of the state, grants must take into account both program needs and fiscal resources. Equalization policy must also include a deliberate varying of the amount of federal funds directly with program needs and inversely with fiscal resources. Finally, equalization policy must also consider the minimum program level desired; then larger amounts of federal funds must go in support of minimum program levels and lesser amounts in support of programs exceeding minimum levels.

REVENUE SHARING: A NEW DIRECTION

IN FEDERALISM

Over the years, power in the American federal system has flowed toward Washington, largely because the national government has the superior taxing powers and therefore the money to deal more effectively with the nation's domestic problems. But the many dissatisfactions with the conditional grant-in-aid system led to appeals for a new approach to federal financial assistance to state and local governments—unrestricted federal grants with no strings attached. For many years Congress debated the idea of "revenue sharing"—the turnover of federal tax dollars to state and local governments for use as they see fit. The idea of revenue sharing assumes that the federal government is better at *collecting* revenue than state or local governments, but state and local governments are better at *spending* it. Consequently, revenue sharing was said to combine the best features of each level of government. More importantly, revenue sharing promised to reverse the flow of money and power to Washington, to end excessive red tape, and to revitalize state and local governments.

The State and Local Fiscal Assistance Act of 1972 is a true landmark in American federalism. This Act establishes general revenue sharing and provides for the distribution of over $5 billion per year of federal monies to states and communities with very few restrictions on its use. This Act was strongly supported by state and local government officials. Two-thirds of these shared revenues go to local governments and one-third to state governments. The formula for allocation to states and cities is based on three factors: population, tax effort, and the income level of the population. These revenues may be used for police and fire protection, sewage and garbage disposal, pollution abatement, transportation, physical facilities, parks and recreation, and many other recognized state-local functions; but the Act denied use of these funds for welfare or education, because these functions were already heavily supported with federal monies. Revenue sharing under this Act does *not* replace any existing grant-in-aid programs, but does provide states and communities with new unrestricted revenues.

Revenue sharing promises to reverse the trend toward centralization of power in Washington. Of course, it still is too early to judge whether revenue sharing will accomplish such a bold objective. Congress will always be under pressure to attach restrictions to the use of any money coming out of the federal treasury. But revenue sharing may mark the beginning of a new phase of American federalism—one in which states and communities acquire new resources and new power.

SOME CONCLUSIONS ABOUT GOVERNMENT SPENDING

Government expenditures provide an overview of American public policy. Our analysis of government spending in this century suggests the following general propositions:

1. Government activity has grown in relation both to the size of the population and to the economy. Government activity now accounts for about one-third of all economic activity in the United States.

2. Government expenditures as a proportion of all economic activity in the nation spurt upward in response to wars and depressions. When these crises subside, government expenditures associated with them decline somewhat, but stabilize at levels higher than before the crisis.

3. War conditions citizens to tolerate major increases in government activity. During war, government domestic spending declines; but after a war, domestic spending displaces defense spending and achieves a higher plateau than before the war.

4. Private expenditures exceed public expenditures in the United States by a two-to-one margin. The balance in favor of the private sector of American society reflects a preference for private over public enterprise.

5. Among public expenditures, national income security (social security, welfare, and social services) takes highest priority. In recent years national defense spending has declined as a percentage of the GNP. Education is the nation's third largest public undertaking.

6. Wars and depressions have helped to shift responsibilities from local and state governments to the national government. However, national power and state-local power are not at opposite ends of a seesaw; national activity has expanded rapidly in the twentieth century, but so has the activity of state and local governments.

7. The national government assumes exclusive responsibility for national defense and related activity, international affairs, space research, social security, and the postal service. Welfare expenditures have been gradually shifted to the national government. State and local governments retain the primary responsibility for education, highways, and health and hospital care, although national involvement in these fields is growing.

8. Federal grants-in-aid to state and local governments have been the principal instrument of the national government's involvement in domestic policy areas. These federal areas payments now make up nearly one-fifth of all state and local government revenue.

BIBLIOGRAPHY

BREAK, GEORGE F., *Intergovernmental Fiscal Relations in the United States.* Washington, D.C.: Brookings Institution, 1967.

MOSHER, FREDERICK C., and ORVILLE F. POLAND, *The Costs of American Governments.* New York: Dodd, Mead, 1964.

SHARKANSKY, IRA, *The Politics of Taxing and Spending.* New York: Bobbs-Merrill, 1969.

National Urban Coalition, *Counterbudget.* New York: Praeger, 1971.

Representatives of Tax Reform Research Group picket White House. UPI Photo

10 BUDGETS AND TAXES:

incrementalism at work

Too often we think of budgeting as the dull province of clerks and statisticians. Nothing could be more mistaken. The budget is the single most important policy statement of any government. The expenditure side of the budget tells us "who gets what" in public funds, and the revenue side of the budget tells us "who pays the cost." There are few government activities or programs that do not require an expenditure of funds, and no public funds may be spent without budgetary authorization. Deciding what goes into a budget (the budgetary process) provides a mechanism for reviewing government programs, assessing their cost, relating them to financial resources, making choices among alternative expenditures, and determining the financial effort that a government will expend on these programs. Budgets determine what programs and policies are to be increased, decreased, lapsed, initiated, or renewed. The budget lies at the heart of public policy.[1]

INCREMENTALISM IN BUDGET MAKING

The incremental model of public policy making is particularly well suited to assist in understanding the budgeting process. Although the systems model helps to identify underlying environmental force affecting

---

[1] See Aaron Wildavsky, *The Politics of the Budgetary Process* (Boston: Little, Brown, 1964).

overall *levels* of public taxing and spending, the *process* by which decisions are reached on taxes and expenditures appears to conform to an incremental pattern.

Budgeting is *conservative* because decision-makers generally consider last year's expenditures as a base. Active consideration of budget proposals is generally narrowed to new items or requested increases over last year's base. The attention of governors and legislators, and mayors and councils, is focused on a narrow range of increases or decreases in a budget. A budget is almost never reviewed as a whole every year, in the sense of reconsidering the value of existing programs. Departments are seldom required to defend or explain budget requests, which do *not* exceed current appropriations; but requested increases in appropriations require extensive explanation, and they are most subject to downward revision by higher political officials.

Budgeting is very *political*. As Aaron Wildavsky was told by a federal executive, "It's not what's in your estimates, but how good a politician you are that matters." [2] Being a good politician involves (1) the cultivation of a good base of support for your requests among the public at large and among people served by the agency; (2) the development of interest, enthusiasm, and support for your program among top political figures and legislative leaders, and (3) skill in following strategies that exploit your opportunities to the maximum. Informing the public and your clientele of the full benefit of the services they receive from the agency may increase the intensity with which they will support the agency's request. If possible, the agency should inspire its clientele to contact governors, mayors, legislators, and councilmen, and to help work for the agency's request. This is much more effective than the agency trying to promote its own requests.

Budgeting is also quite *fragmented*. In theory, the budget office is supposed to bring together budget requests and fit them into a coherent whole, while at the same time relating them to revenue estimates. But often budget offices do little more than staple together the budget requests of individual departments, and it is very difficult for a governor or mayor, and almost impossible for a legislature or council, to view the total policy impact of a budget. Wildavsky explains that the fragmented character of the budgetary process helps to secure agreement to the budget as well as reduce the burden of calculation. Some budgets must be agreed upon by the executive and the legislature if the government is going to continue to function at all, and this pressure to agree often means that conflicts over programs must go unresolved in a budget. Calculations are made in small segments, often by legislative subcommit-

---

[2] *Ibid.*, p. 19.

tees, and must be accepted by the legislature as a whole. If each subcommittee challenged the result of the others, conflict might be so great that no budget would ever be passed. It is much easier to agree on a small addition or decrease to a single program than it is to compare the worth of one program to that of all others.

Finally, budgeting is *nonprogrammatic*. For reasons that accountants have so far kept to themselves, an agency budget typically lists expenditures under the ambiguous phrases: "personal services," "contractual services," "travel," "supplies," "equipment." It is impossible to tell from such a listing exactly what programs the agency is spending its money on. Such a budget obscures policy decisions by hiding programs behind meaningless phrases. Even if these categories are broken down into line items (for example, under "personnel services," the line-item budget might say, "John Doaks, Assistant Administrator, $15,000"), it is still next to impossible to identify the costs of various programs. Reform-oriented administrators have called for budgeting by programs for many years; this would present budgetary requests in terms of end products or program packages, like aid to dependent children, vocational rehabilitation, administration of fair employment practices laws, highway patroling, and so on. Chief executives generally favor program budgeting because it will give them greater control over the policy. But very often administrative agencies are hostile toward program budgeting—it certainly adds to the cost of bookkeeping, and many agencies feel insecure in describing precisely what it is they do. Wildavsky points out that there are some political functions served by *non*program budgeting. He notes that

> Agreement comes much more readily when the items in dispute can be treated in dollars instead of basic differences in policy. Calculating budgets in monetary increments facilitates bargaining and logrolling. It becomes possible to swap an increase here for a decrease there or for an increase elsewhere without always having to consider the ultimate desirability of the programs blatantly in competition. . . . Party ties might be disruptive of agreement if they focused attention on policy differences between the two political persuasions. . . . Consider by contrast some likely consequences of program budgeting. The practice of focusing attention on programs means that policy implications can hardly be avoided. The gains and the losses for the interests involved become far more evident to all concerned. Conflict is heightened by the stress on the policy differences and increased still further by an inbuilt tendency to an all-or-nothing, "yes" or "no" response to the policy in dispute. The very concept of program packages suggests that the policy in dispute is indivisible, that the appropriate response is to be for or against rather than bargaining for a little more or a little less. Logrolling and bargaining are hindered because it is much easier to trade increments conceived in monetary terms than it is to give in on basic policy differences. Problems of calculation are vastly increased by the necessity, if program budgeting is

to have meaning, of evaluating the desirability of every program as compared to all others, instead of the traditional practice of considering budgeting in relatively independent segments.[3]

Program budgeting also provides the opportunity for the introduction of performance standards in the budgeting process. "Performance budgeting" usually involves the designation of some unit of service, for example, one pupil, one hospital patient, or one welfare recipient, and the establishment of standards of service and costs based upon a single unit of service. A common example of performance budgeting is found in school systems, where pupils are designated as a basic unit of service, and standards for numbers of teachers, supplies and materials, auxiliary personnel, building floor space, and many other cost items are calculated on the basis of the number of pupils to be served. Thus, standards may allocate teachers on the basis of 1 to every 25 students, or a full-time principal for every 250 students, or a psychologist for every 1,000 pupils, or $20 worth of supplies for every student, and so on. These formulas are used to determine the allocation of resources at budget time.

One political consequence of the use of formulas in performance budgeting is the centralization of budgetary decision making. Departments are merely asked to provide the number of pupils, or patients, or recipients, or other units of service they expect to serve in the coming fiscal year. A central unit of budget analysis then determines allocations through the application of formulas to the service estimates provided by the departments. Many departments, accustomed to less bureaucratic procedures, feel that the use of formulas is mechanical and inflexible. But it is not surprising in a large and complex bureaucracy to understand the search for equitable patterns in the distribution of resources leading to the use of formulas applied throughout the system. Once a formula has been established, however, it is often difficult to change or adjust the formula from one year to the next. Performance budgeting places great power in the hands of the staff personnel budget officers who devise the formulas. Performance budgeting is generally favored by economy-minded groups, particularly businessmen who are familiar with the application of unit cost procedures to manufacturing enterprise.

THE FORMAL BUDGETARY PROCESS

It is difficult to imagine that prior to 1921, the president played no direct role in the budget process. The secretary of the treasury complied

---

[3] *Ibid.,* p. 136–38.

the estimates of the individual agencies, and these were sent, without revision, to Congress for its consideration. The Budget and Accounting Act of 1921 provided for an executive budget giving the president responsibility for budget formulation, and thereby giving him important means of controlling federal policy. The Office of Management and Budget (OMB), located in the Executive Office, has the key responsibility for budget preparation. In addition to this major task, the OMB has related responsibilities for improving the organization and management of the executive agencies, for coordinating the extensive statistical services of the federal government, and for analyzing and reviewing proposed legislation to determine its effect on administration and finance.

Preparation of the federal budget starts more than a year before the beginning of the fiscal year for which it is intended. OMB, after preliminary consultation with the executive agencies and in accord with presidential policy, develops targets or ceilings within which the agencies are encouraged to build their requests. This work begins a full sixteen to eighteen months before the beginning of the fiscal year for which the

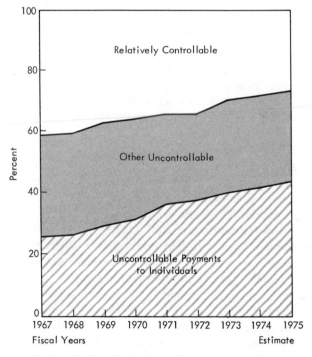

Fig. 10-1 *Controllability of Federal Expenditures—(Percentage)*

Source: The Budget of the United States Government, 1975

budget is being prepared. In other words, work will begin in January or March, 1975, on budget for the fiscal year beginning October 1, 1976, and ending September 30, 1977.

Budget materials and instructions go to the agencies with the request that the forms be completed and returned to OMB. This request is followed by about three months' arduous work by agency-employed budget officers, department heads, and the "grass roots" bureaucracy, in Washington and out in the field. Budget officials at the bureau level check requests from the smaller units, compare them with the previous year's estimates, hold conferences, and make adjustments. The process of checking, reviewing, modifying, and discussing is repeated on a larger scale at the department level.

The heads of agencies are expected to submit their completed requests to OMB by mid-September or early October. Occasionally a schedule of "over ceiling" items (requests above the suggested ceilings) will be included.

With the requests of the spending agencies at hand, OMB begins its own budget review. Hearings are given each agency. Top agency officials support their requests as convincingly as possible. On rare occasions dissatisfied agencies may ask the budget director to bring their cases to the president.

In December the president, with his OMB director, will devote time to the document which by now is approaching its final stages of assembly. They and their staffs will "blue-pencil," revise, and make last-minute changes, as well as prepare the president's message, which accompanies the budget to Congress. After the budget is in legislative hands, the president may recommend further alterations as needs dictate.

Although the completed document includes a revenue plan with general estimates for taxes and other income, it is primarily an expenditure budget. Revenue and tax policy staff work centers in the Treasury Department and not in the Office of Management and Budget.

Congress has two responsibilities in making money available for spending—authorization and appropriation. Authorization in a technical sense refers to the substantive legislation that establishes a program and enables an agency to spend money when appropriations are made. An appropriations measure, on the other hand, allows an agency to obligate the government to pay out funds and spend specified amounts. Before authorization legislation goes to the House or Senate floor, it is considered by appropriate program committees (for example, Aeronautical and Space Sciences, Education, and Labor, or Interior and Insular Affairs).

Until recently, Congressional consideration of the budget was divided between House and Senate Appropriations Committees and subcommittees and the Senate Finance Committee. Moreover, consideration of proposed government spending was divided over twelve to fifteen different appropriations bills, each covering separate broad categories, which arrived on the Congressional Calendar at different times of the year. Finally, taxing measures were considered separately from appropriations measures and by different committees. In short, Congress never took an overall view of the budget—setting priorities among major categories, considering the overall impact of the budget on the economy, or balancing revenues with expenditures. As a result Congress was open to the charge that it dealt irresponsibly with government spending.

Congress attempted to remedy problems of budgetary oversight in 1974 by establishing new Congressional budgetary procedures. Congress created two new House and Senate Budget Committees and a Legislative Budget Office to review the President's budget soon after its submission to Congress. These Committees draft a concurrent resolution setting forth target totals to guide Congressional actions on appropriations and revenue measures considered throughout the year. This initial budgetary guide is enacted by the Congress prior to consideration of specific taxing or spending measures. Thus, Congressional committees considering taxing and spending bills not only have Presidential recommendations to guide them, but also the guidelines established earlier by the Budget Committees. If an appropriation measure exceeds the target set by the earlier resolution, it is sent back to the Budget Committees for reconciliation. A final Congressional budget including all appropriations measures, tax measures, and the debt ceiling—would be passed by Congress before October 1, the new date set for the start of the fiscal year. Of course, it is still too early to judge whether the new procedures will make Congress any more responsible in government spending. But the new procedures clearly reduce Congressional dependence on executive budgetmaking.

Consideration of specific appropriations measures are functions of the Appropriations Committees in both houses. Committee work in the House of Representatives is usually more thorough than it is in the Senate; the committee in the upper House tends to be a "court of appeal" for agencies against House action. Each committee, moreover, has about ten largely independent subcommittees to review the requests of a particular agency or a group of related functions. Specific appropriations bills are taken up by the subcommittees in hearings. Departmental officers are called to the Hill to answer questions on the conduct of their programs and to defend their requests for the next fiscal year. Lobbyists and other witnesses testify.

The appropriation subcommittees are of primary importance in Congressional consideration of the budget. Because neither Congress nor the full committees have the time or understanding necessary to conduct adequate reviews, the subcommittee has become the locus of Congressional budget analysis. Several factors contribute to its preeminent position. Each subcommittee specializes in a relatively small fraction of the total budget. It considers the same agencies and functions year after year. The long tenure characteristic of the membership of the prestigious Appropriations Committees guarantees decades of experience in dealing with particular programs. Although the work of the subcommittee is reviewed by the full committee, in practice it is routinely accepted with the expenditure of little time and debate.

The House Committee on Ways and Means and the Senate Finance Committee are the major instruments of Congress for consideration of *taxing* measures. Through long history and jealous pride they have maintained complete formal independence of the Appropriations Committees, further fragmenting legislative consideration of the budget.

In terms of aggregates, Congress does not regularly make great changes in the executive budget, rarely changing it more than 5 percent. The House normally cuts appropriations, the Senate restores a part, and the inevitable conference committee arrives at an amount close to what the president requested.

The budget is approved by Congress in the form of appropriations bills, from twelve to fifteen of them, each ordinarily providing for several departments and agencies. The number of revenue measures is smaller. As with other bills that pass Congress, the president has ten days to approve or veto appropriations legislation. He lacks the power to veto items in bills, and only rarely exercises his right to veto appropriations bills in their entirety.

Once the budgeted funds are authorized, controls over their expenditure shift to the executive establishment, although not immediately to the departments and agencies. The Bureau of the Budget may establish reserves against appropriations in order to provide for emergencies and to effect economies. The Bureau, after consultation with the agencies, apportions the appropriations, usually on a quarterly basis. A major purpose of apportionment is to prevent an agency from depleting its appropriation before the end of the fiscal year.

Allotment, a second step in federal budget execution, is a device by which the budget officer of each agency allocates funds to bureaus and the lesser units on a monthly or quarterly basis.

THE STABILITY OF PUBLIC POLICY

The most important influence over the size and content of this year's budget is last year's budget. One of the reasons for this is the continuing nature of most governmental programs and outlays. The greatest part of a government budget represents expenditures that are mandated by previous programs—for example, commitments to recipients of social security, commitments to veterans, interest that must be paid on the national debt, the maintenance of a defense establishment, and so on. (See Figure 10-1) Another reason for using last year's budget as a base is the cost that would be involved in generally reconsidering every government program and expenditure. There is not enough time and energy for the decision-making process required to do this, so past programs are assumed to be worthy of continuation at previous levels of expenditures. It is considered a waste of time to view every budget as a blank slate and to ignore past experience. Moreover, the political instability that would ensue if every program were reevaluated every year would be too much for the system; every political battle that has ever been fought over a program would have to be fought all over again every year. Obviously, it is much more practical and political to accept past decisions on programs and expenditures as a base, and concentrate attention on new programs and increases and decreases in expenditures. For all these reasons, the range of decision making actually confronting legislative and executive officials is really quite small, generally within 10 percent of the previous budget!

Political scientist Richard Fenno calculated the percentage change of appropriation to federal agencies over a twelve-year period and found that in one-third of all cases appropriations were within 5 percent of the previous year's appropriations; in one-half of all cases, appropriations were within 10 percent of the previous year; and in three-quarters of all cases appropriations were within 30 percent of the previous year.[4]

The federal budget is such a giant, complex document that no one is really able to view it in a comprehensive, holistic fashion. In such complicated situations we are likely to use simplified rules of thumb to enable us to find satisfactory solutions. Completely rational approaches are simply not possible when the problem is as complicated and multi-faceted as the federal budget. Davis, Dempster, and Wildavsky were able to identify two simple rules of thumb which appeared to explain by far the greatest portion of budgetary allocations in any year: [5]

1. The agency request for a certain year is a fixed mean percentage of the Congressional appropriation for that agency in the previous year plus a random variable for that year.

[4] Richard F. Fenno, *The Power of the Purse: Appropriations Politics in Congress* (Boston: Little, Brown, 1966).

[5] Otto A. Davis, M. A. H. Dempster, and Aaron Wildavsky, "A Theory of the Budgetary Process," *American Political Science Review*, 60 (September 1966), 529–47.

2. The Congressional approximation for an agency in a certain year is a fixed mean percentage of the agency's request in that year plus a variable representing a deviation from the usual relationship between the Congress and the agency for the previous year.

Less than 15 percent of all the budgetary decisions studied deviated significantly from these rules or from related propositions.

In a study of budgetary decisions at the state level (Illinois), Thomas Anton was able to identify several interesting informal practices that grow up among agency heads who understand the incremental nature of budgeting: [6]

1. Spend all of your appropriation. A failure to use up an appropriation indicates that the full amount was unnecessary in the first place, which in turn implies that your budget should be cut next year.
2. Never request a sum less than your current appropriation. It is easier to find ways to spend up to current appropriation levels than it is to explain why you want a reduction. Besides, a reduction indicates your program is not growing and this is an embarrassing admission to most government administrators.
3. Put top priority programs into the basic budget, that is, that part of the budget which is within current appropriation levels. Budget offices, governors and mayors, and legislative bodies will seldom challenge programs which appear to be part of existing operations.
4. Increases that are desired should be made to appear small and should appear to grow out of existing operations. The appearance of a fundamental change in a budget should be avoided.
5. Give the budget office, chief executive, and the legislature something to cut. Normally it is desirable to submit requests for substantial increases in existing programs and many requests for new programs, in order to give higher political authorities something to cut. This enables them to "save" the public untold millions of dollars and justify their claim to promoting "economy" in government. Giving them something to cut also diverts attention away from the basic budget with its vital programs.

Anton also examined the respective roles of the governor, state agencies, the budgetary commission, and the legislature in budget making. Agency heads generally request much more than last year's appropriation. The executive budgetary commission makes heavy cuts into the agencies' requests. The governor makes additional requests to bring his budget into balance with revenues and avoid new taxes. But the general assembly restores many of the cuts in agency requests. The final budget is much higher than last year's appropriations, but much lower than agency requests.

[6] Thomas J. Anton, *The Politics of State Expenditures in Illinois* (Urbana: University of Illinois Press, 1966).

THE FEDERAL BUDGET

The incremental nature of the federal government's budget is revealed in figures showing the percentage of federal expenditures going to various purposes over the years (see Table 10-1). These figures change, but they do not change much. The relative rankings of federal

Table 10-1 *Federal Expenditures Over a Decade*

	1960	1965	1968	1970	1972	1975
			Billions of Dollars			
National Defense	45.9	49.6	80.5	79.4	78.3	87.7
International Affairs	3.0	4.3	4.6	4.1	3.7	9.1
Space Research	.4	5.1	4.7	3.9	3.4	3.3
Agriculture	3.3	4.8	5.9	6.3	7.1	2.7
Natural Resources	1.0	2.0	1.7	2.5	3.8	3.1
Commerce and Transportation	4.8	7.4	8.0	9.4	11.2	13.4
Community Development and Housing	1.0	.3	4.0	3.0	4.3	5.7
Health and Welfare	18.7	27.2	43.5	57.1	82.1	126.4
Education and Manpower	1.3	2.5	7.0	7.5	9.8	11.5
Veterans' Benefits	5.4	5.7	6.9	8.7	10.7	13.6
Interest	8.3	10.3	13.7	17.8	20.6	29.1
General Government	1.3	2.3	2.6	3.6	4.9	6.8
Revenue Sharing	—	—	—	—	—	6.2
Total	92.2	118.4	178.8	197.9	231.9	304.4
			Percentage Distribution			
National Defense	48.8%	41.9%	45.0%	40.1%	32.6%	28.8%
International Affairs	3.3	3.7	2.6	2.1	1.6	1.3
Space Research	0.4	4.3	2.6	2.0	1.4	1.1
Agriculture	3.6	4.1	3.3	3.2	2.9	.9
Natural Resources	1.1	1.7	1.0	1.3	1.6	1.0
Commerce and Transportation	5.2	6.2	4.5	4.7	4.7	4.4
Community Development and Housing	1.1	0.2	2.3	1.5	1.9	1.9
Health and Welfare	20.3	23.0	24.3	28.8	34.2	41.5
Education and Manpower	1.4	2.1	3.9	3.8	4.1	3.8
Veterans' Benefits	5.9	4.8	3.8	4.4	4.5	4.5
Interest	9.0	8.7	7.7	9.0	8.6	9.6
General Government	1.4	1.9	1.5	1.8	2.0	2.2
Revenue Sharing						2.0
Total	100.0	100.0	100.0	100.0	100.0	100.0

Source: Data derived from *The Budget of the United States Government, 1975* (Washington, D.C.: Government Printing Office, 1974).

outlays by function remain the same. Despite a doubling of federal expenditures over a decade, the proportion of federal funds going to various purposes changes very little.

The major incremental changes over the decade have been the gradual drop-off in defense spending as a proportion of the federal budget, and the steady increase in spending for health and welfare, including the social security program. The Vietnam War bolstered military spending from 1965 to 1969 but did not alter the long-term decline in defense spending as a percentage of total federal outlays. Domestic spending has been increasing at a much faster pace than defense spending. The greatest increases have come in the area of health and welfare. Not only have public assistance payments and the costs of medical care for the poor skyrocketed, but the social security program has grown very rapidly. (Of course, social security taxes have been increased to cover the increased costs of social security; social security receipts were the fastest-growing source of federal income over the decade.) The Elementary and Secondary Education Act of 1965 greatly increased federal outlays in education. The space program was important in the mid-1960s, but has been gradually cut back. General revenue sharing—federal money payments to state and local governments with few strings attached—was first authorized in the State and Local Government Fiscal Assistance Act of 1972 and now accounts for 2 percent of total federal outlays.

TAX POLICY: WHO BEARS THE BURDENS OF GOVERNMENT?

The politics of taxation centers about the question of who actually bears the burden or "incidence" of a tax—that is, which income groups must devote the largest proportion of their income to taxes. Taxes that require high-income groups to pay a larger percentage of their incomes in taxes than low-income groups are said to be *progressive*, while taxes that take a larger share of the income of low-income groups are called *regressive*. Note that the *percentage of income* paid in taxes is the determining factor. Most taxes take more money from the rich than the poor, but a progressive or regressive tax is distinguished by the *percentages of income* taken from various income groups.

Progressive taxation is generally defended on the principle of ability to pay; that is, the assumption that high-income groups can afford to pay a larger percentage of their incomes into taxes at no more of a sacrifice than that required of lower-income groups to devote a smaller proportion of their income to taxation. This assumption is based on what economists call "marginal utility theory" as it applies to money: each additional dollar of income is slightly less valuable to an individual than preceding dollars (e.g., a $5,000 increase in the income of an individual already earning $100,000 is much less valuable to him than a $5,000 increase to an individual earning only $3,000 or an individual with no income). Hence, added dollars of income can be taxed at higher *rates* without violating equitable principles.

Opponents of progressive taxation generally assert that equity can only be achieved by taxing everyone at the *same* percentage of their income, regardless of the size of their income. Progressivity penalizes initiative, enterprise, and risk, and reduces incentives to expand and develop the nation's economy. Moreover, by taking incomes of high-income groups, governments are taking money that would otherwise go into business—investments, stocks, bonds, loans, etc.—and hence government is curtailing economic growth.

Regressive taxation is seldom defended as equitable in itself. However, some regressive taxes—notably the general sales tax—are such good revenue producers that they have many adherents. Sales taxes are less visible than income taxes; consumers generally consider them part of the price of an item. They can reach mobile populations whose income or property cannot be taxed by a state or local jurisdiction. When a major segment of the *national* tax structure is progressive, it is sometimes argued that some regressivity in state and local taxation is not inequitable in the light of the overall tax picture. It is also contended that inasmuch as low-income groups benefit from many government services, they ought to share in their costs. Finally, it can be argued that the benefits to low-income groups of increased government expenditures outweigh whatever burdens are imposed by the regressivity of sales taxation.

In considering the burden of incidence of a tax it is important not only to consider the *rate,* but also *economic behaviors* that affect burdens, and the problem of tax shifting. The *rate* simply states the percentage of the *base* (the object of the tax) which will go to taxes—for example, a 4 percent tax on all sales, or 10 percent tax on airline tickets, or a progressive sliding rate from 16 to 60 percent on income. A *rate* may appear to be neither progressive nor regressive, but economic behaviors may operate to make certain income groups more likely to bear the greater burden of the tax. For example, a 10 percent tax on jewelry or yachts does not have a progressive rate, but because high-income groups are presumed to spend a greater percentage of their income on these items than low-income groups, and therefore would spend a larger percentage on the tax on such items, the tax is presumed to be progressive. A 4 percent tax on all sales of consumer items is considered regressive because low-income groups devote a larger percentage, sometimes all, of their income to consumer items and hence bear the full brunt of the tax. High-income groups, which save or invest a sizable proportion of their income and spend only part of it for consumer items, do not allocate the same proportion of their incomes to the payment of a sales tax as low-income groups. When the person taxed, such as a property-owner, can pass on the impact of the tax to other persons, such as renters, the burden of the tax is said to *shift*. Because poor people usually rent, and they must spend a large percentage of their income for housing, property taxes shifted onto them in the form of higher rents are generally considered regressive.

In general, the federal tax structure is progressive, while state and local tax structures are regressive. The federal personal income tax is the only tax that is progressive throughout the entire range of incomes. This means that, in general, if a particular governmental function is financed through state and local revenue systems rather than federal revenues, it is being financed on a regressive rather than progressive revenue basis. Thus, much of the political debate over "federalism,"—that is, over which level of government, state or federal, should provide a particular governmental service—concerns the fact that the federal government tax structure is generally progressive, while the state and local tax structures are generally regressive. If the federal government pays for a particular governmental program it is being paid for out of largely regressive taxes.

Property taxes are quite regressive. This conclusion is based on the assumption that the renter actually pays his property taxes through increased rentals levied by the landlord, and the further assumption that high-income groups have more wealth in untaxed forms of property. State and local sales taxes are generally regressive, but not as regressive as property taxes. The regressivity of sales taxation is based upon the asumption that low-income groups must devote most, if not all, of their income to purchases, while high-income groups devote larger shares of their income to savings. Many states exclude some of the necessities of life from sales taxation, such as packaged food bought in supermarkets, in order to reduce the burden of sales taxation on the poor. Yet, on the whole, sales taxation remains more regressive than income taxation.

Finally, it should be noted that the social security system is financed on a regressive revenue structure. Social security payments are made only on wage and salary income, not on profits, capital gains, interest, and dividends, which provide a large share of the income of upper-income groups. More importantly, the social security payments are only collected on the *first* $7,800 of wage income; thus persons earning more than this amount pay a *lower* percentage of their total income into social security than persons earning less than this amount. Of course, this financing system was established on the principle that social security is an "insurance" program in which participants only received what they paid for; it was not established as an income redistribution system.

Although there is no constitutional requirement that assigns different types of taxes to federal, state, and local governments in America, over the years, these three levels of government have come to rely on separate tax bases (see Figure 10-2). The federal government's principal reliance is on personal and corporate *income* taxes. State governments also rely on income taxes to some extent (two-thirds of the states levy income taxes), but the principal source of state tax revenues is *sales taxation*. Consumers are a notoriously weak pressure group. And it seems easy for taxpayers to dribble pennies away two or three at a time. Sales tax does not require obvious payroll deductions as income taxation or year-end tax bills as property taxation. It is a steady producer of large amounts of revenue. Local governments rely primarily on *property* taxes. Real estate is relatively easy to find for tax purposes, and it cannot be easily moved out of the local jurisdiction. A local sales tax can result in merchants moving beyond city boundaries, and a city income tax can speed the population exodus to suburbia.

TAX REFORM AND TAX "LOOPHOLES"

Incrementalism is a characteristic of tax policy just as it is a characteristic of expenditure policy. A review of major tax decisions of the federal government over the last decade clearly indicates the obstacles to significant change in the tax structure.

Since the adoption of the Sixteenth Amendment in 1913, the income tax has been the chief producer of revenue for the federal government and the chief object of political conflict. Yet despite many efforts at tax "reform"—efforts which, if successful, would result in a

FEDERAL TAX SOURCES

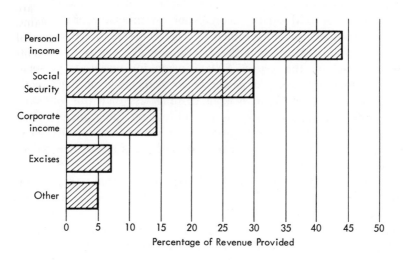

STATE AND LOCAL TAX SOURCES

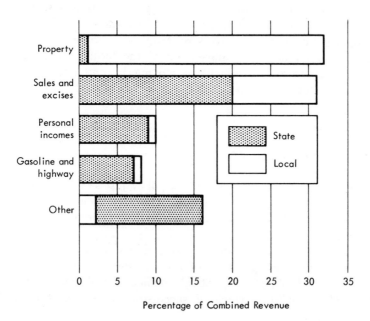

Fig. 10-2 *Federal, State, and Local Tax Sources*

reallocation of burdens among income groups—Congress has never undertaken any comprehensive rewriting of federal tax laws. Instead, tax policy has been characterized by a gradual accretion of decisions.

The actual incidence of the federal income tax is a matter of great controversy. Although nominal rates are very progressive, the actual effective tax rate on income—the rate that income is taxed after exemptions, deductions, capital gains, and other provisions are considered— is much less progressive than generally believed. The Internal Revenue Code is hundreds of pages long, and it contains a long list of exemptions, deductions, and special treatments; these have been expanded by

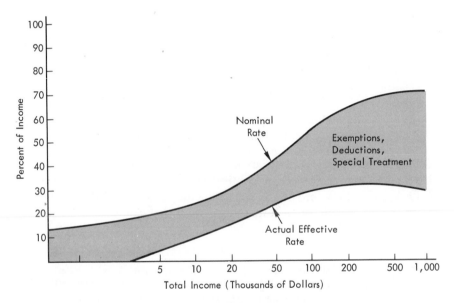

Fig. 10-3 *Actual and Nominal Tax Rates: Federal Personal Income Tax*

Source: Data derived from J. Pechman, *Federal Tax Policy* (Washington: Brookings Institution, 1968).

administrative and court decisions. Almost ritualistically, Congressmen and presidents have pledged to eliminate "loopholes" and "reform" the tax structure. Yet every major effort to do so has failed.

The problem in closing tax loopholes is that what one man regards as a loophole may be regarded as a socially useful tax provision by someone else. (For example, deductions from taxable income for charitable contributions are generally applauded as a useful incentive to charitable giving; but this is also a major source of lost tax revenue.) Almost *half* of total personal income in America is not taxed because of all the exemptions and deductions written into the tax laws.

A great deal of personal income escapes federal income taxation because of the following deductions and exemptions:

1. Personal exemption of $750 per dependent, with double exemptions for the blind and the aged
2. Medical expenses over 3 percent of income and drug expenses over 1 percent
3. Charitable contributions
4. Taxes paid to state and local governments
5. Child-care expenses and alimony payments
6. Casualty losses
7. Interest payments, including home mortgages
8. Income from social security, public assistance, unemployment insurance, and veterans' disability

Although these provisions account for the great bulk of lost revenue, they are seldom the object of political controversy. So many Americans make use of these provisions that they are rarely called "loopholes." In contrast, certain other exemptions and deductions are frequently cited as "loopholes":

1. *Capital gains*—profits from the sale of investments held over six months—are taxed at only 25 percent (35 percent for gains of more than $50,000). This is regarded by some as a necessary incentive for business investment; but regarded by others as special treatment for income derived from investment that is not afforded to income from wages and salaries.
2. *State and local bond interest* is completely exempt from federal income taxation. This is regarded by some as an incentive to buy state and local government bonds for roads, hospitals, schools, environmental improvement, etc.; but regarded by others as a way in which wealthy people can escape taxation on income from their investments.
3. *Oil and gas depletion allowance* permits individuals and companies to deduct 22 percent of income from oil and gas production in recognition of the depreciation of these reserves. This is regarded by some as a necessary incentive in the search for new sources of energy; but regarded by others as a special privilege to oil and gas interests.

4. *Accelerated depreciation of property* permits individuals and companies to calculate the depreciation of their income-producing property in ways that overestimate the actual decline in value. This is regarded by some as a spur to capital investment and economic growth; but regarded by others as an unfair "fast tax write-off."

The history of tax reform legislation reveals a reluctance to radically restructure the tax system and a tendency instead to make only incremental changes in the tax laws. In 1964 Congress reduced the progressivity of tax rates—from the previous 20 to 91 percent to range of 14 to 70 percent—but retained nearly all the traditional exemptions, deductions, and special treatments. In 1968, the costs of the Vietnam war moved Congress to consider an increase in the personal income tax. Again there was considerable controversy over loopholes, but the device finally settled upon was a "surtax" of 10 percent—a uniform 10 percent increase over whatever the individual was already paying. This device again left the basis of the tax structure untouched.

The Tax Reform Act of 1969 caused the most comprehensive review of tax exemptions and deductions, but only minor changes were incorporated into law. For example, after much debate, the oil and gas depletion allowance was reduced from 27.5 to 22 percent. The tax on capital gains was increased for gains in excess of $50,000 from 25 to 35 percent. The tax rates on single persons were reduced to rates at or below the rates paid by married taxpayers. The personal exemption was raised from $600 to $750, and taxes were eliminated on the lowest incomes. Finally, a 10-percent minimum tax was imposed on high incomes, regardless of exemptions, deductions, or exclusions. But these were clearly *incremental* changes, rather than a major restructuring of the tax laws.

Contrary to widespread belief, "soaking the rich" would not lead to any major increase in federal government revenue. For example, if all incomes over $50,000 a year were confiscated by the government, the additional tax revenues would amount to less than $20 billion, or 6.5 percent of the federal government's budget. Closing four tax loopholes (capital gains, state and local bond interest, oil and gas depletion allowance, accelerated depreciation) would increase federal revenues less than $10 billion, or 3 percent of the budget (perhaps less if the changes caused shifting of investments). Taxing the rich may provide some symbolic satisfaction, but it will not produce great revenue. The bulk of taxable income in America is concentrated in the middle classes. Unquestionably, continued increases in governmental activities will result in greater tax burdens on the middle classes.

SPENDING POLICY: WHO ENJOYS THE BENEFITS OF GOVERNMENT?

Expenditures as well as taxes can be progressive or regressive in their impact. Obviously public assistance payments are *progressive* expenditures because they are of greater benefits to low-income families than high-income families. In contrast, interest payments—interest on government bonds paid out to investors—are *regressive* expenditures because they are likely to go to high-income rather than low-income groups. In determining the distributional impact of expenditures, assumptions must be made about the use of government services by various income classes, and the relationship of this use to their total income. We must consider education, health, public assistance, recreation, police and fire, etc., and the use that is made of these governmental services by various income groups.

As we might expect, the most progressive of all government services in its distributional impact is welfare. Three-quarters of all welfare expenditures go to the two lowest-income classes. Social security benefits are also very progressive. Expenditures for public schools and highways tend to benefit middle-income groups more than the poor or the rich. Apparently the poor do not get as much out of public education as the middle class; neither do the wealthy, who limit the size of their family and make greater use of private schools. Public expenditures for higher education are generally regressive, because it is the middle and upper-middle classes who are most likely to send their children to college. Only in the very highest income categories are the benefits of public higher education expenditures diminished, probably because this group relies more on private colleges and universities.

In general, the distributional impact of total government expenditures is moderately progressive.

THE POLITICS OF INCOME REDISTRIBUTION

What factors shape the distribution of government burdens and benefits among classes of people? Let us attempt to identify political systems that distribute burdens and benefits progressively, and systematically distinguish them from political systems that distribute burdens and benefits regressively. Then let us try to observe the environmental and political correlates of progressivity and regressivity and the distributional impact of public policy.

Once again the fifty states provide an excellent opportunity to examine systematically variation in an important policy output and to observe the conditions associated with this variation. Several scholars have attempted to calculate the *net* distributional impact among income classes of state government revenues and expenditures for each of the fifty states.[7] They do so by (1) calculating the amounts paid in revenue and amounts received in benefits by each state government for each income class in their state (they did this by using the assumptions about incidence presented in Figure 10-4; (2) calculating the ratio of revenues paid to benefits received, for each income class in each state; and (3) summing the ratios for three lowest income classes in each state. The result is a measure of the *net* distributional impact of state revenues and expenditures. The higher the ratio, the greater the distributional impact in a progressive direction—that is, in the direction of providing greater benefits for low-income groups while collecting less revenue from these groups.

The net distributional impact of state revenues and expenditures is progressive in every state. However, the *degree* of progressivity varies among the states. Scholars differ over exactly how to compute redistribution ratios, but states such as Massachusetts, California, Connecticut, and Illinois are generally considered highly progressive, while Texas, Virginia and South Dakota are generally considered less progressive.

Progressivity in the distributional impact of state taxes and expenditures is more closely related to urbanization than any other socio-economic condition. The findings presented in Table 10-2 derived from two separate studies, indicate a positive relationship between progressivity and urbanization: the more urban states have somewhat higher ratios of benefits to taxes for low-income groups than the less urban states. Progressivity is also related to income. Wealthy states with well-educated adult populations are somewhat more progressive in their tax and expenditures impact than poorer states with less-educated adult populations.

One might assume that the greater the inequality of income (as measured by the Gini index), the greater the need or demand for redistribution through state revenue and expenditure policies. But progres-

[7] Brian R. Fry and Richard F. Winters, "The Politics of Redistribution," *American Political Science Review,* 64 (June 1970), 508–22; Bernard H. Booms and James R. Halldorson, "The Politics of Redistribution: A Reformulation," *American Political Science Review,* Vol. 67 (Sept., 1973), 924–33.

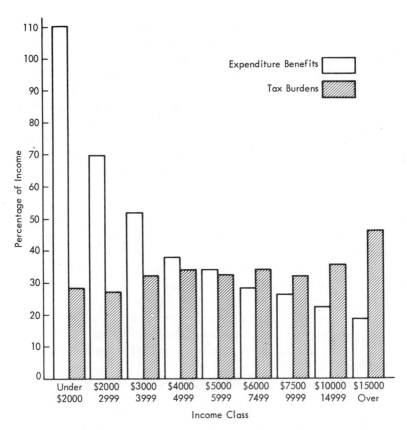

Fig. 10-4 *Total Tax Burden and Expenditure Benefit as Percent of Income by Income Class*

Source: Tax Foundation, Inc., *Tax Burdens and Benefits of Government Expenditures by Income Class* (New York: The Tax Foundation, 1967).

sivity does *not* increase with increases in the Gini index, or with increases in the proportion of poor people in the states.

What about the effect of political variables on distributional policy? Party competition has no discernible effect on distributional policy. Progressivity in distributional impact of state taxing and spending does *not* increase with increases in party competition. However, increased voter participation does appear to be related to greater progressivity. Reformism in state politics—as reflected in the extension of civil service

Table 10-2 *The Linkages Between Environmental Resources, Political System Characteristics, and the Distributional Impact of State Taxing and Spending: Results of Two Separate Studies*

| | CORRELATION COEFFICIENTS WITH PROGRESSIVITY IN DISTRIBUTIONAL RATIOS OF STATE TAXING AND SPENDING | | | |
| | Simple | | Partial | |
	F & W [1]	B & H [2]	F & W [1]	B & H [2]
Level of Environmental Resources				
Income	.17	.65	—.27	.42
Urbanization	.33	.67	.15	.30
Education	—.01	.39	.17	.45
Distribution of Environmental Resources				
Income inequality (Gini)	.00	—.43	.22	.00
Political System Characteristics				
Voter participation	.14	.34	.37	.40
Party competition	—.21	.24	—.14	.14
Civil service coverage	.33	.44	.34	.20
Legislative professionalism	.51	.51	.28	.20

[1] Fry and Winters, op. cit.
[2] Booms and Halldorson, op. cit.

coverage and legislative professionalism—is also associated with progressivity in distributional policy. Civil service coverage, and especially legislative professionalism, are positively correlated with progressivity. The causal linkage in this case is probably not directly from civil service coverage or legislative professionalism to progressive redistribution in state taxing and spending. It is more likely that civil service coverage and legislative professionalism are part of a broader political ethic of reformism, and it is this ethic that produces a tax and revenue system that is more progressive in its distributional impact.

SUMMARY

Incrementalism is particularly descriptive of the budget-making progress. Because budgets are the most important policy statements of governments, incrementalism heavily impacts the entire range of policy making.

1. Budgeting is conservative, because decision-makers generally consider last year's expenditures as a base and focus their attention on a narrow range of increases or decreases in expenditures.

2. Budgeting is fragmented, because agencies and legislative committees generally deal with specific segments of the budget; seldom is there much consideration given to the total policy impact of a budget.

3. Budget is nonprogrammatic, because careful consideration of the policy implications of each expenditure might create irresoluble conflicts. Evaluating the desirability of every program as compared to all other programs would be politically infeasible.

4. The formal budgetary process illustrates the fragmented character of budgetary decision making and the diffusion of responsibility for expenditure policy.

5. The range of decisions actually available to policy-makers in the development of a budget is really quite small, generally within 10 percent of the previous budget.

6. Realizing the incremental nature of budget making, agency heads devise a series of informal budgetary practices designed to minimize the appearance of change and guarantee the gradual expansion of agency activities.

7. Despite a doubling of federal expenditures over a decade, the proportion of federal funds going to various purposes has not changed very much. Defense expenditures have declined somewhat as a proportion of all federal expenditures while welfare and education expenditures have risen.

8. Tax policy is also characterized by incrementalism. Despite rhetoric about eliminating tax loopholes and reforming the tax structure, Congress has preferred to make minor changes in tax laws rather than undertake their major restructuring.

9. Policies that distribute government burdens and benefits among income groups can be identified by calculating the progressivity and regressivity of both taxes and expenditures. Progressivity means that the tax burden is a higher percentage of income of high-income groups than of low-income groups, or that the expenditure benefit is a higher percentage of the income of low-income groups than of high-income groups. Regressivity in tax burdens and expenditure benefits means just the opposite.

10. The burden of all federal taxes is progressive, although not steeply so. The most progressive of all taxes is the federal personal income tax. In contrast, state and local taxes are regressive, owing to the reliance of state and local governments on sales and property taxation.

11. The distributional impact of most government expenditures is moderately progressive. Welfare and social security expenditures are very progressive Expenditures for schools and highways tend to benefit middle-income groups more than the rich or poor. Expenditures for public higher education are generally regressive because more middle- and upper-class families send their children to college.

12. The distributional character of public policy in the American states is related to urbanization and income. Wealthy, urban states have more progressive taxing and spending structures than poorer, rural states. Party competition has no discernible impact on distribution policy; but voter participation is related to progressivity. Reformism—as reflected in civil service coverage and legislative professionalism—is also associated with progressivity in net distributional policy.

BIBLIOGRAPHY

ANTON, THOMAS J., *The Politics of State Expenditures in Illinois*. Urbana, Ill.: University of Illinois Press, 1966.

FENNO, RICHARD, *The Power of the Purse: Appropriations Politics in Congress*. Boston: Little, Brown, 1966.

LINDBLOM, CHARLES E., and DAVID BRAYBROOKE, *The Strategy of Decision*. New York: Free Press, 1963.

WILDAVSKY, AARON, *The Politics of the Budgetary Process*. Boston: Little, Brown, 1964.

The presence of ground troops afford both psychological and military deterrents in conventional war games. Wide World Photos

11 DEFENSE POLICY:

strategies for serious games

Several years ago the Nobel prize-winning mathematician and peace advocate Bertrand Russell observed that the game of "Chicken" was played by youthful degenerates and world leaders. The statement is true. But whether we like it or not, our life, liberty, and security depend upon our national leaders being willing to play the game. For as Russell himself observes,

> Practical politicians may admit all this [the dangers and destructiveness of war], but they argue that there is no alternative. If one side is unwilling to risk global war, while the other side is willing to risk it, *the side which is willing to run the risk will be victorious in all negotiations and will ultimately reduce the other side to complete impotence.* . . . We are, therefore, faced quite inevitably with the choice between brinkmanship and surrender.[1]

Game theory provides an interesting way of thinking about defense policy. Defense policies of major world powers are interdependent. Each major power must adjust its own defense policies to reflect not only its own national objectives but also its expectations of what other major powers may do. Outcomes depend on the combination of choices made in world capitals. Moreover, it is not unreasonable to assume that major powers strive for rationality in defense policy making. Nations

[1] Bertrand Russell, *Common Sense and Nuclear Warfare* (New York: Simon and Schuster, 1959), p. 30.

243

choose defense strategies (policies) that are designed to achieve an optimum payoff even after considering all their opponents' possible strategies. Thus, national defense policy making conforms to basic game-theoretic notions.

Our use of game-theoretic ideas is limited, however, to suggesting interesting questions, posing dilemmas, and providing a vocabulary for dealing with policy making in a competitive, interdependent world. A formal game-theoretic approach would require sophistication in mathematics and logic beyond the scope and purposes of this chapter.

DETERRENCE STRATEGY AND NUCLEAR WAR

In order to maintain peace and protect the national interests of the United States, primary reliance is placed upon the notion of *deterrence*. In a general sense, deterrence means that war and overt aggression can best be prevented by making the consequences of such acts clearly unacceptable to rational leaders of other nations. But there are different levels of deterrence and different defense strategies that need to be explored under the general category of deterrence.

Minimum Deterrence. This is the notion that potential enemies can be dissuaded from aggression or war by the mere possession of enough nuclear weapons and delivery systems to destroy their homeland. The minimum deterrence strategy rests on the belief that nuclear war is now "unthinkable" because of the destruction involved and that no rational leader would choose war as an instrument of national goals. A related notion is that "overkill' is a measure of the effectiveness of the deterrent—that if the U.S. has enough explosive force at its disposal to kill every Russian six times this is enough (or too much) defense. Perhaps it is the widespread ignorance of the American public about defense policy that accounts for the popularity of these notions, or perhaps they are comfortable substitutes for serious thinking about defense requirements. But no serious military analyst today believes that minimum deterrence is sufficient insurance against war, and this view has never prevailed in American defense policy.

Assured Destruction Deterrence. This is the notion that a potential enemy can be dissuaded from aggression or war only by our maintaining the capacity to destroy his society *even after* absorbing a well-executed surprise attack. Assured destruction deterrence assumes the enemy's best possible move—a surprise first strike against our own offensive forces. It emphasizes our "second-strike capability"—the ability of our forces to survive a surprise attack by the enemy and then to inflict an unacceptable level of destruction on his homeland. Generally, U.S. defense analysts believe that an enemy will consider one-quarter to one-third of the enemy's population killed and two-thirds of his industrial capacity destroyed to be "unacceptable" and hence sufficient to deter a nuclear attack.

According to former Secretary of Defense Robert McNamara:

> It is generally agreed that a vital first objective, to be met in full by our strategic nuclear forces, is the capability of Assured Destruction. Such a capability would, with a high degree of confidence, ensure that we would deter, under all foreseeable conditions, a calculated, deliberate nuclear attack upon the United States.[2]

It is extremely important to realize that second-strike capability must be *known* to the enemy if it is to serve as a deterrent. Deterrence is achieved *only* if: (1) the enemy *knows* that you have the capacity to deliver unacceptable damage even after absorbing a first strike, (2) the enemy believes that you would in fact do so if attacked, and (3) the enemy is a rational decision-maker. Deterrence, then, is a *psychological* concept: it is not enough merely to be confident yourself; the potential aggressor must be clearly aware of your capacities and intentions. In other words, your threat must be "credible." This means your capacities and intentions must be fully communicated to the enemy. It would be irrational to keep your second-strike capacity a secret. (Even if you did not have such a capability, you might bluff that you did.) Hence, U.S. policy-makers regularly publicize the strength and size of U.S. strategic offensive forces. The enemy must not suspect that in the event of an attack you would lack the will to use your weapons. Hence, occasional "saber rattling" or "shows of force" can serve a useful psychological purpose.

Note then, that assured destruction deterrence is far more complex than minimum deterrence. It is not sufficient to merely count missiles or megatonnage or "overkill capacity." The key question is the *survivability* of an effective deterrent strike force. Assured destruction deterrence considers what can be done *after* a successful surprise attack by the enemy. The surviving forces will be damaged and not fully coordinated because of the enemy's attacks on communications and command installations. These forces must operate in the confusion of a post-attack environment. The enemy's defenses will be alerted. Yet the

---

[2] Testimony of Robert S. McNamara, Committee on Armed Services, U.S. House of Representatives, 89th Congress, 1st session, February 1965. Reprinted in Mark E. Smith and Claude J. Johns, eds., *American Defense Policy*, 2nd ed. (Baltimore: Johns Hopkins Press, 1968), p. 98.

surviving forces must still retain a *credible* capability of penetrating the best-alerted defenses and inflicting unacceptably high casualties.

In striving for assured destruction deterrence, both the U.S. and the USSR have developed long-range intercontinental ballistic missiles (ICBMs) that can travel between the U.S. and the USSR in less than forty minutes. These are disposed in underground "hardened" silos—concrete structures designed and constructed so that they can be destroyed only by a large explosion very nearby. They are far enough apart so that a single explosion regardless of its size can destroy no more than one missile silo. Thus, for an attacker to eliminate with confidence the defender's entire force on a first strike, he would have to evade early detection of his own salvo release (otherwise the defender's salvo would be fired before the attacker's missiles arrived) and accurately target each of the defender's missile silos, or else fire several warheads at each silo to insure a hit.

Another approach to assured destruction deterrence is to place missiles in submarines. Submarines with underwater-launched missiles (ULMs) are difficult to detect, follow, and destroy. The coordinated destruction of this deterrent on a first strike is very unlikely with the technology available now.

A third approach to assured destruction deterrence is the development of advanced manned bomber forces. In general, manned bomber forces are considered vulnerable to a first strike; one nuclear explosion can destroy all the aircraft at a single base. Bombers are only safe when they are in the air, and keeping a large bomber force in the air at all times is expensive. However, given sufficient warning, bombers can be effective. An advanced bomber (the Defense Department is now planning the B-1) can penetrate defenses by a variety of methods, and it can "stand off" the target and launch nuclear warheads in air-to-surface missiles (ASMs) without ever overflying the target area.

American defense policy relies on the "triad" of land-based missiles, submarine-launched missiles, and manned bombers to provide its assured destruction deterrence. This combination of forces is believed to be a more effective deterrent than reliance on any single weapons system, because the diversity and multiplicity of forces makes it difficult for an enemy to develop a first-strike capability that can take out all three systems simultaneously.

Counterforce. Counterforce is the capacity to reduce the damage inflicted by an enemy. A counterforce strategy assumes that assured destruction deterrence has been provided, but it adds that in the event of the failure of deterrence, whether by accident or miscalculation, it is still essential that forces be provided to limit the damage of an enemy attack. Although most defense analysts accept the assured destruction deterrence notion, there is disagreement over the utility, costs, and effectiveness of counterforce measures. Nonetheless, American defense policy still includes some elements of counterforce thinking.

Strategic offensive forces—ICBMs, ULMs, and even bombers—can be used in a counterforce role *if* they can reach some of the enemy's attacking forces *before* they are launched. But if the enemy is planning a surprise first strike it is unlikely that our offensive forces could significantly reduce the weight of that attack. The best our offensive forces could do would be to destroy enemy residual forces—unlaunched missiles and bombers, refire missile silos, or any other strategic forces the enemy might have withheld for subsequent strikes.

The major dispute over counterforce strategy centers on the development of defensive, antiballistic missile systems (ABMs). ABMs are surface-to-air missiles designed to intercept and destroy incoming missiles. Because an ICBM requires less than forty minutes to travel from the USSR to the U.S., the reaction time of an ABM must be less than twenty minutes. An ABM system could be placed around our ICBM silos in order to protect them and reinforce our assured destruction deterrence, and it could be placed around Washington to insure the survival of command and communications facilities. Or ABM could be used to defend major population centers, but this would require nationwide coverage and very large numbers of missiles.

There are several deficiencies in ABM, however, aside from its cost. First of all, virtually all defense analysts believe that it is technically impossible to build an ABM system capable of keeping U.S. casualties to "acceptable" levels (under 40 million?) in the event of a Soviet first strike against cities. Just as bomber forces have been able to penetrate SAM (surface-to-air missile) defenses, ABMs are unlikely to stop any significant proportion of an attacking missile force. Moreover, offensive countermeasures are cheaper and easier to develop than effective antiballistic missiles. In other words, even if a heavy ABM system were constructed at great cost, the enemy could easily offset its effect by a modest increase in his offensive forces.

An effective nationwide civil defense program could reduce U.S. fatalities from an all-out enemy first strike against cities to 80 million out of a 210-million population. (Without *any* civil defense, U.S. casualties in such an attack might run to 150 million.) The additional civil defense required to reduce casualties below 80 million would be very costly and easily offset by less costly increases in the enemy's offensive striking force. For example, to limit fatalities to 40 million in a large first strike against cities, we would have to spend four times as much as a potential aggressor would have to spend on his offensive forces to offset our efforts. Thus, it is difficult to justify a *heavy* civil defense effort. None-theless, the U.S. has failed to provide even a modest civil defense pro-gram.

More important than the technical and cost problems in counterforce policy is the strategic dilemma that the policy creates. *An increase in one nation's counterforce capabilities is a reduction in the other nations' assured destruction capabilities.* A heavy emphasis on counterforce by one player might be viewed by another player as an attempt to take away his second-strike capability and hence leave him open to a surprise attack. If both players possess credible assured second-strike destruction capabili-ties, then a reasonably stable "balance of terror" situation is said to exist. Each nation is deterred from a first strike by the knowledge that the other nation will have enough forces left to inflict unacceptable damage levels. *But* if either nation builds an effective counterforce (a heavy ABM system, a strong civil defense program with deep shelters or city evacuation plans, etc.), this action may be viewed as an attempt to take away the other nation's second-strike capability and free oneself from the consequences of surprise first strike. Thus, counterforce may be viewed by an opponent as a very aggressive move—perhaps even preparation for a deliberate first strike. At the very least, counterforce would oblige one's opponent to add new strength to his offensive forces to insure that his assured destruction deterrent remains credible and effective.

Credible First-Strike Capability. First-strike capability is the ca-pacity to threaten the enemy with a first strike and to make the threat a credible one. Although the notion that "we will never strike first" is a common one, for many years the United States has provided a protective nuclear shield over Western Europe by pledging to come to aid of NATO nations in the event of an attack. This commitment includes an implied pledge to use our strategic nuclear forces against the Soviet heartland in the event that Soviet troops invade Western Europe. It is generally as-sumed that this threat played a major role in halting Soviet expansion in Europe in the years following World War II. The history of Soviet expan-sion into Eastern Europe—postwar Communist takeovers in Poland, Hun-gary, Czechoslovakia, Bulgaria, Rumania; the use of Soviet troops in East Germany, Poland, and particularly Hungary to maintain Communist governments in these nations; military pressures and blockades of Berlin—all combine to suggest that the Soviets can and will use force in Europe to further their political goals. They clearly have superiority in conven-tional military strength—troops, tanks, artillery, support aircraft, etc. Hence, most defense analysts believe that the threat of nuclear retaliation was an essential component of the defense of Western Europe.

In recent years, the credibility of our threat has been seriously eroded. In the decade following the end of World War II, the United States indeed possessed a credible first-strike threat. It possessed the atomic bomb and long-range bombers to deliver it. More importantly, the Soviet Union did *not* possess atomic weapons and had no significant second-strike capability. The U.S. could threaten to use nuclear weapons knowing that the other side had to believe the threat because the U.S. *could* use them without risking damage to itself. But after the Soviet Union acquired its own second-strike assured destruction capability, the U.S. threat lost much of its credibility. The Soviets began to doubt that the U.S. would risk nuclear destruction on itself in order to save Western Europe. They felt freer to increase pressure on Berlin, eventually creating a Berlin crisis in 1961 that necessitated President Kennedy's historic trip to Berlin and pledge of U.S. support. France also began to doubt the credibility of the U.S. commitment and embarked on its own nuclear weapons-development program. Indeed, the whole fabric of European relations during 1960 to 1970 reflected the decline in the credibility of the U.S. shield.

Note that credible first-strike capability does not simply mean the capability of hurting the other side on a first strike. *Credible* first-strike capability really depends on how much harm the enemy can do in retaliation. A first-strike threat is not really credible if the enemy knows that you know he can inflict unacceptable damages on you in response.

Developing a credible first-strike capability would entail (1) a massive buildup of offensive weapons—enough to take out all or nearly all of the enemy's offensive weapons on a first strike; (2) a massive buildup of counterforce systems to reduce his second-strike damage to acceptable levels; or (3) both of these moves in combination.

Current U.S. defense policy does *not* include the force levels required for a credible first-strike capability. Indeed, in the last few years defense policy-makers have avoided references to "superiority" of force levels and talked instead about "sufficiency." This means that U.S. defense policy has emphasized assured destruction deterrence with some counterforce; but we now recognize the loss of our credible first-strike capability.

THE EVOLUTION OF AMERICAN DEFENSE POLICY

American defense policy has evolved continuously since World War II in response to technological change and to changes in perceived threats to its national interests from other nations.[3] Immediately after

---

[3] For a general introduction to the development of U.S. defense policy, see Morton H. Halperin, *Defense Strategies for the Seventies* (Boston: Little, Brown, 1971).

Table 11-1 *The Language of Defense Policy*

ABM. Antiballistic missile system. Missiles designed to intercept and destroy incoming offensive missiles.

SAM. Surface-to-air-missiles. Short-range missiles designed to intercept and destroy enemy aircraft. U.S. B-52 pilots successfully attacked targets in North Vietnam defended by Soviet SAMs with less than 1 percent attrition rate.

KT OR MT. Kilotons or megatons. Measures of destructive power of weapons. 1 KT is equivalent to a *thousand* tons of TNT and 1 MT is equivalent to a *million* tons.

MINUTEMAN. U.S. solid-fueled missile with intercontinental range. 1,000 minutemen are dispersed in hardened underground silos. Minuteman I carries one MT warhead; advanced Minuteman III carries three 200-KT MIRVed warheads.

MIRV. Multiple independently targetable re-entry vehicle. A U.S. system capable of directing three to ten nuclear warheads at separate targets after being launched from one missile. MIRVs on Minuteman III missiles carry three 200-KT warheads; MIRVs on Poseidon carry ten 50-KT warheads.

MRV. Multiple reentry vehicle. Several warheads launched from a single missile but *not* at separate targets. MRVs hit in a pattern around a target to insure its destruction.

ASM OR SRAM. Air-to-surface missiles or short-range attack missiles. Airborne short-range (60–75 miles) missile with nuclear warhead for attack against surface target designed to give bombers "standoff" capability—the ability to hit a target without flying over it.

STRATEGIC WEAPON. Any weapon, plan, or policy designed to strike the enemy's homeland and destroy his ability to wage war.

TACTICAL WEAPON. Any weapon, plan, or policy designed to defeat the enemy's armies in the field.

SLBM. Submarine-launched ballistic missile. Missile in Polaris and Poseidon nuclear-powered submarines capable of firing under the surface and delivering a 1-MT warhead or, in the case of MIRVed Poseidon, ten 50-KT warheads.

HARDENING. Protecting a land-based missile against nuclear attack by enclosing it in underground silos of concrete and steel.

Table 11-1 *Continued*

B-1 Amsa. B-1 advanced manned strategic aircraft. Long-range U.S. supersonic bomber being developed to replace the antiquated B-52s.

Fobs. Fractional orbital bombardment system. USSR designed and tested system for delivering a nuclear warhead by launching it from a low-orbit earth satellite.

Polaris and Poseidon. U.S. submarine and submarine-launched missile systems. Polaris submarines carry 16 missile launching tubes. New Poseidon missiles are MIRVed to carry 10 separately targetable warheads. Eventually 31 of the 41 U.S. Polaris submarines will be modified for Poseidon missiles.

Trident. A new submarine and submarine-launched missile system that will double the range (3,000 to 6,000 miles) of underwater-launched missiles over current Polaris type. This will give submarines greater hiding space in the oceans. Earliest date for an operational Trident is 1978.

World War II, the United States proceeded to disband its military forces and disarm itself as rapidly as possible. A 15-million-man army was dissolved, and the U.S. was left with an army of slightly over 1 million men and a military budget of only $12 billion. The policy of "demobilization" was extremely short-sighted: the U.S. had entered a new era of worldwide responsibilities, but defense policy failed to reflect America's new role in world affairs. Only gradually did defense policy analysts in the Truman Administration become aware of the Soviet military threat in Europe. Aggressive moves in Europe by the USSR under Stalin [4] convinced President Truman by 1947 of the need to commit the United States to the defense of Western European nations. The first official statement of the "containment" policy came in an address to Congress by President Truman requesting military and economic aid to the Greek and Turkish governments, which were then engaged in civil wars against Communist insurgents. Then the U.S. established the Marshall Plan of economic aid for

---

[4] These moves included (1) the establishment of Communist governments in Eastern European nations in violation of wartime agreement to support "democratic" government "broadly representative" of all factions; (2) military support of Communist takeover in Czechoslovakia in 1948; (3) the breakup of the four-power military control commission that was to govern the occupation of Germany, and the sealing off of the Soviet sector of East Germany; (4) a military blockade of Berlin in 1948 designed to oust American, British, and French occupation authorities; (5) Soviet military advice and support for armed Communist troops in Greece and Turkey; and (6) the continued maintenance of a large Soviet land army in Eastern Europe threatening the security of Western European nations.

the rehabilitation of Western European economies, not only for humanitarian purposes but also to strengthen these nations against Communist aggression. The United States also established and recognized a separate West German government and permitted the establishment of a small West German army. Finally, the United States made an explicit commitment to defend Europe and established the North Atlantic Treaty Organization (NATO). These moves were based upon the widespread belief that World Wars I and II had come about because aggressors had assumed that the United States would remain aloof and permit them to dominate Europe. The NATO defense treaty was a firm commitment of U.S. military support that hopefully would deter Soviet attack.

Although the United States was pledged to defend Western Europe, it was soon clear that its military capabilities did not correspond to the new responsibilities that America's political leaders had assumed. The Truman Doctrine announced America's intention to "support free peoples who are resisting attempted subjugation by armed minorities or by outside pressures," but it was not clear how the United States military forces were supposed to "contain" Communism. The United States had few conventional military forces, and only a small stockpile of atomic weapons. In summary, the United States had undertaken foreign policy commitments for which it had few military backup resources.

Nonetheless, the United States possessed the unprecedented power of the atomic bomb. Each of the two atomic bombs dropped on Hiroshima and Nagasaki to conclude World War II was a thousand times more powerful than any single weapon that had been developed up to that time. Doubtlessly the president and his advisors, and more importantly, the Soviet Union, linked the possession of the bomb with America's efforts to halt the spread of Communism in Europe. Moreover, the bomb lent national status and distinction to U.S. military might, even at a period when U.S. military forces-in-being were very weak. If the Soviet Union was deterred from further expansion in Europe after 1948, it was not because of conventional U.S. forces which could easily be overrun by the huge conventional Red Army. Whatever deterrent value U.S. military forces possessed in the immediate postwar period rested on the possession of the atomic bomb. When the military began to gear up to support foreign policy commitments already made by the president, the atomic bomb quickly became the center of efforts to revitalize the nation's military capability.

It was, in part, the realization of America's *weaknesses* in conventional forces that led to the strategy of nuclear deterrence. Immediately after World War II, the United States thought of the atomic bomb as a weapon to be used in conventional war—a weapon that was larger and more destructive than other weapons but one that would be used essentially in the same fashion to support conventional military operations. But in August 1949 when the USSR exploded its own atomic weapon (many years ahead of America's intelligence estimates), the United States began to reassess its strategic concept. America began to think of nuclear weapons not as a means of defeating a potential enemy in actual combat, but instead as a means of *deterring* an enemy attack. Deterrence strategy is concerned with the *threatened* use of force rather than the *actual* application of force. Indeed, if nuclear weapons were to be employed in battle, then the strategy of deterrence would have failed. In 1950, to reinforce its deterrence strategy the United States proceeded on a top-priority basis with the development of the new hydrogen bomb, which increased the explosive power from 20,000 tons of TNT (the 20-KT atomic explosions of Hiroshima and Nagasaki) to the 10-million-ton (10 MT) nuclear bomb.

Even as the United States began to develop its deterrence strategy, the North Korean Communist government initiated a conventional military invasion of South Korea in June 1950. The Korean war necessitated a vast increase in American defense spending for conventional war capability as well as nuclear deterrence. The defense budget increased to $40 billion a year—almost three times the $15 billion spent previously. The U.S. expanded its conventional forces to a 3½-million-man army, not only to fight the Korean War but also to build up the American forces in NATO. The possibility existed that the Korean War might be a feint on the part of the Communists to draw American power into Asia in order to clear the way for a Soviet attack on Western Europe. The post of Supreme Allied Commander for Europe was created and General Dwight D. Eisenhower was appointed to that position.

The Korean War was unpopular with defense policy analysts in the Eisenhower Administration. Involvement in future "Koreas" could seriously erode America's military capabilities. Communist ground forces could always outnumber America's. America's military superiority was based on the nation's technological advances, and not the size of its ground armies. The United States could not expect to indefinitely fight conventional wars such as those in Korea with ground troops.

When Dwight Eisenhower came into office in 1953 he was committed not only to end the Korean war but also to revise American military strategy. It is generally believed that Eisenhower's threat to use nuclear weapons in a strategic attack on China's homeland brought the Chinese to the Korean peace talks. After the Korean truce agreement was accomplished, the Eisenhower Administration pledged to avoid future "Koreas" and to develop a "new look" in defense policy. The new doctrine was labeled "massive retaliation."

The Massive Retaliation Doctrine placed principal reliance on strategic nuclear attack as a deterrent to aggression. This doctrine recognized that·the United States was short on manpower compared to its Communist adversaries, China and Russia, but was highly advanced technologically. The only way to offset the Communist superiority in local ground forces was to emphasize nuclear weapons and air power. According to Secretary of State John Foster Dulles, "There is no local defense which alone will contain the mighty land power of the Communist world. Local defense must be reinforced by the further deterrent of massive retaliatory power." [5] No longer would the United States merely respond to Communist aggression by committing U.S. ground forces to a limited conventional war. Instead, the United States decided "to depend primarily upon a great capacity to retaliate instantly by means and at places of our own choosing." [6]

The policy of massive retaliation relied on a credible first-strike capability by the United States—a credible threat to unleash the nuclear forces of the Strategic Air Command against Soviet heartland in the event of limited aggression. The massive retaliation strategy gave the Air Force the primary role in American strategy and defense expenditures. Massive retaliation possessed still another advantage: it was less expensive than the maintenance of a large conventional army. Massive retaliation provided "more bang for the buck." The emphasis on strategic air power actually enabled the Eisenhower Administration to present lower defense budgets to Congress than otherwise would have been the case.

An important modification of the massive retaliation strategy of the 1950s came with the development of the "tactical nuclear weapon"— nuclear weapons of low explosive power that might be used by troops on the battlefield. New breakthroughs in technology enabled the United States to develop and deploy among its NATO troops nuclear weapons that could be fired from artillery tanks and support guns. In 1954 the NATO council formally committed itself to the use of tactical nuclear weapons in the event of large-scale fighting on the European front. NATO troop requirements were reduced in the belief that tactical nuclear weapons could substitute for manpower. On the other hand, the development and deployment of these tactical nuclear weapons suggested to the Soviets that the United States might choose a response to aggression in Western Europe that was somewhat less "massive" than an all-out nuclear strike on the Soviet homeland.

The massive retaliation policy provoked criticism from both inside and outside the military establishment. Criticism centered around two

---

[5] John Foster Dulles, *New York Times,* January 13, 1954; also cited in Henry T. Nash, *American Foreign Policy: Response to a Sense of Threat* (Homewood, Ill.: Dorsey, 1973), p. 61.

[6] *Ibid.*

major points. The first was that massive retaliation would not be effective in deterring local, ambiguous, Communist aggressions. Although it might succeed in halting a massive Soviet attack on Western Europe, it would not prevent the Communist bloc from initiating minor aggressions in areas outside of Europe. These minor aggressions would never be serious enough enough in themselves to justify "massive retaliation," but over time the Communist bloc could gradually nibble away at the free world. The threat of massive retaliation was simply not credible in deterring aggression in Asia, Africa, the Middle East, or Latin America— particularly Communist-inspired "wars of national liberation" which relied more heavily on internal subversion than conventional external attack. A second major criticism emerged after the Soviet Union acquired its own capability to deliver a devastating nuclear strike against the United States. This argument contended that the "credibility" of massive retaliation was eroded with the increase in Soviet capabilities in nuclear weapons and strategic delivery systems. Massive retaliation implied a U.S. first strike; the primary weapon was the bomber, which itself was vulnerable to an enemy first strike. By attacking our strategic forces, the Soviet Union could disarm our "scorpion" and not be stung back. Critics began to emphasize the need for well-protected strategic forces that could survive an enemy first strike and could retaliate. This meant that additional defense expenditures would be required for the development of hardened missile sites and improved command and control. Finally, there was the criticism that massive retaliation actually reduced the choices available to the president in the event of aggression. Assuming the failure of massive retaliation to deter the enemy, the president would be faced with only two choices: surrender or nuclear war. Critics of massive retaliation argued that more "flexibility" in response was required, that the president should have a range of alternatives in confronting aggression, and that "balanced" military forces were preferred over exclusive reliance on nuclear bombers. Related to this criticism was the belief that both the United States and USSR had achieved a nuclear standoff, that neither nation would use nuclear weapons in a conflict because of the risk of retaliation, and that therefore conventional military weapons would determine the course of world events.

In the 1960 election, John F. Kennedy successfully employed these criticisms against his Republican opponent, Richard M. Nixon. Kennedy launched a full-scale attack on the Republican Administration's defense posture, criticizing both its failure to develop second-strike capability in offensive missiles (the so-called "missile gap") and the failure to develop flexible, balanced ground, sea, and air forces. Kennedy charged that the "missile gap" threatened the security of the United States by giving the Soviet Union the potential of knocking out our retaliatory bomber forces on the ground. In retrospect it appears that the Soviet Union never had that kind of superiority in missiles, but the psychological impact of Sputnik—the first artificial earth satellite—created the impression of Soviet superiority in technology and military capability. It also proved that they had developed very accurate guidance systems (to put things in orbit), and were therefore capable of launching accurately targeted warheads. Moreover, Kennedy charged—accurately—that the United States had seriously neglected conventional military forces—troops, artillery, tanks, ships, and support aircraft. He cited the need for having the option to fight without the use of nuclear weapons.

Upon taking office, President Kennedy and his influential Secretary of Defense, Robert S. McNamara, former president of the Ford Motor Company, realized that the Minuteman and Polaris missile forces were already being developed. Kennedy ordered deployment of a force of 1,000 Minuteman missiles, and 41 Polaris submarines—the basic strategic offensive force levels that were to remain as America's primary deterrent through the 1970s. Secretary of Defense McNamara developed the notion of assured destruction deterrence and ordered the developmnt of well-protected, accurate missile systems with good command and control. He also talked of the value of a "damage-limiting" counterforce program to save American lives in the event of a nuclear war, and recommended a nationwide fallout shelter program. However, by the mid 1960s McNamara came to believe that increasing Soviet strategic capabilities made counterforce unfeasible. He introduced strict techniques of systems-analysis and cost-effectiveness budgeting in weapons systems, and he determined that the cost of a counterforce strategy could be offset by increases in enemy offensive capabilities. Thus, later in the Johnson Administration, counterforce was deemphasized and *assured destruction* became the primary criterion for designing United States strategic forces. Nonetheless, in 1967 McNamara recommended a deployment of a small ABM system designed to deal with the emerging Chinese nuclear threat. He also reported that the United States was planning to deploy MIRVs (multiple independently targeted reentry vehicles) in its land- and sea-based missiles in 1970.

The Kennedy Administration also launched a program to improve the capability of American forces to fight conventional wars. The size of the army was increased and programs for the development of new conventional weapons—from automatic rifles to tanks—were initiated.

In addition, President Kennedy had come into office determined to improve America's capability of dealing with local guerrilla operations. He believed that the Communist tactic of "wars of national liberation" would become the most significant threat to security in the 1960s. These wars were actually "subconventional"—political subversion and guerrilla warfare, rather than conventional military activity. President Kennedy established the Army "Green Berets" and greatly intensified training for counterinsurgency.

This new "flexible response" and "balanced forces" strategy called for nuclear as well as conventionally armed land forces. Thus, the president would have the option of responding to aggression by the use of counterinsurgency forces, conventionally armed ground troops, nuclear-armed ground troops, or various types of strategic nuclear strikes. Thus, when President Johnson decided in 1965 to send large numbers of U.S. troops to South Vietnam, these forces were available and equipped with nonnuclear weapons.

The failure of the American military to achieve a decisive victory in Vietnam had far-reaching consequences for the military itself and for American society. Humiliation in a jungle war, the heavy loss of men and materials, and the protracted frustration of pursuing a dedicated, elusive enemy seriously demoralized American military forces. The war cost 50,000 American lives. At the height of our involvement in 1968 the U.S. had a force of 560,000 men in Vietnam. The total armed forces of the U.S. included over $3\frac{1}{2}$ million men. The credibility of America's top commanders was impaired by unfounded reports of progress and premature predictions of the enemy's defeat. Discipline deteriorated in the ranks, atrocities against civilians captured public attention, and racial conflict among the troops became commonplace. More importantly, the American public became divided and demoralized over the war. Obvious errors in political and military judgment, prolonged and fruitless combat against a third-rate military power, and the moral and philosophical questions posed by American involvement in a distant war, all combined to undermine confidence in military and civilian defense policy-makers. A decade that had begun with strong pressure to *improve* America's defense capabilities ended with strong Congressional pressure to *reduce* defense expenditures and curtail weapons development.

Upon taking office, Richard Nixon ordered an overall review of defense policy. Defense requirements for the 1970s were to be reevaluated in the light of the Nixon Doctrine, first announced in 1969. The Nixon Doctrine placed primary responsibility for the defense of free nations against Communist insurgency on these nations themselves. The U.S. would provide economic assistance and military supplies to nations resisting internal Communist subversion, but these nations would have to provide their own military forces. Even against conventional military forces of the nations under attack, the U.S. might commit conventional air power—nonnuclear bombing—in support of allied troops, but it would not send American ground troops into combat except under extreme provocation. The draft was ended and the military geared itself for an "all-volunteer" force. Defense expenditures declined as a percent of the Gross National Product.

The Nixon Administration acknowledged America's loss of strategic nuclear "superiority" over the Soviet Union, but argued the necessity of maintaining "nuclear sufficiency." The administration concentrated on the improvement of America's assured destruction deterrent—continued MIRVing of land- and submarine-based missiles, the development of the long-range Trident missile-carrying submarine, and the development of the B-1 bomber. The president attempted to avoid programs that would seem to threaten the *Soviet's* second-strike deterrent capability. Finally, in a historic Moscow summit meeting, the president signed the Strategic Arms Limitation (SALT) agreement.

THE STRATEGIC ARMS LIMITATION AGREEMENT—SALT

In 1972 the U.S. and the USSR concluded two and a half years of talks about limiting the strategic arms race. The Strategic Arms Limitation (SALT) Agreement marks a milestone in the long journey toward arms control. The SALT agreement consists of a formal treaty limiting ABMs and an executive agreement placing a numerical ceiling on offensive missiles. The ABM treaty limits each side to one ABM site for defense of its national capital and one ABM site for defense of an offensive ICBM field. The total number of ABMs permitted is 200 for each side, 100 at each location. (The USSR already has both of its ABM sites constructed; the U.S. has only one site at the Grand Falls, North Dakota, Minuteman field.) Under the offensive arms agreement, each side is frozen at the total number of offensive missiles completed or under construction. The Soviet Union is permitted 1,618 land-based missiles, including 313 new giant SS-9s. The U.S. is permitted to maintain 1,054 land-based missiles and to construct new Poseidon missiles if it dismantles an equal number of older missiles (presumably 54 obsolete Titans). Both sides are limited to the missile-carrying submarines operational or under construction at the time of the agreement; this means 43 for the Soviets and 41 for the U.S. Both sides can replace older submarines and missiles, as long as their number and size remains unchanged. There are *no* limitations on MIRV. As a consequence, the U.S. holds a temporary advantage in deliverable warheads under the agreements (5,700 for the U.S. compared to 2,500 for the USSR), but the Soviets are now MIRVing their own. There are no limitations on bombers. There are no limitations on advanced research on totally new weapons systems. The SALT agreements will last until 1977. Both nations are pledged to continue efforts at further arms control—the SALT II talks.

Why would the U.S. and USSR enter into such an agreement? First of all, the USSR achieved what it had been struggling toward for decades: strategic parity with the U.S. officially recognized in a treaty acknowledging Soviet superiority in the number and size of offensive weapons. The U.S. achieved a slowing of the Soviet momentum in the building of heavy ICBMs (SS-9s) and missile-carrying submarines—a momentum which would have given the Soviet Union even greater superiority in the years to come. The Soviets are free to MIRV their own missiles but the U.S. hopes that Phase II of SALT will resolve this issue before the end of the current five-year agreement. Both sides have agreed *not* to build large-scale ABM system to defend their own cities. This means that each agrees to curtail its counterforce efforts. Satellite reconnaissance makes the SALT agreement self-enforcing; without satellite photography the question of inspection would have doomed negotiations. Each nation holds the population of the other as hostage (a "stabilizing" condition), as long as neither develops a credible first-strike capability. However, further technological advances in MIRV and antisubmarine warfare could threaten the current stability if it gave either or both nations the capacity to take out the other's ICBMs, submarines, and bombers in a coordinated first strike. Hence, to insure stability, the U.S. and USSR must find some way to further curb the technological race.

NUCLEAR WAR GAMES

Thus far, we have examined some of the strategic alternatives available to nations in confronting thermonuclear war. Now let us consider some of the real and potential outcomes.[7]

Is it realistic to view a first-strike nuclear attack as an even remote possibility? One possible cause of nuclear war is accident—mechanical failure or human error. For years Americans have been entertained in movies and novels by the thought of inadvertent war—the failure of "fail-safe" mechanisms or the crazed actions of "Dr. Strangeloves." The actual probability of inadvertent war has been rendered very low by a variety of elaborate safety precautions and devices. But it is important to realize that an increase in safety controls over nuclear weapons lengthens reaction time and reduces assured destruction capability. More-

---

[7] For further inquiry into nuclear war strategies, see Herman Kahn, *On Thermonuclear War* (Princeton: Princeton University Press, 1961); Herman Kahn, *Thinking About the Unthinkable* (New York: Horizon Press, 1962); Henry A. Kissinger, ed., *Problems of National Strategy* (New York: Praeger, 1965).

Table 11-2 *The Balance of Strategic Forces*

U.S.	USSR
The U.S. maintains elements of three separate strategic weapons systems—land-based missiles, sea-based missiles, and bombers. Each system is designed to independently guarantee assured destruction of an enemy's soft targets even after absorbing a surprise thermonuclear attack.	The USSR maintains a superiority in the total number of missiles, and the SS-9 is capable of carrying a much larger warhead than any U.S. missile (25 MT versus 1 MT for Minuteman). The USSR has substantially fewer deliverable warheads because of the U.S. advantage in the MIRV program.[1]

Land-Based Missiles

U.S.	USSR
Total: 1,054	Total: 1,618
Minutemen: 1,000 including MIRVed Minuteman IIIs.	SSGs: 313 including MIRVed. SS-11s; 1,305
Titan: 54 obsolete.	S-8 modified-MIRV. 52 holes under construction.

Sea-Based Missiles

U.S.	USSR
Total: 656 SLBMs including Polaris and MIRVed Poseidons.	Total: 560 SLBMs
Submarines: 41	Submarine: 43

Deliverable Warheads

U.S.	USSR
Total: 5,700	Total: 2,500

Strategic Bombers

U.S.	USSR
Total: 516	Total: 140
B-52s: 440	
FB-11s: 76	
(B-1 under development).	

Other Offensive Weapons

U.S.	USSR
550 tactical fighter bombers in Europe.	730 Intermediate-range missiles (IRBMs). Targeted on Europe and China.
7,000 nuclear warheads in Europe.	

ABM's

U.S.	USSR
100 (Protecting ICBM site).	200 (Protecting ICBM site and Moscow).

[1] In the next few years, perhaps before the expiration of the current SALT agreement in 1977, the USSR should surpass the U.S. in deliverable warheads. In July 1972, U.S. intelligence reported that the USSR was developing a missile more powerful than the SS-9 which could carry twenty 1-MT warheads. It could be launched from existing silos and therefore not violate the SALT agreement. If fully deployed, this missile could give the USSR over 7,000 deliverable warheads.

over, if command and control is centralized in the hands of the president, it is more vulnerable to attack. In contrast, strong assured destruction deterrence reduces the possibility of inadvertent war, because it gives a decision-maker time to evaluate and decide about the size and intentions of incoming attack forces. The defender is not under overwhelming pressure to get his own attack forces safely into the air. Nonetheless, in a period of tension, with exchanges of threats and perhaps limited aggression, an accident or sequence of multiple accidents could be dangerous.

A more likely cause of a first-strike surprise nuclear attack would be the loss of assured destruction second-strike capability by one or both nations. If a nation has no second-strike capability, it may come to believe that its survival depends upon a preemptive strike. Such a first strike would not be undertaken to achieve political goals, but rather to prevent a feared enemy attack. If a nation has no second-strike deterrent, the advantages of striking first are so great that, should there appear to be a high probability of the enemy actually attacking, it may be more rational to accept a relatively small retaliatory strike rather than risk a high probability of receiving a much more destructive first blow. Reciprocal fear of surprise attack may pressure one side to launch a preemptive strike if only because it knows the other side is under similar pressure! Note that such a war would not be a product of accident, but rather the product of rational calculation.

If *both* sides possess credible first-strike capability (which means that neither side possesses second-strike assured destruction capability), the pressure to preempt would be overwhelming. Defense analysts refer to such a situation as "unstable." In contrast, if *both* sides possess second-strike assured destruction capability (which means that neither can launch a first strike without expecting to receive unacceptable damage in a retaliating blow), then it is said that a "balance of terror" exists. War is still a possibility, but defense analysts label such a situation as "stable."

Research and technological advancement are a constant threat to stability. For example, until recently the standard Soviet ICBM, the SS-11, was comparable to the U.S. Minuteman, our primary assured destruction deterrent. Both weapons were relatively equal and both nations had approximately the same number of weapons. In order for the USSR to achieve a credible first-strike capability against the U.S. (that is, in order for them to insure that we could not strike back after a surprise attack), they would need to build two or three times as many SS-11s as we had Minutemen. This is because two or three SS-11s would be needed to *insure* that each Minuteman was destroyed in their initial attack. But in the late 1960s the USSR began to deploy a much larger and more accurate ICBM, the SS-9. Defense analysts estimated that one SS-9 was capable of destroying one Minuteman (although no missile is 100 percent reliable). If the USSR were to build 1,200 or more SS-9s, our Minuteman second-strike deterrent would be taken away. Of course, our Polaris submarine force, with 656 missiles, would still remain as a deterrent. But it was also observed that the USSR was building a large-scale ABM system which, combined with their SS-9, might take away most of our second-strike deterrent. Hence, the SS-9 and the Soviet ABM system were viewed as threats to the relatively stable "balance of terror" that existed.

To counter the perceived threat from a large-scale Soviet ABM system, the U.S. developed a multiple independently targeted reentry vehicle (MIRV) for its Minuteman and Polaris missiles. MIRV enables *each* missile to launch three, six, or even fourteen separate warheads at separate targets while still high in space over the enemy's homeland. The U.S. is currently adding MIRVs to its Polaris and Minuteman missiles; these "MIRVed" missiles will be known as Poseidon and Minuteman III.

MIRV makes *any* ABM system obsolete; it has the potential of multiplying U.S. striking power by six times. A thousand ICBMs with MIRV could deliver 6,000 separately targeted nuclear warheads. Such an attack would easily overwhelm an ABM system and saturate the target areas with multiple hits. Initially the Soviets were behind the U.S. in the development of MIRVs, but now they too have begun to deploy this weapon.

However, even though MIRV is attractive in guaranteeing penetration of any ABM system, it also "destabilizes" the balance of strategic forces. MIRV has the potential capability of removing each side's second-strike capability by destroying every offensive missile in its silo in saturation targeting. Thus, MIRV increases the incentive for both sides to strike first. This is because each side will have lost its second-strike capability to a MIRV saturation-type surprise attack. Although MIRV, even in Soviet hands, may not itself lead to the initiation of nuclear war, it is extremely destabilizing in a period of *crisis*. Each side may realize that the other side knows the advantages of striking first and might reach the conclusion that a nuclear war in which it struck first was preferable to risking a first strike from the other side.

In order to maintain second-strike assured destruction deterrence against a fully developed MIRVed ICBM attack, it is essential that a nation develop an ULM-equipped *submarine deterrent force*. MIRVed missiles have a potential first-strike capability against land-based missiles and aircraft, but they have no ability to attack missile-carrying submarines lurking in the depths of the oceans. If the U.S. and USSR both acquired effective MIRV systems, deterrence would depend upon each nation's capacity to launch a second-strike retaliatory attack with ULMs from submarines that are on station at the time of attack (and not destroyed in port).

The U.S. has 41 missile-launching submarines; each can carry 16 Polaris underwater-launched missiles. This means the U.S. has a total force of 656 Polaris missiles. Ten of these submarines (with 160 launching tubes), known as Poseidons, have been converted to carry new MIRVed warhead missiles. The U.S. Navy is planning to MIRV the rest of missile force in the years ahead, and to build a new submarine, the Trident, capable of launching missiles with intercontinental range— 6,000 miles. (Present maximum range of Polaris is 3,000 miles; the added range will give the submarine much more ocean room in which to hide.) The Soviets are nearing completion of their force of 42 missile-carrying submarines with over 700 underwater-launched missiles.

These submarine forces may become major stabilizing elements in the nuclear war game in the late 1970s. They give each nation a second-strike capability—offensive power that cannot be destroyed in a MIRVed ICBM, saturation-type first strike. Thus, though MIRV appears to threaten stability, submarine forces promise to maintain stability.

Satellite reconnaissance is another major stabilizing force in the nuclear war game. Good intelligence reduces uncertainty about offensive and defensive capabilities, and hence reduces the likelihood of war through miscalculation. One result of the U.S. space program was the development of "spy in the sky" satellites capable of constant photo reconnaissance of enemy territory. These satellites can take amazingly detailed pictures from outer space. (High-altitude airplane overflights of enemy territory—"U-2" flights—are no longer essential.) It is now virtually impossible for the enemy to deploy offensive or defensive weapons without the president knowing about it as soon as construction begins. The development of these satellites also makes arms limitations agreements easier, because each nation can identify cheating in their space photography.

DILEMMAS OF NUCLEAR WAR

Thirty years of peace between the U.S. and the USSR has made the thought of nuclear war unreal. Despite several serious crises—Hungary, 1957; Berlin, 1961; Cuba, 1963—the U.S. and USSR have avoided nuclear war. However, it is a paradox of the nuclear war game that the longer the period of peace and the greater number of crises that are resolved *without* war, the greater the potential danger of war emerging from a new crisis situation. Governments may become more intransigent as the thought of a real war diminishes, particularly if those nations that have stood firm in past crises have won gains against those who have "backed down." In describing the Cuban missile crises, Secretary of State Dean Rusk was quoted as saying: "We were eyeball to eyeball with the Russians and they blinked." If both governments decide on the basis of past experience that the other will certainly back down in the next crisis, and neither "blinks," the possibility of a nuclear exchange is greatly enhanced.

Controlled Reprisal—"Tit for Tat." Even if assured destruction deterrence prevents a surprise all-out nuclear attack, a limited strategic nuclear exchange is still a possibility. Although many laymen have visualized *any* nuclear war beginning with a full-salvo city-busting attack, most defense policy analysts consider a "controlled," limited nuclear exchange as a more likely prospect. For example, consider the following "scenario": The USSR decides that the U.S. would not really go to nuclear war to defend Berlin and Western Europe. Soviet troops quickly capture Berlin, and heavy Soviet divisions pour into West Germany. The Soviets make no direct attack on the U.S. but they warn the U.S. that nuclear retaliation on our part will result in the complete destruction of American society. American "deterrence" has failed to protect Berlin, West Germany, and Western Europe from a conventional military attack, and neither the U.S. nor other NATO countries have sufficient conventional forces—troops, tanks, artillery, tactical air support—to halt the Russian advance. Is the president faced with the choice between all-out nuclear war or the surrender of Western Europe? Perhaps not—even if he has previously told the USSR that he would order an all-out nuclear attack in response to such aggression. (It may be rational to *threaten* to go to all-out war to deter an aggression, and also rational *not* to do so even if the threat fails to deter the aggression.) Instead, the president may choose to launch a controlled demonstration attack on a single Soviet city to convince the Soviets of our firm resolve to resist aggression; at the same time he would demand a halt to the Soviet advance and threaten additional damage if they did not acquiesce in our demand. This move might convince the Soviets of our seriousness of purpose and strength of will. On the other hand, the Soviets might retaliate with a limited controlled attack of their own on three or four American cities, demonstrating their greater firmness of will. They would couple such an attack with a peace offering and a threat that we had better acquiesce in the surrender of Europe or face even greater destruction. At this point, both sides would be engaged in a superdestructive game of Chicken.

As bizarre as this scenario may appear, most defense policy analysts believe that the threat of controlled reprisal is a more credible deterrent to aggression than the threat of mutual annihilation.

The Targeting Dilemma. The choice of targets—cities versus military installations—presents still another strategic problem. Most laymen assume that a surprise first strike by the Soviet Union would be directed against American cities. (It is easy to assume that the enemy is vindictive and malevolent; but defense policy analysts must assume that he is rational.) Yet it is *irrational* for an attacker to merely try to hurt the defender. The rational first-strike attacker will try to destroy the defender's retaliatory power in order to escape destruction himself. An all-out first strike against *cities* would be senseless, because it could only cause the defender to retaliate with a destructive counterblow. Thus, *first-strike* targets will be offensive missile sites, submarines, and bomber bases. Indeed, a rational first-strike attacker may wish to see some part of the defender's population "saved" so that they might be held as hostages against a retaliatory blow. The attacker might couple his first strike against military targets with an announcement that any second-strike retaliation by the defender would result in the destruction of the rest of the defender's civilian population.

In contrast, the defender (presumably the United States) would not achieve much in a second-strike response by attacking *empty* missile sites, *empty* submarines, and bases whose bombers are already in the air. Indeed, it would be a more rational second-strike deterrent to threaten to respond by attacking the enemy's *cities. A surprise attack might best be deterred by appearing to be irrevocably committed to an all-out mass killing of civilians in retaliation.* But if deterrence fails and the U.S. has already absorbed an enemy first strike, what rational purpose is served by destroying his civilian population? Aside from revenge, there would be little to gain from such an attack. In other words, it may be rational to *threaten* a nuclear holocaust, but irrational to carry through on the commitment.

"Broken-Backed" War. Some defense policy analysts believe that after the first great exchange of nuclear salvos, a war between the U.S. and USSR would then be fought by surviving conventional military forces. Conditions on both sides would be chaotic and military units would be forced to fight with little support from a disabled homeland— hence, the reference to a "broken-backed" war. However, it is next to impossible for war planners to formulate defense policies based on the assumption of national disaster at the outset of hostilities. Even if efforts were made to insure the survivability of some conventional military forces, it is impossible to predict the effects of popular panic, adminis-

trative disorganization, or panic among the troops. Moreover, most (but not all) military analysts today believe that strategic bombardment would be decisive in a nuclear war.

CONVENTIONAL WAR GAMES

Because of the high risks and costs of all-out nuclear war, and the *recognition* of these risks and costs by the U.S. and the USSR, limited conventional war is a more likely occurrence than a thermonuclear exchange. The notion of deterrence in nuclear war strategy involves the *psychological* use of very destructive weapons. But conventional war strategy is much more likely to involve the *actual* use of less destructive weapons—artillery, tanks, troops, and tactical aircraft.

America's active involvement in limited conventional wars in Korea and Vietnam has made most Americans realize that "war" is not a single, simple, or uniform action. Wars come in different varieties and sizes. Sometimes it is difficult for Americans to understand why this is so—why the United States does not seek "total victory" in every war and use any and every weapon in its arsenal to achieve that victory.

War is an instrument of national policy. Victory in war is not an end in itself; the purpose of war is to achieve some national objective—security, survival, credibility, protection of an ally, vital territory, resources, etc. Nations are continually asserting their wills in conflict situations with other nations and using a variety of means of influence and coercion. At some point these conflicts become "war." War, then, is a matter of the degree and intensity of international conflict. It is not undisciplined mass violence. The size and nature of a war must be related to its political purposes. Karl Von Clauswitz, the famous German military theorist of the nineteenth century, explains the importance of keeping the political purposes of a war constantly in the forefront of military operations:

> War is nothing but a continuation of politics by other means . . . war can never be separated from political intercourse, and if this occurs, all the threads of relations are broken, and we have before us a senseless thing without an object.

War, then if it is to be employed at all, must be employed in a rational fashion to serve national purposes. War is not simply a way of giving vent to hatred, malevolence, or sadism. Crushing the enemy is not the measure of success, but whether we have achieved our national purposes at a reasonable cost. For war to be a rational policy—that is, for its benefits to outweigh its costs—several conditions must be met. First of all, policy-makers must clearly understand the objectives of the war and commit military forces in rough proportion to the value of these objectives. War is a very crude instrument of policy. Its violence and destruction can set off a chain of consequences that overshadow and defeat the original purposes of the war. Costs in lives and resources can easily spiral all out of proportion to the original objectives of the war. An increase in costs may itself cause a nation to expand its original objectives in order to rationalize higher costs. The enemy must then commit larger forces to prevent greater losses. Hence the necessity for close control and supervision of the level of violence. Diplomats must make continuing efforts to maintain political talks toward a negotiated settlement on the basis of national objectives.

If the object of war becomes total victory over the enemy, there will be no limit on the enemy's use of force. Total victory for one nation implies total defeat for its opponent—a threat to national survival, justifying unlimited levels of violence. Political objectives are set aside for possible resolution after the war, and every effort is directed toward the complete destruction of the enemy's war-making power. As the dimensions of violence and destruction increase, the war arouses passionate fears and hatreds which themselves come to replace rational objectives in the conflict. As the level of suffering and sacrifice increases, the goal becomes the blind unreasoning destruction of the enemy.

In a "stable" nuclear balance of terror—where each side possesses assured destruction second-strike capability—conventional war becomes a more likely possibility. America's strategic nuclear forces have been designed to deter a direct attack on continental United States and a major attack on Western Europe. In *all* other conflicts the United States will probably rely on conventional weapons, or perhaps in extremely rare circumstances, "tactical" nuclear weapons. *Exclusive* reliance on nuclear weapons would place the United States in a terrible dilemma in confronting limited aggression—involving a choice between either surrender or nuclear war. In contrast, if the United States maintains a balance of forces—strategic nuclear, tactical nuclear, nonnuclear conventional, counterinsurgency—it will be able to confront aggression anywhere in the world with weapons and forces appropriate to the situation.

Apart from their strictly military purposes, conventional forces also have an important psychological role to play. The deployment of U.S. troops in Berlin, West Germany, and Western Europe serves notice to the USSR that it cannot send Soviet divisions across the borders without engaging U.S. troops. Even though these U.S. troops are no match for the massive Soviet armies, nonetheless, the very fact that American troops would have to be killed in a Soviet attack in Western Europe *insures* U.S. involvement in such a conflict. U.S. troops in Europe form a "plate-glass window": the Soviets *know* that to take Western Europe they would have to kill American troops, and this knowledge is a further deterrent to such an attack. Deploying U.S. troops in Europe notifies friend and foe alike of the seriousness of our commitment to defend the area.

U.S. troops in Europe are equipped with tactical nuclear weapons. Obviously this fact has additional deterrent value. Not only do the Soviets know that U.S. troops would be immediately involved in any defense against aggression, but they also know that such a defense would involve the use of nuclear weapons, at least at the tactical level.

Perhaps the most important objectives at stake in conventional war situations are the perceived political effects of various outcomes. The actual territories, resources, or people being fought over may be relatively unimportant. In general, the superpowers have justified military intervention in local conflicts by citing the long-range threats that might occur if a particular area is allowed to fall. In Korea and Vietnam the United States was concerned with the lessons that allies and enemies would draw from its actions. If the U.S. had withdrawn precipitously and permitted Hanoi to win a military victory, potential enemies would have been encouraged to believe that U.S. commitments have little meaning and the danger of future aggressions would be increased. Moreover, our allies would begin to doubt our willingness to defend them if they came under attack and were forced to acquiesce in enemy demands. It would be harder for the United States to convince both allies and enemies of the seriousness of its commitments if it permitted one of its allies to be taken by military violence.

In the Kennedy-Johnson Administrations, the policy of flexible response and balanced forces meant that the U.S. should prepare itself to respond to various levels of aggression with weapons and forces appropriate to the threat. Moreover, the U.S. should be prepared to fight several of these conflicts simultaneously. Specifically, this country should be prepared to fight simultaneously two conventional wars, with or without tactical nuclear weapons, on two continents (presumably Europe and Asia), with a small military contingent left over to handle one minor conflict. This became known as the "2½ war" force level.

The Nixon Doctrine asserts that nations being threatened by aggression must assume primary responsibility for their own security. The U.S. will no longer provide military advisors or counterinsurgency forces to governments threatened by Communist-inspired "wars of national liberation"; U.S. aid would be limited to economic assistance and military supplies. In the case of a conventional war, the U.S. now expects any nation under attack by the conventional forces of another nation to be responsible for the burden of providing its own ground forces. Even in a major conventional war (e.g., North Korean attack on South Korea; North Vietnam attack on South Vietnam; Chinese attack on Taiwan; etc.) the U.S. would attempt to limit its military role to sea and air support.

Under the Nixon Doctrine, U.S. force levels have been reduced to a "1½ war" capability—the capability of fighting one conventional war, with or without tactical nuclear weapons, and a minor conflict simultaneously. This reduction in force levels from Kennedy-Johnson years permits the U.S. to end the draft and rely on an all-volunteer army.

Limited wars are wars fought in relatively small geographic areas with restrictions on both sides on weapons and targets. The Korean war was limited to the Korean peninsula and the Vietnam war to Indochina. In the Korean war the Chinese never attacked U.S. bases in Japan and the U.S. never attacked Chinese territory. In the Vietnam war the U.S. did not target population centers or industry, although these were occasionally hit in attacks aimed at nearby military or transportation facilities. Not using nuclear weapons has been the most significant limitation on U.S. actions in limited wars. But it is difficult to predict the specific military actions that would be taken in any *future* limited war. The conduct of limited wars is determined by specific international and local political conditions at the time of the conflict. Limits are not a product of any agreement between the countries involved, but instead a product of internal decisions about the benefits and costs of various military actions.

SOVIET AND CHINESE DEFENSE POLICY

In its strategic confrontation with the United States, the Soviet Union's primary concern has been the deterrence of American nuclear attack. In the immediate post–World War II period, Soviets had no significant capability of attacking the American homeland. Their primary military deterrent was a large ground army capable of seizing and holding Western Europe. In addition, the Soviet Union placed great emphasis on air defense. It developed the SAM missile system very early and has continued to improve its heavy air defense system (known in the West as the Tallinn system). The Soviets have always spent relatively more on counterforce efforts than the United States, and their larger land area and dispersed population give them a greater natural advantage in damage limitation.

Immediately following World War II, the Soviets launched a crash program for the development of nuclear weapons. They developed their atomic and hydrogen bombs even more quickly than the United States. At the same time they began a similar program for the development of intercontinental ballistic missiles. The Soviets did not develop a bomber force as large as that of the United States, but instead concentrated on large missiles capable of carrying large-megatonnage nuclear weapons. In October 1957, the Soviets launched the first artificial earth satellite—Sputnik—suggesting Soviet superiority IBMs. In the early 1960s the Soviets exploded a 100-megaton nuclear warhead—the largest ever exploded on earth.

Soviet strategic thinking closely parallels American thought. The Soviets are aware of the importance of developing assured destruction forces that are relatively invulnerable to a first strike. The Soviet SS-11 ICBM is liquid-fueled, but otherwise it resembles a Minuteman. The Soviet SS-9 is a much larger missile, capable of carrying three large warheads; the Soviets are now proceeding to MIRV warheads. Although historically Soviet military doctrines stressed land forces, in the late 1960s the Soviets began to deploy a submarine force closely resembling U.S. Polaris forces. Each Soviet "Y-class" submarine has sixteen missile tubes; it is nuclear-powered and can fire from under water. The development of this force suggests that the Soviet Union is concerned with the vulnerability of its land-based missiles to American MIRVed Minuteman missiles.

In 1957 the Soviets acknowledged the great destruction that would result from a nuclear war between the Soviet Union and the United States. Premier Khrushchev publicly rejected the Marxist-Leninist notion of the inevitability of war with Capitalist nations. This "deviation" from Communist ideology helped to create the split with the Chinese. The Soviets continued to believe in the ultimate success of worldwide Communist revolution, and Premier Khrushchev publicly predicted that Communism would eventually "bury" Capitalist nations. But the Soviets stressed that the destructiveness of general nuclear war made it necessary to direct the course of the worldwide revolution along less dangerous channels. They acknowledged that the early stages of a nuclear war can be decisive, but in contrast to American military thinking, they continued to discuss the notion of "broken-backed war." The Soviets expect that a strategic nuclear exchange would be followed by large-scale ground fighting which would determine the ultimate outcome of the war. In this ground fighting, the Soviets assume that they can invade and capture Western Europe.

Although the Soviet Union has publicly rejected *nuclear war* as an instrument of expanding worldwide Communism, it has certainly not rejected the use of *conventional* military forces to achieve that goal. The Soviet Union has maintained a large standing army in Eastern Europe. These forces were actually used in East Germany, Hungary, and Czechoslovakia to maintain Communist governments in these nations. The Soviet forces in Eastern Europe are armed with tactical nuclear weapons, and they are capable of fighting both conventionally and with these nuclear weapons.

The major Soviet use of military force against Western Europe has been centered on Berlin. The Soviets have attempted to use their conventional superiority to force the Western powers out of that city. Thus far, American steadfastness has prevented the Soviets from achieving this goal.

The Cuban missile crisis was a direct product of Soviet efforts to achieve nuclear parity with the United States before its ICBM force was fully operational and deployed. The Soviets sought unsuccessfully to place intermediate-range ballistic missiles (IRBM) in Cuba to threaten massive destruction of the United States in the event of general war. In October of 1963 President Kennedy declared a naval blockade of Cuba and a quarantine on Soviet ships delivering offensive missiles to the island. At the same time he readied America's strategic missile and bomber forces to react in the event of a Soviet military response. After an exchange of communications, Premier Khrushchev announced that Soviet missile-carrying ships would return home and that offensive missiles would be removed from Cuba. At a later date, President Kennedy announced that U.S. IRBMs would be removed from American bases in Turkey. At the time it appeared as if the Soviet Union had backed down in the face of American nuclear power. Premier Khrushchev never again recovered his prestige in the Soviet Union and he was soon replaced. Now, with the full deployment of Soviet ICBM forces and the achievement of superiority in the number of these missiles, it is no longer necessary for the Soviets to attempt to gain advanced bases for IRBMs.

During the 1960s the Soviet defense policy became concerned with the possibility of a military conflict with China. There was a substantial buildup of conventional Soviet forces on the Soviet-Chinese border, and there were several armed border clashes between these two Communist powers. The developing nuclear capability of the Chinese has created great concern in the Soviet Union. On several occasions, Soviet diplomats have attempted to probe the attitude of the American government toward a Soviet preemptive first strike against China's nuclear installations. The Chinese have publicly accused the Soviets of preparing such an attack.

In contrast to the Soviet Union, Chinese military strategy reflects the "correct" Marxist-Leninist line that war is a legitimate instrument of worldwide Communist revolution. Chairman Mao Tse-tung teaches that power comes from the barrel of a gun. The Chinese do *not* believe that nuclear war would lead to world destruction. On the contrary, they believe that Communism, not Capitalism, would survive as the worldwide system of government after a nuclear war, and that China itself would survive as the major political power. They argue that "the United States is a paper tiger" and that nuclear weapons cannot destroy China.

There is an element of rationality in the apparently irrational attitude of the Chinese toward nuclear war. They have only a small number of nuclear weapons and are facing two potential opponents with massive nuclear strength. By publicly denying the destructiveness of nuclear war, they communicate to their potential enemies that they do not fear nuclear power. Playing the role of a lunatic can be a source of strength in some situations. If the Chinese can convince their opponents that they are not afraid of their opponents' weapons, then they can not be blackmailed by such weapons. (On the other hand, their lunacy may be a source of weakness if it convinces the Soviets that a preemptive strike is essential because the Chinese are lunatics and will use their nuclear weapons as soon as they are developed.)

Although publicly discounting the importance of nuclear weapons, nonetheless, the Chinese have devoted great resources to the development of their own nuclear capability. Nuclear weapons are important to the Chinese not only in confronting Capitalist nations but also as a means of increasing their power within the Communist world. In the 1970s the Chinese possessed nuclear weapons but only a limited capability of delivering them on an enemy homeland. At present the Chinese appear to be relying upon bombers with a limited range and perhaps IRBMs. American intelligence does not estimate a significant ICBM capability for the Chinese until 1980. The Chinese have demonstrated their willingness to use conventional war as an instrument of their foreign policy on several occasions. In 1951, they sent their armies into Korea to prevent the collapse of the North Korean Communist regime. In 1965, Chinese armies conquered Tibet and made it a satellite of the Peking government. The Chinese have used limited military force for specific purposes in the Taiwan straits and on the Indian border.

Note, however, that the actual use of Chinese military forces has been limited to territories immediately adjacent to Chinese homeland. Despite an ideological commitment to use force as an instrument of foreign policy, the Chinese have been cautious in the actual application of force. The U.S. commitment to defend Taiwan has effectively deterred a Chinese invasion of that island. Maoist military doctrine holds that an enemy should be strategically despised but tactically respected. This means that even though the Chinese are convinced that in the long run they will defeat their enemies, in the short run they must recognize their enemies as being stronger and thus deserving of respect. Maoist military doctrine stresses the notion of going from a weak position to a strong position over a period of time, by the proper application of short-run tactics and long-run strategic·(Maoist) thinking. The Red Chinese used this as their strategy in the long civil war in which they came to power. Maoism holds that a very small force can triumph ultimately against overwhelming odds by gradually increasing its strength while diminishing the strength of its enemies. Currently the Chinese believe that the best way to advance the cause of worldwide revolution and bring about the overthrow of Capitalist and Imperialist governments is through "wars of national liberation." But the seriousness of the Chinese conflict with the Soviet Union has caused them to seek a détente with the United States.

SUMMARY

Decisions about defense policy in Washington, Moscow, Peking, and other world capitals are interdependent—the future of mankind depends on what is done at each of these major power centers and how each responds to the decisions of others. Game theory provides a vocabulary and way of thinking rationally about decision making in competitive interdependent situations. Let us set forth several summary ideas about defense policy.

1. Minimum deterrence strategy is the belief that potential enemies can be dissuaded from war simply because the U.S. possesses nuclear weapons and delivery systems. It is considered insufficient by most military analysts because it fails to consider the enemy's best possible move—a surprise first strike against our offensive forces.

2. Assured destruction deterrence strategy is the basis of current national defense policy. It seeks to prevent nuclear war by making the consequences of a first strike unacceptable to a potential enemy by providing assured second-strike capability. The U.S. maintains a "triad" of forces—land-based missiles, submarine-launched missiles, and manned bombers—to assure survival of enough offensive forces after a surprise first strike to deliver an "unacceptable" level of destruction on the enemy's homeland.

3. The success of deterrence strategy rests on its credibility. It assumes that aggression can be prevented if the enemy is convinced that the U.S. has the capacity and the will to deliver unacceptable damage after a first strike. Moreover, it assumes that the enemy is a rational decision-maker.

4. Counterforce strategy attempts to limit the damage inflicted by an enemy attack. But counterforce measures are expensive, unreliable, and easily offset by increases in the enemy's offensive capabilities. More importantly, counterforce strategy reduces the enemy's assured second-strike capability and encourages him to strike first; it replaces a "balance of terror" in which each side has assured second-strike capability, with an unstable relationship.

5. It is widely assumed that Soviet expansion into Western Europe after World War II was halted by America's credible first-strike threat. The Soviets

have always enjoyed supremacy in conventional military strength in Europe, but in the early Cold War years the U.S. maintained supremacy in nuclear weapons and strategic bombers. However, when the Soviets developed their own second-strike capability, the credibility of our threat declined, the NATO alliance eroded, and Western European nations began to make their own security arrangements.

6. The evolution of U.S. defense policy reflects changing strategic concepts in response to the growing nuclear capabilities of the Soviet Union and changing notions of the threats posed by potential enemies. For example, "massive retaliation" reflected America's early nuclear supremacy and credible first-strike capability. Assured destruction deterrence and nuclear "sufficiency" reflects America's response to the vastly improved strategic nuclear capacities of the Soviet Union. Flexible response and balanced forces strategies reflected President Kennedy's belief that limited aggression and "wars of national liberation" posed a serious threat to U.S. interests. Recent reductions in U.S. troop strength reflects the Nixon Doctrine thinking that the primary responsibility for defense against Communist aggression rests on the nations directly involved.

7. The SALT agreements between the U.S. and USSR limit certain counterforce measures (ABMs) and restrict the total number of missiles. But unlimited use of MIRVs and unrestricted research and development of new weapons system threaten to upset the "balance of terror" by taking away each nation's assured destruction deterrent.

8. Rational policy making in a nuclear world requires defense analysts to "think about the unthinkable." If deterrence fails, what strategies could be pursued to limit damage and protect American security? Three "scenarios" were posed as examples of strategic problems: controlled reprisal or "tit for tat," targeting choices after absorbing a full-salvo first strike, and "broken-backed" war.

9. Rational thinking in conventional war requires that the political purposes of the war should guide military operations. Unlimited, uncontrolled violence is not a rational strategy in a conventional war. For conventional war to be a rational policy, the benefits must outweigh the costs.

10. Soviet strategic thinking closely resembles our own. The Soviets have worked to acquire and maintain assured destruction deterrence; indeed, their progress in missile development may soon give them the capacity to take out our land-based missile force on a first strike. The Soviets have given somewhat higher priority to counterforce measures than the U.S., and their population and land area give them an advantage in damage limitation. The Chinese have publicly stated their disregard of nuclear weapons, apparently to take away the U.S. and Soviet psychological advantage. Yet the Chinese have devoted great resources to the rapid development of their own nuclear capability. They have used conventional troops to protect and expand their own borders.

BIBLIOGRAPHY

HALPERIN, MORTON H., *Defense Strategies for the Seventies*. Boston: Little, Brown, 1971.

KISSINGER, HENRY A., *Nuclear Weapons and Foreign Policy*. New York: Harper and Row, 1957.

SCHELLING, THOMAS C., *Arms and Influence*. New Haven: Yale University Press, 1966.

SMITH, MARK E., and CLAUSE J. JOHNS, eds., *American Defense Policy*, 2nd ed. Baltimore: Johns Hopkins Press, 1968.

Workmen post new speed limits on nation's highways, after President Nixon signed into law a bill establishing a maximum speed of 55 miles per hour to conserve energy. UPI Photo

12 INPUTS, OUTPUTS, AND BLACK BOXES:

a systems analysis of state policies

EXTENDING THE BOUNDARIES OF POLICY ANALYSIS

Political science has been so preoccupied with describing political institutions, behaviors, and processes that it has frequently overlooked the overriding importance of environmental forces in shaping public policy. Of course, political scientists generally recognize that environmental variables affect politics and public policy, but these variables are often slighted, and occasionally ignored, in specific policy explanations. The problem seems to be that the concepts and methods of political science predispose scholars to account for public policy largely in terms of the *internal* activities of political systems. Political science never lacked descriptions of what goes on within political systems; what it has lacked is a clear picture of the *linkages* between environmental conditions, political activity, and public policy.

What is the environment? By the environment we mean anything that lies outside the boundaries of the political system yet within the same society. Needless to say, this takes in a great deal of territory. Environmental variables include such things as the level of technological development, the extent of urbanization, the literacy rate, the level of adult education, the character of the economic system and its level of development, the degree of modernization of the society, the occupational structure, the class system, racial composition and ethnic diversity, mobility patterns, prevailing myths and beliefs, and so on. Any variable that is distinguishable from the political system itself yet lies within the same society is part of the environment.

From the almost unlimited number of environmental conditions that might influence public policy outcomes, we must choose only a limited number for inclusion in our research. Although we are fortunate today that computer technology enables us to handle far more environmental variables than would ever be possible without such technology, we are still obliged to reduce our studies to manageable proportions by making some selection. Let us begin by reviewing the research literature on the impact of economic development on public policy.

ENVIRONMENTAL RESOURCES AND PUBLIC POLICY:
PREVIOUS RESEARCH

Economists have contributed a great deal to the systematic analysis of public policy. Economic research very early suggested that government activity was closely related to the level of economic development in a society.[1] Economic development was broadly defined to include levels of wealth, industrialization, urbanization, and adult education.

Systematic analysis of the economic determinants of *state and local* government expenditures began with the publication of Fabricant's *The Trend of Government Activity in the United States Since 1900*.[2] Fabricant employed comparative analysis of state and local spending in all of the states to observe relationships between three socioeconomic measures (per capita income, population density, and urbanization) and per capita expenditures of state and local governments. Using data for 1942, Fabricant found that variations in these environmental variables in the states accounted for more than 72 percent of the variation among the states in total state and local spending. Of these three variables, he found that per capita *income* showed the strongest relationship to expenditures.

Another economist, Glenn F. Fisher, continued Fabricant's analysis into the 1960s.[3] He found that Fabricant's original three socioeconomic variables were somewhat *less* influential in determining levels of state and local government spending than they had been two decades before. The three variables that had explained 72 percent of the variation in state

---

[1] See, for example, Bruce R. Morris, *Problems of American Economic Growth* (New York: Oxford, 1961); Walter Krause, *Economic Development* (Belmont, Calif.: Wadsworth, 1961); W. W. Rostow, *The Process of Economic Growth*, 2nd ed. (New York: W. W. Norton, 1962).

[2] Solomon Fabricant, *Trend of Government Activity in the United States Since 1900* (New York: National Bureau of Economic Research, 1952).

[3] Glenn F. Fisher, "Interstate Variation in State and Local Government Expenditures," *National Tax Journal*, 17 (March 1964), 57–74.

and local spending in 1942 explained only 53 percent variation in spending in 1962. However, by adding other economic variables (e.g., percentage of families with less than $2,000 annual income, percentage increase in population, percentage of adult education with less than five years schooling), Fisher was able to explain even *more* of the interstate differences in state and local per capita spending than Fabricant's original analysis. And, like Fabricant, Fisher found that per capita *income* was the strongest single environmental variable associated with state and local expenditures.

Economists Seymour Sachs and Robert Harris added to this research literature by considering the effect of federal grants-in-aid on state and local government expenditures.[4] By 1960 it appeared that environmental resources were losing some of their explanatory power in relation to state-local spending, particularly in the areas of welfare and health. Sachs and Harris also noted that the ability of income, population density, and urbanization to explain interstate variation in total state-local spending had declined from 72 percent in 1942 to 53 percent in 1960 (see Table 12-1). They particularly noted the decline in the explanatory power of

Table 12-1 *The Linkages Between Environmental Resources, Federal Aid, and State-Local Spending*

PERCENT OF STATE-LOCAL SPENDING DETERMINED BY:

State-Local Expenditures	Economic Development [1]				Environmental Resources plus Federal Aid [2]
	1942	1957	1960	1970	1970
Total Expenditures	72	53	53	62	72
Education	59	62	60	52	67
Highways	29	34	37	50	86
Public Welfare	45	14	11	17	48
Health and Hospitals	72	46	44	37	38
Police	81	74	79		
Fire Protection	85	67	74	}	63
General Control	59	45	52		

Note: Figures are coefficients of multiple determination (R^2) for 48 states.

[1] Economic development is defined as per capita income, population density, and percent urbanization.

[2] Three economic development variables plus per capita federal aid.

Source: Adapted from Seymour Sachs and Robert Harris, "The Determinants of State and Local Government Expenditures and Intergovernmental Flow of Funds," *National Tax Journal,* 17 (March 1964), 78–85. 1970 findings by the author.

[4] Seymour Sachs and Robert Harris, "The Determinants of State and Local Government Expenditures and Intergovernmental Flow of Funds," *National Tax Journal,* 17 (March 1964), 78–85.

these three variables in the areas of welfare (from 45 percent in 1942 to 11 percent in 1960) and health (from 72 percent in 1942 to 44 percent in 1960).

They suggested that the decline in the explanatory power of economic resources could be attributed to the intervening effect of federal grants-in-aid, particularly in the welfare and health fields. They reasoned that federal grants were freeing the states from the constraints of their own economic resources. Federal grants were "outside money" to state and local government officials which permitted them to fund programs at levels beyond their own resources. Hence the decline in the closeness of the relationship between economic resources and state-local spending, particularly in the fields with the heaviest federal involvement: welfare and health.

Table 12-1 is a replication of the Sachs and Harris study. We have updated their research to 1970. The Table shows some decline over time in the importance of economic resources in explaining state-local spending. But it also shows what happens when federal grants-in-aid are included among the explanatory variables: federal grants add considerably to the explanation of state-local spending. The proportion of total state-local spending explained by economic resources alone is 62 percent; but by considering federal grants-in-aid in addition to economic resources, 72 percent of total state-local spending can be explained. Note that in the welfare field the proportion of explained variance leaps from 17 percent to 48 percent by the inclusion of federal aid. This means that a state's economic resources have relatively little to do with its welfare spending; federal policy is the primary determinant of state-local spending in this field. It should be noted, however, that income remains the single most important determinant of state-local spending for all other functions. Sachs and Harris, on the basis of regression analysis, conclude: "Per capita income remains the most important determinant of expenditures even after the federal aid variables are added."

ENVIRONMENTAL RESOURCES AND LEVELS OF PUBLIC SPENDING AND SERVICE

There is little doubt that levels of government revenue, expenditures, and services are closely linked to environmental resources. Although there are some notable exceptions, virtually all the systematic evidence points to this fact: environmental resources (particularly income) are the most important determinants of *levels* of government taxing, spending, and service. Socioeconomic measures such as per capita income, adult education, and urbanization consistently turn out to be the most influential variables in systematic analysis of public policies when public policies are defined as levels or amounts or averages of taxes, expenditures, or services.

Table 12-2 presents a typical selection of public policy outcomes in the American states defined in terms of levels of taxing, spending, benefits, and service. These are important policy outcomes in education,

Table 12-2 *The Relationship Between Environmental Resources and Levels of Spending and Service in the Fifty States, 1970*

LEVELS OF SPENDING AND SERVICE	SIMPLE CORRELATION COEFFICIENTS			TOTAL	
	Income	Education	Urban	Multiple Coefficients	Percent Explained
Education					
Per Pupil Expend.	.76	.53	.30	.79	63
Average Teacher Salary	.90	.54	.54	.91	83
Teacher-Pupil Ratio	−.12	−.32	−.18	.48	23
Per Capita Educ. Expend.	.56	.63	.14	.72	52
Welfare					
Per Capita Welfare Expend.	.32	.18	.41	.42	17
Per Capita Health Expend.	.54	.14	.31	.61	37
Unemploy. Benefits	.80	.49	.61	.81	66
OAA Benefits	.50	.30	.14	.53	28
ADC Benefits	.70	.59	.33	.74	55
Gen. Assist. Benefits	.79	.53	.56	.80	64
OAA Recipients	−.50	−.49	−.11	.61	37
ADC Recipients	−.02	−.21	.32	.51	26
Unemploy. Recipients	.58	.20	.31	.62	39
Gen. Assist. Recipients	.58	.35	.55	.63	40
Highway					
Per Capita Highway Expend.	.07	.29	−.43	.71	50
Public Regulation					
Numbers of Laws	.47	.30	.41	.47	22
Public Employees Per Popul.	.13	.41	.00	.46	21
Public Employee Salary	.90	.55	.51	.90	81
Per Capita Corrections Expend.	.69	.58	.32	.72	52
Police Protection	.57	.37	.73	.75	56
Finance					
Per Capita Total Expend.	.78	.54	.34	.79	62
Per Capita Total Revenue	.64	.26	.08	.67	45
Per Capita Tax Revenue	.77	.65	.54	.80	64
Per Capita Debt	.59	.30	.61	.67	45

health and welfare, highways, public regulation, and taxing and spending. Let us summarize the environmental policy linkages revealed in this table. First of all, differences in educational expenditures among the fifty states are closely related to differences in income. (Figure 12-1 is a graphic portrayal of this relationship.) Income also explains most of the differences among the states in measures reflecting the level of educational service, such as average teacher salaries and pupil-teacher ratios. In contrast, environmental resources are not as influential in explaining health and welfare expenditures as they are in explaining education expenditures. Per capita welfare expenditures do not correlate with measures of environmental resources, and this can be attributed to the effect of federal participation in welfare financing. (The federal government provides half the funds spent on public assistance, and federal percentages of total public assistance expenditures declined with increases in state income levels. This means that federal policy offsets the effect of wealth so that per capita welfare expenditures do not reflect income levels in the states.) However, the impact of environmental resources on benefit levels in health and welfare programs is quite obvious. Benefits per recipient for unemployment, old age assistance, aid to families with dependent children, and general assistance are closely related to income levels in the states. In these programs receiving federal aid—old age assistance, aid to families with dependent children, and unemployment—poorer states provide assistance to more recipients per population than richer states. But in general assistance programs, which are not federally aided, richer states provide assistance to more recipients than do poorer states.

Highway expenditures in the states are also related to environmental conditions, although in a somewhat different fashion than health, welfare, and education expenditures. Rural states spend *more* per capita on highways than do urban states.

The legislatures of wealthy urban states introduce and enact more laws than do the legislatures of poor rural states. Moreover, there are more public employees per capita in wealthy urban states than in poor rural states. Finally, the average monthly salaries of public employees in wealthy urban states is greater than in poor rural states. All this suggests that the level of government activity and public service is a function of the availability of resources. Police protection (as well as the crime rate) is related to urbanization, and per capita correctional expenditures are related to wealth.

There is little doubt that the overall ability of states to raise revenue and spend money is a function of their level of economic resources. Both per capita expenditures and per capita revenues are closely related to wealth. Per capita tax levels are also related to wealth, as is the ability to carry larger per capita debt levels.

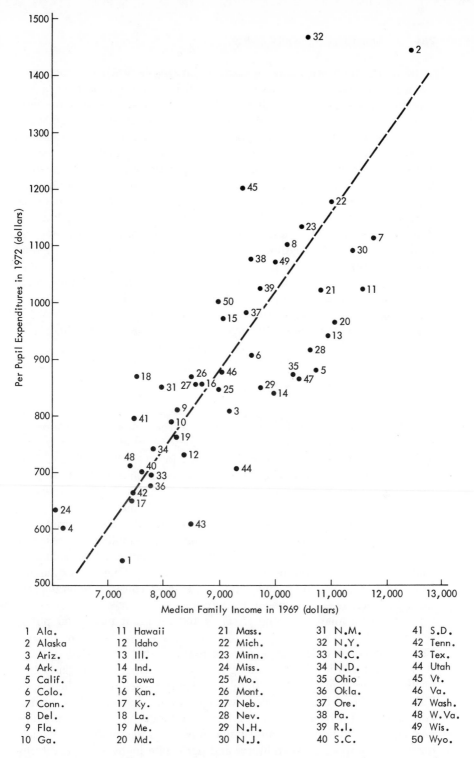

Fig. 12-1   *The Fifty States Arranged According to Median Family Income and Per Pupil Expenditures for Education*

1 Ala.	11 Hawaii	21 Mass.	31 N.M.	41 S.D.
2 Alaska	12 Idaho	22 Mich.	32 N.Y.	42 Tenn.
3 Ariz.	13 Ill.	23 Minn.	33 N.C.	43 Tex.
4 Ark.	14 Ind.	24 Miss.	34 N.D.	44 Utah
5 Calif.	15 Iowa	25 Mo.	35 Ohio	45 Vt.
6 Colo.	16 Kan.	26 Mont.	36 Okla.	46 Va.
7 Conn.	17 Ky.	27 Neb.	37 Ore.	47 Wash.
8 Del.	18 La.	28 Nev.	38 Pa.	48 W.Va.
9 Fla.	19 Me.	29 N.H.	39 R.I.	49 Wis.
10 Ga.	20 Md.	30 N.J.	40 S.C.	50 Wyo.

In short, there are many significant linkages between environmental resources and policy outcomes in the states. Levels of government taxing, spending, benefits, and service are related to income, urbanization, education. It is possible, of course, to focus attention on *un*explained variations in policy outcomes. (Unexplained variation is 1 minus the explained variation: for example, environmental resources explain 63 percent of variations among the states in per pupil expenditures, and the remaining 37 percent is unexplained by environmental resources.) Environmental variables fail to explain half of the total variation in half of our policy variables. Certainly there is room for continued research on additional determinants of public policy. But social science rarely produces complete explanations of anything. Unexplained variation may be a product of poor measurement or a product of the combined efforts of thousands of other factors influencing political systems. The fact that only three environmental variables—income, education, and urbanization—can explain half of the variation in levels of public spending and service is evidence of the importance of environment in explaining public policy.

FEDERAL GRANTS AS "OUTSIDE MONEY"

Federal grant-in-aid money is now a very important resource of state and local governments in America. Federal grants now account for one-third of all state government revenues and one-sixth of all local government revenues. State and local government officials tend to view federal grants as "outside money" to help support programs in education, welfare, health, highways, housing, urban renewal, and a myriad of other programs. This "outside money" tends to free states and communities from some of the constraints of their own limited economic resources and, therefore, reduce somewhat the impact of state and local economic resources on levels of public spending and service. Thus, in explaining levels of public spending and service, we must consider federal grant money as well as environmental resources.

Our own analysis of the effect of federal grant money on public policy in the states confirms the ideas of economists Sachs and Harris. Federal money is indeed an important resource that helps explain interstate variation in levels of spending and service. This is particularly true in the two areas of greatest federal involvement—welfare and highways. Table 12-3 shows the explanatory value of adding federal aid to income, education, and urbanization in regression problems on levels of spending and service. Adding federal aid significantly raises the multiple coefficient for per capita welfare expenditures and per capita highway expenditures.

Table 12-3 *Environmental Resources, Federal Aid, and Levels of Spending and Service in the Fifty States, 1970*

LEVELS OF SPENDING AND SERVICE	ENVIRONMENTAL RESOURCES		ENVIRONMENTAL RESOURCES AND FEDERAL AID	
	Multiple Coefficients	Percent Explained	Multiple Coefficients	Percent Explained
Education				
Per Pupil Expend.	.79	63	.80	64
Average Teacher Salary	.91	83	.92	85
Teacher-Pupil Ratio	.48	23	.49	24
Per Capita Educ. Expend.	.72	52	.82	67 *
Welfare				
Per Capita Welfare Expend.	.42	17	.69	48 *
Per Capita Health Expend.	.61	37	.61	38
Unemployment Benefits	.81	66	.81	66
OAA Benefits	.53	28	.53	28
ADC Benefits	.74	55	.75	56
Gen. Assist. Benefits	.80	64	.80	64
OAA Recipients	.61	37	.64	41
ADC Recipients	.51	26	.57	32
Unemployment Recipients	.62	39	.62	39
Gen. Assist. Recipients	.63	40	.65	43
Highways				
Per Capita Highway Expend.	.71	50	.93	86 *
Public Regulation				
Numbers of Laws	.47	22	.47	22
Public Employes Per Population	.46	21	.79	62 *
Public Employee Salaries	.90	81	.92	85
Per Capita Corrections Expend.	.72	52	.72	52
Police Protection	.75	56	.76	58
Finance				
Per Capita Total Expend.	.79	62	.81	66
Per Capita Total Revenue	.67	45	.86	75 *
Per Capita Tax Revenue	.80	64	.80	64
Per Capita Debt	.67	45	.67	45

* An asterisk indicates a significant increase in explained variance by the addition of federal aid to multiple regression problem.

STABILITY AND CHANGE
IN INPUT-OUTPUT RELATIONSHIPS

Do relationships between environment and public policy persist over time? Most of the linkages described so far are based on data from the last decade. Can these same linkages be observed in other time periods? Are there any changes over time in the nature of the relationships between environment and public policy?

To explore these questions, we traced the relationships between several environmental variables and levels of public spending in the states over a period of eight decades—1890 to 1970. The results are shown in Figure 12-2. Each of the three diagrams traces the strength of the relationships (measured in terms of the size of the simple correlation coefficients) between environmental variables and total state-local spending, spending for education, and spending for welfare, in the fifty states.

Wealth has *always* been an important determinant of levels of total spending for public services in the American states. A half-century ago, states and communities relied primarily on property taxes, and hence the value of property for revenue. Property value was the principal determinant of total state-local spending. In more recent decades personal income has been an even more influential determinant of public spending and services. There is no indication of any weakening over time in the relationships between wealth and government spending.

In contrast, urbanization, and particularly industrialization, are losing their influence over time as determinants of public spending. At one time, differences in the degree of industrialization among the fifty states helped to account for differences in spending policies. But in recent years, as all states became industrialized, differences in the degree of industrialization ceased to be a determinant of public policy. The same decline in influence of public policy can be observed in urbanization, although this variable has not yet lost all of its influence. But certainly urbanization is not as important today as it was a few decades ago.

Education has a strong and persistent impact on public policy. The educational level of the adult population has a significant impact on total spending, and an even greater impact on spending for education.

In general, then, we can say that income and education are persistent determinants of levels of government spending in the states. However, one important exception must be noted: environmental inputs have lost much of their influence over state-local welfare spending over the last few decades. The reason for this seems clear: when the federal government stepped into the welfare field during the New Deal, federal funds relieved the states of dependence on their own resources. Thus, after the 1930s the relationship between environmental resources and welfare spending in the states declined. The obvious effect of federal intervention in the welfare field on input-output relationships suggests

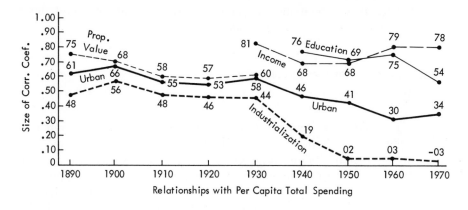

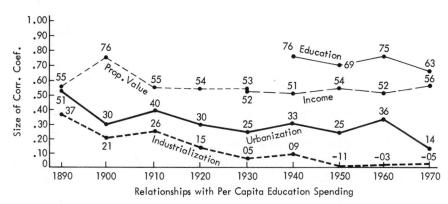

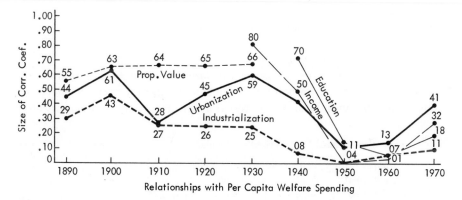

Fig. 12-2 *Stability and Change in Relationships Between Environmental Resources and Levels of Public Spending Over Time*

once again that federal money must be viewed as an important input variable determining state-local policy.[5]

POLITICS, ENVIRONMENT, AND POLICY:
PREVIOUS RESEARCH

The political system functions to transform demands generated in the environment into public policy. The traditional literature in American politics instructed students that characteristics of the political system, particularly two-party competition, voter participation, and apportionment did have direct bearing on public policy.[6] Because political scientists devoted most of their time to studying what happened *within* the political system, it was natural for them to believe that the political processes and institutions which they studied were important in terms of public policy outcomes. Moreover, the belief that competition, participation, and equality in representation had important consequences for public policy squared with the value placed upon these variables in the prevailing pluralist ideology.

The assertion that political variables, such as party competition, voter participation, and malapportionment, affected public policy rested more upon a priori reasoning than upon systematic research. It seemed reasonable to *believe* that an increase in party competition would increase educational spending, welfare benefits, numbers of welfare recipients, highway spending, health and hospital care, and so on, because competitive parties would try to outbid each other for public favor by offering such inducements, and the overall affect of such competition would be to raise levels of spending and service. It also seemed reasonable to believe that increased voter participation would influence public policy, presumably in a more liberal direction.

However, in order to assess the *independent* effect of politics on public policy, it was important to control for the intervening effects of environmental variables. Early research in state politics demonstrated

[5] See also Richard I. Hofferbert's "Ecological Development and Policy Change in the American States," *Midwest Journal of Political Science,* 10 (November 1966), 481–92; and his "Socioeconomic Dimensions of the American States: 1890–1960," *Midwest Journal of Political Science,* 12 (August 1968), 401–18.

[6] V. O. Key, Jr., *American State Politics: An Introduction* (New York: Knopf, 1956); also his *Southern Politics in State and Nation* (New York: Knopf, 1951); Duane Lockard, *New England State Politics* (Princeton: Princeton University Press, 1959); Malcolm Jewell, *The State Legislature* (New York: Random House, 1962); Duane Lockard, *The Politics of State and Local Government* (New York: Macmillan, 1963); John H. Fenton, *People and Parties in Politics* (Glenview, Ill.: Scott, Foresman, 1966).

conclusively that party competition and voter participation were themselves heavily influenced by environmental variables. A number of
scholars—Ranney and Kendall, Key, Schlesinger and Golembiewski, for
example—indicated that economic development affects the level of inter-
party competition; they reported statistically significant associations between urbanism, income, industrialization, and classifications of party
competition among the states.[7] Knowledge of this linkage between the
environment and the political system, coupled with knowledge about the
linkage between the environment and public policy, clearly suggested that
scholars should test to see if party competition *independently* affected
public policy, or whether both party competition and public policy were
products of economic development. For example, if it was shown that, in
general, wealthy states have more party competition than poor states, it
might be that differences in the level of welfare benefits of competitive
and noncompetitive states are really a product of the fact that the former
are wealthy and the latter are poor. If this was the case, policy differences
between the states might be attributable to wealth rather than to party
competition. In order to isolate the effect of party competition on education and welfare policies from the effect of environmental variables, it is
necessary to control for these variables.

The first hint that political variables might not be as influential in
determining levels of public taxing, spending, and service as commonly
supposed came in an important research effort by Richard E. Dawson and
James A. Robinson in 1963.[8] These political scientists examined the linkages between socioeconomic variables (income, urbanization, industrialization), the level of interparty competition, and nine public *welfare*
policies. They concluded that "high levels of interparty competition are
highly interrelated both to socioeconomic factors and to social welfare
legislation, but the degree of interparty competition does not seem to
possess the important intervening influence between socioeconomic factors and liberal welfare programs that our original hypothesis and
theoretical schemes suggested." These researchers failed to uncover any
evidence that a competitive political system devoted any more resources
to welfare functions than a noncompetitive system *at the same level of*

[7] Austin Ranney and Wilmoore Kendall, "The American Party System," *American Political Science Review*, 48 (1954), 477–85; V. O. Key, Jr., *American
State Politics*, p. 99; Joseph A. Schlesinger, "A Two-Dimensional Scheme
for Classifying State According to the Degree of Inter-Party Competition,"
American Political Science Review, 49 (1955), 1120–28; Robert T. Golembiewski, "A Taxonomic Approach to State Political Party Strength," *Western
Political Quarterly*, 11 (1958), 494–513.

[8] Richard E. Dawson and James A. Robinson, "Inter-Party Competition, Economic Variables, and Welfare Policies in the American States," *Journal of
Politics*, 25 (May 1963), 265–89.

economic development. Thus, Dawson and Robinson raised serious doubts about the relevance of a political variable—party competition—which most political scientists had believed to be an influential determinant of public policy. Perhaps more importantly, the Dawson-Robinson article inspired political scientists to undertake comparative systematic research into the determinants of public policy.

In 1965, this author published a comprehensive analysis of public policy in the American States.[9] Employing Easton's systems model, the linkages between the four economic development variables, four political system characteristics, and over ninety separated policy output measures in education, health, welfare, highways, corrections, taxation, and public regulation were described. This research produced some findings that were very unsettling for many political scientists. Four of the most commonly described characteristics of political systems—(1) Democratic or Republican control of state government, (2) the degree of interparty competition, (3) the level of voter turnout, and (4) the extent of malapportionment—were found to have *less* affect on public policy than environmental variables reflecting the level of economic development—urbanization, industrialization, wealth, and education. Quoting that text, "the evidence seems conclusive: economic development variables are more influential than political system characteristics in shaping public policy in the states." The reasoning in this was similar to that of Dawson and Robinson: Most of the associations that occur between political variables and policy outcomes are really a product of the fact that economic development influences *both* political system characteristics *and* policy outcomes. When political factors are controlled, economic development continues to have a significant impact on public policy. But when the effects of economic development are controlled, political factors turn out to have little influence on policy outcomes. Several policy areas were pointed out where political factors remained important (notably the division of state versus local responsibilities for public services), and certain policy areas were also identified in which federal programs tended to offset the impact of economic development levels on state policies. Yet in an attempt to generalize about the determinants of public policy, it was concluded that, *on the whole,* economic development was *more* influential in shaping state policies than any of the political variables previously thought to be important in policy determination.

Several additional studies in the mid-1960s appeared to confirm the idea that political variables were less influential than the economic environment in determining levels of government taxing, spending, and service. Several articles employed systematic comparative analysis to

[9] Thomas R. Dye, *Politics, Economics, and the Public* (Chicago: Rand McNally, 1966).

assess the impact of apportionment practices on policy outcomes in the fifty states while controlling for the effects of environmental factors.[10] It turned out that there were few measurable policy differences between states that were well-apportioned and states that were malapportioned, and that economic variables were *more* influential in determining policy outcomes than apportionment practices. Another study reported that the organizational structure of state executive branches and formal powers of governors were not as influential as economic measures in determining the level of government activity in the states.[11] A comprehensive study by Richard I. Hofferbert examined the relationships between environmental variables, malapportionment, party competition, and welfare policies. He concluded: "Structural characteristics and, if one prefers to give partisan variables a separate berth, the nature of the party system and its operation do not seem to go very far toward explaining the kinds of policies produced in the states. . . . We see by the data presented here and elsewhere, however, clear indication that there is a relationship between the environment and policy." [12]

Most of these systematic policy studies were based upon comparative observations made at one point in time. To confirm that linkages between environment, system, and policy persisted *over time*, Hofferbert studied the relationships between environmental forces, political conditions, and public policy in the American states from 1890 through 1960. He detected a slight *decline* in the strength of the relationships between environmental forces and policy outcome over this time period. He reasoned that a generally high level of economic development provides political decision-makers with greater latitude in policy choices, and tends to free them from the restraints imposed by limited resources. Although environmental forces continue to be the major determinant of public policy, the implication of Hofferbert's study is that in the future *the attitudes of political leaders* may be increasingly important in determining levels of public spending and service.

A partial challenge to the general direction of these findings was entered by Ira Sharkansky and Richard I. Hofferbert. These political scientists "factor-analyzed" twenty-one specific socioeconomic variables, fifty-three specific political system variables, and thirty-four specific ex-

10 Thomas R. Dye, "Malapportionment and Public Policy in the States," *Journal of Politics*, 65 (August 1965), 586–601; Herbert Jacob, "The Consequences of Malapportionment: A Note of Caution," *Social Forces*, 43 (December 1964), 256–61.

11 Thomas R. Dye, "Executive Power and Public Policy in the States," *Western Political Quarterly*, 22 (December 1969), 926–39.

12 Richard I. Hofferbert, "The Relation Between Public Policy and Some Structural and Environmental Variables in the American States," *American Political Science Review*, 60 (March 1966), 73–82.

penditure and service measures for the American states. These efforts gave birth to two *environmental* factors: "industrialization" and "cultural enrichment"; two political *system* factors: "turnout-competition" and "professionalism-local reliance"; and three *policy outcome* factors: "welfare-education," "highways-natural resources," and "public safety." Their next step was an examination of the correlations between these factors. "Cultural enrichment" correlated with "turnout-competition" and "industrialization" correlated with "professionalism-local reliance." Among the policy outcome factors, "public safety" correlated most closely with "cultural enrichment" and "highway-natural resources" correlated most closely with "industrialization." However, "welfare education" correlated more closely with "turnout-competition" than with "industrialization" or "cultural enrichment." In other words, one policy outcome factor was more closely associated with a political system factor than with either environmental factor. "We shall conclude that systematic linkages exist between dimensions of state politics and public services that are independent of socioeconomic characteristics." [13]

The importance of all this research was that political scientists were using comparative systematic research methods to explain public policy, and they were looking beyond the confines of the political system itself to the social, economic, and cultural environment in their search for the forces shaping public policy. Their most important and controversial set of findings was that certain political variables which had previously claimed a great deal of attention from political scientists—notably party competition, voter participation, and malapportionment—were not as influential in determining levels of government taxing, spending and service as environmental variables reflecting a level of economic development. Some scholars reacted to these findings as if political science had a vested interest in finding that traditional political variables were the most important factors in explaining public policy, and as if the discovery that economic or other environmental variables are more important is somehow damaging to the discipline.[14] A more balanced view, of course, is that political science derives its importance from what it seeks to explain— public policy.[15] The important thing to achieve is the most effective and efficient explanation of policy outcomes. If economic or other environ-

[13] Ira Sharkansky and Richard I. Hofferbert, "Dimension of State Politics, Economics, and Public Policy," *American Political Science Review*, 63 (September 1969), 867–79.

[14] See John H. Fenton, *People and Parties in Politics* (Glenview, Ill.: Scott, Foresman, 1966), pp. 31–49; and Duane Lockard, "State Party Systems and Policy Outputs," in Oliver Garceau, ed., *Political Research and Political Theory* (Cambridge: Harvard University Press, 1968), pp. 190–220.

[15] William Keech and James W. Prothro set forth a truly professional view of the relationships between research findings, professional interests, and ideo-

mental variables explain public policy more clearly than political variables, so much the better. The object is to explain public policy, and not to assert the primacy of politics or economics in determining policy outcomes.[16]

PLURALISM AND PUBLIC POLICY

The political system includes *all* the institutions, structures, processes, and behaviors that function to transform demands into governmental decisions. This includes political party activity, voting behavior, the structure and behavior of executive and legislative bodies, interest-group activity, and lobbying, formal constitutional arrangements, the political attitudes of both elites and masses, political customs and traditions, the apportionment system, the structure and behavior of courts, the formal and informal power of governors, etc. The list of political syst m characteristics that might conceivably affect public policy is boundless!

A review of the traditional literature on American politics reveals an especially intense interest among political scientists in electoral system variables—party competition and voter participation. These variables are highly valued in pluralist political ideology. High voter participation and intense party competition suggest a normative model of plur 'st democracy which is current in the literature of American political science. In contrast, low voter participation and an absence of party competition suggest a type of political system that has been widely deplored by

---

logical commitments. In referring to this author's *Politics, Economics, and the Public* these scholars stated:

> This research has produced some findings that have been unsettling for many political scientists. Dye concludes that "the evidence seems conclusive: economic development variables are more influential than political system characteristics in shaping public policy in the states." Some have reacted to these and earlier findings as if political science had a vested interest in political phenomena, and as if the discovery that economic or other variables are more important than political variables in explaining policy is somehow to damage the discipline. A more balanced view is that political science derives its importance from its dependent variables, the phenomena it seeks to explain. Thus the important thing to achieve is the most effective and efficient explanation of political variables. If economic or other independent variables explain policy more clearly than political variables, so much the better. The point is that we must seek out the best explanations, not that they must be political.

See William Keech and James W. Prothro, "American Government," *Journal of Politics* (May 1968), pp. 438–39.

[16] The best critical review of this literature is Herbert Jacob and Michael Lipsky's "Outputs, Structure, and Power: An Assessment of Changes in the Study of State and Local Politics," *Journal of Politics*, 30 (May 1968), 510–38.

American political scientists.[17] Hence, it is very important that we inquire about the impact of these particular system variables on public policy.

Let us examine the relationship between party competition and voter participation and policy outcomes reflecting levels of government taxing, spending, benefits, and services in the American states.

In Table 12-4 party competition appears closely related to a number of important policy outcomes. States with a high degree of party competition tend (1) to spend more money per pupil per public school, (2) to pay higher teacher salaries, (3) to enjoy lower pupil-teacher ratios, (4) to pay more liberal welfare benefits, (5) to grant unemployment compensation and several assistances to more persons, (6) to pay higher salaries to their public employees, (7) to spend more total public monies, and (8) to raise more total revenue and tax revenue than states with less competitive party systems. Political participation also appears closely associated with levels of government activity. In the field of education, higher voter participation in the states is associated with higher per pupil expenditures, higher teachers' salaries, lower pupil-teacher ratios. Better participation is also associated with increased welfare benefits. There is also a tendency for states with higher participation rates to spend more money on highways, have more public employees per population, pay higher salaries for public employees, and have higher correctional expenditures. Finally, political participation is associated with increased total government spending and increased revenues and taxes.

It should be noted, however, that pluralism in the American states—as measured by party competition and voter participation—is *also* related to environmental resources—income, education, and urbanization. High levels of income, education, and urbanization tend to foster party competition. Voter participation is notably higher in states with higher incomes and well-educated adult populations.

These relationships in the American states between environmental resources and political participation and competition may be of significance to the study of political systems generally. There is reason to believe that environmental resources such as wealth, urbanization, and education are prerequisite to the development of liberal pluralist democracy, including voter participation and party competition, in any political system. Students of comparative government have identified the relationship between economic development variables and the political systems of

[17] Competition and participation are conceptually linked in pluralist political thought. Statistic analysis reveals that competition and participation are also linked empirically; states with competitive parties are also states with high voter turnouts. The coefficient for this relationship in the fifty states is .72. Even after controlling for the effects of the environment (income, urbanization, and education), competition and participation are still significantly, and independently, associated; the partial coefficient for the relationship between competition and participation controlling for three environmental variables is .45.

Table 12-4 *Pluralism and Levels of Government Activity in the Fifty States*

LEVELS OF GOVERNMENT
ACTIVITY

PLURALISM

	Party Competition	Voter Participation
Education		
Per Pupil Expenditures	.59 *	.48 *
Average Teachers Salaries	.49 *	.34 *
Teacher-Pupil Ratio	.64 *	.62 *
Per Capita Educ. Expend.	.46 *	.38 *
Welfare and Health		
Unemployment Benefits	.52 *	.42 *
OAA Benefits	.55 *	.54 *
ADC Benefits	.69 *	.63 *
Gen. Assist. Benefits	.52 *	.46 *
OAA Recipients	—.48 *	—.38 *
ADC Recipients	—.17	—.09
Unemployment Benefits	.35 *	.29
Gen. Asst. Benefits	.38 *	.44 *
Per Capita Welfare Expend.	.03	.06
Per Capita Health Expend.	—.20	.06
Highways		
Per Capita Highway Expend.	.25	.27
Public Regulation		
Numbers of Laws	—.17	—.19
Public Employees per Population	.24	.21
Ped Capita Corrections Expend.	.42 *	.31 *
Policemen per Population	.25	.13
Taxing and Spending		
Total Per Capita Expend.	.61 *	.53 *
Total Per Capita Revenue	.47 *	.38 *
Total Per Capita Taxes	.59 *	.51 *
Total Per Capita Debt	.21	.11
Environmental Resources		
Income	.66 *	.52 *
Education	.62 *	.49 *
Urbanization	.29	.18

* An asterisk indicates a significant relationship.

nation-states. Seymour Lipset found that economic development variables and rates of change in these variables were related to stable democratic government as opposed to unstable democratic government or dictatorship.[18]

[18] Seymour Martin Lipset, *Political Man* (New York: Doubleday, 1960); and "Some Social Requisites of Democracy: Economic Development and Political Legitimacy," *American Political Science Review*, 53 (1959), 69–105.

The importance of these environment–to–system linkages for policy analysis are clear: because competitive, participatory political systems stand higher on measures of wealth, education, and urbanization than noncompetitive, nonparticipatory systems, policy differences between them may not necessarily be the product of competition or participation itself. Policy differences may *really* be a product of their differing levels of wealth, urbanization, and education rather than a direct product of competition or participation. Later we will control for the effects of environmental resources in order to observe the independent effect of competition and participation on policy outcomes.

REFORMISM AND PUBLIC POLICY

Another set of political system characteristics that has interested both scholars and statemen over the years centers about reform, professionalism, and innovation in government. Reformism has been an important political movement in American state and local government for over a century.[19] The reform style of politics emphasizes, among other things, the replacement of political patronage practices with a civil service system; the professionalization of government service; the reorganization of government to promote efficiency and responsibility; and a preference for an antiseptic, "no politics" atmosphere in government.[20] At the *municipal* level reformism has promoted the manager form of government, nonpartisan elections, home rule, at-large constituencies, and comprehensive planning; it is fairly easy to distinguish between "reformed" and "unreformed" cities by looking at these structural characteristics. It is somewhat more difficult to identify *states* in which reform has had an identifiable impact. However, we have selected two variables that are conceptually linked to reformism at the state level—civil service coverage of state employees, and professionalism in the state legislature.

The percentage of state employees covered by civil service is directly related to one of the primary objectives of the reform movement in state and local government. It is reasonable to assume that this variable taps the broader political ethic of reformism and progressivism in state politics. It is not so much that civil service itself would affect the content of public policy, but that civil service is an indicator of reformism, and reformism may influence the level of public taxing, spending, benefits, and services.

Some state legislatures are highly "professional" while others are not. By "professional" we mean that in some legislatures the members are well-paid and tend to think of their jobs as full-time ones; members and

[19] See Richard Hofstadter, *The Age of Reform* (New York: Knopf, 1955).
[20] See Thomas R. Dye, *Politics in States and Communities* (Englewood Cliffs, N.J.: Prentice-Hall, 1969), Chapter 10.

committees are well-staffed and have good informational services available to them; and legislative assistance, such as bill drafting and statutory revision, is available. In other legislatures, members are poorly paid and regard their legislative work as part-time; there is little in the way of staff for members or committees; and little or nothing is provided in the way of legislative assistance and services. The Citizens Conference on State Legislatures has graded each state legislature on a variety of professional criteria, including professional staff, adequacy of compensation, length of sessions, facilities, leadership structure, rules and procedures, work management, and regulation of lobbying.[21] The Citizens Conference ratings are our measure of "legislative professionalism."

The indicators of reformism in state politics are related to a number of measures of public benefits and services in the fifty states (see Table 12-5). States with comprehensive civil service programs tend to (1) spend more money per pupil for public schools, (2) pay higher teachers' salaries, (3) spend more for health services, (4) pay more liberal welfare benefits, (5) enjoy better police protection, (6) and tax and spend more than states with less comprehensive civil service coverage. States with more "professional" legislatures also provide somewhat higher levels of benefits and services than do states with less professional legislatures. Moreover, it is interesting to note that (1) professional legislatures pass more laws than nonprofessional legislatures, and (2) professional legislatures spend *less* money on highways (frequently the pork barrel of state government) than nonprofessional legislatures.

Of course, we must remember that relationships that are shown in simple correlation coefficients do not necessarily mean that reformism *causes* particular policy outcomes. Relationships between reformism and public policy may occur because both reformism and public policy are affected by environmental forces. Note in Table 12-5 that civil service coverage and legislative professionalism are closely related to income and urbanization. Because we know that these environmental forces are linked to the same policies, we must consider the possibility that environment is shaping both reformism and public policy.

THE RELATIVE IMPORTANCE OF ENVIRONMENTAL
AND POLITICAL FORCES IN SHAPING PUBLIC POLICY

So far we have talked only about the relationships between (a) environmental resources and political system characteristics; (b) political system characteristics and public policy, and (c) environmental resources and public policy.

---

[21] Citizens Conference on State Legislatures, *The Sometimes Governments* (New York: Bantam Books, 1971).

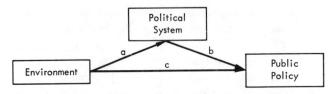

We have established linkages between levels of government taxing, spending, benefits, and services, and both the level of environment resources and the character of the political system; and we also know that levels of environmental resources are closely linked to the character of political systems.

But we have not yet examined the *relative importance* of environmental resources and political system characteristics in the determination of public policy. Are public policies determined primarily by environmental resources, with political system variables having only a marginal impact on policy (linkage c)? Or are political system variables really more influential in determining the content of public policy than environmental resources (linkage b)?

In order to assess the relative influence of environmental and political variables in shaping public policy we have constructed a series of multiple regression problems using various combinations of independent (environmental and political) variables. The multiple correlation coefficients tell how much of the total variation in a policy outcome can be explained by *all* of the environmental and political variables entered into the multiple regression problem. More importantly, partial correlation coefficients tell us the policy impact of each environmental and political variable while controlling for the effects of all other environmental and political variables in the problem. In other words, the partial coefficients give us a very good idea of the relative influences of each of our environmental and political variables in producing variation in levels of public taxing, spending, benefits, and service.

A series of multiple regression problems were performed on all the measures of levels of government activity in the American states. The results obtained with per pupil expenditures for education, per capita expenditures for welfare, per capita expenditures for highways, per capita total revenues, average weekly unemployment benefits, average monthly ADC payments, and police protection per population are representative of the results obtained with our other policy measures. These are presented in Table 12-6.

The first set of multiple regressions in Table 12-6, under the label "Problem 1: Environment," shows the combined effects of our environmental variables—income, education, urbanization, and federal aid—on each of our policy measures. Note the size of the multiple correlation coefficients obtained by using only these four environmental variables: a significant proportion of the variation in all our policy measures can be attributed to environmental forces alone. An asterisk indicates the single most influential independent variable in each of the problems. Income is the single most influential variable in determining per pupil expenditures for education, unemployment benefits, ADC benefits, and tax revenue;

Table 12-5 *Reformism and Levels of Government Activity in the Fifty States*

LEVELS OF GOVERNMENT ACTIVITY	REFORMISM	
	Civil Service Coverage	Legislative Professionalism
Education		
Per Pupil Expenditures	.41 *	.32 *
Average Teachers Salaries	.50 *	.48 *
Teacher-Pupil Ratio	−.10	.05
Per Capita Educ. Expend.	.09	−.10
Welfare and Health		
Unemployment Benefits	.19	.16
OAA Benefits	.50 *	.30 *
ADC Benefits	.36 *	.31 *
Gen. Assist. Benefits	.41 *	.16
OAA Recipients	.43 *	.24
ADC Recipients	.42 *	.41 *
Unemployment Recipients	−.17	−.26
Gen. Assist. Recipients	−.10	.08
Per Capita Welfare Expend.	.53 *	.38 *
Per Capita Health Expend.	.10	.32 *
Highways		
Per Capita Highway Expend.	−.10	−.62 *
Public Regulation		
Numbers of Laws	.29	.51 *
Public Employees per Popul.	.03	−.24
Per Capita Corrections Exp.	.42 *	.17
Policemen per Population	.45 *	.52 *
Taxing and Spending		
Total Per Capita Exp.	.31 *	.32 *
Total Per Capita Revenue	.25	−.02
Total Per Capita Taxes	.32 *	.33 *
Total Per Capita Debt	.39 *	.53 *
Environmental Resources		
Income	.49 *	.36 *
Education	.19	−.01
Urbanization	.40 *	.61

* An asterisk indicates a significant relationship.

Table 12-6 Multivariate Analysis: The Relative Importance of Environmental and Political Forces in Explaining Levels of Spending and Benefits in the Fifty States

PARTIAL COEFFICIENTS IN REGRESSION PROBLEMS ON:

INDEPENDENT VARIABLES	Per Pupil Expenditures	Per Capita Welfare Expend.	Unemployment Benefits	ADC Benefits	Per Capita Highways	Police Protection	Per Capita Tax Revenue
Problem 1: Environment							
Income	.68 *	−.02	.51 *	.56 *	−.21	.18	.50 *
Education	.09	.21	.20	.31	.35	−.09	.31
Urbanization	−.28	.42	.06	−.26	−.10	.62 *	.12
Federal Aid	.15	.79 *	.05	−.19	.67 *	.23	.08
Multiple Coefficient	.80	.81	.81	.75	.84	.76	.80
Problem 2: Environment and Pluralism							
Income	.64 *	−.13	.50 *	.56 *	−.22	.13	.45 *
Education	.07	.18	.21	−.03	.34	.05	.13
Urbanization	−.26	.53	.06	−.14	−.12	.58 *	.17
Federal Aid	.15	.83 *	.06	−.18	.68 *	.22	.08
Party Competition	.09	.12	.09	−.08	−.18	.20	.09
Voter Participation	−.04	.00	.06	.38	−.14	−.23	.10
Multiple Coefficient	.80	.86	.81	.79	.85	.78	.80
Problem 3: Environment and Reformism							
Income	.52 *	−.37	.43 *	.38	.00	.04	.30
Education	.25	.27	.23	.40	.38	−.01	.43 *
Urbanization	−.40	.18	−.00	−.34	−.30	.57 *	−.04
Federal Aid	.22	.83 *	.07	−.14	.68 *	.21	.17
Civil Service	.16	.21	−.06	.15	.06	.22	.10
Legislative Professionalism	.33	.04	.04	.23	−.37	.06	.35
Multiple Coefficient	.82	.86	.82	.77	.86	.78	.83

* An asterisk indicates the strongest independent variable in each problem.

urbanization is the single most influential variable in determining police protection; and federal aid is the single most influential variable in determining per capita expenditures for welfare and highways.

Now let us combine our environmental variables with measures reflecting pluralism in the political systems of the fifty states as in our second set of regressions, "Problem 2: Environment and Pluralism." When measures of pluralism—party competition and voter participation—are added to our environmental variables, there is *no really significant increase* in explanatory power. The multiple coefficients for Problem 2 are not significantly higher than those for Problem 1. A knowledge of the extent of pluralism in a political system does *not* enable us to predict levels of government activity with any more accuracy than merely knowing the level of environmental resources. Moreover, in every case, the single most influential independent variable remains an environmental variable even after the addition of our pluralist measures to the regression problems. In no case does party competition or voter participation emerge as more influential than the most influential environmental variable in determining policy.

If we combine environmental variables with measures reflecting reformism in political systems, "Problem 3: Environment and Reformism," the relative strength of the environmental variables is undiminished. On the whole, reformism as a political system characteristic is *less* influential than environmental resources in determining levels of public spending and services.

A CLOSER LOOK: CAUSAL MODELS IN POLICY DETERMINATION

What are the *causal* implications of the research on public policy? So far we have examined the *relative importance* of environmental resources and political variables in the determination of levels of government spending and service. But we really have not yet specified the *causal* linkages between environment, system, and policy.[22]

Let us construct a diagrammatic model that sets forth some specific notions about *how* environmental conditions might influence political system characteristics and public policy. Figure 12-3 is a diagrammatic portrayal of several causal ideas. First of all, it suggests that income, urbanization, and education may affect public policy *indirectly*, by stimulating party competition, which in turn increases political partici-

---

[22] An earlier attempt at testing causal model in state policy analysis is in Charles F. Cnudde and Donald J. McCrone, "Party Competition and Welfare Policies in the American States," *American Political Science Review*, 63 (September 1969), 858–66.

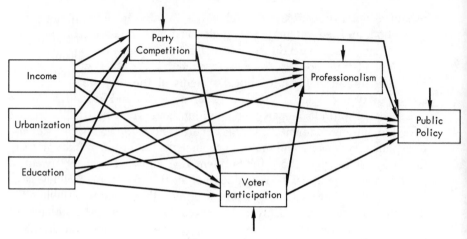

Fig. 12-3 *A Path-Analytic Model for the Explanation of Public Policy*

pation, which in turn stimulates legislative reform, which in turn affects public policy. The diagram also portrays *direct* linkages from income, urbanization, and education to public policy, and direct linkages from party competition and political participation to public policy. Thus, a number of possible direct and indirect causal paths to public policy are represented by the arrows. (The short arrows coming from open spaces remind us that public policy, as well as legislative professionalism, party participation, and party competition may also be affected by forces not mentioned in our model.)

A technique known as "path analysis" permits us to test the adequacy of the causal ideas set forth in Figure 12-3. It provides an overall estimate of the explanatory power of our model, and more importantly, it permits us to test both direct and indirect causal paths to public policy.

The results of "path-analytic" testing of our causal model are shown in Figure 12-4 for four policy variables in the American states: (1) per pupil educational spending, (2) average benefit levels in Aid to Dependent Children programs, (3) police protection, and (4) per capita tax revenues. Notice that a number of linkages (arrows) are missing from these diagrams. These are hypothesized causal paths which turned out *not* to be influential in the determination of the particular policy under study. It turns out that *per pupil expenditures* are affected by income and urbanization *directly*, with no completed indirect causal paths through professionalism, participation, or competition. In contrast *AFDC welfare benefits* are affected *directly* by income, and *indirectly* by paths from competition through participation and paths through legislative professionalism. *Police protection* in the states is affected only by urbanization *directly;* there are no indirect paths through political

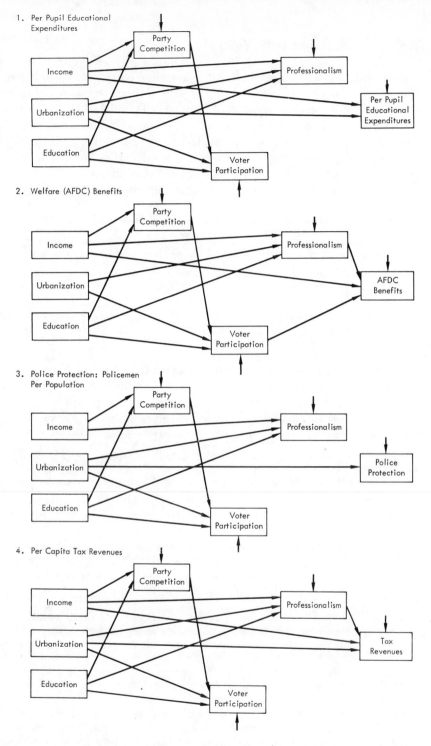

1. Per Pupil Educational Expenditures

2. Welfare (AFDC) Benefits

3. Police Protection: Policemen Per Population

4. Per Capita Tax Revenues

Fig. 12-4 *Path Analysis: Four State Policies with Environment, Competition, Participation, and Professionalism*

system variables. In contrast, *tax levels* are affected by income and education *directly,* and *indirectly* by the path through legislative professionalism. Other causal paths that proved influential: legislative professionalism is affected by income, urbanization, and education, but not voter participation or party competition; voter participation is affected by party competition and urbanization and education but not income; party competition is affected by income and education.

This brief excursion into causal modeling suggests that:

1. Different policy measures have different causal structures
2. Some public policies are influenced directly by environmental forces and political system characteristics have little or no impact on these policies
3. Other public policies are influenced directly by environmental forces, *and* indirectly by political system characteristics.

SUMMARY

The policies dealt with in this analysis reflected *levels* of taxing, spending, benefits, and services in education, health, welfare, highways, police, and government finance. It is important to remember that the results obtained in analyzing *levels* of government activity may not be the same as those obtained in analyzing *distributional* policies or qualitative policies. Moreover, we investigated only a limited number of political system characteristics—pluralism and reformism. It is possible that other political system characteristics might be related to some policy outcomes in a different fashion. However, let us set forth some general propositions about public policy which are suggested by our analysis:

1. Economic development is an important determinant of overall levels of government taxing, spending, and service. Wealth, as measured by per capita personal income, is the single most important environmental variable associated with levels of government taxing, spending, and service.
2. Federal grants-in-aid, considered "outside" money to state and local governments, help to release these governments from their dependence upon economic conditions within their jurisdictions and permit them to spend at higher levels than they would otherwise be able to do. Federal grants reduce the impact of a state's own economic resources on its level of spending and service. Thus, in explaining levels of public spending and service in the states, one must consider federal grants as well as environmental resources.
3. Wealth and education have been consistent determinants of the level of government spending and service over time. In contrast, industrialization has been losing influence as a determinant of government spending. Where the federal government has intervened and offset disparities among the

states, the influence of environmental variables has been significantly reduced.

4. The traditional literature in American politics asserted that characteristics of political systems—particularly party competition and voter participation —had an important impact on the content of public policy. But recent systematic research suggests that the characteristics of political systems are not as important as environmental conditions in shaping public policy. Most of the correlations between political system variables and public policy measures are a product of the fact that environmental forces shape *both* the political system and public policy.

5. Pluralism implies that factors such as party competition and voter participation are important determinants of public policy. And it is true that states with competitive parties and high voter turnouts have generally higher levels of taxing, spending, benefits, and service in a variety of policy areas. But these same states also tend to be wealthy urban states with well-educated adult populations.

6. Reformism—as measured by civil service coverage and professionalism in legislatures—is associated with higher levels of taxing, spending, benefits, and service in the states. However, reformism is also associated with environmental conditions—income, urbanization, and education.

7. Multivariable analysis indicates that, in many policy areas, environmental variables—income, urbanization, education, and federal aid—are more influential in determining levels of taxing, spending, benefits, and service, *than* either pluralism or reformism in the political system. Reformism is somewhat *more* influential *than* pluralism in determining some policy outcomes, but in most cases the single strongest determinant of government activity is an environmental variable.

8. The testing of alternative causal models in policy determination leads us to reject the proposition that environmental forces shape public policy *only* through changes which are made in the political system. We must also reject the idea that the character of the political system must be changed in order to change public policy. Environmental resources can affect public policy directly regardless of the character of the political system. However, in some policy areas environmental forces shape public policy both directly and indirectly through political variables.

BIBLIOGRAPHY

DYE, THOMAS R., *Politics, Economics, and the Public: Policy Outcomes in the American States.* Chicago: Rand McNally, 1966.

FRANCIS, WAYNE, *Legislative Issues in the Fifty States: A Comparative Analysis.* Chicago: Rand McNally, 1969.

HOFFERBERT, RICHARD I., and IRA SHARKANSKY, eds., *State and Urban Politics.* Boston: Little, Brown, 1971.

JACOB, HERBERT, and KENNETH VINES, eds., *Politics in the American States,* 2nd ed. Boston: Little, Brown, 1971.

SHARKANSKY, IRA, *Spending in the American States.* Chicago: Rand McNally, 1968.

Supreme court rules against absolute right of executive privilege. UPI Photo

13 THE POLICY-MAKING PROCESS:

getting inside the system

THE BLACK BOX PROBLEM

It is vitally important that we understand what goes on in the little black box labeled "political system." The systems approach employed in the previous chapter deals with aggregate characteristics of *whole* political systems; this model does not say much about what goes on *within* political systems. Our comparative analysis focused attention on the linkages between environmental resources, system characteristics, and public policy, and dealt with numbers of whole political systems. But we also want to know what happens *within* political systems. We want to know how public policy is generated within the political system, how institutions and processes function to handle demands generated in the environment, and how parties, interest groups, voters, governors, legislators, and other political actors behave in the policy-making process.

Let us try to illustrate the differences between a *comparative systems* approach and a *within-system* approach. Finding a high correlation between cigarette smoking and the incidence of cancer among human systems is important. But this correlation does not in itself reveal the functioning of cells within the human body: we still want to know *how* cancers are formed and how they behave. So also finding a high correlation between urbanization and police protection does not in itself reveal the functioning of political systems; we will want to know *how* a political system goes about transferring demands arising from the socio-economic environment into public policy.

In describing the political process, however, it is important to remember that the activities of the various political actors are greatly constrained by environmental conditions. We have already described the great influence environmental resources have on the character of the political system and the content of public policy. It is true that not *all* the variance in public policy can be explained by environmental resources. However, the activities of parties, groups, and individuals *within* the political system are heavily influenced by the nature of the environment. So our initial systems approach has warned us not to expect the activities of individuals, groups, parties, or decision-makers to produce policies at variance with environmental resources and constraints.

MASS OPINION AND PUBLIC POLICY

The influence of public opinion over government policy has been the subject of great philosophical controversies in the classic literature on democracy. Edmund Burke believed democratic representatives should serve the *interest* of the people but not necessarily conform to their *will* in deciding questions of public policy. In contrast, some democratic theorists have evaluated the success of democratic institutions by whether or not they facilitate popular control over public policy.

The philosophical question of whether public opinion *should* be an important independent influence over public policy may never be resolved. But the empirical question of whether public opinion *does* constitute an important independent influence over public policy can be tackled by systematic research. However, even this empirical question has proved very difficult to answer.

The problem in assessing the independent effect of mass opinion on the actions of decision-makers is that their actions help to mold mass opinion. Public policy may be in accord with mass opinion but we can never be sure whether mass opinion shaped public policy or public policy shaped mass opinion.

In V. O. Key's most important book, *Public Opinion and American Democracy,* he wrote:

> Government, as we have seen, attempts to mold public opinion toward support of the programs and policies it espouses. Given that endeavor, perfect congruence between public policy and public opinion could be government *of* public opinion rather than government *by* public opinion.[1]

[1] V. O. Key, Jr., *Public Opinion and American Democracy* (New York: Knopf, 1967), pp. 422–23.

Although Key himself was convinced that public opinion did have some independent effect on public policy, he was never able to demonstrate this in any systematic fashion. He lamented:

> Discussion of public opinion often loses persuasiveness as it deals with the critical question of how public opinion and governmental action are linked. The democratic theorist founds his doctrines on the assumption that an interplay occurs between mass opinion and government. When he seeks to delineate that interaction and to demonstrate the precise bearing of the opinions of private citizens on official decision, he encounters almost insurmountable obstacles. In despair he may conclude that the supposition that public opinion enjoys weight in public decision is a myth and nothing more, albeit a myth that strengthens a regime so long as people believe it.[2]

Yet Key compiled a great deal of circumstantial evidence supporting the notion that elections, parties, and interest groups, do institutionalize channels of communication from citizens to decision-makers.

But there is very little *direct* evidence in the existing research literature to support the notion that public opinion has an important influence over public policy. Many surveys reveal the absence of any knowledge or opinion about public policy on the part of masses of citizens. This suggests that mass opinion has little influence over the content of public policy. How can mass opinion be said to affect public policy when there *is* no mass opinion on a great many policy questions? Studies suggesting that the masses of people have little knowledge of, interest in, or opinion about a great many policy questions clearly imply that public opinion has little impact on the content of public policy. Likewise studies that indicate that public opinion is unstable and inconsistent also imply that public opinion has little policy impact.

In a careful study of the relationship between mass opinion and Congressional voting on policy issues, Warren E. Miller and Donald Stokes found very low correlations between the voting records of Congressmen and the attitudes of their constituents on social welfare issues, and even lower correlations on foreign policy issues.[3] Only in the area of civil rights did Congressmen appear to vote according to the views of a majority of their constitutents. In general, "the representative has very imperfect information about the issue preferences of his constitu-

---

[2] *Ibid.*, p. 411.

[3] Miller and Stokes, "Constituency Influence in Congress," *American Political Science Review*, 57 (March 1963), 55–65; see also Charles F. Cnudde and Donald J. McCrone, "The Linkage Between Constituency Attitudes and Congressional Voting Behavior," *American Political Science Review*, 60 (March 1966), 66–72.

ency, and constituency's awareness of the policy stands of the representative is ordinarily slight." With the possible exception of civil rights questions, most congressmen are free from the influence of popular preferences in their legislative voting.

This is not to say that policy-makers are completely free from the influence of mass opinion. On the contrary, the voting behavior of Congressmen on roll-call votes correlates very closely with characteristics of their constituencies. Districts of different social and economic makeup produce different political orientations and voting records for Congressmen. For example, Congressmen from urban-industrial districts are more likely to vote "liberal" than are Congressmen from rural, agricultural districts, regardless of party affiliation. Congressmen from suburban, high-income, white-collar districts have different voting records than do Congressmen from big-city, low-income, political machine-dominated districts.

Because a Congressman is a product of the social system in his constituency, he shares its dominant goals and values. He has deep roots in the social system of his constituency—many organizational memberships, many overlapping leadership positions, lifetime residency, close ties with social and economic elites, shared religious affiliations, and so on. A Congressman is so much "of" his constituency that conflicts seldom occur between his own views and the dominant views in his constituency.

Thus English political philosopher Edmund Burke's classic question about representation—Should the legislator be guided by his party, his constituents, or his personal judgment?—is an artificial one for the Congress. A majority of legislators in America *say* they follow their conscience in decision making, because this reflects the popular image of the Congressman as an independently courageous defender of the public interest who acts out of his own personal virtue and conviction, regardless of the consequences. But most Congressmen do not perceive many conflicts between the wishes of their constituents, their party, and their own judgment. Even where conflict is perceived, Congressmen usually attempt to balance conflicting demands rather than represent a party, a constituency, or self exclusively.

ELITE ATTITUDES AND PUBLIC POLICY

When V. O. Key wrestled with the same problem confronting us—namely, the determination of the impact of popular preferences on public policy—he concluded that "the missing piece of the puzzle" was "that thin stratum of persons referred to variously as the political elite, the political activists, the leadership echelons, or the influentials."

The longer one frets with the puzzle of how democratic regimes manage to function, the more plausible it appears that a substantial part of the explanation is to be found in the motives that activate the *leadership echelon,* the values that it holds, the rules of the political game to which it adheres, in the expectations which it entertains about its own status in society, and perhaps in some of the objective circumstances, both material and institutional, in which it functions.[4]

In view of our inability to find any direct links between public policy and popular preferences, it seems reasonable to ask whether the preferences of elites are more directly reflected in public policy than the preferences of masses. Do elite attitudes independently affect public policy? Or are elite attitudes so closely tied to environmental conditions that elites have relatively little flexibility in policy making and therefore little independent influence over the content of public policy?

Elite preferences are more likely to be in accord with public policy than mass preferences. This finding is fairly well-supported in the existing research literature. Of course this does not *prove* that policies are determined by elite preferences. It may be that government officials are acting rationally in response to events and conditions, and well-educated, informed elites understand the actions of government better than masses. Hence, it might be argued that elites support government policies because they have greater understanding of and confidence in government, and they are more likely to read about and comprehend the explanations of government officials. On the other hand, the correspondence between elite opinion and public policy may also indicate that elite opinion determines public policy.

Elite Opinion and the War in Vietnam. Let us consider, for example, the relationship between elite and mass opinion and the Vietnam War. Early in the war, well-educated Americans gave greater support to the war than less-educated Americans. The masses had greater doubts about the advisability of the war than the elites. However, the Johnson Administration went ahead with a policy of escalation, increasing U.S. combat forces in Vietnam. By 1968 elite opinion was divided, and in the 1968 elections both Democratic and Republican presidential candidates gave only guarded support for the policy of the Administration. By 1969, elite opinion had shifted dramatically; nearly two out of every three well-educated Americans had come to believe that U.S. involvement in Vietnam was a "mistake." Mass opposition to the war had also grown to a point where a majority now felt U.S. policy was a mistake. But mass opinion never shifted as dramatically as elite opinion. It was at this point that the policy of escalation was reversed, and President Nixon began his

[4] V.O. Key, Jr., *Public Opinion and American Democracy,* p. 537.

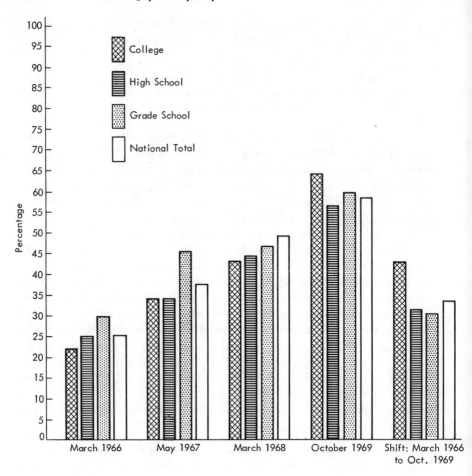

Fig. 13-1 *Agreement That U.S. Involvement in Vietnam Was a Mistake, by Education Levels*

Source: Gallup Opinion Index (October 1969), p. 15.

policy of gradual U.S. combat troop withdrawal and "Vietnamization" of the war.

Many other policy areas display the same elite-mass opinion linkages. It is usually the most highly educated, prestigiously employed, wealthy people who are highly supportive of government policies. Policy change more closely corresponds to changes in elite opinion than changes in mass opinion.

Elite Opinion and Desegregation. Another indication of the influence of elite opinion on policy is found in sociologist Crain's important study, *The Politics of School Desegregation.*[5] Crain systematically measured and compared the desegregation policies of eight Northern cities, specifically in terms of their acquiescence to the demands of civil rights groups.

Perhaps the most interesting finding presented by Crain is that the ideological orientation of the school board members is the *most* important factor in determining how a community responds to demands for changes in racial patterns in the schools. Crain ranked his cities according to their acquiescence to civil rights demands and then searched for community factors that appeared to influence the degree of acquiescence.[6] Certainly the intensity of the demands of civil rights activists did not lead to acquiescence; in fact the relationship was just the opposite; nonacquiescent cities were faced with the most militant civil rights activity.

Although the cities with the largest black populations were most likely to have acquiescent school boards, the correlation was not as good as one would expect ($r = .53$). The potential black vote was *not* a very strong influence on school board policy making. Perhaps one reason why the percentage of blacks does not correlate very well with acquiescence to black demands is that cities with the largest black populations have more anti-black sentiment among whites. But in an apparent paradox, it also turned out that the status characteristics of white populations, particularly at high educational levels, which might be expected to correlate with acquiescence to black demands, did not appear to influence board policy. Thus, Crain concludes that neither the characteristics of the community nor the activities of the civil rights movement (other than their initial presentations of the issue) had much influence on board policy.

The most important factor influencing desegregation policy was the civil rights attitude of school board members. Figure 13-2 plots the median civil rights liberalism (obtained by analyzing responses to questionnaires filled out by board members) against the acquiescence of the school board. The overall correlation (.65) is not very high. However,

[5] Robert Crain, *The Politics of School Desegregation* (Chicago: Aldine, 1968).

[6] Crain's acquiescence scale was as follows: (1) Pittsburgh: adoption of open enrollment after hearing parents' testimony; (2) Baltimore: decision by ad hoc committee to eliminate districting (June 1963); (3) San Francisco: decision to close Central Junior High School (August 1962); (4) Newark: adoption of open enrollment to settle suit (January 1962); (5) St. Louis: receipt and adoption in general terms of Maher committee report (June 1963); (6) Lawndale: refusal to change woodside boundaries (January 1961); (7) Bay City: fruitless discussion of de facto segregation prior to the first boycott (June 1963); (8) Buffalo: designation of Woodlawn school boundaries (March 1963).

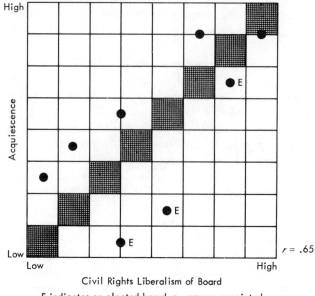

Fig. 13-2 *Civil Rights Liberalism of School Boards and Acquiescence in De-segregation in Northern Cities*

Source: Robert Crain, *The Politics of School Desegregation* (Chicago: Aldine Publishing Co., 1968). Copyright © 1968 by National Opinion Research Center. Reprinted by permission of Aldine-Atherton, Inc.

the pattern reveals an important difference between elected and appointed boards: the three cities that fall below the line of regression, being less acquiescent than we would expect from the liberalism score of the members, all have *elected* boards; the other five all have appointed boards. Apparently elected school board members do not inject their own liberalism into board policy as much as appointed board members. Elected board members with the same liberalism scores as appointed board members are less acquiescent in the demands of civil rights groups.

Thus, public policy is more likely to conform to elite opinion than to mass opinion. (Additional evidence to support this conclusion is presented in Chapter 3, "Civil Rights: Elite Mass Interaction.") But elites themselves must be responsive to environmental forces; these forces generate demands for governmental activities and provide the necessary resources to support public policy. It is unlikely that elites can operate independently of environmental forces for very long. Decision-makers are heavily constrained by the availability of resources, if nothing else. And they cannot long ignore pressing environmental problems. Virtually every public official and elected representative complains of the many specific demands and constraints placed upon him in decision making— demands and constraints that severely limit his policy choices. The question of how much *independent* effect elite opinion has on public policy remains unresolved.

PARTY INFLUENCE ON PUBLIC POLICY

Parties are important institutions in the American political system, but it would be a mistake to overestimate their impact on public policy. It makes relatively little difference in the major direction of public policy whether Democrats or Republicans dominate the political scene. American parties are largely "brokerage" organizations, devoid of ideology and committed to winning public office rather than to advancing policy positions. Both the Democratic and Republican parties and their candidates tailor their policy positions to societal conditions. The result is that the parties do not have much independent impact on policy outcomes.

Both American parties subscribe to the same fundamental political ideology. Both share prevailing democratic consensus about the sanctity of private property, a free enterprise economy, individual liberty, limited government, majority rule, and due process of law. Moreover, since the 1930s both parties have supported the same mass-welfare domestic programs of social security, fair labor standards, unemployment compensation, and graduated income tax, a national highway program, a federally aided welfare system, countercyclical fiscal and monetary policies, and government regulation of public utilities. Finally, both parties have supported the basic outlines of American foreign and military policy since World War II—international involvement, anticommunism, the cold war, European recovery, NATO, military preparedness, selective service, and even the Korean and Vietnam wars. A change in party control of the presidency or Congress has not resulted in any significant shifts in the course of American foreign or domestic policy.

Yet there are nuances of differences between the parties that can be observed in the policy-making process. The social bases of the Democratic and Republican parties are slightly different. Both parties draw support from all social groups in America, but the Democrats draw disproportionately from labor, big-city residents, ethnic voters, blacks, Jews, and Catholics; while Republicans draw disproportionately from rural, small-town, and suburban Protestants, businessmen and professionals. To the extent that the policy orientations of these two broad groups differ, the thrust of party ideology also differs. However, the magnitude of this difference is not very great.

Conflict between parties occurs most frequently over issues involving social welfare programs, housing and urban development, Medicare, antipoverty programs, and the regulation of business and labor. Party conflict is particularly apparent in the budget, the most important policy document of the national government. The budget is identified as the product of the president and carries the label of his party. On some issues, such as civil rights and appropriations, voting will follow party lines during roll calls on preliminary motions, amendments, and other preliminary matters, but swing to a bipartisan vote on passage of the final legislation. This means that the parties have disagreed on certain aspects of the bill, but compromised on its final passage.

What are the issues that cause conflict between the Democratic and Republican parties? In general, Democrats have favored lower tariffs; federal subsidies for agriculture; federal action to assist labor and low-income groups through social security, relief, housing, and wage-hour regulation; and generally a larger role for the federal government in launching new projects to remedy domestic problems. Republicans, on the other hand, have favored higher tariffs, free competition in agriculture, less government involvement in labor and welfare matters, and reliance on private action (see Table 13-1).

What then is the basis of party cohesion where it exists? Is party cohesion a product of effective party organization and discipline? Or is it really a result of similarities in the constituencies represented by each party? For example, is Democratic party cohesion a result of party organization pressures? Or is it the fact that Democrats typically are elected from metropolitan centers with strong labor groups, many Catholic voters, racial and ethnic minorities, and persons with few skills and poor education, and it is really constituency similarities that hold the Democratic legislators together? Could it be that Republican cohesion is a product of the fact that Republicans typically represent middle-class suburbs, small towns, and rural areas, and these types of constituencies have similar ideas about public policy?

It is unlikely that party organization and discipline alone is the cause of party voting, for organization and discipline can only be effective under certain conditions. The weight of evidence seems to support the hypothesis that *party influence is only effective where the parties represent separate and distinct socioeconomic coalitions.* Where the constituencies of a state are divided along social and economic lines, and where the party division coincides with these constituency divisions, only

Table 13-1 *Party Division on Selected Key Votes in Congress*

HOUSE VOTES

	Republicans		Democrats	
	Yes	No	Yes	No
Medicare (1965)	65	73	248	42
Establish Department of Housing and Urban Development (1965)	9	118	208	66
Federal Aid to Education (1965)	35	96	228	57
Model Cities Programs (1966)	16	81	162	60
Rat control in cities (1967)	22	148	154	59
Anticrime grants to states (1967)	172	4	84	143
Turnover Poverty Program to states (1970)	103	63	60	168
Override Nixon's veto of Labor-Welfare funds (1970)	27	156	199	35

SENATE VOTES

	Republicans		Democrats	
	Yes	No	Yes	No
Medicare (1965)	13	14	55	7
Repeal Taft-Hartley "right to work" provisions (1965)	5	26	40	21
Reduction in spending 5% across all items (1965)	26	5	17	41
Antiballistic missile (ABM) system (1970)	29	14	21	36

Source: Congressional Quarterly, varoius issues, 1965–1970.

then will party program and discipline be effective in shaping policy in legislative chambers.[7]

INTEREST GROUPS AND PUBLIC POLICY

Interest-group activity also provides a linkage between environmental forces and public policy. The interest-group structure of a society clearly reflects its socioeconomic composition. Modern urban institutional societies spawn a multitude of diverse interest groups. The resulting multiplicity and diversity reduces the likelihood that any single interest group can determine policy working in all fields. In contrast, poor, rural, agricultural societies produce fewer interest groups, but the opportunity

[7] Hugh L. LeBlanc, "Voting in State Senates: Party and Constituency Influences," *Midwest Journal of Political Science*, 13 (February 1969), 33–57.

Table 13-2 *Relationships Between Environment, Interest Group Structure, and Party System in the American States*

ENVIRONMENT	INTEREST GROUPS	PARTIES	INTEREST-GROUP INFLUENCE
Wealthy, urban, industrial	many, diverse	competitive, cohesive	indirect, moderate
Poor, rural, agricultural	fewer, consolidated	noncompetitive, faction-ridden	direct, strong

for these interest groups to dominate policy making in underdeveloped economies is greater.

Interest-group activity is also linked to party competition, which in turn is related to economic development. Interest groups are more directly influential in policy making in societies where the party system is weak and undeveloped. In the absence of strong cohesive parties, interest groups play a direct role in legislative affairs, with little moderation of their influence by intervening party influences. In contrast, where parties are strong and cohesive, interest groups may be more numerous and active, but their influence must be filtered through, and moderated by, party affairs.

Union Protesters in Washington. Photo by Fletcher Drake

On what kinds of decisions are interest groups most likely to exercise influence? Party and constituency influence are most important on broad social and economic issues. But on narrower issues, parties are less likely to take a stand, and constituents are less likely to have either an interest or an opinion. The legislator is, therefore, freer to respond to the pleas of organized groups on highly specialized topics than he is on major issues of public interest. The absence of both party and constituency influence on certain types of issues contributes to the effectiveness of organized interests. Economic interests, seeking to use the law to improve their competitive position, are a major source of group pressure on these specialized topics. Of course, these arguments are phrased in terms of "the public interest." As Malcolm Jewell reports in Kentucky:

> Representatives of horse racing interests write that the introduction of dog racing would damage not only them but the state's way of life. The chiropractors are upset by a bill sponsored by the state medical association. Bank presidents wire to prevent a bill that would permit small loan companies to loan larger amounts. Florists and nurserymen want license laws to limit competition. Local dairies want legislation to guarantee orderly market practices and undercut methods used by chain stores.[8]

Particularly active in lobbying are the businesses subject to extensive government regulation. The truckers, railroads, and liquor interests are consistently found to be among the most highly organized and active lobbyists in state capitals. Organized pressure also comes from associations of governments and associations of government employees. State chapters of the National Education Association (NEA) are persistent in presenting the demands of educational administrators and occasionally the demands of the dues-paying teachers as well.

The actual policy impact of interest groups is difficult to measure. A majority of state legislators report that they have never been persuaded to *change* their views on a particular policy question because of lobbying activity.[9] Yet it is very likely that lobbying can be effective on issues on which legislators held no prior opinions. These are likely to be the specialized economic issues.

A systematic study of the overall policy consequences of interest-group activity is political scientist Lewis A. Froman's study of special advantages and privileges written into state constitutions.[10] Professor Fro-

8 Malcolm Jewell, *The State Legislature* (New York: Random House, 1962), p. 70.

9 Harmon Zeigler and Michael Baer, *Lobbying: Influence and Interaction in American State Legislatures* (Belmont, Calif.: Wadsworth, 1969).

10 Lewis A. Froman, "Some Effects of Interest Group Strength in State Politics," *American Political Science Review*, 60 (December 1966), 952–62.

man found that in states in which interest groups are stronger, a larger number of special privileges and advantages will be granted by state constitutions. The stronger the interest groups in the state, the greater the length of the state constitution, the greater the number of proposed amendments, and the greater the number of amendments adopted. States with strong interest groups tend to have long constitutions, which deal directly with questions of public policy (labor practices, regulation of utilities, transportation problems, and so on). Typically, interest groups press for constitutional provisions to protect their interests because they are unwilling to trust future legislatures in matters of public policy. Thus, strong interest-group states are likely to have lengthy constitutions, which specify, among other things, public tariffs and charges, limit the taxing powers of the states and communities, place restrictions on state debt, specify the duties and powers of public service commissions and the regulation of utilities, set forth regulations on insurance companies, specify the hours and duties of local government officials, set the salaries of the state and local officeholders, exempt certain industries from taxation, regulate school systems, and so on. Froman concludes that constitutions are one of the means by which advantages and disadvantages are distributed in political systems, and that the strength of interest groups in gaining special constitutional advantages can be observed in the length of state constitutions and in amending activity.

BUREAUCRATIC, EXECUTIVE, LEGISLATIVE INTERACTION

The process approach to government devotes a great deal of attention to the formal and informal relationships between administrative agencies, chief executives, and legislative aides. Students of this approach concentrate their attention on the powers of chief executives over administrative agencies and over legislative proposals, and the powers of legislative aides over the actions of administrative agencies and chief executives. But the impact of patterns of administrative, executive, and legislative interaction on the *content of public policy* is largely unexplained.

One of the rare studies of the interaction between administrative agencies, governors, and legislatures that focuses on the impact of this interaction on budgetary outcomes is political scientist Ira Sharkansky's analysis of the budgetary process in nineteen states.[11] Professor Sharkansky examined the relationships between agency requests, governors'

---

[11] Ira Sharkansky, "Agency Requests, Gubernatorial Support and Budget Success in State Legislatures," *American Political Science Review*, 62 (December 1968), 1220–31.

recommendations regarding these requests, and legislative appropriations vis-à-vis agency requests and governors' recommendations. First he measured the "acquisitiveness" of executive agencies by the agency's request for the coming budget period as a percentage of current expenditures. Then he measured the "governors' support" of the agency's request by the governors' recommendation for each agency as a percentage of its requests. He measured the "governors' success" by legislative appropriations as a percent of the governors' recommendations. Finally, he measured "budgetary short-term success" in the legislature by legislative appropriations as a percent of agency requests, and "budgetary expansion" by legislative appropriations as a percentage of the agency's current expenditures.

Several interesting ideas emerge from the analysis of this data:

1. More acquisitive agencies get their requests cut down more by governors and legislatures than less acquisitive agencies. However, the more acquisitive agencies end up with generally higher appropriations than the less acquisitive agencies.
2. The governors' support appears to be a critical ingredient in the success enjoyed by executive agencies in their budgetary requests to the legislature. Legislatures respond more to governors' recommendations than to agency requests. Agencies with the largest budget expansions were those that enjoyed the greatest gubernatorial support.
3. The governors who enjoyed the greatest budgetary success in the legislature tended to be those who could be reelected. Governors with high tenure potential were better able to elicit legislative cooperation in funding requests than those who could not expect to remain in office because of constitutional limitations on their terms.

POLICY INNOVATION

Policy innovation has been a central concern of students of the policy processes.[12] Policy innovation is simply the readiness of a government to adopt new programs and policies. Several years ago, Jack L. Walker constructed an "innovation score" for the American states based upon elapsed time between the first state adoption of a program and its

[12] Victor Thompson, *Bureaucracy and Innovation* (University of Alabama Press, 1969); Lawrence B. Mohr, "Determinants of Innovation in Organizations," *American Political Science Review*, 63 (March 1969), 111–26; Michael Aiken and Robert R. Alford, "Community Structure and Innovation: The Case for Public Housing," *American Political Science Review*, 64 (September 1970), 843–64; Jack L. Walker, "The Diffusion of Innovations Among the American States," *American Political Science Review*, 63 (September 1969), 880–99.

later adoption by other states. Walker monitored eighty-eight different programs adopted by twenty or more states, and he averaged each state's score on each program adoption to produce an index of innovation for each state. "The larger the innovation score, the faster the state has been on the average in responding to new ideas or policies." [13] Walker proceeded to explore relationships between innovation scores in the fifty states and socioeconomic, political, and regional variables. It turned out that innovation was more readily accepted in urban, industrialized, wealthy states.

However, in a subsequent study of policy innovation in the American states, Virginia Gray argued persuasively that no general tendency toward "innovativeness" really exists—that states which are innovative in one policy area are not necessarily the same states which are innovative in other policy areas. She examined the adoption of twelve specific innovations in civil rights, welfare, and education, including the adoption of state public accommodations, fair housing, and fair employment laws, and merit systems and compulsory school attendance. States that were innovative in education were not necessarily innovative in civil rights or welfare. Nonetheless, she discovered that "first adopters" of most innovations tended to be wealthier states.[14]

Let us try to explain why wealth, urbanization, and education are associated with policy innovation. First of all, *income* enables a state to afford the luxury of experimentation. Low incomes place constraints on the ability of policy-makers to raise revenues to pay for new programs or policies: high incomes provide the *tax resources* necessary to begin new undertakings. We can also imagine that *urbanization* would be conducive to policy innovation. Urbanization involves social change and creates demands for new programs and policies, and urbanization implies the concentration of creative resources in large cosmopolitan centers. Rural societies change less rapidly and are considered less adaptive and sympathetic to innovation. Finally, it is not unreasonable to expect that *education* should facilitate innovation. An educated population should be more receptive toward innovation in public policy, and perhaps even more demanding of innovation in its appraisal of political candidates. In summary, wealth, urbanization, and education, considered together, should provide a socioeconomic environment conducive to policy innovation.

We might also expect both party competition and voter participation to affect policy innovation. Closely contested elections should encourage parties and candidates to put forward innovative programs and ideas to

---

[13] "Diffusion of Innovations Among the American States," p. 883.

[14] Virginia Gray, "Innovation in the States," *American Political Science Review*, Vol. 67 (December 1973), 1174–85.

capture the imagination and support of the voter. Competitive states are more likely to experience turnover in party control of state government. Innovations in policy are more likely when a new administration takes office. An increase in political participation should also encourage policy innovation.

The decision-making milieu itself—characteristics of the legislative and executive branches of state government—can also be expected to influence policy innovation. Specifically, we expect that the ethic of "professionalism" among legislators and bureaucrats is a powerful stimulus to policy innovation. Professionalism involves, among other things, acceptance of professional reference groups as sources of information, standards, and norms. The professional bureaucrat attends national conferences, reads national journals, and perhaps even aspires to build a professional reputation that extends beyond the boundaries of his own state. Thus, he constantly encounters new ideas, and he is motivated to pursue innovation for the purpose of distinguishing himself in his chosen field. Moreover, one might argue that professional bureaucrats are also moved to propose innovative programs in order to expand their authority within the bureaucracy—"empire building."

All these factors—income, urbanization, education, tax revenue, party competition, voter participation, civil service coverage, and legislative professionalism—are *related* to policy innovation. Table 13-3 shows the simple correlation coefficients between each of these explanatory variables and the policy innovation scores.

Table 13-3 *Correlates of Policy Innovation In the American States*

	Figures are simple correlation coefficients for relationships with the innovation index		
Income	.56	Party Competition	.34
Urbanization	.54	Voter Participation	.28
Education	.32	Civil Service Coverage	.53
Tax Revenue	.28	Legislative Professionalism	.62

Further causal analysis reveals that "professionalism" in the legislative and executive branches of state government appears to be the most direct source of policy innovation. We might speculate that professionalism among both legislators and bureaucrats encourages the development of national standards for governmental administration. Professionals know about programmatic developments elsewhere through professional meetings, journals, newsletters, etc. More importantly, they view themselves as professional administrators and governmental leaders and they seek to adopt the newest reforms and innovations for their own states. As Jack Walker comments, "They are likely to adopt a more cosmopolitan perspective and to cultivate their reputations within a national professional community rather than merely within their own state or agency." [15] Even if individual legislators themselves do not think in professional terms, legislatures with professional staffs may be influenced by these values.

Education, participation, and innovation appear to be linked in a causal fashion. This lends some limited support to the *pluralist* contention that an educated and active political constituency can have an impact on public policy—at least to the extent that such a constituency seems to promote novelty and experimentation in programs and policies. In summary, the explanation of policy innovation turns out to be one that emphasizes professionalism in legislature and bureaucracies, and an educated and politically active population.

SUMMARY

Systems theory helps us to conceptualize the linkages between the environment, the political system, and public policy, but it does not really describe what goes on inside the "black box" labeled "political system." Although political science has traditionally concerned itself with describing political institutions, processes, and behaviors, seldom has it systematically examined the impact of these political variables on the *content* of public policy. Let us try to set forth some general propositions about the impact of political processes and behaviors on policy content.

1. It is difficult to assess the independent effect of public opinion on public policy. Public policy may accord with mass opinion but we can never be certain whether mass opinion shaped public policy or public policy shaped mass opinion.
2. Public policy is more likely to conform to elite opinion than mass opinion. Elite opinion has been particularly influential in the determination of civil rights policy. However, it is unlikely that elites can operate independently of environmental resources and demands for very long.
3. The Democratic and Republican parties have agreed on the basic outlines of American foreign and domestic policy since World War II. Thus, partisanship has not been a central influence on public policy. However, there have been some policy differences between the parties. Differences have occurred most frequently over questions of welfare, housing and urban development, antipoverty efforts, health care, and the regulations of business and labor.
4. Most votes in Congress and state legislatures show the Democratic and Republican party majorities to be in agreement. However, when conflict

[15] *Ibid.*, p. 895.

occurs it is more likely to occur along party lines than any other kind of division.

5. Party influence is only effective where parties represent separate and distinct socioeconomic environments. Party voting on policy questions is more likely to occur when Democrats represent urban constituencies with strong labor groups, Catholic voters, racial and ethnic minorities, and working-class groups; and Republicans represent middle-class suburbs, small towns, and rural areas. It is unlikely that party organization or ideology has much independent effect on public policy.

6. Interest groups have more independent influence on policy questions involving narrow economic interests. A rural, agricultural or non-diversified, single-industry environment is conducive to the emergence of powerful interest groups. But interest groups in urban, diversified economies also exercise great influence on specialized economic issues.

7. Acquisitive executive agencies have their budget requests cut down more by governors than less acquisitive agencies, but they end up with generally higher appropriations. The support of the chief executive is essential to budgetary requests. Legislatures respond more often to governors' recommendations than to agency requests. The most successful governors in legislative interaction are those who can run for reelection at the end of their term.

8. Policy innovation—the readiness of a government to adopt new programs and policies—is linked to urbanization, education, and wealth, as well as competition, participation, and professionalism. Specifically, policy innovation appears to be a product of professionalism in legislatures and bureaucracies, and an educated and politically active population.

BIBLIOGRAPHY

EDELMAN, MURRAY, *The Symbolic Uses of Politics.* Urbana, Ill.: University of Illinois Press, 1964.

KEY, JR., V. O., *Public Opinion and American Democracy.* New York: Knopf, 1967.

LIPSET, SEYMOUR MARTIN, *Political Man.* New York: Doubleday, 1963.

POMPER, GERALD, *Elections in America.* New York: Dodd, Mead, 1968.

SCHATTSCHNEIDER, E. E., *The Semi-Sovereign People.* New York: Holt, Rinehart & Winston, 1960.

ZEIGLER, HARMON, *Interest Groups in American Society.* Englewood Cliffs, N.J.: Prentice-Hall, 1964.

Speaker's chair, House of Representatives. THE NEW YORK TIMES, George Tames

14 POLICY IMPACT:

finding out what happens after a law is passed

ASSESSING THE IMPACT OF PUBLIC POLICY

Americans generally assume that once we *pass a law* and *spend money,* the purpose of the law and expenditure should be achieved in whole or in part. We assume that when Congress adopts a policy and appropriates money for it, and when the executive branch organizes a program, hires people, spends money, and carries out activities designed to implement the policy, the effects of the policy will be felt by society and will be those intended by the policy. Unfortunately, these assumptions are not always warranted. The national experiences with the "war on poverty," public housing, urban renewal, public assistance, and many other public programs indicates the need for careful appraisal of the real impact of public policy. There is a growing uneasiness among policy-makers and the general public about the effectiveness and the costs of many public service and social action programs. America's problems cannot always be resolved by passing a law and throwing a few billion dollars in the general direction of the problem in the hope that it will go away.

We must distinguish between "policy output" and "policy impact." The impact of a policy is its *effect on real-world conditions.* The impact of a policy includes:

1. Its impact on the target situation or group
2. Its impact on situations or groups other than the target ("spillover effects")

327

3. Its impact on future as well as immediate conditions
4. Its direct costs, in terms of resources devoted to the program
5. Its indirect costs, including loss of opportunities to do other things.

All the benefits and costs, both immediate and future, must be measured in terms of both *symbolic* and *tangible* effects.

Identifying the target groups means defining the part of the population for whom the program is intended—e.g. the poor, the sick, the ill-housed, etc. Then the desired effect of the program on the target group must be determined. Is it to change their physical or economic circumstances—for example, the "life chances" of blacks, the income of the poor, the housing conditions of ghetto residents? Or is it to change their knowledge, attitudes, awareness, interests, or behavior? If multiple effects are intended, what are the priorities among different effects—for example, is a high payoff in terms of positive attitudes toward the political system more valuable than tangible progress toward the elimination of black-white life chances? What are the possible unintended effects (side effects) on target groups—for example, does public housing achieve better physical environments for many urban blacks at the cost of increasing their segregation and alienation from the white community? What is the impact policy on the target group in proportion to total need? Accurate data describing the unmet needs of the nation are not generally available, but it is important to estimate the denominator of total need so that we know how adequate our programs are. Moreover, such an estimate may also help in estimating symbolic benefits or costs; a program that promises to meet a national need but actually meets only a small proportion of it may generate great praise at first but bitterness and frustration later when it becomes known how small its impact is relative to the need.

Policy impact is not the same as policy output. It is important *not* to measure benefits in terms of government activity. For example, the number of dollars spent per member of a target group (per pupil educational expenditures, per capita welfare expenditures, per capita health expenditures) is not really a measure of the *impact* of a policy on the group. It is merely a measure of government activity—that is to say, a measure of *policy output*. We cannot be content with measuring how many times a bird flaps its wings, we must assess how far the bird has flown. In *describing* public policy, or even in *explaining* its determinants, measures of policy output are important. But in assessing the *impact* of policy, we must find identity changes in the environment or the political system that are associated with measures of government activity.

All programs and policies have differential effects on various segments of the population. Identifying important nontarget groups for a policy is a difficult process. For example, what is the impact of the welfare reform on groups other than the poor—government bureaucrats, social workers, local political figures, working-class families who are not on welfare, taxpayers, others? Nontarget effects may be expressed as benefits as well as costs, such as the benefits to the construction industry of public housing projects. And these effects may be symbolic as well as tangible— for example, wealthy liberals enjoy a good feeling from participation in an antipoverty program, whether the program helps the poor or not.

When will the benefits or costs be felt? Is the program designed for short-term, emergency situations? Or is it a long-term, developmental effort? If it is short-term, what facts will prevent the processes of incrementalism and bureaucratization from turning it into a long-term program, even after the immediate need is met? Many impact studies show that new or innovative programs have short-term positive effects—for example, operation Headstart and other educational programs. However, the positive effects frequently disappear as the novelty and enthusiasm of new programs wear off. Other programs experience difficulties at first, as in the early days of Social Security and Medicare, but turn out to have "sleeper" effects, as in the widespread acceptance of the Social Security idea. Not all programs aim at the same degree of permanent or transient change.

Programs are frequently measured in terms of their direct costs. We generally know how many dollars go into program areas, and we can even calculate (as in Chapter 9) the proportion of total governmental dollars and the proportion of the Gross National Product devoted to various programs. Government agencies have developed various forms of cost-benefit analysis, such as Program, Planning, and Budgeting Systems (PPBS) and operations research, to identify the direct costs (usually, but not always, in dollars) of government programs.

But it is very difficult to identify the indirect and symbolic costs of public programs. Rarely can all these cost factors be included in a formal decision-making model. Often political intuition is the best guide available to the policy-maker in these matters. What are the indirect symbolic costs for poor whites of the federal government's activities on behalf of blacks? What are the costs of public housing and urban renewal in the effects of relocation on the lives of slum dwellers? What are the symbolic costs for the working poor of large numbers of welfare recipients? What were the costs of the Vietnam War in terms of American morale and internal division and strife?

Moreover, it is very difficult to measure benefits in terms of general social well-being. Cost accounting techniques developed in business were designed around units of production—automobiles, airplanes, tons of steel,

Table 14-1 *Assessing Policy Impact*

	BENEFITS		COSTS	
	Present	**Future**	**Present**	**Future**
Target Groups and Situations	Symbolic Tangible	Symbolic Tangible	Symbolic Tangible	Symbolic Tangible
Nontarget Groups and Situations (Spillover)	Symbolic Tangible	Symbolic Tangible	Symbolic Tangible	Symbolic Tangible
	Sum	Sum	Sum	Sum
	Present Benefits	Future Benefits	Present Costs	Future Costs
	Sum All Benefits	—	Sum All Costs	
		Net Policy Impact		

etc. But how do we identify and measure units of social well-being? In recent years, some social scientists have begun the effort to develop "social indicators"—measures of social well-being of American society.[1] This movement is just beginning; we are still a long way from assessing the impact of public policy on general social indicators or rationally evaluating alternative public policies by weighing their costs against gains in social indicators.

All these aspects of public policy are very difficult to identify, describe, and measure. Moreover, the task of calculating *net* impact of a public policy is truly awesome. The *net* impact would be all the symbolic and tangible benefits, both immediate and long-range, minus all the symbolic and tangible costs, both immediate and future (see Table 14-1). Even if all the immediate and future and symbolic and tangible costs and benefits are *known* (and everyone *agrees* on what is a "benefit" and what is a "cost"), it is still very difficult to come up with a net balance. Many of the items on both sides of the balance would defy comparison—for example, how do you subtract a tangible cost in terms of dollars from a symbolic reward in terms of the sense of well-being felt by individuals or groups?

[1] See U.S. Department of Health, Education and Welfare, *Toward a Social Report* (Washington: Government Printing Office, 1969); Bertram M. Gross, ed., *Social Intelligence for American's Future* (Boston: Allyn and Bacon, 1969).

THE SYMBOLIC IMPACT OF POLICY

The impact of a policy includes both its *symbolic* and *tangible* effects. Its symbolic impact deals with the perceptions that individuals have of government action and their attitudes toward it. Even if government policies do not succeed in reducing dependency, or eliminating poverty, or preventing crime, and so on, this may be a rather minor objection to them if the failure of government to *try* to do these things would lead to the view that society is "not worth saving." Individuals, groups, and whole societies frequently judge public policy in terms of its good intentions rather than its tangible accomplishments. The general popularity and public appraisal of a program may be unrelated to the real impact of a program in terms of desired results. The implication is that very popular programs may have little positive impact, and vice versa.

The policies of government may tell us more about the aspirations of a society and its leadership than about actual conditions. Policies do more than affect change in societal conditions; they also help hold men together and maintain an orderly state. For example, a government "war on poverty" may not have any significant impact on the poor, but it reassures moral men, the affluent as well as the poor, that government "cares" about poverty. Whatever the failures of the antipoverty program in tangible respects, its symbolic value may be more than redeeming. For example, whether the fair housing provisions of the Civil Rights Act of 1968 can be enforced or not, the fact that it is national policy to forbid discrimination in the sale or rental of housing reassures men of all races that their government does not condone such acts. There are many more examples of public policy serving as a symbol of what society aspires to be.

The subjective condition of the nation is clearly as important as the objective condition. For example, white prejudices about blacks in schools, in public accommodations, or in housing may be declining over time. But this may not reduce racial tensions if blacks *believe* that racism is as prevalent as it ever was. Blacks may be narrowing the gap between black and white income, jobs, and housing through individual initiative and opportunity within the existing system. But if blacks *believe* that only massive government intervention in income, employment, and housing will assist them, this belief will become a critical factor in policy making.

Once upon a time "politics" was described as "who gets what, when, and how." Today it seems that politics centers about "who *feels* what, when, and how." The smoke-filled room where patronage and pork were dispensed has been replaced with the talk-filled room where rhetoric and image are dispensed. What governments *say* is as important as what governments *do*. Television has made the image of public policy as important as the policy itself. Systematic policy analysis concentrates on what governments *do*, why they do it, and what difference it makes. It devotes less attention to what governments *say*. Perhaps this is a weakness in policy analysis. Our focus has been primarily upon activities of governments rather than the rhetoric of governments.

EVALUATING ONGOING PROGRAMS:
WHY GOVERNMENTS DO NOT KNOW THE IMPACT
OF THEIR OWN POLICIES

Policy impact can be studied by evaluating ongoing programs (policy evaluation) or by deliberately experimenting with alternative policies or programs (policy experimentation). Attempts at policy evaluation are common in government programs; frequently government analysts and administrators report on the conditions of target groups before and after their participation in a new program and some effort is made to attribute observed changes to the new program itself. Policy experimentation is less frequent; seldom do governments systematically select experimental and control groups of the population, introduce a new program to the experimental group only, and then carefully compare changes in the conditions of the experimental group with a control group that has not benefited from the program. Let us turn first to some of the problems confronting policy evaluation studies; later we will describe policy experimentation.[2]

1. The first problem confronting anyone who wants to evaluate a public program is to determine what the goals of the program are. What are the target groups and what are the desired effects? But governments often pursue incompatible goals to satisfy very diverse groups. Overall policy planning and evaluation may reveal inconsistencies of public policy and force reconsideration of fundamental societal goals. Where there is little agreement on the goals of a public program, evaluation studies may engender a great deal of political conflict. Government agencies generally prefer to avoid conflict, and hence to avoid studies that would raise such questions.

2. Many programs and policies have primarily symbolic value. They do not actually change the conditions of target groups but merely make these groups feel that government "cares." A government agency does not welcome a study that reveals that its efforts have no tangible effects; such a

[2] For an excellent discussion of policy evaluation, see Edward A. Suchman, *Evaluative Research* (New York: Russell Sage Foundation, 1967).

revelation itself might reduce the symbolic value of the program by informing target groups of its uselessness.

3. Government agencies have a strong vested interest in "proving" that their programs have a positive impact. Administrators frequently view attempts to evaluate the impact of their programs as attempts to limit or destroy their programs, or to question the competence of the administrators.
4. Government agencies usually have a heavy investment—organizational, financial, physical, psychological—in current programs and policies. They are predisposed against finding that these policies do not work.
5. Any serious study of policy impact undertaken by a government agency would involve some interference with ongoing program activities. The press of day-to-day business generally takes priority over study and evaluation in a governmental agency. More important, the conduct of an experiment may necessitate depriving individuals or groups (control groups) of services to which they are entitled under law; this may be difficult, if not impossible, to do.
6. Program evaluation requires funds, facilities, time, and personnel which government agencies do not like to sacrifice from ongoing programs. Policy impact studies, like any research, cost money. They cannot be done well as extracurricular or part-time activities. Devoting resources to study may mean a sacrifice in program resources that administrators are unwilling to make.

Government administrators and program supporters are ingenious in devising reasons why negative findings about policy impact should be rejected. Even in the fact of clear evidence that their favorite programs are useless or even counterproductive, they will argue that

1. The effects of the program are long-range and cannot be measured at the present time.
2. The effects of the program are diffuse and general in nature; no single criteria or index adequately measures what is being accomplished.
3. The effects of the program are subtle and cannot be identified by crude measures or statistics.
4. Experimental research cannot be carried out effectively because to withhold services from some persons to observe the impact of such withholding would be unfair to them.
5. The fact that no difference was found between persons receiving the services and those not receiving them means that the program is not sufficiently intensive and indicates the need to spend *more* resources on the program.
6. The failure to identify any positive effects of a program is attributable to inadequacy or bias in the research itself, not in the program.

Recently Harvard Professor James Q. Wilson formulated two general laws to cover all cases of social science research on policy impact:

Wilson's First Law: All policy interventions in social problems produce the intended effect—*if* the research is carried out by those implementing the policy or their friends.

Wilson's Second Law: No policy intervention in social problems produces the intended effect—*if* the research is carried out by independent third parties, especially those skeptical of the policy. [Interestingly, Wilson was commenting on the Armor study and Armor's critics, particularly Thomas F. Pettigrew.]

Wilson denies that his laws are cynical. Instead he reasons that

> Studies that conform to the First Law will accept an agency's own data about what it is doing and with what effect; adopt a time frame (long or short) that maximizes the probability of observing the desired effect; and minimize the search for other variables that might account for the effect observed. Studies that conform to the Second Law will gather data independently of the agency; adopt a short time frame that either minimizes the chance for the desired effect to appear or, if it does appear, permits one to argue that the results are "temporary" and probably due to the operation of the "Hawthorne Effect" (i.e., the reaction of the subjects to the fact that they are part of an experiment); and maximize the search for other variables that might explain the effects observed.[3]

PPBS, SOCIAL INDICATORS, AND OTHER
EVALUATIVE TOOLS

Despite these difficulties, however, there has been substantial progress in recent years in policy evaluation research. Increasingly, decision-makers are turning to analysts to ask questions about the effectiveness of ongoing and proposed programs—What is it doing? Why do we need it? What does it cost? They do not always get good answers yet, but the need for systematic policy research is now recognized.

For example, variations of PPBS—Planning, Programming, Budgeting Systems—have been widely adopted by government agencies in recent years. Despite an elaborate terminology, PPBS is merely an attempt to rationalize decision making in a bureaucracy. It is part of the budgetary process—but the focus is on the *uses* of expenditures and the *output* provided for rather than on dollar amounts allocated by agency or department. The aim of PPBS is to specify, and hopefully to quantify, the output of a government program, and then to minimize the cost of achieving this output and to learn whether benefits exceed the cost. The first step in PPBS is to define program objectives. The next, and perhaps critical step, is to develop indices or measures of the level of accomplishment under each program—the "output." Then the costs of the program

---

[3] James Q. Wilson, "On Pettigrew and Armor," *The Public Interest*, Number 31 (Spring 1973), pp. 132–34.

can be calculated *per unit of output*. Presumably this enables the decision-maker to view the real cost-benefit ratio of a program (e.g., how much it costs to teach one pupil per year, or train one worker in a manpower program, or keep one child in a day-care center, etc.). This also provides a basis for more elaborate comparisons of the costs and benefits of alternative programs, or to analyze the "cost effectiveness" of alternative programs (to see which achieves a given goal at least cost).

Some of the early enthusiasm for PPBS and related tools has cooled. PPBS was first introduced by Secretary Robert N. McNamara in the Defense Department in 1961 as a systematic method of determining the relative costs and benefits of alternative weapons systems. But establishing units of output and their costs and estimating the costs of alternative programs in *domestic* policy fields has proven more complex than similar tasks involving weapons systems.

First of all, it is difficult to establish prices for certain social outcomes, which are not usually sold and therefore have no price. How can we establish the value of finding a cure for cancer? How can we compare the value of finding a cure for cancer with the value of teaching poor children to read and write? A strict cost-benefit comparison would require that we add up the costs and benefits of each and choose the program with the higher excess of benefits over costs. But the benefits of certain programs may be of inestimable value. How do we set values on freedom from fear, good health, the pleasures of clean air, the joys of outdoor recreation, and so forth?

Second, different programs benefit different people. Public funds for higher education benefit middle-class groups more than public funds for literacy training. How do we calculate the benefits of college education for some groups in relation to the benefits of literacy training for other groups, even if costs were the same?

Finally, decision-makers are constrained by the political process. They and their constituents have intuitive notions about the relative benefits of health, education, housing, or welfare programs, which are not likely to be changed by cost-benefit estimates.

A number of social scientists have advocated the development of a set of indicators to show social progress (or retrogression). They have urged the preparation of an annual "Social Report" similar to the President's Economic Report but designed to assess the social condition of the nation. Most Americans can agree on the values of a healthy, well-educated, adequately housed, and affluent population, even if they cannot agree on public policies designed to achieve these values. Perhaps a general assessment of the nation's progress toward these goals would be helpful in an overall evaluation of the effectiveness of public policy. At least that is the idea behind this "social indicator" movement. "Social indicators" are defined simply as quantitative data that serve as indices to socially important conditions of a society.

Presumably a set of social indicators and a social report would accomplish two things: first, it would focus attention on certain social conditions and thus make possible more informed judgments about national priorities, and second, by showing how different measures of social well-being change over time, it might help evaluate the success of public programs. In exploring the feasibility of social reporting, a team of social scientists working for the Department of Health, Education and Welfare suggested the development of a variety of measures similar to those shown in Table 14-2. Some of these social measures deal with health, education, and welfare; others with social trends such as women in the labor force, voter turnout, and vacations and leisure time. But more than anything else, this initial study revealed great gaps in available information about the health and happiness of the American people.

But the task of choosing social indicators raises many *political* questions.[4] First of all, the choice of a particular indicator suggests a societal goal. Most people agree on the value of a longer life span and lower infant mortality rates. But should everyone graduate from college? Should every community have a community college? Should a large female labor force be a national goal? Should the government provide free family planning services to low-income families? And how do we set priorities among these goals?

There is a hidden political bias in the social indicators movement itself—a bias on behalf of liberal reform and social welfare. Proponents of social indicators and a Social Report are generally committed to long-range government planning, bettering the lot of the poor and of minorities, and using government power to insure social welfare. Conservatives have reason to be suspicious of a movement which assumes that government can select society's goals and monitor progress toward these goals. Moreover, there is the assumption behind the social indicators idea that social measures can and should be affected by government policies. Government monitoring of social indicators *implies* government responsibility for social conditions. Finally, there is a concern that social accounting will lead to a totalitarian society in which every aspect of life is monitored and controlled by government. Even a supporter of social reporting writes:

> Any kind of Social Report would, in the eyes of many, entail a danger: it could involve government in making the kinds of judgments of value

---

[4] For an excellent discussion of the political implications of social measurement, see Peter J. Henriot's "Political Questions About Social Indicators," *Western Political Quarterly*, 23 (June 1970), 235-55.

Table 14-2 *Suggested Social Indicators*

INDICATOR	PRESENT EXPERIENCE	1976–79 GOAL
1. Infant Mortality (per 1,000 live births)	22.1 (1967)	12
2. Maternal Mortality (per 100,000 live births)	28.9 (1967)	15
3. Family Planning Services (for Low-Income Women 15–44)	1 million (1968)	5 million
4. Deaths from Accident (per 100,000 population)	55.1 (1967)	50
5. Number of Persons in State Mental Hospitals	426,000 (1967)	50,000
6. Expectancy of Healthy Life	68.2 years (1966)	70.2 year
7. Three- to five-year-olds in school or pre-school	35.2% (1967)	95%
8. Persons 25 and older who graduate from high school	51.1% (1967)	65%
9. Persons 25 and older who graduate from college	10.1% (1967)	15%
10. Persons in Learning Force	100 million (1967)	150 million
11. Percent of Major Cities with public Community Colleges	66% (1968)	100%
12. Number of first-year students in Medical Schools	10,000 (1967)	18,000
13. Handicapped Persons Rehabilitated	208,000 (1968)	600,000
14. Average Weekly Hours of Work—Manufacturing	40.6 (1967)	37.5
15. Labor Force Participation Rate for Women Aged 35–64	48% (1967)	60%
16. Average Annual Paid Vacation—Manufacturing	2 weeks (1967)	4 weeks
17. Housing Units with Bathtub or Shower	85% (1960)	100%
18. Percent of Population Illiterate	2.4% (1960)	0
19. Voters as a Percentage of Voting Age Population	63% (1964)	80%
20. Private Philanthropy as a percent of GNP	1.9% (1967)	2.7%
21. Public and Private Expenditures for Health, Education and Welfare as a percent of GNP	19.8% (1968)	25%
22. Percent of Population in Poverty	12.8% (1968)	0
23. Income of Lowest Fifth of population	5.3% (1967)	10%
24. Persons who work during the year	88 million (1967)	110 million
25. Life Expectancy	70.2 year (1966)	72 years

Source: U.S. Department of Health, Education and Welfare, *Toward a Social Report* (Ann Arbor: University of Michigan Press, 1970).

that, in our political order, are the prerogatives of the individual citizen or of the organizations of which he is a voluntary member. This danger is not imaginary. If—perhaps one should say when—we do have a Social Report, it will be necessary to subject it to rigorous and skeptical criticism.[5]

There is also an implicit political elitism in the notion of social indicators—the view that social scientists are the best judges of what is "good" for the people. In a democratic society, demands for public programs are supposed to originate in the political process from the felt needs of the people. But social accounting implies that social scientists will become "philosopher-kings" deciding what "problems" confront society and what are the "best" solutions for them.

Establishing a government agency to monitor social progress in the nation raises still other political questions: How will social indicators, and by implication social goals, be chosen? What influences will lobbying pressures have on the selection of indicators and the gathering of data? What safeguards are necessary in the "management" of data? To whom will the data used for social indicators be made available? What are the dangers to privacy that an extensive system of social records might involve?

EXPERIMENTAL POLICY RESEARCH:

THE GUARANTEED INCOME EXPERIMENT

Many policy analysts argue that "policy experimentation" offers the best opportunity to determine the impact of public policies. This opportunity rests upon the main characteristics of experimental research: the systematic selection of experimental and control groups, the application of the policy under study to the experimental group only, and the careful comparison of differences between the experimental and the control group after the application of the policy.

Perhaps the best-known example of an attempt by the federal government to experiment with public policy is the New Jersey Graduated Work Incentive Experiment funded by the Office of Economic Opportunity. The experiment was designed to resolve some serious questions about the impact of welfare payments on the incentives for poor people to work.[6] In order to learn more about the effects of the present welfare

---

[5] Irving Kristol, "Social Indicators, Reports and Accounts," *The Annals* (March 1970), p. 11.

[6] See Harold M. Watts, "Graduated Work Incentives: An Experiment in Negative Taxation," *American Economic Review*, 59 (May 1969), 463–72.

system on human behavior, and more importantly, to learn more about the possible effects of proposed programs for guaranteed family incomes, the OEO funded a three-year social experiment involving 1,350 families in New Jersey and Pennsylvania.

Debates over welfare reform had generated certain questions which social science presumably could answer with careful, controlled experimentation. Would a guaranteed family income reduce the incentive to work? If payments are made to poor families with employable male heads, will the men drop out of the labor force? Would the level of the income guarantee, or the steepness of the reductions of payments with increases in earnings make any difference in working behavior? Because current welfare programs do not provide a guaranteed minimum family income, make payments to families with employable males, or graduate payments in relation to earnings, these questions could only be answered through *policy experimentation*. But policy experimentation raised some serious initial problems for OEO. First of all, any experiment involving substantial payments to a fair sampling of families would be expensive. For example, if payments averaged $1,000 per year per family, and if each family had to be observed for three years, and if 1,000 families were to be involved, a minimum of $3 million would be spent even *before* any consideration of the costs of administration, data collection, analysis and study, and reporting. Ideally a *national* sample should have been used, but it would have been more expensive to monitor than a local sample, and differing employment conditions in different parts of the country would have made it difficult to sort out the effects of income payments from variations in local job availability. By concentrating the sample in one region, it was hoped that local conditions would be held constant. Ideally *all* types of low-income families should have been tested, but procedure would have necessitated a larger sample and greater expense. So only poor families with an able-bodied man age 18 to 58 were selected; the work behavior of these men in the face of a guaranteed income was of special interest.

To ascertain the effects of different levels of guaranteed income, four guarantee levels were established. Some families were chosen to receive 50 percent of the Social Security Administration's poverty level income, others 75 percent, others 100 percent, and still others 125 percent. In order to ascertain the effects of graduated payments in relation to earnings, some families had their payments reduced by 30 percent of their outside earnings, others 50 percent, and still others 70 percent. Finally a control sample was observed—low-income families who received no payments at all.

The experiment was begun in 1968 and planned to run for three years. But political events move swiftly and soon engulfed the study. In

1969 President Nixon proposed the Family Assistance Plan (FAP) to Congress, which, initially at least, guaranteed all families a minimum income of 50 percent of the poverty level and a payment reduction of 50 percent of outside earnings. The Nixon Administration had not waited to learn the results of the OEO experiment before introducing FAP. Nixon wanted welfare reform to be his priority domestic legislation and the bill was symbolically numbered HR 1 (House of Representatives Bill #1).

After the FAP bill had been introduced, the Nixon Administration pressured OEO to produce favorable supporting evidence in behalf of the guaranteed income—specifically, evidence that a guaranteed income at the levels and graduated sublevels proposed in FAP would *not* reduce incentives to work among the poor. The OEO obliged by hastily publishing a short report, "Preliminary Results of the New Jersey Graduated Work Incentive Experiment," which purported to show that there were no differences in the outside earnings of families receiving guaranteed incomes (experimental group) and those who were not (control group.)[7]

The director of the research, economics professor Harold Watts of the University of Wisconsin, warned that "the evidence from this preliminary and crude analysis of the earliest results is less than ideal." But he concluded that "no evidence has been found in the urban experiment to support the belief that negative-tax-type income maintenance programs will produce large disincentives and consequent reductions in earnings." Moreover, the early results indicated that families in all the separate experimental groups, with different guaranteed minimums and different graduated payment schedules, behaved in a fashion similar to each other and to the control group receiving no payments at all. Predictably, later results confirmed the preliminary results, which were produced to assist the FAP bill in Congress.

PROBLEMS IN POLICY EXPERIMENTATION

The whole excursion into government-sponsored policy impact experimentation raises a series of important questions.[8] First of all, are

[7] U.S. Office of Economic Opportunity, "Preliminary Results of the New Jersey Graduated Work Incentive Experiment," February 18, 1970. Also cited in Alice M. Rivlin, *Systematic Thinking for Social Action* (Washington, D.C.: Brookings Institution, 1971).

[8] For an excellent discussion of the problems and prospects of experimental policy research, see Frank P. Scioli and Thomas J. Cook, "Experimental Design in Policy Impact Analysis," *Social Science Quarterly*, 54 (September 1973), 271–91.

government-sponsored research projects predisposed to produce results supportive of popular reform proposals? Are social scientists, whose personal political values are generally liberal and reformist, inclined to produce findings in support of liberal reform measures? Would the OEO have rushed to produce "preliminary findings" in the New Jersey experiment *if* they had shown that the guarantees did in fact reduce the incentive to work? Or would such early results be set aside as "too preliminary" to publish? Because the participants in the experiment knew that they were singled out for experimentation, did they behave differently than they would have if the program had been applied universally? Would the work ethic be impaired if *all* American families were guaranteed a minimum income for life rather than a few selected families for a temporary period of time? Thus, the questions raised by this experiment affect not only the issues of welfare policy but also the validity of policy experimentation itself.

Experimental strategies in policy impact research raise still other problems. Do government researchers have the right to withhold public services from individuals simply to provide a control group for experimentation? In the medical area, where the giving or withholding of treatment can result in death or injury, the problem is obvious and many attempts have been made to formulate a code of ethics. But in the area of social experimentation, what are we to say to control groups who are chosen to be similar to experimental groups but denied benefits in order to serve as a base for comparison? Setting aside the legal and moral issue, it will be politically difficult to provide services for some people and not others. Perhaps only the fact that relatively few Americans knew about the New Jersey experiment kept it from becoming a controversial topic.

Another reservation about policy impact research centers on the bias of social scientists and their government sponsors. "Successful" experiments—where the proposed policy achieves positive results—will receive more acclaim and produce greater opportunities for advancement for social scientists and administrators than will "unsuccessful" experiments. Liberal, reform-oriented social scientists *expect* liberal reforms to produce positive results. When reforms appear to do so, the research results are immediately accepted and published; but when results are unsupportive or negative, social scientists may be inclined to go back and recode their data, or redesign their research, or reevaluate their results because they believe a "mistake" must have been made. The temptation to "fudge the data," "reinterpret" the results, coach participants on what to say or do, and so forth will be very great. In the physical and biological sciences, the temptation to "cheat" in research is reduced by the fact that research can be replicated and the danger of being caught and disgraced is very great. But social experiments can seldom be replicated perfectly, and replication seldom brings the same distinction to a social scientist as the original research.

People behave differently when they know they are being watched. Students, for example, generally perform at a higher level when something—anything—new and different is introduced into the classroom routine. This "Hawthorne effect" [9] may cause a new program or reform to appear more successful than the old, but it is the newness itself that produces improvement rather than the program or reform.

Another problem in policy impact research is that results obtained with small-scale experiments may differ substantially from what would occur if a large-scale nationwide program were adopted. In the New Jersey experiments, if only one family received income maintenance payments, its members may have continued to behave as their neighbors did. But if everyone had been guaranteed a minimum income, community standards might have changed and affected the behavior of all recipient families.

Despite these problems, the advantages of policy experimentation are substantial. It is exceedingly costly for society to commit itself to large-scale programs and policies in education, welfare, housing, health, and so on without any real idea about what works. Increasingly, we can expect the federal government to strive to test newly proposed policies and reforms before committing the nation to massive new programs.

THE LIMITS OF PUBLIC POLICY

Never have Americans expected so much of their government. Our confidence in what governments can do seems boundless. We have come to believe that governments can eliminate poverty, end racism, ensure peace, prevent crime, restore cities, clean the air and water, and so on, if only they will adopt the right policies.

Perhaps confidence in the potential effectiveness of public policy is desirable, particularly if it inspires us to continue to search for ways to resolve societal problems. But any serious study of public policy must also recognize the limitations of policy in affecting societal conditions. Let us summarize these limitations:

[9] The term is taken from early experiments at the Hawthorne plant of Western Electric Company in Chicago in 1927. It was found that worker output increased with any change in routine, even decreasing the lighting in the plant. See David L. Sills, ed., *International Encyclopedia of the Social Siences,* Vol. 7 (New York: Free Press, 1968), p. 241.

1. Some societal problems are incapable of solution because of the way in which they are defined. If problems are defined in *relative* rather than *absolute* terms, they may never be resolved by public policy. For example, if the poverty line is defined as the line which places one-fifth of the population below it, then poverty will always be with us regardless of how well-off the "poor" may become. Relative disparities in society may never be eliminated. Even if income differences among classes were tiny, then tiny differences may come to have great symbolic importance, and the problem of inequality may remain.

2. Expectations may always outrace the capabilities of governments. Progress in any policy area may simply result in an upward movement in expectations about what policy should accomplish. Public education never faced a "dropout" problem until the 1960s when, for the first time, a majority of boys and girls were graduating from high school. At the turn of the century, when high school graduation was rare, there was no mention of a dropout problem. Graduate rates have been increasing every year, as has concern for the dropout problem.

3. Policies that solve the problems of one group in society may create problems for other groups. In a plural society one man's solution may be another man's problem. For example, solving the problem of inequality in society may mean redistributive tax and spending policies which take from persons of above-average wealth to give to persons with below-average wealth. The latter may view this as a solution, but the former may view this as creating serious problems. There are *no* policies which can simultaneously attain mutually exclusive ends.

4. It is quite possible that some societal forces cannot be harnessed by governments, even if it is desirable to do so. It may turn out that government cannot stop urban migration patterns of whites and blacks, even if it tries to do so. Whites and blacks may separate themselves regardless of government policies in support of integration. Some children may not be able to learn much in public schools no matter what is done. Governments may be unable to forcibly remove children from disadvantaged environments because of family objections even if this proves to be the only way to ensure equality of opportunity, and so on. Governments may not be *able* to bring about some societal changes.

5. Frequently people adapt themselves to public policies in ways that render the policies useless. For example, we may solve the problem of poverty by government guarantees of a high annual income, but by so doing we may reduce incentives to work and thus swell the number of dependent families beyond the fiscal capacities of government to provide guarantees. Of course, we do not really *know* the impact of income guarantees on the work behavior of the poor, but the possibility exists that adaptive behavior may frustrate policy.

6. Societal problems may have multiple causes, and a specific policy may not be able to eradicate the problem. For example, job training may not affect the hard-core unemployed if their employability is also affected by chronic poor health.

7. The solution to some problems may require policies that are more costly than the problem. For example, it may turn out that certain levels of public

disorder—including riots, civil disturbances, and occasional violence—cannot be eradicated without the adoption of very repressive policies—the forceable break-up of revolutionary parties, restrictions on the public appearances of demagogues, the suppression of hate literature, the addition of large numbers of security forces, and so on. But these repressive policies would prove too costly in terms of democratic values—freedom of speech and press, rights of assembly, freedom to form opposition parties. Thus, a certain level of disorder may be the price we pay for democracy. Doubtless there are other examples of societal problems that are simply too costly to solve.

8. The political system is not structured for completely rational decision making. The solution of societal problems generally implies a rational model, but government may not be capable of formulating policy in a rational fashion. Instead the political system may reflect group interests, elite preferences, environmental forces, or incremental change, more than rationalism. Presumably, a democratic system is structured to reflect mass influences, whether these are rational or not. Elected officials respond to the demands of their constitutents, and this may inhibit completely rational approaches to public policy. Social science information does not exist to find policy solutions even if there are solutions. Moreover even where such information exists, it may not find its way into the political arena.

BIBLIOGRAPHY

RIVLIN, ALICE M., *Systematic Thinking for Social Action* (Washington: Brookings Institution, 1971).

SUCHMAN, EDWARD A., *Evaluative Research* (New York: Russell Sage Foundation, 1967).

U.S. Department of Health, Education and Welfare, *Toward A Social Report* (Washington, D.C.: Government Printing Office, 1969).

INDEX